American English Grammar

American English Grammar introduces students to American English in detail, from parts of speech, phrases, and clauses to punctuation and explaining (and debunking) numerous "rules of correctness," integrating its discussion of Standard American grammar with thorough coverage of the past sixty years' worth of work on African American English and other ethnic and regional non-Standard varieties. The book's examples and exercises include 500 real-world sentences and longer texts, drawn from newspapers, film, song lyrics, and online media as well as from Mark Twain, Stephen King, academic texts, translations of the Bible, poetry, drama, children's literature, and transcribed conversation and TV and radio shows. Based on twenty years of classroom testing and revision, *American English Grammar* will serve as a classroom text or reference that teaches students how to think and talk not only about the mechanics of sentences but also about the deep and detailed soul and nuance of the most widely used language in human history.

Seth R. Katz is Associate Professor and Associate Chair in the Department of English at Bradley University, USA.

D1595728

American English Grammar

An Introduction

Seth R. Katz

Routledge
Taylor & Francis Group

NEW YORK AND LONDON

First published 2020
by Routledge
52 Vanderbilt Avenue, New York, NY 10017

and by Routledge
2 Park Square, Milton Park, Abingdon, Oxon, OX14 4RN

Routledge is an imprint of the Taylor & Francis Group, an informa business

© 2020 Taylor & Francis

Library of Congress Cataloging-in-Publication Data
A catalog record for this book has been requested

ISBN: 978-0-367-21935-2 (hbk)
ISBN: 978-0-367-21940-6 (pbk)
ISBN: 978-0-429-26888-5 (ebk)

Typeset in Times New Roman
by Apex CoVantage, LLC

Visit the eResources: www.routledge.com/9780367219406

To my family and my students

Contents

Introduction

Language Variety and Grammar

A book like this one—a "grammar book"—is typically expected to deal with one variety of English, often called "Standard English" (SE). People tend to think of the Standard variety as "proper" or "grammatically correct" or "the best English." But SE is just one variety of English: a variety commonly associated with school and professional life, with very formal contexts of speaking and writing, and with the speech of formally educated middle- and upper-class people. But it is certainly not, in every situation, "the best English." If I were to speak my best professor-in-the-classroom SE—or write it in an email or text message—to my wife, my children, or my friends, they would all wonder what's wrong and if am I angry at them. Similarly, African Americans from predominantly Black working-class communities who speak SE among their friends and family risk being accused of "talking White" and acting "uppity." Think how odd it would be if the old folk song:

> It ain't gonna rain no more, no more,
> It ain't gonna rain no more,
> How in the heck can I wash my neck
> If it ain't gonna rain no more?

were instead sung:

> It is not going to rain anymore, anymore,
> It is not going to rain anymore,
> How do you suppose that I will be able to wash my neck
> If it is not going to rain anymore?

Clearly, different varieties of English are appropriate for different rhetorical situations: we speak—and write—different versions of English depending on who our audience is, the message we are delivering, and our purpose for delivering it. English has many varieties, all of which are a significant part of how we perform, and thereby show, our membership in different groups, including our families, different groups of friends, our ethnic groups, faith communities, peers, colleagues, and teammates. We also vary our language to perform other individual roles and relationships, whether with the boss, the people who work under us, the checker at the grocery store we see weekly, the checker we have never met before, the friend we are happy to run into, the stranger we bump into accidentally—the list goes on and on. Think about it: you don't tell the same story the same way to your best friend and to your parents. You will change pronunciation, articulation, word choice, and even grammar.

Non-Standard varieties of English have often been denigrated as "broken," and people who speak non-Standard varieties are often regarded—even by members of their own speech communities!—as sounding "uneducated." Just start using the word "ain't" routinely in class, or among formally educated middle-class people, and see what happens. The reality, however, is that people who speak non-Standard varieties can communicate their interests and needs to those who speak SE varieties, and they certainly have no trouble making themselves understood in their own speech communities. Indeed, members of those speech communities are expected to use the non-Standard variety in interactions within the group; if they don't, they will mark themselves as different from the group, outside of its norms, or even rebellious against the group. Just think of the teen who drops an f-bomb at the family dinner table or a teen who will not use the f-word with a group of friends who routinely do so.

Far from being "broken," all varieties of English are equally rule governed and orderly—that is, equally grammatical—and each variety partakes of exactly the same blueprint; indeed, that grammatical blueprint, and the resulting mutual intelligibility despite variation, is the very definition of a "language." No native speaker of any variety of English would find the following acceptable as an intelligible sentence: *bought bicycle red boy the*. There are languages in which this sentence order is accommodated by the blueprint, putting the verb first, followed by the direct object and ending with the subject, and placing adjectives and articles after the noun they are connected to. But not English. Likewise, any native speaker of any variety of English will answer the following question in the same way: given the following words, how would you assemble them into a single noun phrase?

girls, young, the, French, three

Native speakers will, with little hesitation, respond that *the three young French girls* is the "correct" phrase. This is evidence of just one of the many "rules of English"—lines marking firm walls on the blueprint of the language—that all native speakers internalize.

Varieties of the language are possible because, although the walls of the blueprint can't be changed, some features of the interior are not fixed in place.

While many people may "know" that *Him and me went to the store* is not "Standard," it remains perfectly intelligible even to people who would never say it. Likewise, with *I ain't got no money*, no native speaker of English takes the "double negative" as implying the positive meaning *I have money*. But rules on when to use subject (*he*; *I*) versus object (*him*; *me*) pronouns, and whether or not multiple negation is acceptable, are flexible among varieties of English (in fact, these two sentences are acceptable in more varieties of English than not). Unlike hard rules, as in the examples of the *bicycle* and the *girls* above, these walls are not yet established within the English blueprint—as much as some language authorities would like them to be.

People who speak non-Standard varieties also have no trouble communicating their interests and needs to those who speak SE varieties because the number of ways in which non-Standard varieties differ from SE varieties is very small. For example, out of thousands upon thousands of grammatical rules in English, there are only about forty ways in which the grammar of African American Vernacular English (AAVE)[1] varieties may differ from SE. The fact that some of these forty differences are so distinctive to speakers of other varieties of English is a mark of both how discerning our ear for language is—how closely attuned we are to its nuances—and of how quick we are to judge people we regard as different from us, as not part of "our group." As many have noted, the judgements we make about other people's language are not primarily about the language at all but about the people speaking.

It is useful to learn to use the variety of English that is correct or most appropriate for any situation and audience. Students who write, *I ain't got no money*, in a formal classroom paper will likely not be awarded a good grade, no matter how brilliant their ideas. Likewise, the employee in an office job who uses *ain't* in a spoken or written report to a client is unlikely to receive a positive performance review. There is nothing wrong with the varieties of English we use at home and in all of the day-to-day, comfortable, familiar contexts we encounter. But to succeed, to "get ahead" in the world, the more varieties of English we can self-consciously understand—and even use—the better off we will be.

Unlike most "grammar books," this one—*American English Grammar* (*AEG*)—will address not only the "rules" of written and spoken Standard English, and provide you with concepts and terminology to analyze, discuss, and argue the merits of sentences in SE, but it will also apply those concepts and terminology to the most notable non-Standard features of other varieties of English, including regional American Englishes, AAVEs, Chicano Englishes, Vietnamese- and Native-American Englishes, advertising language, poetry, song lyrics, informal varieties, and others so that you will understand the rules that underlie those distinctly non-Standard features and be ready to analyze and discuss the grammatical structures of a much greater range of English sentences.

The Point of the Book

The point of this book, and indeed, the object of studying grammar (as far as I'm concerned), is to help you develop a command of grammatical concepts and terminology and their application. We apply that terminology in "parsing" sentences: taking sentences into their "constituent parts." Once you know how to identify and name the constituents of a sentence, you then have the ability to do a couple of things well. First, you will be able to talk very precisely about what makes different varieties of English different and how the rules of different varieties work. And second, you will be able to talk about what makes a good or well-formed and rhetorically effective sentence versus a bad, poorly formed, or ineffective sentence. Learning how to talk about the details of sentence structure leads you to understand the conventions of speaking and writing that govern people's judgments of whether a sentence is good or bad. That ability to articulate why we judge sentences as good or bad leads you to be more conscious of your own speaking and writing: it leads you to see how to make your own sentences—and paragraphs—both spoken and written, more effective for a particular communicative context.

While some of you may just enjoy the puzzle of parsing sentences, parsing is, in itself, about as useful as last Sunday's *New York Times* crossword: once you finish it, you throw it away. But as with learning the techniques, relationships, jargon, and concepts of any complex activity, learning to parse sentences helps us naturalize an activity that is otherwise unnatural. Ordinarily, we do not analyze the language we use (though we often critique the language that other people use). If we tried to parse our sentences as we were speaking or writing them, we would be unable to communicate; it would be much the same as if, while walking down the street, we tried to analyze all of the muscle interactions involved in walking: we would soon stumble and fall down. We live in language in much the same way that we live in our bodies, in air, or under the influence of gravity: it is unnatural—and therefore difficult—to try to separate ourselves far enough from these essential features of life to analyze them. The study of grammar, and learning to parse sentences, allow us to denature the apparently natural process of producing and decoding language, the better to understand how it works, and so to improve on our own nature.

We should also note that, traditionally, the study of grammar is exclusively about single, isolated sentences, not about paragraphs. I see this approach as wrong-headed: as we shall see very quickly, the sentences in a paragraph work together to guide how we interpret their structure and the meanings of their words. Later in the book, we will also see that there are grammatical elements in sentences that serve to connect sentences to one another within—and even between—paragraphs. The focus of traditional grammar on single sentences is inadequate because some elements in sentences are always structured as they are so that sentences will connect to each other. And, in the real language world (as opposed to the ideal language world of most grammar books), we *never* use single sentences alone without any other context. For the most part, this textbook will use single-sentence examples only to illustrate basic points about sentence structure and to help you in learning to identify and analyze those structures. Exercises will use both artificial single sentences (the shallow end of the pool) and real-world texts taken from various sources (the deep end, where we usually swim).

Something else we need to get out of the way: you may have been brought up to expect that a grammar book is a kind of rule book that contains all of the correct guidelines to which writers and speakers must conform.

As should be evident by now, *AEG* is not that kind of "grammar book."

In talking about sentences and grammar, there are two major schools of thought: one is *prescriptive*, largely comprising sets of arbitrary rules about what one should and should not do in writing. Rules such as "never start a sentence with *because*," or "never end a sentence with a preposition," or "never use multiple negation," or "always use *fewer* with count nouns but *less* with mass nouns," or "never split an infinitive" are prescriptive rules, best thought of as rules of language etiquette. People who know and care about them will notice if you don't follow them; but if someone doesn't know the rule, or if you are in a situation where the rule simply doesn't matter, then no one will notice if you don't follow it. When you cheer for your team, or when you write a text message to a friend, it would be strange for someone to criticize you for splitting an infinitive.

The other school of thought, and the one we will mostly be working with, is *de*scriptive grammar. We will be looking at what people actually do in writing and speaking as we develop a set of terms and concepts that is broad enough and powerful enough that it allows us to describe the vast majority of sentences in English. We will frequently find that there is more than one way to describe or analyze a sentence or phrase. Each different interpretation or analysis will have strengths and weaknesses that I will try to elucidate. I will try to give you multiple avenues of interpretation by way of being true to the reality of language. And I will give you multiple avenues of interpretation by way of emphasizing the point that parsing sentences is, like other systems of human thought and analysis (e.g. science, law, military or sports strategy, or deciding on the meaning of poetry and fiction) a matter of interpretation: how we identify the form and function of particular words within a sentence may depend wholly on our understanding of the speaker or writer's *intention*, rather than on a pre-assigned form or function label. However, from years of teaching experience, I know that students are curious about and often anxious to be "correct" according to prescriptive rules. And so, along the way, I will at times explain the reasoning behind the sorts of prescriptive rules listed above. Such rules are invariably rooted in English grammar, but rather than reflecting the actual lines on the blueprint, they express someone's idiosyncratic notion of correctness that, having been uttered with enough authority and repeated often enough, have risen to the status of Rules, even though, far from being actual walls, they may really be no more than some people's idea of how best to arrange the furniture.

A Summary of the Book

Now, some nitty gritty. Chapter 1 will provide an overview of the major features of sentences: subjects, predicates, and sentence-modifying adverbials that fall outside the subject-predicate structure but provide context for it. Chapter 1 will also introduce lexical classes (a.k.a. "parts of speech") and the phrases that are associated with them, such as nouns and noun phrases. Chapters 2 through 9 will then focus on the individual "lexical classes" and their phrases. I have chosen to examine these lexical classes and their phrases using three lenses:

- The forms they can take.
- The functions they can perform in sentences.
- The kinds of meanings that we use those phrases to express.

I understand that the last of those three lenses—meaning—will set off alarm bells for some instructors who are considering whether to use this text, but I incorporate considerations of meaning as a deliberate choice for several reasons. First, it is the approach to understanding lexical classes that will be most familiar and comfortable to most students because it is the approach still routinely taken in K–12 instruction, as well as by many college composition instructors. Second, although the linguists' scholarly pendulum has swung about as far away as possible from explicitly including considerations of word meaning in discussions of sentence structure, there is some evidence that the pendulum may be beginning its inevitable swing back because we really can't ever generalize the analysis of syntax to the point where it takes no consideration of how people actually use words. Much of the work of recent linguistics has come to focus primarily on "bottom up" approaches to language, approaches that attempt to isolate, abstract, and generalize cognitive processes related to the production and recognition of phonetic (sound), phonologic (sound and meaning), morphologic (word building), and syntactic (sentence building) processes. These efforts to figure out the subconscious algorithms of language have tried to separate those processes from the messier businesses of semantics (meaning) and pragmatics (actual social use of language). I simply disagree with this approach, especially in that it is examples from those very messy realities and oddities of language that very often drive the interest of the scholar seeking the rules of the underlying subconscious processes. So while I will be taking advantage of many of the rich insights provided by the past sixty years of work in syntactic theory, I will be blending those ideas with a variety of other approaches, including not only some traditional ideas and terminology but work in corpus-based linguistics, historical linguistics, cognitive linguistics (especially prototype theory), linguistic structuralism, dialectology, ethnolinguistics, pragmatics (especially linguistic politeness theory), language education, and guides to style and usage. I believe that this eclectic approach, which I have developed over my three decades as a college instructor in courses not only in grammar and linguistics but in literature and writing, serves to provide students with a broader understanding of the mundanities, rigidities, complexities, and rich flexibilities of English and its grammar.

In this book, we will deal with eight parts of speech: nouns (N), prepositions (P), adjectives (ADJ), determiners (D), pronouns (PRON), verbs (V), adverbs (ADV), and conjunctions (CONJ). Of these parts of speech, the category of determiners is likely new to you; this part of speech comprises a set of words that only function in noun phrases (NP), appearing at the front of the NP, ahead of the noun and a preceding adjective (e.g. *that green book*). The most common and familiar determiners are the articles (*a, an, the*). Also, the chapter on conjunctions includes a detailed discussion of the forms and functions of punctuation, which primarily works to conjoin phrases and clauses.

Chapter 10 will examine independent clauses (a.k.a. sentences) and dependent clauses. All clauses have subjects and predicates, but as their name implies, dependent clauses cannot stand alone but occur as dependent constituents within other phrases and clauses, functioning like noun phrases (nominally), adjective phrases (adjectivally), or adverb phrases (adverbially). The emphasis on those three categories of dependent clauses leads us into Chapter 11, in which we will focus on all of the kinds of phrases and clauses that can function as nominals, adjectivals, and adverbials and take a new approach to categorizing adverbials by their scope of reference and where they can be placed in a phrase or clause.

Chapter 12 deals with the most complex part of English grammar: participle and infinitive phrases, known collectively as non-finite verb phrases. These phrases look like predicates in that they contain verbs along with the phrases that commonly complement—complete the meaning of—the verb, but they can function as nominals, adjectivals, and adverbials. Many grammar textbooks simply avoid dealing with them at all, which annoyed me enough that it started me down the road of writing this book. Non-finite verb phrases are a significant feature of English style, providing us with interesting ways to vary our sentence structures. My experience has shown that upper-division college students are ready to handle them.

The book concludes with Chapter 13, in which students perform a Grand Review Exercise. For the exercise, the students are given a 600-word essay from a popular magazine and asked to identify, in succession, all of the types of phrases and clauses they have studied in this book. Students identify each complete example of each type of constituent, its form, function, and interior constituent structure, as appropriate. Although this review exercise is time consuming (it typically takes up the last three weeks of a semester-long course), these final rounds of repetition serve not only to review and reinforce what the students have studied but to show them how much they have learned. Students who have not previously been confident about their mastery of the course material are reassured by both the repetition of the more common constituents and structures and by their ability to articulate possible parsings of more difficult or unusual structures. Students also start to see patterns in the grammatical structures and how particular sorts of patterns and repetitions in the grammar create prosodic and rhetorical effects.

Each chapter is accompanied by exercises, about which I have a general recommendation: students <u>must</u> do the exercises in order to internalize the alien concepts and terms—indeed, the whole alien way of thinking—that a course in grammar comprises. For most students, if they don't do the exercises and keep up with them, they will quickly drown in the alien bog of concepts and terms. However, grading such exercises is a drag for the instructor, and attaching a grade to the exercises is, in my experience, counter-productive: students tend to fixate on their grade rather than focusing on whether they understand the terms and concepts.

Here's what I do: I assign the exercises and immediately provide my students with the answers. Students do the exercises, check their work before the next class session, then come to class with questions. I devote the first twenty minutes of the next class session to addressing students' questions—which invariably overlap and help me identify things I need to explain better. And the discussion helps students engage more with the material and practice using the terms and concepts. As I walk students through the process of parsing sentence constituents, I model the thinking processes involved in grammatical analysis; we discuss a few of the pedestrian examples, but mostly students hone in on the problematic examples; thus—best of all—the discussion shows the students that grammar and sentence parsing are, in fact, matters of discussion and interpretation, rather than God-given rules about what is "correct."

The coverage of grammar in *AEG* is deliberately designed to be more thorough than that of most college grammar texts. I have been classroom testing this material in evolving drafts of this book since 2002, and my experience has shown me that my students, the majority of whom have been college juniors and seniors heading for careers in teaching and professions that will require skill in writing and editing, need a language that will help them understand, explain, teach, and apply concepts of grammar and usage. *AEG*, and the course I teach with it, are constructed so that concepts and terms build on each other, and between traversing the book *and* doing the "Grand Review Exercise," students work through the complete material of the book twice. The goal of the repetition and the unusual thoroughness of the coverage is that students should become more alert to and aware of language—and so learn how to *think* like grammarians. After about week six of the course, when the students start coming into class complaining that they can't avoid spotting adverb clauses, phrasal verbs, and puzzling constructions that they aren't sure how to parse *in their reading for other classes*, or on the Internet, or in their friends' Snap Chat posts, then I know that the class is working, that grammatical analysis has gotten under their skin, and that they are ready to teach grammar or become editors, writers, and communicators who have the conceptual and technical vocabulary to discuss how and why sentences work.

Key Points

- Like all languages, American English has many varieties.
- All these varieties of English are mutually intelligible because they share a common blueprint.
- The grammatical differences among varieties, while distinctive, are relatively few.
- Even in their distinctively different features, all varieties are governed by grammatical rules.
- We choose the variety of English we use to suit the rhetorical context (our audience, message, and purpose).
- As distinct from the grammatical rules—the walls of the blueprint—of English, prescriptive grammar focuses on "rules" that govern "correct language etiquette": how the furniture is arranged.
- Descriptive grammar focuses on how people actually use language, in terms of both the blueprint and the furniture.
- Grammatical structures (phrases and clauses) can be understood, discussed, and interpreted in terms of form, function, and meaning.

A Guide to Non-Standard American Varieties

Unlike most grammar textbooks, *AEG* incorporates substantial treatment of features of the grammars of non-Standard American English varieties. And unlike those few books that offer some limited treatment of a few features of non-Standard varieties, rather than placing those odd bits in a separate chapter on "Non-Standard English" or "Black English," *AEG* includes non-Standard variants in its more general discussions of those portions of English grammar. Thus, for example, the discussion of AAVE "habitual *be*" is included with the discussion of other Standard and non-Standard aspectual verbs.

Here follows a complete guide to all of the features of non-Standard American English varieties discussed in *AEG* and where they are included in the book:

- Nouns: pluralization:
  - Plural -*s* deletion
    - In ESL speech and AAVE (p. 31).
    - With plural demonstrative determiner *dem* in the Gullah English variety of the coastal islands of South Carolina and Georgia, and in AAVE (p. 31).
    - With nouns of measurement in Southern-based rural vernaculars (p. 31).

- ○ Regularization of irregular plurals in most vernacular varieties of American English (pp. 31–32).
- ○ Double marking pluralization by adding -*s* to irregular plurals in some American English vernacular varieties (p. 32).
- Nouns: reduplicated subject or predicate marker in AAVE and other varieties (pp. 40–41).
- Prepositions:

  - ○ AAVE *up* (p. 48).
  - ○ Northeastern *wait on line* (p. 56)
  - ○ Age- and class-graded use of *on accident* and *based off of* (pp. 56, 59n16).

- Adjectives: comparatives and superlatives:

  - ○ Regularization of irregular comparatives and superlatives in most American English vernaculars (pp. 61–63).
  - ○ Use of -*er* and -*est* on adjectives of two or more syllables, where the Standard variety uses *more* and *most* (pp. 61–62).
  - ○ Double marking of comparatives and superlatives in some American English vernaculars (pp. 62–63).

- Determiners:

  - ○ Absent possessive suffix *'s* in AAVE (pp. 68–69).
  - ○ Use of the third-person plural pronoun *them* as a demonstrative determiner in American English vernacular varieties (p. 71).

- Pronouns:

  - ○ Regularization of the possessive pronoun *mines* in AAVE (p. 82).
  - ○ Use of possessive forms ending in -*n* in Appalachian English and other rural varieties (p. 82).
  - ○ Regularization of reflexive *hisself* and *theirselves* in many American English vernaculars, including AAVE and Chicano English (p. 83).
  - ○ Object pronoun forms in subject position in many spoken American varieties (p. 84).
  - ○ Plural *you* in American vernaculars, including Northern *youse*, Pittsburgh *yinz*, and Southern *y'all* (p. 84).
  - ○ Personal dative use of object pronoun forms in Southern and other American vernaculars (p. 84).
  - ○ Associative plurals in AAVE and some Southern varieties (p. 85).
  - ○ Appositive pronouns in AAVE (p. 85).

- Verbs: tense:

  - ○ Deletion of -*s* in third-person singular in many vernacular varieties, including AAVE (p. 101).

- ○ Leveling of all present tense forms of *be* to *is* and all past tense forms to *was* in vernacular varieties (p. 102).
- ○ Regularization of irregular verb forms in Chicano English (p. 102).
- ○ Deletion of the past-tense marker *-ed* in ESL or varieties still influenced by other languages, such as Vietnamese English and Native American Indian English in the Southwest (p. 102).
- ○ Unmarking of the verb in habitual contexts in Native American Indian English in the Southwest (p. 103).
- ○ Historical present in European American vernaculars and AAVE (p. 103).
- ○ Narrative tense in AAVE (p. 103).

- Verbs: modal auxiliaries and semi-modal verbs:

  - ○ Future *be* in AAVE (p. 108).
  - ○ *Be fixin' to/finna/fidna/fitna* in Southern and AAVE varieties (p. 108).
  - ○ *Imma* in AAVE (pp. 108–109).
  - ○ *(Su)poseta* in some American varieties (p. 109).
  - ○ NEED + PAST PARTICIPLE in some Midwest varieties (p. 109).
  - ○ Double modals in Southern vernaculars and other varieties (p. 109).

- Verbs: aspect auxiliaries and aspectual verbs:

  - ○ Completive *done* in Southern varieties and AAVE (pp. 115–116).
  - ○ Modal completive, and resultative, *be done* in Southern varieties and AAVE (p. 116).
  - ○ Imperfect aspect with completive *done* in AAVE (p. 116).
  - ○ Imperfect aspect with reinforcing *like* in the ordinary speech of younger Americans (pp. 116–117).
  - ○ Habitual *be* in AAVE and some Southern varieties (p. 117).
  - ○ Intensified stative *be* in AAVE (pp. 117–118).
  - ○ Remote time stressed *been* and unstressed *been* in AAVE (pp. 118–119).[2]
  - ○ Perfective *be* in some varieties of American English (p. 119).
  - ○ Indignant *come, go,* and *start* in AAVE and informal varieties (pp. 119–120).

- Verbs: voice: passive *get* in vernacular American English varieties (p. 122).
- Verbs: absent *be* or "zero copula" in AAVE and Southern American English; *be*-deletion in questions (pp. 131–132).
- Verbs: leveling of subjunctive *were* to *was* with first- and third-person singular subjects in all varieties (p. 129).
- Verbs: complementation: quotatives:

  - ○ *Be like, go,* and *be all* among Americans under age 40, and AAVE *say* (pp. 150–151).
  - ○ Subject-auxiliary inversion with quotatives in AAVE (pp. 157, 213).

- Adverbs:

  - ○ Absent *-ly* in Southern mountain varieties such as Appalachian and Ozark English (p. 170).

- *Liketa* in Appalachian English (p. 173).
- Intensifying adverbs (*right, plumb, slam, clean*) in some Southern vernaculars (pp. 173–174).
- *Steady* in AAVE (p. 174).
- *Ain't but* and *don't but* for only in AAVE (p. 174).
- *Fucking* in American vernacular varieties (p. 174).

• Adverbs: negation:

- Tag-question *no?* in Hispanic English (p. 176).
- *Ain't* in all American vernacular varieties (pp. 176–177).
- *Don't* with habitual *be* in AAVE (p. 177).
- Multiple negation or "negative concord" in all American vernacular varieties, including negative auxiliary inversion in Southern varieties and AAVE (pp. 177–179).
- Leveling to *were* with negative past tense *be* in some coastal dialect areas of the American Southeast (pp. 179–180).
- Leveling of *doesn't* to *don't* in virtually all vernacular American varieties (p. 180).

• Relative Pronouns:

- *What* in place of *that*, *who*, or *whom* in all vernacular American varieties (p. 227).
- *Which* as a coordinating conjunction in general American English (p. 227).
- Relative pronoun functioning as a subject deleted from the adjective clause in Southern vernaculars and in AAVE (pp. 227–228).

• Noun Clauses:

- *That*-clause: AAVE non-Standard *that*-clause with SUBJ-AUX inversion instead of a complementizer (p. 229).
- *Wh*-clause: *whosever* as a variant of *whoever's* (both as a pro-determiner and a contraction of *whoever is* and *whoever has* in American spoken varieties (p. 232).

• Sentences:

- Interrogatives without inversion of the subject and auxiliary verb in AAVE (p. 213).
- Interrogatives with auxiliary deletion in American informal varieties (p. 213).
- Existential *there* constructions in which the form of *be* does not agree in number with the agent in vernacular varieties of American English (p. 215).
- *It* or *they* instead of existential *there* in vernacular varieties of American English (p. 215).

Acknowledgements

Thanks to the hundreds of students who have taken my grammar classes over the past twenty-seven years and who have been variously tolerant, angry, joyous, frustrated, and enlightened, sometimes all in the course of a few minutes. They have been the patient guinea pigs for each iteration of this book, and all have contributed to its making. For their particular insights, thanks to Kristen Zidon, Elizabeth Liddell, Ebonee Younger, Melissa Smith, Chris Douglas, Brian Hyken, Rhea Breese, and Kristin Henrichs.

Thanks to colleagues Rob Prescott, Peter Dusenbery, Demetrice Worley, Anne Herbert, and especially Bob DeGise for many fascinating discussions about oddities of the English language. Thanks to the staff and resources of the Bradley University Cullom Davis Library: your fingerprints are all over this book.

Credit and thanks are due to the digital resources that led me to the hundreds of real-world examples used throughout the book: *Corpus of Contemporary American English, EBSCOhost, Google Books, Hathi Trust Digital Library, Internet Archive, JSTOR, Nexis Uni, ProQuest, Project Muse*, and the Internet itself.

Thanks to Ze'ev Sudry at Routledge, who believed enthusiastically in this project, and Helena Parkinson for facilitating all of the details of production. Thanks to Julie Tetel Andresen at Duke University, Amanda Athon at Governors State University, and David Crowe at Augustana College, who provided generous feedback on the manuscript that only served to improve the final product, and especially to William C. Spruiell at Central Michigan University, whose sage suggestions saved me from several gaffes and helped me to replace some muddy thinking with a modicum of clarity and grace. All remaining gaffes and muddiness are fully my responsibility.

Thanks to Larry and Lynn Seitzman, whose friendship enriches both my life and my work.

Thanks to my in-laws, Sandy and Bobbie Fedderly, for their support and encouragement.

Thanks to my parents, Marilyn Noskin Katz (1931–1988) and Arthur J Katz (1927–2018), and my brothers Curtis (1953–2011) and Ken, who raised me in a home full of books, music, movies, theater, news, ideas, information, wordplay, parody, comedy, crosswords, comics, cartoons, and conversation and with a love of words. They made it normal to laugh with delight while reading the greatest short story anthology of them all: the dictionary.

And, as always, my deepest thanks and love go to my wife Barb and our children Mara, Sophie, and Elie, who never fail to indulge, encourage, and play with me with the English language. At the Katz house, puns will fly, and the dictionary is always close to the dinner table.

Credits

Bad, Bad Leroy Brown

Words and Music by Jim Croce

Imma Be

It's So Easy

Tik Tok

The Truth

Abbreviations and Conventions

AAVE	African American Vernacular English	PARTP	Participle Phrase
ACT	Active Voice	PASS	Passive Voice
ADJ	Adjective	PAST	Past Tense
ADJCL	Adjective Clause	PCOMP	Complement of a Preposition
ADJP	Adjective Phrase	PERF	Perfect Aspect
ADV	Adverb	PL	Plural Number
ADVC	Adverbial Complement	POSS	Possessive Case
ADVCL	Adverb Clause	PP	Prepositional Phrase
ADVP	Adverb Phrase	PRED	Predicate
CCONJ	Coordinating Conjunction	PRES	Present Tense
CONJ	Conjunction	PROADJ	Pro-adjective
CORRELCONJ	Correlative Conjunction	PROADV	Pro-adverb
D	Determiner	PROD	Pro-determiner
DO	Direct Object	PROG	Progressive Aspect
DP	Determiner Phrase	PRON	Pronoun
F	Feminine Gender	PRONP	Pronoun Phrase
IND	Indicative Mood	PV	Phrasal Verb
INFP	Infinitive Phrase	QUOT	Quotation
INTERJ	Interjection	RELPROADV	Relative Pro-adverb
IO	Indirect Object	RELPROCL	Relative Pro-clause
LC	Locative Complement	RELPROD	Relative Pro-determiner
M	Masculine Gender	RELPRON	Relative Pronoun
MC	Manner Complement	SC	Subject Complement
MOD	Modifier	SCONJ	Subordinating Conjunction
MV	Main Verb	SE	Standard English
N	Noun	SENT	Sentence
N'	N-bar	SENTMOD	Sentence Modifier
NCL	Noun Clause	SG	Singular Number
NEU	Neuter Gender	SPEC	Specifier
NOM	Nominative Case	SUBJ	Subject
NP	Noun Phrase	TC	Temporal Complement
OBJ	Objective Case	V	Verb
OC	Object Complement	VC	Verb Complement
P	Preposition	VP	Verb Phrase

Notes

1. In an effort not to offend, I have chosen to use "African American Vernacular English" (AAVE) as an overarching term to name one set of varieties of American English. I understand well that there are a number of contending terms, with African American Language, African American English, Black English Vernacular, Black English, and Ebonics being the chief terms of use during the past forty years, and that each term carries with it particular associations, affiliations, and political implications. I apologize for any dissatisfaction resulting from my choice.

2. For a unified treatment of the AAVE system for expressing time and events, see Lisa J. Green and Walter Sistrunk. "Syntax and Semantics in African American English." *The Oxford Handbook of African American Language.* Ed. Sonja Lanehart. New York: Oxford University Press, 2015. 355–370. For a detailed account of the system of tense, mood, and aspect in AAVE, see Charles E. DeBose. "The Systematic Marking of Tense, Modality, and Aspect in African American Language." In Lanehart, op. cit. 371–386.

Chapter 1

Sentences; Parts of Speech and Their Phrases

1.1 Sentences: Subjects, Verbs, Verb Complements, and Sentence Modifiers

Traditionally, the study of grammar focuses on sentences without context, not on paragraphs or other sets of connected sentences, such as conversations. In actual use, sentences always work together with each other and the context (words, physical surroundings, experience, knowledge) to guide how we interpret their structure and the meanings of their words. Later in the book, we will also see that there are grammatical elements in sentences that serve to connect sentences to one another within—and even between—paragraphs. For the most part, this textbook will only use single-sentence examples to illustrate basic points about sentence structure and to help you learn to identify and analyze those structures. Exercises will use both artificial single sentences (the shallow end of the pool) and real-world texts taken from various sources (the deep end, where we usually swim). In our study of grammar, we will take several different approaches to the same material, each one further refining how we analyze sentences. Here is a first approach.

Sentences typically comprise four major constituents: the subject, the verb, the verb complement, and sentence modifiers. In general, sentences must have a subject and a verb: these constituents are obligatory. Typically, you can't have a well-formed sentence in English without a subject and a verb.[1] Most verbs take some kind of complement: a constituent that <u>completes</u> the meaning of the verb. So, for example, in the sentence *Nancy likes avocadoes*, *avocadoes* is the complement. Without it, the sentence sounds incomplete: **Nancy likes* (the asterisk is a conventional way to mark that an example is not grammatical—that it does not fit the blueprint of English). For a subset of verbs—e.g. *smiles*—a complement is not required: *Nancy smiles* needs no complement.

Sentence modifiers are optional: with or without them, a sentence can still be grammatically well formed. In the sentence *Yesterday, Ed carried the groceries*, *yesterday* is a sentence modifier. It is optional in that we can remove it, and we will still have a well-formed sentence: *Ed carried the groceries*.

Let's drill down a little further. The easiest way to parse a sentence—to identify its constituent parts so as to analyze how it works—is to start with the verb, the word that names the action being performed by the subject. In the preceding example about Ed, the verb is *carried*, the only word in the sentence that names an action. The verb in a sentence may comprise more than one word: in a sentence like *The groceries were being carried by Ed*, the complete verb is *were being carried*. We will sometimes differentiate between the complete verb (e.g. *were being carried*) and its constituents, the main verb (e.g. *carried*) and auxiliary verbs (e.g. *were* and *being*; see Chapter 6).

Once you have found the verb, the next step in parsing a sentence is to ask *Who or what did the action?* In the case of the sentence *Yesterday, Ed carried the groceries*, the question is, *Who or what carried?* The answer to that question—*Ed*—names the subject of the verb. The subject of a verb is always some kind of nominal and most commonly a noun phrase (NP). An NP is a word or group of words comprising a noun (obligatory) and its dependent modifiers (optional); an NP can, among other functions, serve as the subject of a verb. We will abbreviate the phrase "noun phrase functioning as a subject" by the shorthand "NP:SUBJ," where the colon means "functioning as" and "SUBJ" is an abbreviation for "Subject." We will define NPs in more detail in Chapter 2. The complete NP:SUBJ—the noun and its modifiers—we call the complete subject; when we isolate the noun from the NP:SUBJ, we call the noun by itself the simple subject.

A good test for locating the subject of the sentence is

> **The subject question test**: Once you have identified a verb, ask *Who or what*, followed by the appropriate form of the verb. The answer will be the subject of the verb.

Taken together, the simple subject and the complete verb constitute the kernel sentence (e.g. *Ed carried*). It is often useful to identify the kernel sentence when we are puzzled as to what a sentence is about or when we are trying to revise a sentence for clarity or organization.

We must also distinguish between the form and function of sentence constituents. "NP" is a form, as are the categories identified by part-of-speech names (e.g. adjective, adverb, preposition, etc.). "Subject" is a function: a role an NP may perform within a sentence. In the sample sentence, *Ed* has the form of NP, and it functions as the SUBJ. As we will learn, NPs can have a great variety of different constituent structures: along with a noun, an NP can include a variety of modifiers with a variety of forms, but all NPs can fulfill the same functions within sentences. That is, part of what defines the form of an NP is the kind of functions it can perform.

Coming back to the example sentence, the phrase *the groceries* is, like *Ed*, an NP in form, comprising a noun (*groceries*) and a determiner (D) (*the*). The

NP *the groceries* is functioning as a verb complement: it completes the sense or meaning of the verb *carried*. To identify the function of the NP *the groceries*, we need to ask, *What did Ed carry?* The answer to the question—in this case, *the groceries*—identifies a very common type of verb complement, a direct object (DO; see Chapter 7). We now have a first test for identifying verb complements:

> **The verb complement question test**: Once you have identified a verb and its subject, ask, *Whom or what did the subject verb?* The answer will be the complement of the verb—more specifically, the direct object (DO).

When we ask, *Whom or what did Ed (subject) carry (verb)?* the answer—*the groceries*—is the verb complement.[2]

Taken together, the verb and its complement (or complements: some verbs take more than one; see Chapter 7) and modifiers (verbs can take modifiers, just like nouns can; see Chapters 6) constitute a verb phrase (VP) functioning as the predicate of the sentence (VP:PRED). Sometimes we will refer to the verb and its complements and modifiers, taken altogether, as the complete predicate, while we will sometimes refer to the complete verb of a sentence, taken by itself, as the simple predicate.

Now you know how to identify the guts—the subject and predicate—of any sentence. You also know how to identify a common sort of verb complement. Many English sentences are about someone or something (named by an NP:SUBJ) doing something (an action named by a V) to someone or something (an NP:DO). English is thus often referred to as a SUBJECT-VERB-OBJECT (SVO) language since that is our preferred and predominant sentence order. Other languages prefer a different order for the major sentence constituents. In our study of English grammar, parsing the vast majority of sentences or clauses (a set of words that includes a subject and a predicate) will begin with asking the question, *Who is doing what?* or *Who is doing what to whom?* Sentences in English most commonly comprise an NP:SUBJ and a VP:PRED.

While subjects and predicates are obligatory in sentences, and most verbs require complements, the fourth major part of a sentence—sentence modifiers—are, as we noted above, optional. In our example sentence, *Yesterday, Ed carried the groceries*, *yesterday* is a sentence modifier. We know it is optional because, if we drop it from the sentence, the remaining string of words is still a well-formed sentence. In traditional grammar, *yesterday* would be analyzed as an adverb modifying the verb *carried*—telling when the carrying happened. But it's not just that the *carrying* happened yesterday; it's the specific incident of *Ed carrying the groceries* that happened *yesterday*. And, unlike the word *the*, which is tightly connected to the word *groceries* and cannot be moved away from *groceries*, *yesterday* is not "tied" closely to the verb *carried*. In the grammar we will study here, a modifier is a word that shapes or limits the meaning of its head (the word, phrase or clause it modifies) and that is tied to its head—that is, within the sentence, the modifier has to be located close to the constituent it modifies. While *the* cannot be moved away from *groceries* and still be understood as related to *groceries, yesterday* can potentially appear in three different places in the sentence without altering the meaning of the sentence:

> *Yesterday, Ed carried the groceries.*
> *Ed carried the groceries yesterday.*
> *?Ed, yesterday, carried the groceries.*

Sentence modifiers like *yesterday* can, usually, appear at the beginning of the sentence; at the end of the sentence; and, often, between the subject and the predicate. The last example, *?Ed, yesterday, carried the groceries*, is, admittedly, a trifle odd; the question mark indicates that native speakers might find the sentence strange, though not necessarily unacceptable (as noted above, a sentence that is outright badly formed or unacceptable within the English blueprint will be marked with an asterisk). Now, though, consider these examples:

> *Because they don't think they're smart, too many kids quit science.*
> *Too many kids, because they don't think they're smart, quit science.*
> *Too many kids quit science because they don't think they're smart.*[3]

Because they don't think they're smart, like *yesterday* in the sentence about *Ed*, functions as a sentence modifier. "Sentence modifier" is a function performed by the broad class of adverbials, which includes the part-of-speech category "adverb." The function of a constituent will sometimes dictate how we label its form. For example, depending on its context of use, the form of the word *yesterday* can be either:

- An adverb (e.g. in *Yesterday, Ed carried the groceries*; *yesterday* is an adverb functioning as a sentence modifier—ADV:SENTMOD).
- A noun (e.g. *Yesterday was a good day*; *yesterday* is an NP:SUBJ).

The form label is not an inherent feature of the word itself but arises from its context of use. *Because they don't think they're smart* is a dependent clause; specifically, it is an adverb clause (ADVCL), and, like *yesterday*, it is functioning as a sentence modifier (ADVCL:SENTMOD). "Dependent clause" and "adverb clause" are forms, just like "noun."

There are two good tests for identifying sentence modifiers:

> **The optionality test for sentence modifiers**: Given a constituent word, phrase, or clause at the beginning or end of a sentence, or between the subject and the verb, a constituent that you think functions as a sentence modifier, if you can drop that constituent from the sentence, and

the remaining words still constitute a well-formed sentence in English, then the constituent you have removed was probably a sentence modifier.

The movability test for sentence modifiers: Given a constituent word, phrase, or clause at the beginning or end of a sentence, or between the subject and the verb, a constituent that you think constitutes a sentence modifier, if you can move that constituent from its position to one or both of the other sentence modifier positions without changing the essential meaning of the sentence, then the constituent you have moved is probably a sentence modifier.

The movability test is, by itself, the better test for sentence modifiers. However, if both tests work (the constituent is optional, <u>and</u> it can be moved without altering the meaning of the sentence), then the constituent in question is a sentence modifier.

1.2 Parts of Speech and Their Phrases

Traditional grammar books begin by defining what are called the "parts of speech": classes of words, defined by the kinds of meanings they are used to convey. We will stick with this meaning-based (or "semantic") approach to defining classes of words; it is also the approach that dictionaries commonly use, and sometimes the dictionary will be a helpful reference for figuring out which part-of-speech label to assign to a word or phrase. But we will add two other ways of thinking about classes of words. The first of these I have already mentioned: along with the semantic definitions, the parts of speech can be defined by the function of a word or phrase in the context of a sentence. We can take a single word (e.g. *play*) to provide a clear example:

>*play* **functioning as a <u>verb</u>**: *I <u>play</u> baseball every day.*
>*play* **functioning as a <u>noun</u>**: *She made a good <u>play</u>.*

We can identify *play* in the first sentence as a verb (lexical category) because it is filling a particular functional slot in the sentence, performing a sentence function that we identify with verbs: naming the action performed by a subject (*I*) while filling the role of "head" in the predicate. Likewise, in the second sentence, we can identify *play* as a noun because it is filling the slot—performing the function—of direct object—naming the thing acted upon—a sentence function we identify with nouns, NPs, and other nominals.

The other way we will talk about classes of words is in terms of form. One feature of form, at the level of words, has to do with inflections: the ways in which the words in a part-of-speech category can be changed, often by adding an ending (or "suffix"). So, for example, let's make up a noun: *plek*, as in, *I went to Lowe's to buy a <u>plek</u>*. To change the form to indicate that we are talking about more than one *plek*, you would readily tell me to "add an -*s*," as in, *The clerk told me they were out of pleks*. As part of the knowledge native speakers of English acquire about nouns and how they work—even if we have never heard the term "noun"—we know that to pluralize a noun—to indicate we have more than one of a thing—we add the sound [s].[4]

Verbs commonly change form as well. Again, let's make up a verb: *kadow*. Now let's conjugate it—that is, let's give all the forms it has in the present tense, as in the sentence *Today I kadow*: *I kadow*; *you kadow*; *he/she/it kadows*; *we kadow*; *you kadow*; *they kadow*. Once again, as a native speaker, you know to change the form with *he/she/it* from *kadow* to *kadows*. Likewise, if I ask you what form the verb takes in the following contexts, you would have no problem knowing how to change it:

> *Yesterday, we kadowed.*
> *I can't talk right now—I'm busy kadowing!*
> *Of course I have kadowed before.*

Only nouns change form by adding -*s* to mark the plural; only verbs change form by adding -*s* to mark the third-person singular or -*ed* and -*ing* to mark other forms and functions (see Chapter 6).

We need to pause here to consider a couple of further distinctions about words, forms, and part-of-speech labels. First, I proposed that the same word, *play*, might function as a verb or a noun, depending on the context in which it is used. Another way to think of this is that, whatever the common history of *play*$_{VERB}$ and *play*$_{NOUN}$ in current English, we have two homonymous-but-separate words. This makes sense in that *play*$_{VERB}$ can take the addition of the present participle ending -*ing* (*I am playing*), while *play*$_{NOUN}$ cannot, and *play*$_{NOUN}$ can take the plural marker -*s* (*I made two key plays yesterday*), while *play*$_{VERB}$ cannot. This idea is further bolstered by the variety of words ending in -*ing* that, although they remain usable as verbs, also have clearly distinct homonymous adjectives, e.g. *boring* (meaning "causing boredom" or "dull"):

> **boring** functioning as a <u>verb</u>: *This book is boring me.*
> **boring** functioning as an <u>adjective</u>: *This is a boring book.*

The adjective is gradable (*a more boring book*), while the verb is not. Contrast this example with the participle *moseying*, which can be used as a verb (*He was moseying into town*) or an adjective (*the moseying horse*) but is ungradable (**the more moseying horse*). Clearly, we have a well-established adjective form of *boring* but no such well-established adjective form of *moseying*. In *AEG*, I will do my best to treat pairs like *play*$_{VERB}$ and *play*$_{NOUN}$ and *boring*$_{VERB}$ and *boring*$_{ADJECTIVE}$ as separate homonyms, but in some instances, it will prove difficult to make a clear distinction. We will find that, far from being neat, separate boxes, the part-of-speech categories are radial, having clear, central, prototypical examples but becoming less distinct as we move away from those centers and often overlapping with each other.

One more note about how the forms of words interact with how we might place them in lexical categories. Words can take two different kinds of affixes: inflectional affixes and derivational affixes. Inflectional affixes in English are all suffixes: endings added to words to help show that a word is a member of a lexical category. A word that can take an inflectional ending is, by definition, part of the lexical category of words that can take such endings. There are eight inflectional endings in English, all of which we will discuss at greater length in the chapter on the relevant part of speech:

Nouns:

Plural -*s* (*the word<u>s</u>*)
Possessive *'s* (*Frost'<u>s</u> poem*)

Verbs:

Third-person singular present -*s* (*She work<u>s</u> well.*)
Present participle -*ing* (*She is work<u>ing</u> well.*)
Past tense -*ed* (*She work<u>ed</u> well.*)
Past participle -*en*/-*ed* (*She has eat<u>en</u>/work<u>ed</u>.*)

Adjectives and Adverbs:

Comparative -*er* (*the bigg<u>er</u> one; arrived soon<u>er</u>*)
Superlative -*est* (*the bigg<u>est</u> one; arrived soon<u>est</u>*)

Note that inflectional affixes do not change a word's part of speech: *word* and *words* are still both nouns.[5]

Derivational <u>prefixes</u> change a word's meaning but do not change its part of speech (e.g. *lock*$_v$; *unlock*$_v$). Derivational <u>suffixes</u> change a word's meaning and typically (though not always) change its part of speech. Thus, while the word *arouse* is always a verb, when we add the derivational ending -*al*, it becomes the noun *arousal*, a word that is always a noun. English has over 100 derivational prefixes and several hundred derivational suffixes. Here are a few more examples of derivational suffixes:

V→ADJ (*fix* + **able**)
V→N (*speak* + **er**)
N→N (*king* + **dom**)
N→ADJ (*cube* + **ic**)
N→V (*vapor* + **ize**)
ADJ→ADJ (*green* + **ish**)
ADJ→V (*modern* + **ize**)
ADJ→ADV (*quiet* + **ly**)
ADJ→N (*stupid* + **ity**)

The field of linguistics that deals with affixes and the rules of affixation—in short, how words are constructed—is called *morphology*. Alhough we do not have time to delve into English morphology, how words are constructed from smaller bits clearly overlaps with how they are organized to construct sentences, and concepts from morphology will be significant at other points in this book.

At the level of phrases, "form" involves what kinds of constituents a phrase may include and in what order. Determiners—for example, *the*—only appear in NPs and only appear before the noun. If we encounter the word *the*, we know that the form of the phrase in which it is a constituent is almost certainly an NP. Thus, along with the semantic and functional definitions of the parts of speech and their phrases, we will talk about form as a way of identifying the lexical categories of words and phrases.

I have now used the word "phrase" several times. Although most words can function alone as constituents within a sentence, all may, and some must, act as constituents within phrases. A phrase is a group of words that together form a single, more complex constituent within another phrase or within a clause or sentence. We will see that for most of the parts of speech (e.g. "nouns"), there are related phrases (e.g. "noun phrases"). We will spend more time talking about phrases (e.g. "noun phrases") than about single words (e.g. "nouns").

In this text, we will deal with eight parts of speech: nouns (N); prepositions (P); adjectives (ADJ); determiners (D); pronouns (PRON); verbs (V); adverbs (ADV); and conjunctions (CONJ). Traditional grammar generally includes one more minor part-of-speech category: interjections (INTERJ). As defined by Warriner, "an interjection is a word that expresses emotion and has no grammatical relation to other words in the sentence."[6] An interjection is often followed by an exclamation point to indicate the strength of the emotion expressed (e.g. *Oh dear! Ouch! Wow!*).

Two distinctions worth noting: first, these part-of-speech classes are commonly divided into two general subgroups: "content words" and "function words." Content words are classes of words that are thought of as primarily conveying substantive meaning and include nouns (which name things), adjectives (which name qualities of things), verbs (which name actions), and adverbs (which name such qualities as manner, reason, and duration). Function words are classes of words that are usually thought of as relating content words to each other or nuancing the meaning of content words. The categories of function words include determiners (which "specify" the meaning of the noun in terms of definiteness, number, amount, possession, etc.), prepositions (which relate a following noun phrase to other content words), pronouns (which take, hold, or mark the place of a noun phrase or other nominal), some adverbs (such as intensifiers like *so* and *very* and negators like *not* and *never*), and conjunctions (which link together sentence constituents that have the same function).

Second, content words are commonly considered "open classes," in that new members of those classes routinely enter the language. Speakers and writers create new nouns, verbs, adjectives, and adverbs every day. Some gain a lasting place in the language (e.g. *email* as a noun, verb, and adjective), while some come and go quickly (e.g. the nouns *flivver* and *jalopy*, both referring to a cheap car in poor condition). Function words are commonly considered "closed classes," in that we cannot create new members of the class, and we generally do not stop using existing members. It has been hundreds of years since English has adopted a new preposition, pronoun, adverbial negator, or conjunction.

The next several chapters will be devoted to each part of speech and its associated phrase. Of the eight parts of speech listed above, all but conjunctions commonly form the core or head of a phrase. We will see that there are tests for identifying members of most part-of-speech classes or types of phrase, tests that will be based both on the kinds of meaning that the members of the class may convey and on the kinds of functions that members of the class can perform. We will also think of the functions of words and phrases in terms of the "slots" a type of phrase can "fill" in a sentence.

Remember that the subject of a sentence always consists of a nominal, and the most common type of nominal is the noun phrase (NP). The first parts of speech we will examine will be nouns (and NPs), along with some of the other parts of speech and related phrases that can be constituents of NPs: prepositions and prepositional phrases; adjectives and adjective phrases; and determiners and determiner phrases. We will look at the meanings, forms, and functions of these parts of speech and their related phrases.

Key Points

- Sentences typically comprise four major constituents: the subject and verb (obligatory), the verb complement (obligatory for most verbs), and sentence modifiers (optional).
- The easiest way to parse a sentence—to identify its constituent parts—is to start with the verb, the word that names the action being performed by the subject.
- The answer to the question, *Who or what did the action named by the verb?* is the subject of the verb.
- The complete NP:SUBJ is the complete subject; the head noun of the NP:SUBJ is the simple subject.
- The VP:PRED comprises the complete verb, its complement(s), and modifiers; the complete verb, taken by itself, is the simple predicate.
- Sentence modifiers can appear at the beginning or end of the sentence and, often, between the subject and the predicate.
- There are eight parts of speech, also known as lexical categories; these lexical categories are sub-divided into open classes of content words (nouns, verbs, adjective, and most adverbs) and closed classes of function words (prepositions, pronouns, determiners, some adverbs, and conjunctions).
- Members of each lexical category can be identified by their form, function, and meaning.

- Members of all lexical categories (except conjunctions) can form phrases; phrases commonly comprise a head word (obligatory) and may also include a complement/s (obligatory) and/or modifiers (optional) as dependent constituents.

1.3 Exercises: Sentences

A. Made-up sentences:[7]

- For each sentence 1–10, identify the complete subject and the complete predicate.
- For each sentence 1–10, identify the simple subject and the simple predicate.
- If you can, identify any sentence modifiers that appear in these sentences.

1. The discovery of the vitamins was a major scientific achievement in our understanding of health and disease.
2. In 1912, Casimir Funk coined the term "vitamin."
3. The major period of discovery ran from the early nineteenth century to the mid-twentieth century.
4. The puzzle of each vitamin was solved through the work and contributions of epidemiologists, physicians, physiologists, and chemists.
5. Scientific work on vitamins proceeded through a slow, stepwise series of setbacks, contradictions, refutations, and some chicanery.
6. Research on the vitamins began when the germ theory of disease was dominant.
7. Soon clinicians recognized scurvy, beriberi, rickets, pellagra, and xerophthalmia as specific vitamin deficiencies.
8. After many different kinds of studies, experimental physiology with animal models greatly shortened the period of human suffering from vitamin deficiencies.
9. Ultimately the chemists isolated the various vitamins, deduced their chemical structure, and developed methods for synthesis of vitamins.
10. Since the initial period of discovery our understanding of the vitamins has evolved because of the careful labor of innumerable scientists.

B. A real text:[8] same instructions as in A.

(1) A dog belonging to Princess Anne attacked a royal maid five days after it fatally mauled one of Queen Elizabeth II's beloved Corgis, Buckingham Palace said. (2) Florence the bull terrier bit the maid's leg at the royal Sandringham estate in eastern England, the palace said. (3) The woman was treated for a minor bite following Saturday's attack and did not need to go to the hospital. (4) Five days earlier, Florence savaged a Corgi named

Pharos at Sandringham, injuring him so badly that he had to be put down. (5) Media reports had widely blamed another of Princess Anne's bull terriers, Dotty, for the Corgi incident, but Buckingham Palace cleared her Tuesday and blamed Florence instead. (6) Buckingham Palace refused to comment on whether Florence would have to be put down after biting the maid, who was in her 50s, according to a report in the *Sun* newspaper. (7) British media reported that Florence had no history of violent behavior, unlike Dotty, who bit two children in a park in 2002 and landed Princess Anne with an $880 fine.

Figure 1.1

Notes

1. I have just said "typically" and "in general" because the definition of "sentence" is controversial. Really. For example, imperative voice sentences (e.g. *Close the door.*) have no stated subject. Rather, the subject and a modal auxiliary verb are implied (e.g. *You must* close the door.). This example opens the question of whether, in parsing sentences, we should analyze just what is actually written or said, or we should also consider what is only implied. Also, as you will see in analyzing real-world written examples, very often a string of words punctuated as a "sentence" seems to comprise whatever an author wants to place between an initial capital letter and a final punctuation mark: for example, the second "sentence" of this footnote comprises a single word, "really," which, while formally not a sentence is, in many contexts, a stylistically acceptable "sentence fragment." Grammar and style curmudgeons attack fragments, although the best writers use them routinely. In spoken language, there are no "sentences" *per se*; rather, there are "breath units" (all the words one can utter before having to pause for breath), intonation curves (to mark statements and questions) and pauses. "Sentences" are an attempt to formally represent the features of speech in writing. Paragraphs are a similar attempt to formalize the ways topics are chunked in spoken language. I may be starting with a strong definition of "sentence." But, as a result of the realities of actual English usage, when I introduce and define terms and concepts, my frequent practice will be to offer alternative definitions and interpretations, and we will discover that context plays a strong role in how we define and apply terms.

2. You will already be thinking, "But what about a verb like *be* in a sentence like *Ed is here*: in that case, the complement isn't a *what*, it's a *where*." There are many

different kinds of verb complements that we'll get to in Chapter 7. Direct objects are just a very common type and easy to start with.

3. Alexandra Ossola. "Too Many Kids Quit Science Because They Don't Think They're Smart." *theatlantic.com*. 3 Nov 2014.

4. Which is sometimes pronounced [z], as in *bugs*, or pronounced [əz] and spelled *-es* as in *buses*.

5. Actually, there is one exception: adding possessive *'s* to a N (*Frost's*) or NP (e.g. *the famous poet's*) changes the N or NP to a determiner (D) or determiner phrase (DP). See 4.2.

6. John Warriner. *English Grammar and Composition*. Fourth Course. Orlando: Harcourt Brace Jovanovich, 1982 [1948]. 24.

7. Sentences based on Richard D. Semba. "The Discovery of the Vitamins." Abstract. *International Journal for Vitamin and Nutrition Research* 82.5 (Oct 2012): 310.

8. "Princess Anne's Dog Bites Royal Maid." Associated Press. 1 Jan 2004.

Chapter 2

Nouns (N) and Noun Phrases (NP)

2.1 Noun Features

Nouns are a category of content words. In traditional grammar, nouns are defined semantically as words that name things, whether concrete things (e.g. people, places, animals, or objects) or abstract things (e.g. ideas or qualities). Thus, nouns and noun phrases, are constituents that tell *who* or *what*. Nouns are commonly also defined by four contrastive categories: proper/common; singular/plural; mass/count; and generic/specific.

1. Proper versus common nouns: The main semantic distinction of proper nouns is that they name specific and, within the context of use, unique places (*Peoria*), people (*Carrie Underwood*), things (*Peoria Journal Star*; *Empire State Building*), or events (*World War II*). The main formal distinction is that proper nouns are always capitalized. By contrast, common nouns are not usually capitalized, and most do not name unique places, people, or things; rather, they name classes or types of things (e.g. not *Peoria* but *city/cities*; not *Carrie Underwood* but *singer/s*; not *Peoria Journal Star* but *newspaper/s*; not *Empire State Building* but *office building/s*).

2. Singular versus plural nouns: As the names imply, we use singular nouns to refer to single objects (e.g. *cat*) or groups considered as units (e.g. *audience*) and plural nouns to refer to a group of individuals (e.g. *cats*) or a group of groups (e.g. *audiences*). Plural nouns can also be used to refer (1) to the sum of all of a type of object present in some limited space: *Today in our store, balls are on sale* and (2) to the generic category of an object, as when we say *Dogs like to run*, meaning, "it is generically true of dogs that they like to run." We usually turn singular nouns to plural nouns by a change in form: adding *-s* (*book/books*) or *-es* (*bus/buses*; *flurry/flurries*), with spelling conventions applying. There are a limited set of exceptional plurals that don't take *-s* or *-es*, both from the Anglo-Saxon roots of English (e.g. *child/children*, *ox/oxen*, *woman/women*, *moose/moose*, *mouse/mice*), from Latin (e.g. *alumna* or *alumnus/alumni*; *datum/data*; *medium/media*), and from Greek (e.g. *schema/schemata*; *phenomenon/phenomena*).

Non-Standard plurals: According to Wolfram and Schilling-Estes,[1] there are three distinct ways in which non-Standard varieties of English form plurals that differ from those found in "general American English." In the first two, the plural marker -s can be deleted because a separate word—a determiner preceding the noun (see 4.2)—indicates that the noun is plural in reference and therefore the -s is semantically redundant.

First, in varieties of English "where another language was spoken in the recent past," the plural suffix may simply be absent, as in *Lots of boy_ go to the school. All the girl_ liked the movie. Two boy_ just left.* This "absent plural" is also found to a limited degree in AAVE[2] but not often—only one to ten percent of the time, according to studies done to date.[3] Dillard observes that, while the -s plural marker may be absent "after a numeral or some other expression which clearly denotes plurality, where other modifiers do not so clearly point out plurality," the -s plural marker will be used.[4] Although it may occur in only a small percentage of instances in AAVE usage, to the ears of speakers of varieties that routinely include the plural marker on the noun, the absence would sound strange. So while not using the plural -s marks the speaker as a member of one group, at the same time it marks the speaker as not being a member of other groups, often to the speaker's disadvantage.

The plural demonstrative determiner *dem* (derived from *them*) is commonly used in AAVE varieties to mark plurality. And in the Gullah English variety of the coastal islands of South Carolina and Georgia, as in Caribbean English creoles,[5] *dem* may appear before a noun with the plural -s deleted from the noun as being redundant, as in *dem book_.*[6]

Second, "in Southern-based rural vernaculars," the absence of the plural marker is limited to "nouns of weights and measures" and even some nouns that name units of time that are preceded by a quantifying determiner or a cardinal number, as in *four pound; three ton; two foot; twenty mile; two year, five month; a lot of bushel*:

> *The station is four **mile_** down the road. They hauled in a lotta **bushel_** of corn.*

Again, arguably, if the noun is preceded by a plural quantifier, then the plural marker -s on the end of the noun is redundant and therefore unnecessary.

In the third variety of non-Standard pluralization, irregular plural noun forms are regularized to match the more general pattern of using -s to mark the plural in nouns:

> *They saw the **deers** running across the field.*
> *The **firemans** liked the conversation.*[7]

This regularization occurs for at least some words in most vernacular varieties of American English and may occur with words of three different sorts:

- Those in which the plural is "not overtly marked in general American English": so *deers* and *sheeps* as opposed to SE *deer* and *sheep*, which are used for both the singular and the plural.

- Those words that have irregular plural suffixes in SE: so *oxes* as opposed to SE *oxen*.
- Those words in which the plural is marked in the SE variety by changes in a vowel: so *firemans* and *snowmans* as opposed to SE *firemen* and *snowmen*.

In some vernacular varieties, plurals may also be double marked, as in *mens* and *childrens*.[8] Smitherman argues that, in AAVE, this double marking may be attributable to hypercorrection: if a speaker understands that plurals are always marked with -*s* and is not taught the irregular nouns as exceptions, then it would seem perfectly reasonable to mark all plurals with -*s* so that one would say *mans* or *mens*, *childs* or *childrens*.[9] Wolfram and Schilling-Estes[10] conclude that some of these regularized forms are quite widespread among the vernacular varieties of English (e.g. regularizing non-marked plurals such as *deers*), whereas others (e.g. double marking *mens*) are more limited.

3. Mass vs. count nouns: Mass nouns refer to masses of material (e.g. *water, sugar, applesauce, steel*) or things that conventionally cannot be counted (e.g. *soccer, homework*), while count nouns refer to countable objects (e.g. *dream, letter, inauguration, arm*). Traditionally, when we refer to amounts of things, we refer to mass nouns with the words *more* and *less* (e.g. *more water*; *less water*), but we refer to countable nouns with the words *more* and *fewer* (e.g. *more dreams*; *fewer dreams*). Fowler describes this distinction between *less* and *fewer* as a "modern tendency,"[11] while Lovinger[12] and even Grammar Girl[13] state it as a firm rule. But *less* and *fewer* were actually interchangeable from the earliest days of English until 1770, when Robert Baker offered the opinion that *fewer* sounded more "proper and elegant" with count nouns.[14] Although the rule seems to have become increasingly entrenched in the twentieth century, my students regularly say and write *less* for both mass and count nouns, and it even shows up in the media and published academic writing:

> Pumpkin pie has *less* calories than pecan pie.[15]
> Dulles or Reagan or BWI, they all have very good fencing and usually have *less* problems with deer.[16]

If the next generation has its way, in another thirty years, I predict that *less* with a count noun will be judged "more correct" than *fewer*.

4. Generic vs. specific nouns: We have already used the term "generic" above: generic nouns (or, more properly, generic NPs) refer to the general category of an object. The sentence *Dogs like to run* implies that it is generally true of *dogs* as a category that they like to run. By contrast, a specific noun or NP refers to a particular individual member of a category. In the sentence *My dog likes to run*, the NP *my dog* refers to one specific dog.

The four pairs of contrastive categories I have just described interact in some interesting ways. Count nouns have both a singular and a plural (e.g.

dream/dreams), except for a few that already end in *-s* and are idiosyncratically plural, such as things that are described as coming in pairs (e.g. *scissors, pants*). However, mass nouns are only singular (e.g. *soccer/*soccers*). When it appears that we can pluralize a mass noun, we're actually using it as a count noun:

> *Heteropolysaccharides are formed from several different <u>sugars</u>.*[17] (meaning "different <u>kinds</u> of sugar")
> *Please bring us three <u>waters</u>.* (meaning "three <u>glasses</u> of water")

Generic nouns may be either singular or plural; however, the singular generic must always be preceded by the determiners *a, an,* or *the*:

> <u>*Dogs*</u> *are a species of carnivorous mammal.*
> *The <u>dog</u> is a species of carnivorous mammal.*
> *A <u>dog</u> is a carnivorous mammal.*

Specific NPs may be either singular or plural, depending on whether they refer to a specific individual (e.g. <u>*My dog Rover*</u> *likes to run*) or a specific group (e.g. <u>*Our neighbor's dogs*</u> *won't stop barking!*).

Common count nouns can be pluralized (e.g. *city/cities*), but typically, a proper noun cannot (*Peoria/*Peorias*). There are contexts in which a proper noun takes the plural *-s*, as when we make a claim like, *Three times around the country means that we've already hit all the <u>New Yorks</u> and <u>LAs</u> and now we were playing the <u>Kalamazoos</u> and <u>Poughkeepsies</u>.*[18] In this context, the pluralized proper nouns each mean something like "cities like New York" and "cities like Poughkeepsie." What we are doing in such a context is turning the uniquely referring proper noun into a count noun: counting cities that are like New York is like counting New Yorks. This is like using the pluralized mass noun *waters* to mean *glasses of water*. Similarly, in talking about marathons, one might say or write, *Of all the <u>New Yorks</u> I've watched, the one I remember most is 1992.*[19] *New Yorks* is short for *New York Marathons*; the latter phrase is countable, but in the context of talking about marathons, it is enough to just say *New Yorks* to mean the longer phrase. These distinctions (singular vs. plural; mass vs. count) will become more significant when we study determiners in 4.2.

Proper nouns are generally easy to identify because they are capitalized names of specific people, places, things, events, or ideas. Common nouns, however, can sometimes be harder to identify, especially since the same word can be used as more than one part of speech:

> **Verb**: *I <u>run</u> for exercise.* **Noun**: *I think I'll go for a <u>run</u>.*
> **Adjective**: *I bought a <u>green</u> soccer ball.* **Noun**: <u>*Green*</u> *is my favorite color.*
> **Adverb**: *I want to go <u>home</u>.* **Noun**: <u>*Home*</u> *is where the heart is.*

In SE usage, there are three tests for identifying common nouns:

> **The general noun-slot tests**: Functionally, a noun can be defined most easily by the kind of slot it can fill in a sentence. If a word can be used in the open slot in one of the following sentences, or in similar slots in other sentences, then, in that sentence context, the word is functioning as a noun.
>
> *The* _____ *is/are/was/were good.*
> _____ *is/are/was/were good.*

> **The *the* test for common nouns**: If a word can be used with the determiner *the*, then that word is a common noun. This test is very reliable, although to make the test work with some abstract nouns (e.g. *honesty, caution, justice*), the noun must be followed by a <u>modifying phrase</u> (e.g. "*The caution* <u>practiced by our predecessors</u> should guide us.").[20]

> **The pluralization test for common count nouns**: If a word can be used in the plural, then that word is a common count noun. This test is also very reliable. Remember that it does not work for mass nouns since they cannot typically be pluralized (e.g. *milks [which, like *waters*, can be used to mean "glasses of milk"]; *lightnings; *homeworks). However, if a word can ordinarily be pluralized, then it is a common noun.[21]

Warnings: First, in the second sentence of the general noun-slot test, some pronouns will also fit the slot: *He/she/it/this is good*; *We/you/they/these are good*. You just need to know that these are pronouns (see Chapter 5). Second, as with all of the tests we will use throughout this book for identifying parts of speech and types of phrases and clauses within sentences, when applying the *the* test, remember to do so within the context of the original sentence. Otherwise, you might change the lexical category, or the form, of the word, phrase, or clause. Also, when you have more than one test for a constituent class, try all of them. They may not all agree, but the answer given by the majority of the tests will usually be the correct one.

2.2 Noun Phrases

So far, we have defined "noun" by the meaning and form of individual nouns. But in addition to these two kinds of definition, we will also define parts of speech, phrases, and clauses in terms of their functions. A noun functions as the <u>head</u> of a noun phrase (NP). Whether it appears by itself or, as is often the case, accompanied by dependents, including adjectival modifiers and determiners, a noun is always the head of an NP. Determiners, while dependents of the noun within the NP, are not always optional: if we drop a determiner, it may make the sentence ill formed. For example, in the sentence *The green ball is not for sale*, the determiner *the* is obligatory, while the adjectival modifier *green* is optional (see 4.2). From here on out, we will mostly talk about NPs (rather than nouns), as an NP may comprise just a noun by itself.

The general structure of an NP can be stated as follows:

[DETERMINER PHRASE] + {ADJECTIVE PHRASES} + NOUN + {ADJECTIVAL POST-MODIFIERS}

The items in curly brackets—"Adjective Phrases" and "Adjectival Post-Modifiers"—are modifiers and are optional. I have put square brackets around "Determiner Phrase" because determiners are not always optional and cannot merely be lumped in with the other modifiers. Also, a number of types of constituents can be "adjectival post-modifiers" of nouns; the list includes adjectival prepositional phrases (Chapter 3); adjective clauses (10.2.1); and adjectival participle phrases and adjectival infinitive phrases (Chapter 12). Be aware that when an adjectival modifier comes after a noun, if that adjectival modifier is modifying the preceding noun, then it is a constituent of the NP of which that noun is the head. Students often think an NP ends with the head noun. Sometimes it does; sometimes it doesn't. Be careful.

In the following examples, in the NP:SUBJ of each sentence, [determiners] are in square brackets, {modifiers} are in curly brackets, *adjective phrases* in italics, adjectival post-modifiers are underlined, and the head **nouns** are in bold face:

[The] {*large, green*} **ball** {with the yellow spots} is not for sale.
[The] **ball** {with the yellow spots} is not for sale.
[The] {*large, green*} **ball** is not for sale.
[The] {*large*} **ball** is not for sale.
[The] {*green*} **ball** is not for sale.
[The] **ball** is not for sale.
[The] **balls** are not for sale.
*{*Green*} **ball** is not for sale.
{*Green*} **balls** are not for sale.
***Ball** is not for sale.
Balls are not for sale.

In these sentences, note that all of the modifiers—whether *adjective phrases* or adjectival post-modifiers—are optional: they can be dropped or kept in any combination, and the sentence remains well formed. However, with a singular common noun (e.g. *ball*), the determiner (e.g. *the*) is not optional. But with a plural noun (e.g. *balls*), the determiner is, like the modifiers, optional: if we drop the determiner from before the plural noun, the sentence is still well formed. Yes, the meaning of the NP and the sentence change, as they do when we drop modifiers, but the grammaticality—the well-formedness—of the sentence does not change.

Even with a plural common noun, the determiner is not optional with regard to meaning: semantically, there is a distinct difference between *The balls are not for sale* and *Balls are not for sale*: the first sentence means that some particular set of balls is not for sale, while the second sentence means that all of the balls are not for sale—or, in general, balls are not for sale. Nonetheless, although determiners are not the same as modifiers, determiners, like adjective phrases and adjectival post-modifiers of nouns, are dependents of nouns within an NP since they "depend" on the head noun for their meaning. Determiners only function as constituents within NPs (see 4.2).

Adjectival post-modifiers in NPs can be phrases or clauses: prepositional phrases, participle phrases, infinitive phrases, and adjective clauses (a.k.a. relative clauses):

> NP containing **adjectival post-modifiers** of the noun:
> Prepositional Phrase: *The ball **in the grass** is yellow.*
> Participle Phrase: *The ball **lying in the grass** is yellow.*
> Infinitive Phrase: *The ball **to use for today's game** is on the shelf.*
> Adjective Clause: *The ball **that I want you to use for today's game** is on the shelf.*

Common nouns may take pre-modifying adjective phrases and adjectival post-modifiers, but proper nouns typically do not take determiners or pre-modifiers. However, proper nouns may take adjectival post-modifiers, most commonly adjective clauses:

> Determiner + **Proper Noun**: **The **Franz** had never played in the World Cup final.*
> Adjective + **Proper Noun**: **Happy **Franz** had never played in the World Cup final.*
> **Proper Noun** + Adjective Clause: ***Franz**, who had never played in the World Cup final, was ecstatic.*

When a proper noun takes an adjective clause as a post-modifier, that adjective clause typically provides non-essential information: the information provided by the adjective clause is not required for the reader or hearer to understand which particular object the writer or speaker is naming with the proper noun. With or without the clause *who had never played in the World Cup*, we would understand what particular person the proper noun *Franz* refers to. By contrast, in the sentence *The ball that I want you to use for today's game is on the shelf*, the adjective clause *that I want you to use for today's game* is an essential modifier: this adjective clause functions as a post-modifier of the noun *ball*, identifying which particular ball the speaker is referring to and distinguishing it from other balls that might be present. This adjective clause is essential because, without it, the listener would not know which ball the speaker means. Several times during our study of grammar, we will encounter this distinction between essential modifiers and non-essential modifiers (also known as restrictive and non-restrictive modifiers, respectively).

Nominal appositive phrases: One important type of non-essential modifier that we find as a modifier of a noun is called an appositive phrase. An appositive phrase is an NP (or adjective phrase; see 4.1) acting as a modifier of a noun. The appositive phrase is set next to—in <u>apposition</u> to—a noun phrase:

> *My older brother <u>Thomas</u> is twenty-one.*
> *My aunt and uncle, <u>the Giovannis</u>, own a store, <u>the Empire Shoe Shop on Main Street</u>.*[22]

Each appositive NP modifies an adjoining noun by providing adjectival information about the object referred to by the noun: the apposed NP *Thomas* tells *which older brother*; *the Giovannis* tells *which aunt and uncle*; *the Empire Shoe Shop on Main Street* tells *which store*. The appositive phrase takes the form of an NP (a head noun with dependent determiners and modifiers), but the appositive phrase <u>functions</u> as an adjectival modifier of a noun. Also, in these sentences, each appositive phrase is a non-essential modifier: although each appositive provides adjectival information about a noun, none of the appositives are essential to the hearer or reader's understanding of the reference of that noun.

Appositive NPs can also appear <u>before</u> a noun: *<u>A good all-around athlete</u>, Roland is a promising candidate for the decathlon.*[23]

2.3 Noun Phrase Functions

NPs have several functions:

Subject of a clause: In both of the following examples, *Franz* is the subject of the verb *bought*.

> **Independent Clause** (a.k.a. sentence): *<u>Franz</u> bought the ball with the yellow spots.*
> **Dependent Clause**: *The ball that <u>Franz</u> bought had yellow spots.*

Complement of a preposition: In *Franz bought the ball with <u>the yellow spots</u>*, the NP *the yellow spots* complements or "completes" the sense of the preposition *with*. Together, the preposition and the NP make a prepositional phrase.

Complement of a verb: In *Franz bought <u>the ball with the yellow spots</u>*, the NP *the ball with the yellow spots* is the complement of the verb *bought*. More specifically, it is the direct object (DO) of the verb. "Direct object" is one type of verb complement; NPs can function as other types of verb complement (see Chapter 7):

NP:DIRECT OBJECT: *Franz bought the ball with the yellow spots.*
NP:INDIRECT OBJECT: *Franz bought his teammates the ball with the yellow spots.*
NP:SUBJECT COMPLEMENT: *Franz is an excellent player.*
NP:OBJECT COMPLEMENT: *The team elected Franz captain.*

Identifying NPs: Let's come back to the sentence *Franz bought the ball with the yellow spots*. When you are asked to identify all of the NPs in this sentence, you have to be careful to note that there are three: the subject NP (NP:SUBJ) *Franz*, the direct object NP (NP:DO) *the ball with the yellow spots*, and the complement of the preposition (NP:PCOMP) *the yellow spots*. All three are distinct NPs with their own functions, even though *the yellow spots* is a constituent of—is contained within—the prepositional phrase *with the yellow* spots, which is, in turn, contained within the NP *the ball with the yellow spots*. When asked to identify NPs, you need to be careful and methodical: as I will often note, in parsing sentences, the devil is always in the details.

Modifier of a noun: A word that seems to be a noun in terms of its meaning and common function can also serve to modify another noun in two ways: as an adjective and as a nominal appositive.

Noun functioning as an adjective: In the sentence *Franz bought the soccer ball*, we might parse *soccer ball* as a compound noun: two or more nouns that are commonly used together to name a thing. English has a vast number of nouns that commonly appear together as compounds. Compound nouns may be closed, as in *baseball* or *moonlight*, or open, as in *soccer ball, tennis ball, fly fishing, stop sign*, or *tater tots*. Over time, commonly used open compounds, such as *base ball*, may be joined, first with a hyphen and then into closed compounds, as has happened with *electronic mail*, which was then clipped and hyphenated as *e-mail* and has most recently been joined into the closed compound *email*. Commonly, compound nouns are pronounced with greater stress on the first syllable.

It makes sense to analyze a compound noun as a single noun. If we are talking about *excellent fly fishing*, we are really not talking about *fishing* that was both *excellent* and *fly*; rather, *excellent* tells what kind of *fly fishing* there was. It is also reasonable to analyze *soccer ball* as a single noun. However, it is also true that the compound has an interior structure in which *soccer* tells *what kind of ball*; *soccer* thus seems to be functioning as if it were an adjective: an adjective modifying a noun tells *which* or *what kind of* thing the noun names. Without any other context, we usually think of the word *soccer* as a noun since it names a game—that is, a thing. Thus, within the context of the compound noun, we might think of *soccer* as a noun functioning as an adjective (N:ADJ). This will be the first of many encounters with the inherent fuzziness of the lexical categories.

Compound nouns can be quite complex. *United States of America* or *People's Republic of China* are NPs with analyzable structures, but in actual use, we treat them as if they were just elaborate single words. You can analyze them either way.

Nominal appositive: In the sentence *My aunt and uncle own a store, the Empire Shoe Shop on Main Street*, the NP *the Empire Shoe Shop on Main Street* does not function in a nominal role: by itself, it is not the subject of the sentence or the complement of a verb or preposition. Rather, as we saw above, this NP is a modifier of the noun *store* and provides non-essential adjectival information about that noun by telling *which store*.

Adverbial: An NP may function as an adverbial modifier of an adverb or an entire clause. Adverbial constituents can provide various sorts of modifying information about an action or event named by a clause (e.g. *when* or *where* it happened) or about a quality named by an adjective or another adverb (e.g. *how much* or *how* [in what manner] that quality exists). In *This morning, Franz bought the ball*, the NP *this morning* tells when the whole action in the sentence happened. And the NP can be moved to the end of the sentence or to the slot between the subject and the verb: *Franz bought the ball this morning. Franz, this morning, bought the ball*. The NP *this morning* functions here as a sentence modifier—a function typically filled by some type of adverbial.

In *Five days earlier, he bought new shin guards*, the NP *five days* tells how much *earlier*—that is, it modifies the adverb *earlier*. We will find that locative and temporal NPs—NPs that name places and times—that tell *where* (e.g. *home*) and *when* (e.g. *yesterday*; *Tuesday*)—can function as adverbials (see 11.3).

Pronouns and pronoun phrases (Chapter 5) are NPs, as we can see in the following sentences. In each case, the NP functioning as the subject (NP:Subj) is in brackets:

> *[The woman who drove the red Porsche] went to the store.*
> *[The woman] went to the store.*
> *[She] went to the store.*

A pronoun is traditionally defined as a word that is used to replace a noun. Actually, we use a pronoun to fill the same slot as would be occupied by a complete NP. This suggests that, to identify a complete NP, we could use a pronoun replacement test:

> **The pronoun replacement test for NPs**: Any noun phrase can be replaced by an appropriate third-person pronoun (*he, she, it, they, this, that, these, those*). The pronoun will thus replace—and identify—the complete noun phrase.[24]

We have already seen in the preceding examples how the pronoun *she* replaced the NPs *the woman who drove the red Porsche* and *the woman*. We can see how the pronoun replacement test works for identifying where an NP starts and ends in the following sentences:

1. *The large, green ball with the yellow spots rolled in the grass.*
2. *It rolled in the grass.*
3. **The large green it with yellow spots rolled in the grass.*
4. **The large green it rolled in the grass.*
5. **It with the yellow spots rolled in the grass.*

Numbers 3, 4, and 5 are ill formed because the pronoun has been used only to replace part of the original NP rather than the entire NP. This is the proof that the pronoun does not just replace the noun itself. Also, 3, 4, and 5 show us that we can use the pronoun replacement test to identify where a complete NP begins and ends.

The pronoun replacement test works only based on the function of a constituent, not its form. Although a constituent may look like an NP, if it is not functioning in a nominal role, the pronoun replacement test fails:

NP functioning adjectivally:

Franz bought the <u>soccer</u> ball.
*Franz bought the <u>it</u> ball.
My cousin, <u>the soccer player</u>, is upstairs.
?My cousin, <u>he</u> is upstairs.

NP functioning adverbially:

<u>This morning</u>, Franz bought the ball.
*<u>It</u>, Franz bought the ball.
<u>Five days</u> earlier, he bought new shin guards.
*<u>It</u> earlier, he bought new shin guards.
Franz went <u>home</u>.
*Franz went <u>it</u>.

This failure of the pronoun replacement test suggests that function trumps form: even though, formally, *soccer* and *five days* may look like they are NPs, when those phrases are placed in a context where they function adjectivally or adverbially, then they become, essentially, what their function says they are.

Non-Standard reduplicated subject or predicate marker: Stepping back for a moment to the example of an NP functioning adjectivally, ?*My cousin, he is upstairs*: while we cannot paraphrase the NP functioning adjectivally with a PRON, we find a usage with the same pattern in some non-Standard varieties of English, most notably in AAVE. SE speakers often misunderstand *he* as an appositive, and commonly this is referred to as a "reduplicated subject." Dillard, however, offers a different analysis: in AAVE we often find sentences like:

Ray sister <u>she</u> got a new doll baby.
Ray sister go to school at Adams <u>she</u> got a new doll baby.
Ray sister seven-year-old go to school at Adams <u>she</u> got a new doll baby.

Dillard argues that *seven-year-old* and *go to school at Adams* are adjective clauses with the relative pronoun *who* understood and that the pronoun *she* serves to mark where the subject ends and the predicate begins.[25] In SE, these sentences would read:

Ray's sister got a new doll baby.
Ray's sister, who goes to school at Adams, got a new doll baby
Ray's sister, who is seven years old, and who goes to school at Adams, got a new doll baby.

Semantic or Form-and-Function: Which Description Works Better?

Nouns can be adjectives or adverbs? NPs can function adjectivally or adverbially? What's up with that? The problem arises from the clash of thinking about words—and their associated phrases—in two different ways. In traditional grammar, parts of speech (and, by implication, their associated phrases) were defined in terms of meaning (that is, semantically) and out of context: the word *soccer* must be a noun because it names a thing; the word *green* must be an adjective because it names a quality that relates to things—that is, the adjective can be used to modify a noun. But in the second half of the twentieth century, linguists and grammarians began to think more about the patterns of English sentences and to try to define parts of speech and their associated phrases in terms of their forms (e.g. what inflectional affixes they can take) and functions within the contexts of sentences (that is, syntactically). So if the word *soccer* appears between *the* and a noun, then *soccer* is functioning adjectivally. If the word *green* appears as the subject of a sentence, then *green* is functioning nominally.

Which approach is right? For our purposes, and for the purposes of talking about writing and clarity, both approaches are useful. It is important to know that when we use an unexpected form in a particular functional slot, it can confuse a reader or create an unexpected effect, as when Gerard Manley Hopkins writes in his poem "The Windhover," *The achieve of, the mastery of the thing,*[26] using the verb form *achieve* in a functional slot we associate with nouns.

Throughout this book, we will approach grammar from both sides: the traditional, semantic approach and the more recent form-and-function approach. This dual approach will lead us to say sometimes that a particular constituent is, in its form, an NP or other nominal functioning as an adverbial or adverbially or, in form, an adjective phrase but functioning as a nominal or nominally. We will use question tests (e.g. an NP or nominal is a constituent that tells *who* or *what*; an adjective phrase or adjectival constituent tells *which one* or *what kind of*; an adverb phrase tells *when, where, how, how long, how much*, etc.) together with formal and functional analyses (What inflectional affixes could a word take in the context? What role is this constituent filling relative to the constituents around it?). When thinking about sentence constituents, it often proves useful to have both kinds of information in mind.

Key Points

- Nouns are defined semantically as words that name things: people, places, animals, objects, ideas, or qualities.
- Nouns and noun phrases tell *who* or *what*.
- Nouns are also defined by four contrastive categories: proper/common; singular/plural; mass/count; and generic/specific.
- Three tests for identifying nouns are the general noun-slot tests (function); the *the* test for common nouns (function); and the pluralization test for common count nouns (form).
- A noun functions as the head of a noun phrase (NP).
- A noun phrase must include a N:HEAD and may include a determiner and/ or adjectival modifiers.
- An NP may function as the subject of a clause, a verb complement, or the complement of a preposition. In these functions, a complete NP can always be identified by the pronoun replacement test.
- An NP may also function adjectivally (in a compound noun; as an appositive) or adverbially (particularly NPs that name periods of time).

2.4 Exercises: Noun Phrases

A. Made-up sentences:[27]

- For each sentence, identify all complete NPs. Sometimes there are complete NPs inside other complete NPs.
- For each NP, identify the head noun.
- For each NP, <u>try</u> to identify its function.

1. Elizabeth Cady Stanton, the chief philosopher of the women's suffrage movement, formulated the agenda for the struggle for women's rights.
2. She was born on November 12, 1815 in Johnstown, New York.
3. Stanton received her formal education at the Johnstown Academy and at Emma Willard's Troy Female Seminary in New York.
4. Her father was a noted lawyer and state assemblyman, and young Elizabeth gained an informal legal education from her interactions with his colleagues and guests.
5. A well-educated woman, Stanton married abolitionist lecturer Henry Stanton in 1840 and became active in the anti-slavery movement.

6. While on her honeymoon in London to attend a World's Anti-Slavery convention, Stanton met abolitionist Lucretia Mott, who, like her, was also angry about the exclusion of women at the proceedings.

7. Mott and Stanton, now fast friends, vowed to call a women's rights convention when they returned home.

8. Eight years later, in 1848, Stanton and Mott held the first Woman's Rights Convention at Seneca Falls, New York.

9. Stanton authored "The Declaration of Sentiments," which expanded on the Declaration of Independence by adding the word "woman" or "women" throughout.

10. This pivotal document called for social and legal changes to elevate women's place in society.

B. A real text: Same instructions as in A. Use the passage from Exercise 1.3B on pages 27–28, "Dog Belonging to Princess Anne Attacks Royal Maid."

Notes

1. Walt Wolfram and Natalie Schilling-Estes. *American English.* 2nd ed. Malden, MA: Blackwell, 2006. 381.
2. Ibid.
3. John Russell Rickford and Russell John Rickford. *Spoken Soul: The Story of Black English.* New York: John Wiley, 2000. 110; Geneva Smitherman. *Talkin' and Testifyin': The Language of Black America.* Boston: Houghton Mifflin, 1977. 28.
4. J. L. Dillard. *Black English: Its History and Usage in the United States.* New York: Vintage Books, 1972. 61.
5. A *creole* is derived from a *pidgin*. A *pidgin* is a makeshift contact language that arises when two groups who do not speak the same language meet (think of trying to buy a souvenir in a foreign country from someone who does not speak any English). A *creole* is the more complex language that arises when a pidgin becomes the language that children are born into: the vocabulary grows, and the grammar becomes more complex. English can be understood as an elaborate creole, emerging from interactions of Anglo-Saxon with other languages: Gaelic, Latin, Danish, Norman French, and every other language in the world whose people English speakers have lived, fought, or traded with.
6. Rickford and Rickford, op. cit. 111.
7. Wolfram and Schilling-Estes, op. cit. 381.
8. Ibid.
9. Smitherman, op. cit. 9.
10. Op. cit. 381.
11. Henry W. Fowler. *A Dictionary of Modern English Usage.* 2nd ed. Ed. Sir Ernest Gowers. New York: Oxford University Press, 1965. 330.
12. Paul W. Lovinger. *The Penguin Dictionary of American Usage and Style.* New York: Penguin Reference, 2000. 134.
13. Mignon Fogarty. "Less versus Fewer." *Grammar Girl: Quick and Dirty Tips for Better Writing. Episode 453.* 30 Jan 2015. <http://grammar.quickanddirtytips.com/>.
14. *Merriam-Webster's Dictionary of English Usage.* 2nd ed. Springfield, MA: Merriam-Webster, 1995. 592.

15. Lisa Drayer. "Take It Off Today: Lisa Drayer of *Women's Health* Magazine Shows How to Cut Calories off of Thanksgiving Dinner." *The Today Show.* NBC-TV. 19 Oct 2007.

16. Ashley Halsey, III. "Airplanes, Animals Have a Turbulent Relationship." *Washington Post.* 11 Oct 2014.

17. John W. Pelley. "Structure and Properties of Biologic Molecules." *Elsevier's Integrated Biochemistry.* Amsterdam: Elsevier, 2007. <www.sciencedirect.com/topics/nursing-and-health-professions/glycosidic-bond>.

18. Marty Friedman. "Story Behind the Song—'True Obsessions'." Online posting. 9 Sep 2002. <www.martyfriedman.com>.

19. Joe Henderson. "Ernie's Return." Online posting. *Running Commentary.* 26 Dec 1998. <www.joehenderson.com/>.

20. Mark Lester. *Grammar and Usage in the Classroom.* 2nd ed. New York: Longman, 2000. 21.

21. Ibid. 24.

22. John E. Warriner. *English Grammar and Composition.* Fourth Course. Orlando: Harcourt Brace Jovanovich, 1982 [1948]. 78.

23. Ibid.

24. Lester, op. cit. 39.

25. Dillard, op. cit. 59.

26. *Poems of Gerard Manley Hopkins.* Ed. Robert Bridges. London: Humphrey Milford, 1918. 29.

27. Sentences based on Debra Michals. "Elizabeth Cady Stanton." *National Women's History Museum.* 2017. <www.womenshistory.org/>.

Chapter 3

Prepositions (P) and Prepositional Phrases (PP)

3.1 Prepositions: Form and Function

Prepositions (P) are a category of function words that convey meaning about the relative locations and movements of actions and objects in space (*on, to, in, by*, etc.) and time (*before, after, until*, etc.), as well as more abstract relations like possession (*of*), source (*by*—as in authorship; *according to*) and a host of other literal and metaphoric relationships.

A preposition may comprise one, two, three, or even four words, although one-word prepositions are the most common. Prepositions are commonly regarded as a closed class of function words, and while this is clearly true for one-word prepositions, it appears that we can generate new examples of multi-word prepositions, based on the models in the list below. And although prepositions are generally thought of as function words, they often carry a lot of the meaning and force of sentences because the relationships they express are meaningful. Just think of the differences in meaning of the following sentences, carried entirely by the prepositions: *The cat is **under** the table. The cat is **on** the table. The cat is **above** the table.*

Grammatically, a preposition functions as the head of a prepositional phrase. A preposition always requires a nominal, most often an NP, as a complement.

What follows is a fairly comprehensive list of single-word prepositions, as well as representative lists of two-, three-, and four-word prepositions.

One-Word Prepositions:

aboard	astride	circa	like	pending	towards
about	at	concerning	minus	per	under
above	bar	considering	near	plus	underneath
across	barring	despite	notwithstanding	regarding	unlike
after	before	down	of	round	until
against	behind	during	off	save	up
along	below	except	on	since	upon
alongside	beneath	excepting	onto	than	versus

(Continued)

(Continued)

amid	beside	excluding	opposite	through	via
amidst	besides	for	out	throughout	vis-à-vis
among	between	from	outside	till	with
amongst	beyond	in	over	to	within
around	but	inside	past	toward	without
as	by	into			

Two-Word Prepositions:

according to	because of	instead of	preparatory to
across from	but for	irrespective of	prior to
ahead of	close to	near to	regardless of
along with	contrary to	next to	save for
apart from	depending on	on board	thanks to
aside from	due to	opposite to	together with
as for	except for	other than	up against
as of	forward of	out of	up to
as to	in between	outside of	up until
away from	inside of	owing to	

Three and Four-Word Prepositions:

as far as	in exchange for	in spite of	on behalf of
at the hands of	in favor of	in the face of	on the matter of
by virtue of	in front of	in the process of	on pain of
by means of	in lieu of	in view of	on the part of
for the sake of	in need of	in common with	on the strength of
for want of	in place of	in comparison with	on top of
in addition to	in relation to	in compliance with	with/in reference to
in back of	in return for	in contact with	with/in regard to
in case of	in search of	on account of	with the exception of
in charge of			

Some things to notice about the words in the preceding lists: As we go along, we will see that a number of words we identify here as prepositions can also function as other parts of speech. A number of prepositions can also function as adverbs:

Prepositions or Adverbs

aboard	around	beside	in	out	throughout
about	as	besides	inside	outside	to
above	astride	between	like	over	under
across	before	beyond	near	past	underneath
after	behind	but	off	round	up
along	below	by	on	since	within
alongside	beneath	down	opposite	through	without

P: *The car rolled **down** the hill.* **Adverb**: *The market went **down**.*
P: *The bird flew **out** the window.* **Adverb**: *Punxsutawney Phil came **out**.*
P: *Dorothy went **over** the rainbow.* **Adverb**: *The soccer game was **over**.*

Notice that the prepositions are always followed by an NP, while the adverbs are not (for more on adverbs and their functions, see Chapter 8).

Of the prepositions listed above, the following eleven can also function as subordinating conjunctions (SConj): *after, as, as far as, before, even after, even before, just after, just before, like, since, than, until, up until.* Subordinating conjunctions mark the beginning of an adverb clause (10.2.3). If one of these words is complemented not just by an NP but by an entire clause, then the word is functioning as an SConj and not as a preposition:

P: *This yarn is light **as** a feather.*
SConj: ***As** Franz approached the goal, the crowd cheered.*
P: *Everything was fine **until** this morning.*
SConj: *I won't leave **until** I see Franz play.*

Some words that function as prepositions can also function as verbs (V):

P: ***Considering** the terrible weather, Franz played surprising well.*
V: *Franz is **considering** his next move.*
P: ***Excluding** Bartonville, all of the teams have paid their entrance fee.*
V: *We are **excluding** Bartonville from the next competition.*

And the word *but* not only can function as a preposition (meaning *except*) but is more commonly used as a coordinating conjunction (CConj):

P: *All **but** Franz caught the bus.*
CConj: *Pele played well, **but** Franz played better.*

Many words that function as prepositions can also function as particles in phrasal verbs. In a phrasal verb, the Verb + Particle combination functions as a single constituent (like a compound noun) and can often be paraphrased by a single word. Compare the following examples:

The bear went over the mountain. The class went over the notes.

In the first sentence, *over the mountain* is a PP, comprising the preposition *over* and the NP *the mountain*. The PP functions as a constituent unit of the sentence, with an adverbial meaning: the PP tells *where* the bear went. Also, the PP can be paraphrased by a single word:

The bear went over the mountain. The bear went there.

In the second example, *over the notes* is not a PP, nor is it a constituent within the sentence. Unlike *over the mountain, over the notes* does not tell *where* the class went—and it cannot be paraphrased by *there*, since *over the notes* is not a location. Rather, *went over* is a phrasal verb, which can be paraphrased by the single word *reviewed*:

> *The class went over the notes. The class reviewed the notes.*

We will examine phrasal verbs in 7.1.4. For now, you should know that there are over 12,000 phrasal verbs in English.

To and **of**: The common preposition *to* functions not only as a preposition and a particle: *to* functions as part of semi-modal verbs (e.g. *want to, have to*) and multi-word imperfect aspectual verbs (e.g. *start to, try to, manage to*; see 6.1.2.2), and *to* marks the infinitive form of verbs (e.g. *to do, to drive*; see 12.2). In addition, the common preposition *of* also functions as a "link" in a number of determiners (e.g. *one of, some of, part of*; see 4.2.1).

Non-Standard AAVE *up*: In AAVE, the preposition *up* is commonly used as an "intimacy marker,"[1] indicating that the location being named in the <u>PP</u> that follows *up* is "familiar and comfortable."[2]

> *We sittin' **up** <u>at Tony's</u>.*
> *Don't be sittin' **up** <u>in my house</u> askin' where's the money.*
> *It was buck naked people **up** <u>in my house</u>.*
> *I ain't got no food **up** <u>in my house</u>.*
> *I was gettin' comfortable watchin' TV **up** <u>in bed</u>.[3]*

In the first sentence, *up* indicates that "Tony is a friend of yours." In the second, third, and fourth sentences, *up* emphasizes that "my house" is an intimate, comfortable place for its owner, and likewise for the "bed" in the fifth sentence. By contrast, **We was waitin' **up** <u>at the dentist's</u>* would be incorrect AAVE "because the dentist's office is a place you probably don't go that much and experience little comfort in."[4]

3.2 Prepositional Phrases: Form and Function

A PP always comprises a preposition followed by a nominal that is functioning as the complement of the preposition (P + Nominal:PComp). That nominal is most commonly a noun phrase (NP:PComp).

Here's a common occurrence that traditional grammar books never notice: within a PP, the **preposition** can also take an <u>adverbial modifier</u>:

> *Judge lined a double <u>just</u> **inside** the left-field foul line to score Hicks and Jacoby Ellsbury.[5]*

*The militant departure with the hostages from this place, took place <u>not</u> <u>very long</u> **before** the raid happened.*[6]
*The British media is abuzz with news that a triplet was born <u>eleven years</u> **after** her twin sisters.*[7]

In the first sentence, *just* is an adverb phrase functioning as a modifier of the preposition *inside* (ADVP:MOD OF P), telling *how far* or *to what degree inside*. In the second sentence, *not very long* is a somewhat more complex ADVP that modifies *before*, telling *how long before*. In the third sentence, *eleven years* is an NP, functioning as an adverbial, functioning as a modifier of *after*, telling *how long after*.

PPs can function as either adjectivals or adverbials: that is, like adjectives, they can modify nouns (though unlike adjectives, adjectival PPs always follow the noun they modify), or, like adverbs, PPs can modify whole sentences, adjectives, or verbs, or function as adverbial complements of verbs.

Adjectival PPs: A PP functioning as an adjectival can only function as a **post-modifier of a noun**, as in *The monsters **under my bed** were hungry*. We can identify an adjectival PP functioning as a post-modifier of a noun (PP:ADJECTIVAL:MOD OF N) using:

> **The adjectival question test (version 1)**: If a PP follows a noun and, with reference to that noun, the PP answers the question *which* or *what kind of*, then the PP is adjectival and modifies the preceding noun.

In the sentence *The monsters under my bed were hungry*, if we want to know whether *under my bed* is an adjectival PP, we first check if it is following a noun—it is preceded by the noun *monsters*—and then ask, does this PP tell *which* or *what kind of monsters?* In this case, the PP *under my bed* does limit the meaning of *monsters* by telling *which monsters*. Therefore, *under my bed* is an adjectival PP.

Note that the noun that a PP modifies will sometimes not be directly before the PP, since a noun may take more than one post-modifier. For example, in the sentence *The house on the hill with the big bay window is empty*, both *on the hill* and *with the big bay window* are adjectival PPs. However, while *on the hill* tells *which house*, and thus is a post-modifier of *house*, *with the big bay window* does not tell *which hill* and thus is <u>not</u> a modifier of the noun that precedes it. Rather, *with the big bay window* answers the question *which house* and is a second post-modifier of *house*. So both PPs are adjectival and function as post-modifiers of the noun *house* (PP:ADJECTIVAL:MOD OF "house").

Sometimes we encounter strings of PPs where the PPs are nested inside each other: each PP is a post-modifier in the NP in the preceding PP. In the sentence *I bought the house by the factory with the big smokestack*, the PP *with the big smokestack* tells *which factory*; it modifies the noun *factory*. The PP *by the factory with the big smokestack* tells *which house*; it modifies the noun *house*. So we have a large NP, *the house by the factory with the big smokestack*, which contains a PP, *by the factory with the big smokestack*, which contains an NP, *the factory with the big smokestack*, which contains a PP, *with the big smokestack*, which, of course, also contains an NP, *the big smokestack*. We can illustrate this structure graphically:

> *I bought* [*the house* [*by* [*the factory* [*with* [*the big smokestack*]]]]].

Or, to put it another way:

> *I bought* [*the house by the factory with the big smokestack*]$_{[NP:DIRECT OBJECT OF "bought"]}$.
> *I bought the house* [*by the factory with the big smokestack*]$_{[PP:ADJECTIVAL:MOD OF "house"]}$.
> *I bought the house by* [*the factory with the big smokestack*]$_{[NP:PCOMP OF "by"]}$.
> *I bought the house by the factory* [*with the big smokestack*]$_{[PP:ADJECTIVAL:MOD OF "factory"]}$.
> *I bought the house by the factory with* [*the big smokestack*]$_{[NP:PCOMP OF "with"]}$.

The pronoun replacement test for NPs helps us see that the PP:ADJECTIVAL is a constituent of an NP. When we substitute an appropriate third-person pronoun for less than all of the NP, the reference of a PP that is modifying the noun in the NP will change:

> *I bought the house by the factory with the big smokestack.*
> **I bought **it** by the factory with the big smokestack.*

Substituting *it* for *the house* changes the reference of the PP *by the factory with the big smokestack* from telling *which* house to telling *where* the house was purchased—as though I bought the house from a realtor located *by the factory*.

> *I bought the house by the factory with the big smokestack.*
> **I bought **it** with the big smokestack.*

Substituting *it* for *the house by the factory* changes the reference of the PP *with the big smokestack* from telling which factory to telling how I bought the house—as though I paid for the house by using *the big smokestack* for barter, or it might mean I bought the house, and the seller threw in the smokestack as a sweetener for the deal (i.e. *I bought the house together with the big smokestack*). By contrast, we can replace any of the complete NPs with a third-person pronoun without changing the meaning of the sentence:

> *I bought the house by the factory with the big smokestack.*
> *I bought the house by the factory with **it**.*

I bought the house by it.
I bought it.

To maintain the reference of the original NPs, we need to substitute *it* for a complete NP, in this case, those NPs whose head nouns are *smokestack, factory*, and *house*, respectively.

Identifying adjectival PPs: If we were asked to identify all of the PPs in the preceding sentence, there are two: *by the factory with the big smokestack*, which is functioning as an adjectival modifier of *house* (PP:ADJECTIVAL:MOD OF "house"), and *with the big smokestack*, which is functioning as an adjectival modifier of *factory* (PP:ADJECTIVAL:MOD OF "factory"). Each PP has a preposition (*by; with*) as its head and an NP (*the factory with the big smokestack; the big smokestack*) as its complement.

Adverbial PPs: PPs functioning as adverbials can have four functions:

- **Modifier of Verb**: *Elise slept in the guest room.*
- **Complement of Verb**: *Carol went into the store.*
- **Modifier of an Adjective**: *Ciara had everyone green with envy.*[8]
- **Sentence Modifier**: *In the evening he informed members of Congress.*[9]

In all of their adverbial functions, PPs can be identified by:

> **The adverbial question test**: If a constituent word, phrase, or clause (let's call it *a*) answers an adverbial question about another constituent word, phrase, or clause (let's call it *b*), then the constituent (*a*) is probably adverbial; if you can delete (*a*) and still have a well-formed sentence, then (*a*) is an adverbial modifier of the constituent (*b*). Adverbial questions include *when, where, why, how, how often, how long*, etc.[10]

We will see this test again in 8.2.

Adverbial PPs functioning as modifiers of verbs: When an adverbial PP functions as the modifier of a verb (PP:ADVERBIAL:MOD OF V), it typically appears directly after the verb:

Elise slept in the guest room.
Yuri yelled with delight.[11]
We waited in the back of the room.

In all three sentences, the PP answers an <u>adverb question</u> about the verb: <u>where</u> *did Elise sleep? In the guest room.* <u>How</u> *did Yuri yell? With delight.* <u>Where</u> *did we wait? In the back of the room.* We also know that these PPs are modifiers because if we remove them, the sentence that remains is still a well-formed English sentence: *Elise slept. Yuri yelled. We waited.*

Typically, modifiers are tied closely to the constituent they modify. An adverbial constituent that modifies a sentence or dependent clause can be moved to the beginning, the end, and sometimes between the SUBJ and the PRED because it modifies the whole sentence or clause. An adjective modifying a noun must appear in the slot between the determiner and the noun, and other adjectival constituents modifying a noun must appear right after the noun. An adverbial constituent modifying a verb must appear close to the verb—either right before or right after it and sometimes in the middle of a multi-word verb. Also, typically, an adverbial modifier of a verb cannot be moved from its position in the sentence without changing its reference or making the sentence ill formed. In addition, we will discuss below how some verbs take adverbials as complements—which also, typically, can't be moved.

It will be most useful to remember that modifiers—whether adjectival or adverbial—are optional constituents: if they are dropped, the sentence remains grammatically well formed and still has the same basic meaning.

Adverbial PP functioning as the complement of a verb: A complement is a constituent that is required in order to complete another constituent so that a sentence will be grammatically well formed. For example, a preposition requires an NP or other nominal as its complement to complete a PP. Most verbs require some kind of constituent as a complement.

When an adverbial PP functions as the complement of a verb, like a PP:ADVERBIAL:MOD OF V, it also typically appears directly after the verb. There are five types of adverbial verb complement, each of which can be a PP:

> PP:ADVERBIAL:SUBJECT COMPLEMENT (SC): *Imelda is **at the shoe store**.*
> PP:ADVERBIAL:LOCATIVE COMPLEMENT (LC): *Carol went **into the house**.*
> PP:ADVERBIAL:TEMPORAL COMPLEMENT (TC): *Elise walked **until noon**.*
> PP:ADVERBIAL:MANNER COMPLEMENT (MC): *Franz played **with confidence**.*
> PP:ADVERBIAL:OBJECT COMPLEMENT (OC):*She put the book **on the table**.*

We will examine each of these types of verb complement in Chapter 7. For now, don't sweat the details too much, but learn to recognize that in each of the preceding sentences with adverbial verb complements, the PP answers an <u>adverb question</u> involving the **verb**:

> <u>Where</u> **is** Imelda? At the shoe store.
> <u>Where</u> did Carol **go**? Into the house.
> <u>When</u> did Elise **walk**? Until noon.
> <u>How</u> did Franz **play**? With confidence.
> <u>Where</u> did she **put** the book? On the table.

However, we know that these PPs are not modifiers because if we remove them, the sentence that remains is no longer well formed:

*Imelda is.
?Carol went.
?Elise walked.
?Franz played.[12]
*She put the book.

And since we know that they are not modifiers, we don't even have to check whether they can be moved to other locations in the sentence to determine whether they are modifying the whole sentence (although you can try it).

Just as we can replace a complete NP with a pronoun, we can usually replace each of these adverbial complements with a single word adverb phrase. Adverbial complements that name locations—that tell *where*—can be replaced with *here* or *there*; adverbial complements that name times—that tell *when*—can be replaced with *now* or *then*; and adverbial complements that name the manner in which something was done—that tell *how*—can be replaced with *well*:

Imelda is **there**.
Carol went **there**.
Elise walked **then**.
Franz played **well**.
She put the book **there**.

These examples suggest an "adverbial replacement test," much like the pronoun replacement test for NPs. However, such a test is not as consistently accurate, since we can also use these adverbs to replace NPs, as in *Carol went up there* (i.e. *up the hill*) and *Elise walked until then* (i.e. *until the evening*). In checking for complete adverbial complements, we will have to use this replacement test carefully.

Adverbial PPs functioning as modifiers of adjectives: Typically, a PP:ADVERBIAL:MOD OF ADJ appears after an adjective when that adjective is the head of an adjective phrase that is functioning as the complement of a verb:[13] *Alex became green **with envy**. Elise was tired **of walking**.* In each sentence, the full adjective phrase (*green with envy*; *tired of walking*) completes the meaning of the verb; without the adjective phrase, the sentence is ill formed.

An adverbial **PP** cannot modify an <u>adjective</u> when the adjective is modifying a <u>noun</u>: **Have you met the <u>green</u> **with envy** <u>boy</u>?* In the sentences about Alex and Elise, we know that the PPs are adverbial modifiers of the adjectives they follow because they answer adverb questions about the adjectives: *How/in what manner green? With envy. How/in what manner tired? Of walking.* We also know that the PPs are modifiers because if we drop them, the sentences are still well formed: *Alex became green. Elise was tired.*

There is no question that these PPs are only modifying the adjectives they follow because we cannot move them anywhere else in the sentence and still have a well-formed sentence with the same meaning as the original (try it).

And with a PP:ADVERBIAL:MOD OF ADJ, we cannot even move the PP in front of the adjective it modifies without sounding like Yoda: *Alex became **with envy** green. *Janet was **of walking** tired.

Adverbial PPs functioning as modifiers of sentences and other clauses: As we have seen above, an adverbial PP functioning as a sentence modifier can appear at the beginning of a sentence, at the end, or sometimes between the subject and the predicate:

> **In the evening** he informed members of Congress.
> He informed members of Congress **in the evening**.
> ?He, **in the evening**, informed members of Congress.

We know that the PP is adverbial because it answers an adverb question about the whole sentence: *When did he inform members of Congress? In the evening.* We know the PP is a modifier because we can drop it and still have a well-formed sentence: *He informed members of Congress.* We know it is a sentence modifier because we can move it to two, possibly three, different slots, and the sentence remains well formed and has the same meaning as the original. We have already seen the movability test for identifying adverbial constituents functioning as sentence modifiers (ADVERBIAL:SENTMOD). Adverbials are very common in English, and we will make a lot of use of this test.

We can sum up the features that define each of the functions of adverbial PPs that we have seen so far:

Adverbial PPs: Functions and Features

	Is the PP required or optional in this function?		In this function, is the PP movable?	In this function, where is the PP located?
	required	optional		
COMP OF V	X		No	Usually after the verb
MOD OF V		X	Not usually	Usually after the verb
MOD OF ADJ		X	Not usually	Usually after the ADJ
SENTMOD		X	Yes	At the beginning or end of the clause or between the SUBJ and PRED

The problem of locative PPs: We are already learning a lot about adverbials; by the time we talk about adverbs, much of what we discuss will be repetition. However, in the context of discussing PPs, it is useful to talk about locative adverbials, phrases that identify a location—a *where*. As we noted above in the adverb question test, *where* is an adverb question. But locative phrases can function as both adjectivals <u>and</u> adverbials, and it can sometimes be hard to say whether a locative PP is adjectival or adverbial. Consider the following examples:

*I met a boy **in a red jacket**.*
*I met a boy **in the park**.*
*The boy **in the park** had a yellow ball.*

The problem arises when the locative PP follows a noun, and it is unclear whether the PP is adjectival and modifies the preceding noun (PP:ADJECTIVAL:MOD OF N) or the PP is adverbial and functions as a SENTMOD (PP:ADVERBIAL:SENTMOD). To check, we simply have to apply the tests we have already learned: if the PP is modifying the noun, then the pronoun replacement test will show that the PP is a constituent of the NP. If the pronoun replacement test fails and the movability test for an ADVERBIAL:SENTMOD works, then it is likely that the PP is adverbial and functioning as a SENTMOD. In each example sentence above, the PP follows a noun and is located where a SENTMOD could be: in the first two sentences, the PP is at the end of the sentence; in the third sentence, the PP is apparently between the subject (*the boy*) and the predicate (*had a yellow ball*). All three <u>might</u> be SENTMODS.

Let's walk through it a little bit. In the sentence *I met a boy in a red jacket*, we can substitute an appropriate pronoun for *a boy in a red jacket* but not for just *a boy*:

*I met a boy **in a red jacket**.*
I met him.
I met him **in a red jacket.* (which would mean that <u>I</u> was wearing the red jacket)

Therefore, *in a red jacket* must be an adjectival PP functioning as a post-modifier of the noun *boy* (PP:ADJECTIVAL:MOD OF "boy").

Just as a double-check, let's see if we might parse the PP *in a red jacket* as an adverbial sentence modifier:

*In a red jacket *I met a boy.*
?*I, **in a red jacket**, met a boy.*

When we move the PP to the beginning, the sentence is no longer well formed; when we move it to the slot between the subject and the predicate, the sentence is a little awkward, but its meaning changes: the PP no longer refers to the *boy* but instead may refer to *I*: *While I was wearing a red jacket, I met a boy*. In this sentence, it does not seem that we can parse the PP *in a red jacket* as a sentence modifier. Now we can apply the adjectival question test: in the original sentence, does the PP *in a red jacket* tell us *which* or *what kind of boy*? It does: *a boy in a red jacket*. If we apply the adverb question test, the answer we get is ridiculous: *where did you meet a boy? *In a red jacket*—as if *a red jacket* were a place! So we have confirmed that in this sentence, the PP *in a red jacket* is not movable and answers an adjective question about the noun it follows, so we have confirmed that the PP *in a red jacket* is a PP:ADJECTIVAL:MOD OF N.

Try the same process with the other two sentences. What happens? In each case, is the PP *in the park* adjectival or adverbial?

3.3 Prepositions and Language Variation

The use of prepositions and particles is highly idiomatic. Some of these idioms vary by region: Northeasterners say *wait on line*, while *wait in line* is the idiom in the rest of the United States. They also vary by generation. Someone may have called you out for writing *based off of* instead of *based on*, or saying *on accident* instead of *by accident*:

> *I broke my user's agreement on accident.*[14]
> *Were Pokémon's Arceus and Giratina based off of the story of God and Satan?*[15]

These changes tend to start with younger people, and with people from poor and working-class communities, and then to move up the age and socio-economic scale. In terms of these two examples, people in their mid-50s would be far more likely to say *by accident* and *based on*. But both forms fit within the blueprint of English: *by accident* treats the *accident* metaphorically as a device that caused the event or as a location one happened to be near. *On accident*, presumably modelled on *on purpose*, treats the accident metaphorically as a location where the event occurred. *Based on* treats *the story* metaphorically as a foundation on which *Arceus and Giratina* were built. *Based off of* treats *the story* metaphorically as a location from which *Arceus and Giratina* set out or began. Both versions (and *on line* and *in line*) work within the blueprint of the English language. Only social convention makes one more "correct" than the other.[16]

Key Points

- Prepositions are function words that convey meaning about locations and movements in space and time, as well as more abstract relations like possession, source, and other literal and metaphoric relationships.
- A preposition functions as the head of a prepositional phrase (PP).
- A PP always requires a nominal, most often an NP, as a complement of the preposition.
- A PP may function as an adjectival or an adverbial.
- An adjectival PP may function as a post-modifier of a noun.
- An adverbial PP may function as a modifier of a verb; a complement of a verb; a modifier of an adjective; or a sentence modifier.

3.4 Exercises: Prepositional Phrases

A. Made-up sentences:[17]

For each sentence,

- Identify each complete PP.
- Identify each preposition.
- Identify each complete NP:PC_{OMP}.
- For each complete PP, **try** to identify whether it is adjectival or adverbial.
- For each complete PP, **try** to identify its function (e.g. "M_{ODIFIER} _{OF} *noun*" or "S_{ENT}M_{OD}").

Sometimes, there are PPs inside other PPs. **Remember**: not all prepositions are part of PPs, and some words that look like prepositions may be functioning as other parts of speech.

> Example: *Franz liked the field in the park.*
> C_{OMPLETE} PP: *in the park*
> P: *in*
> NP:PC_{OMP}: *the park*
> A_{DJECTIVAL} or A_{DVERBIAL}: adjectival
> F_{UNCTION}: M_{ODIFIER} _{OF} "field"

1. Egypt has opened a 4,000-year-old tomb near Giza, home to the famous pyramids, for the first time.
2. The tomb of Mehu is located in the Saqqara region.
3. Dating to the 6th dynasty, the tomb held Vizier Mehu, a high-ranking advisor close to the king.
4. It was discovered in 1940 by Egyptologist Zaki Saad.
5. The public was able to visit it for the first time in history this weekend.
6. Images on social media showed visitors queueing to enter and taking photographs of the interior.
7. The colors inside are different from many other tombs in the necropolis as the brightness of them is somewhat unusual.
8. Many of the paintings inside are unique to the time period, with images of a crocodile marrying a turtle and celebration dances depicted on the walls.
9. The tomb doesn't just contain Mehu but also his son Meren Ra and his grandson Heteb Kha.
10. Mehu held forty-eight titles during the reign of King Pepi, which were found on the walls of the tomb.

B. A real text: same instructions as in A. Use the passage from Exercise 1.3B on pages 27–28, "Dog Belonging to Princess Anne Attacks Royal Maid."

C. Another real text:[18] same instructions as in Exercise A:

(1) Jackson Stands Before Prospective Jurors
(2) *By LINDA DEUTSCH, AP Special Correspondent*
(3) SANTA MARIA, Calif.—Dressed in a bright white suit and a jewel-trimmed vest and belt, Michael Jackson on Monday stood before the first group of prospective jurors who could decide his fate on charges he molested a teenage cancer patient and plied the boy with alcohol at his Neverland Ranch.
(4) The pop superstar, accompanied by four defense lawyers, stood and smiled as he faced prospective jurors for the start of jury selection in what could become the most sensational celebrity trial the world has ever seen. (5) He greeted the clerk with a handshake at the courthouse in this small city in central California about 15 miles from the coast.

Notes

1. John McWhorter. *Talking Back, Talking Black: Truths about America's Lingua Franca*. New York: Bellvue Literary Press, 2017. 39.
2. Ibid. 38.
3. Ibid. 37.
4. Ibid. 39.
5. Billy Witz. "Yankees Keep Pace with Red Sox." *The New York Times*. 27 Sep 2017.
6. Karen DeYoung. *PBS NewsHour*. 21 Aug 2014.
7. Mary Forgione. "British Triplet Born More Than a Decade after Twin Sisters—Any More Coming?" *The Los Angeles Times*. 29 Dec 2010.
8. "Ciara Has Everyone Green with Envy Over Her All-Green Outfit and Dramatic Hair." *Footwearnews*. 7 May 2019.
9. Kacy Burdette. "Photos of Richard Nixon's Last Days as President." *Fortune.com*. 16 Jun 2017.
10. Note that adverbials are a complicated category and adverbial questions need a little elaboration. In particular, *how* is a general version of several more specific questions: *in what manner*; *in what context*; *by what means*. We will see the list of adverbial questions expand as we study more adverbs and adverbial constituents.
11. Robin Cook. *Vector*. New York: GP Putnam's Sons, 1999. 182.
12. Of course, we can create contexts in which *Carol went, Elise walked*, and *Franz played* are well-formed sentences without a verb complement, but the complement has to be implied in the context, as in, "You don't need to go to the store. Carol went." Here, the verb complement—the constituent that tells *where Carol went*—is given by the preceding sentence. A marvelous extended example can be found in Dr. Seuss's *Marvin K. Mooney Will You Please Go Now!*. New York: Random House, 1972. The book goes on for many pages providing complements that tell the manner or time of Marvin's going: "You can go by foot. You can go by cow. Marvin K. Mooney, will you please go now!" The book creates such a weight of context that, in the end, the book can acceptably close, "I said GO and GO I meant. The time had come, SO Marvin WENT." However, this again brings up the question of whether to parse what is implied by a sentence or only what is stated explicitly.
13. However, consider the sentence **Green with envy**, *Alex refused to talk to his rival*. Traditional grammar would argue that the AdjP *green with envy* is modifying *Alex*. But one might also argue that *green with envy* is not, here, functioning adjectivally:

it can readily be paraphrased with an adverb clause: ***Because he was green with envy***, *Alex refused to talk to his rival.* Although it looks like an adjective phrase in form, *green with envy* also seems to function as an adverbial. This problem of interpretation arises from *green with envy* being a <u>non-essential</u> modifier that, as we will see later, can be interpreted as functioning either adjectivally or as an adverbial of concurrent action.

14. Soren. "I Broke My Users Agreement on Accident." *Nintendo Support Forums.* 19 Mar 2019. <https://en-americas-support.nintendo.com>.

15. "Were Pokémon's Arceus and Giratina Based Off of the Story of God and Satan?" *Quora.com.* 2 Apr 2015.

16. For more information on *on accident* versus *by accident*, see Leslie Barratt. "What Speakers Don't Notice: Language Changes Can Sneak In." *TRANS: Internet-Zeitschrift für Kulturwissenschaften* 16 (26 Jun 2006); Mignon Fogarty. "On Accident versus by Accident." *Grammar Girl Quick and Dirty Tips for Better Writing. Episode 63.* 22 Jun 2007. <http://grammar.quickanddirtytips.com/>. For more about *based off*, see Jan Freeman. "Off Base: A Phrase That's Hard to Picture." *The Boston Globe.* 13 Jan 2008.

17. Based on Kara Godfrey. "Egypt Opens 4000-year-old Tomb in a Pyramid Near Giza for the First Time in the World." *Express.* 10 Sep 2018 <www.express.co.uk/travel/>.

18. Adapted from Linda Deutsch. "Jackson Stands Before Prospective Jurors." Associated Press. 31 Jan 2005.

Chapter 4

Adjectives (ADJ) and Adjective Phrases (ADJP); Determiners (D) and Determiner Phrases (DP)

Adjectives are content words, traditionally defined as modifiers of nouns. By "modifying," we mean that they qualify, limit, contextualize, or more closely define the thing that is being named by the noun. But, as modifiers, grammatically, they are optional constituents: if we drop an adjective phrase (ADJP) from an NP, the NP will still be well formed. We will use the word "adjective" to refer to what are sometimes called descriptive adjectives. Descriptive adjectives are words such as *tall, beautiful, happy, miserable*, and *blue* that name qualities possessed by the things named by nouns: they *describe* nouns.

Later in the chapter, we will examine a category of function words called determiners. Traditional grammar commonly fails to distinguish determiners from adjectives since, like adjectives, determiners function in NPs and fill slots preceding the noun. However, within NPs, determiners always precede the ADJP; as we will see below, determiners differ from adjectives in several key features—most notably that adjectives are gradable (e.g. *big, bigger, biggest*), while determiners (e.g. *the, their, seven*) typically are not.

4.1 Adjective Forms

Adjectives come in two forms: gradable and absolute (or non-gradable). Gradable adjectives have three forms or degrees: the base, the comparative, and the superlative:

> **Base**: *close, desirable, good*
> **Comparative**: *closer, more desirable, better*
> **Superlative**: *closest, most desirable, best*

The examples show the three ways in which the different degrees are formed. Most single-syllable adjectives are regular and take the endings *-er* and *-est* to mark the comparative and superlative, while most multi-syllable adjectives are regular and take the words *more* and *most*. *Good/better/best* is one of a small set of irregular exceptions, along with *well/better/best*; *bad/worse/worst*; *far/farther/farthest*; and *far/further/furthest*.

Absolute or non-gradable adjectives do not show degree. Examples include *main*, *electronic*, and *stone* (as in "a *stone* wall"). Something cannot be *mainer or *more main, *electronicer or *more electronic. Nouns functioning as adjectives, such as *stone*, are also typically absolute, as in *soccer ball* and *elbow room*. Present participles (verb forms ending in -*ing*) can often function as adjectives. The degree to which a present participle is gradable varies from non-gradable, as in <u>running</u> water (*the <u>runninger</u> water/*the more running water) to fully gradable with *more* and *most*, as in *the interesting/more interesting/most interesting question*, depending on how firmly established the participle is as an adjective. Past participles (verb forms typically ending in -*ed*) may be non-gradable or weakly gradable when used as adjectives. Whether the following examples sound like "proper" English will depend on your home variety:

> *the burned building*
> *?the more burned building (of the two)*
> *?the most burned building (of all)*

The word *unique*, which started as non-gradable, has, in much common usage, become gradable: for many English speakers, something can now be *more unique* or *the most unique*. While this grates on some speakers' ears, its use in writing has been slowly growing since the 1820s.

Non-Standard comparatives and superlatives: Wolfram and Schilling-Estes observe that "most vernacular varieties of English indicate some comparative and superlative adjective and adverb forms that are not found in Standard varieties. Some forms involve the regularization of irregular forms."[1] Thus, instead of *bad/worse/worst*, we find *bad/badder/baddest*, as in:

> *And it's bad, bad Leroy Brown*
> *The **baddest** man in the whole damn town*
> ***Badder** than old King Kong*
> *And meaner than a junkyard dog.*[2]

> *The $1,000 Titan X truly is the **bestest**, **baddest**, most firebreathing single-GPU graphics card in all the land.*[3]
> *Mirror, mirror on the wall, who's the **goodest**, cleanest, and fairest of them all?*[4]

Some irregular forms "involve the use of -*er* and -*est* on adjectives of two or more syllables (e.g. *beautifulest*, *awfulest*), where the Standard variety uses *more* and *most*";[5] however, Crystal observes that these forms were SE through-out the nineteenth century[6] and seem only to have become consistently non-Standard in the twentieth century. Note the following two nineteenth-century examples, the former from Herman Melville and the latter from Eugene Field, both of which are arguably "Standard":

> *Separately, and together, we brand thee, in thy every lung-cell, a liar;—*
> *liar, because that is the **scornfullest** and **loathsomest** title for a man;*
> *which in itself is the compend of all infamous things.*[7]

> *But the gingham dog and the calico cat*
> *Wallowed this way and tumbled that,*
> *Employing every tooth and claw*
> *In the **awfullest** way you ever saw—*
> *And oh! How the gingham and calico flew!*[8]

A reflection of the transition of such words from Standard to non-Standard may perhaps be seen in their use in the non-Standard "dialect speech" of literary char-acters, as in Mark Twain's *Huckleberry Finn* (1884), where the doctor describes Jim as "faithfuler"[9] or when Jim says, "Well, den, I reck'n I did dream it, Huck; but dog my cats ef it ain't de <u>powerfullest</u> dream I ever see."[10] The history of the shift in this usage from Standard to non-Standard has yet to be studied.

Wolfram and Schilling-Estes also state that, "in some instances, compara-tives and superlatives are doubly marked, as in *most awfulest* or *more nicer*":

> *As far as the economy, the news is getting "**less awfuller**," he said.*[11]
> *Why would you want to develop a greater understanding of nature? Well,*
> *first of all it is everywhere! It's free to visit! It makes a sunny day all that*
> *much **more nicer**!*[12]
> *The **most beautifullest** thing in this world, is just like that!!*[13]

Fries[14] argues that such double markings were not originally redundant. Origi-nally, most gradable adjectives took the *-er/-est* endings as inflections, while *-more/-most* initially developed as comparative and superlative suffixes, as in words like *furthermore* and *outermost*. Then, gradually, the words *more* and *most* came into use as adverbs of degree to mark the comparative and superla-tive. There was a period of overlap when using *more/most* and *-er/-est* together was a SE usage,[15] and we find numerous examples:

> *Brutus shall lead; and we will grace his heels*
> *With the **most boldest** and best hearts of Rome.*[16]

> *This was the **most unkindest** cut of all.*[17]
> *A wall'd town is **more worthier** than a village.*[18]
> *After the **most straitest** sect of our religion I lived a Pharisee.*[19]

Gentle Asper,
*Contain your Spirit in **more stricter** Bounds,*
And be not thus transported with the Violence
Of your strong Thoughts.[20]

This usage only comes to be condemned as a double marking of degree (and therefore a needless redundancy) first by John Dryden, who calls it "gross" (1672),[21] and then with increasing vigor by the late eighteenth-century prescriptive grammarians Robert Lowth (1762), Charles Coote (1788), and Lindley Murray (1795).[22] In his 1940 study, Fries found that while SE speakers tend to use the *-er/-est* inflectional endings about half of the time (using adverbs like *more/most* to mark degree otherwise), non-Standard speakers tend to use the older *-er/-est* inflections ninety percent of the time.[23] This helps explain why the "overuse" or "misuse" of *-er/-est* inflections stands out as a feature of non-Standard varieties.

Wolfram and Schilling-Estes[24] enumerate three non-Standard ways of marking the comparative and superlative degrees of adjectives, all of which are currently in use in many varieties of English: regularization of irregular forms; use of *-er* and *-est* with adjectives of two or more syllables; and double marking. However, when we make judgments about SE versus non-Standard varieties, we should always remember that those judgments really only apply to the current status quo. Regularization is a routine process in language change, and the other two "non-Standard" forms for marking degree were once features of SE.

Identifying adjectives: There are four tests for identifying adjectives:

> **The adjective slot test**: If you can place a word in the slot between the determiner *one* and a singular common noun (e.g. *one ____ house*) or in the slot between the determiner *two* and a plural common noun (e.g. *two ____ houses*), then the word is an adjective.
> **The predicate adjective test**: If you can place a word in the slot after *seems* in *He/she/it seems ____*, then the word is an adjective. This test does not work for nouns functioning as adjectives: **It seems **stone**.*
> **The *very* test** (only works with the base form of gradable adjectives): If a noun modifier can be used with *very*, then the modifier is an adjective.
> **The adjectival question test (version 2)**: If a noun modifier answers the question *which* or *what kind of*, then it is an adjectival. For example, if we have the sentence *Large furry monsters lurked under my bed*, and we want to know if *large* and *furry* are adjectives, we simply ask, *Which monsters lurked under my bed?* or *What kind of monsters lurked under my bed?* And the answer, *large furry ones*, tells us that *large* and *furry* are adjectives.

The adjective question test works for identifying determiners along with adjectives but not for distinguishing between adjectives and determiners: if the sentence read, *The first sixteen large furry monsters lurked under my bed*, and we applied the adjective question test by asking, *Which monsters lurked under my bed?* the answer would be, *The first sixteen large furry ones*. As we shall see below, while traditional grammar categorizes determiners (*The first sixteen*) together with adjectives (*large furry*), there are distinct grammatical differences between these two categories of words. In particular, determiners are almost never gradable.

4.1.1 Adjective Phrases: Forms and Functions

An adjective functions as the head of an adjective phrase (ADJP). Whether it appears by itself, or, as is sometimes the case, accompanied by adverbial modifiers, an adjective is always the head of an ADJP. An ADJP may consist of an adjective alone, or it may include an adverb phrase preceding the ADJ, an adverbial PP following the ADJ, or both:

> **ADJ**: *They ran a **close** race. It's **cold**.*
> <u>ADVP</u> + **ADJ**: *Most polls show a <u>very</u> **close** race.*[25] *It's <u>too</u> **cold**.*
> *Obviously, it would be <u>highly</u> **desirable** to avoid such a scenario.*[26]
> **ADJ** + PP:ADVERBIAL: *They were **green** <u>with envy</u>. She's **high** <u>on life</u>.*
> *I'm **anxious** <u>about the exam</u>.*
> <u>ADVP</u> + **ADJ** + PP:ADVERBIAL: *We're <u>seriously</u> **green** <u>with envy</u> over this floral number.*[27] *She's <u>just</u> **high** <u>on life</u>. I'm <u>so</u> **anxious** <u>about the exam</u>.*

ADJPs only have two functions: <u>modifier of a noun</u>, as in *This is a <u>very close</u> race*,[28] and <u>complement of a verb</u>, as in *The race is <u>very close</u>*[29] (ADJP:SUBJECT COMPLEMENT [SC]) and *He considers the risks <u>minimal</u>*[30] (ADJP:OBJECT COMPLEMENT [OC]; see 7.1.3.2). There is a small limit on which forms of ADJP can perform which functions. While any kind of ADJP can be a verb complement, typically only the simplest ADJP—an adjective preceded by an adverb or a brief adverb phrase—can modify a noun. The ADJP *very highly placed* in the NP *a very highly placed* source is about as complex a phrase as we will normally find in the adjective slot between the determiner and the noun. Generally, we want to put any lengthy adjectival material in the post-modifier slot after the noun. There are, as always, informal contexts that violate this sort of general statement, as in a sentence like the following with a complex <u>pre-nominal ADJP</u>: *We need a "<u>seriously green with envy</u>" emoticon!*[31] In writing, such oddities will commonly be hyphenated or marked with quotation marks (creating a sort of compound ADJ).

We can, of course, place several brief ADJPs in the slot between the determiner and the noun, as when we write or say, *On Sesame Street there were several **large, intensely blue, very furry** monsters*. In this sentence, we have three separate ADJPs before the noun: *large*, followed by *intensely blue*, followed by *very furry*. In traditional grammar we think of each of these as a separate ADJP, conjoined by commas, each modifying the noun *monsters*: each one tells *which* or *what kind of monsters were on Sesame Street*.

There is, however, another strong interpretation of such a string of ADJPs in an NP. In some ways it seems that each of the ADJPs isn't just modifying the noun but that each ADJP modifies everything that follows it in the NP. While the ADJP *very furry* tells us *which monsters*, the ADJP *intensely blue* tells us *which very furry monsters* (*the intensely blue* ones—*the intensely blue, very furry monsters*, as opposed to some other monster, such as Elmo, who is intensely red); and the ADJP *large* tells us *which intensely blue very furry monsters* (*the large intensely blue very furry* ones—like Herry—as opposed to small, intensely blue very furry monsters like Grover). To describe this sense that there is a series of nested relationships among ADJPs that modify a noun, more recent grammatical theory proposes that there is an intermediate structure between the N and the NP, called an "N-BAR" and symbolized by N'. The N' is used to label the structures that are not complete NPs but that help illustrate the internal complexity of the modification within the NP:

monsters [N]
very furry [ADJP:MOD OF "monsters"]
very furry monsters [N']
intensely blue [ADJP:MOD OF N' "very furry monsters"]
intensely blue, very furry monsters [N']
large [ADJP:MOD OF N' "intensely blue very furry monsters"]
large, intensely blue, very furry monsters [N']
several [D:SPECIFIER OF N' "large, intensely blue, very furry monsters"]
several large, intensely blue, very furry monsters [NP:COMPLEMENT OF "were"]

You can analyze the relationships among ADJPs and the noun within an NP either way: both satisfy different features of our sense of how those relationships work. Most people you talk to about grammar will remember the traditional analysis and not know about N-BARS. But it will prove useful to remember that there is usually more than one way to think about any grammatical analysis.

Adjectival appositive phrases: Just as an NP may function as a non-essential modifier of a noun, there are also adjectival appositive phrases:

Happy with his new purchase, *Franz left the store.*
Franz, **happy with his new purchase,** *left the store.*
Franz left the store, **happy with his new purchase.**

Happy is an adjective, and *with his new purchase* is a PP:ADVERBIAL:MOD OF "happy." The adjectival appositive tells us something about Franz. Like some nominal appositives, however, this sort of adjectival appositive seems to be both adjectival—telling us something about Franz—and adverbial—describing a state that existed at the same time as the action named in the clause. After all, we can move the modifying phrase in the same manner we can move an ADVERBIAL:SENTMOD, moving it away from the noun it apparently modifies. So is *happy with his new purchase* adjectival or adverbial? We will further discuss this blurring of the line between non-essential adjectival modifiers and adverbial modifiers in Chapter 12.

4.2 Determiners and Determiner Phrases

Determiners—as a category of function words—appear <u>only</u> in NPs. They appear in the slot before the ADJP:MOD OF N, as the first constituent of the NP. In traditional grammar, the category we are identifying as determiners is simply lumped in with adjectives; after all, like adjectives, determiners conventionally precede nouns and seem to specify and identify what a noun is referring to just as much as adjectives do. However, determiners are distinct from adjectives in several ways, most notably in that determiners are not modifiers. Remember that modifiers are <u>always optional</u> constituents: if we drop them, the sentence is still grammatically well formed. We cannot always drop determiners: ***determiners*** are <u>obligatory</u> with **singular count nouns**:

Singular count noun:

*Franz bought **the** green **ball**.*
*Franz bought **the** **ball**.*
Franz bought green **ball.*
Franz bought **ball*

Plural count noun:

*Franz bought **the** green balls.*
*Franz bought **the** balls.*
Franz bought green balls.
Franz bought balls.

Also, adjectives can function as verb complements (see Chapter 7), but determiners cannot function in any other role besides specifying the meaning of nouns, and they cannot be placed anywhere but in the slot at the beginning of the NP:

Adjective functioning as verb complement: *The ball was **green**.*
Determiner functioning as verb complement: **The ball was **the**.*

For these reasons, we will not say that a determiner phrase <u>modifies</u> a noun but that a determiner phrase functions as a <u>specifier</u> of a noun (DP:SPEC OF N).

4.2.1 Determiner Forms

As with prepositions (Chapter 3) and pronouns (Chapter 5), the most common determiners simply constitute a list that we must learn to recognize. Below, I list ten types of determiners that I also group into large categories—"Central," "Pre-," and "Post-determiners"—based on where they commonly appear within a DP. Central determiners are the most commonly used and often appear alone, with neither a Pre- nor a Post-determiner. Pre-determiners often appear before a Central determiner, and, indeed, some may not be used without a following Central determiner. Similarly, Post-determiners often appear after a Central determiner and sometimes may not be used without a preceding Central determiner. A DP may include all three categories of determiner and may even include four or more determiners. Note: the term "Pre-determiner" has nothing to do with anything being "predetermined"; it just means that these categories of determiners can appear before a Central determiner.

Central Determiners

* Articles: *the, a, an.*
* Demonstratives: *this, that, these, those; which, what.*
* Possessives: *my, your, his, her, its, our, their; whose.*
* Possessive NP (NP + *'s*): *Fred's; dogs'; the Peoria Symphony's.*

Pre-Determiners: Amounts

* Quantifiers: *all, another, any, both, each, either, few, little, many, neither, none, plenty, several, some, every, no.*
* Partitives: *few of/a few of, little of/a little of, a lot of, a/the pound of, a/the quart of,* etc.[32]
    * Many quantifiers + *of*: *all of, another of, any of, each of, either of,* etc.
    * Fractions (see below) + *of*: *one-third of, three-fourths of, two-fifths of,* etc.; *half of, a/the quarter of,* etc.
    * Cardinal numbers (see below) + *of*: *one of, two of, three of,* etc.
* Multipliers: *once, twice, three times,* etc.; *double, triple,* etc.
* Fractions: *one-third, three-fourths, two-fifths,* etc.; *half, a/the quarter,* etc.

Post-Determiners: Numbers

* Cardinal numbers: *one, two, three,* etc.
* Ordinal numbers: *first, second, third,* etc.; *next, last.*

The articles (*the, a, an*) can <u>only</u> be determiners, so they are the best examples to use as models in testing whether other words are determiners. When followed by *of*, quantifiers, partitives, fractions, and cardinals can also only be determiners. All of the other categories of determiners, including quantifiers, fractions, and cardinals without *of*, can function as indefinite pronouns (see 5.1) and therefore can be harder to identify when they are used as determiners.

Four notes about the preceding list of determiner forms: Note (1): **the difference between quantifiers and partitives**: A quantifier limits the reference of a noun to the totality of some set of things named by the noun. A partitive limits the reference of a noun to some part of a set of things named by the noun. In *Some books lay on the table, some* is a quantifier that limits the reference of the noun *books* to all of the books that were on the table. In the sentence *Some of the books were old, some of* is a partitive that limits the reference of the noun *books* to some portion of—"some, but not all of"—the books.

Note (2): All possessive NPs are determiners: As soon as we put *'s* at the end of an NP, it becomes a possessive determiner and behaves like a single word. Even fairly complex NPs can become determiners simply by adding *'s* as a possessive marker. In each of the following sentences, the underlined phrase is a possessive determiner:

> That is *Franz's* ball.
> *The goalie's* gloves were bright yellow.
> Things got a little wild in *the winning team's* clubhouse after the game.[33]

This is very much like when we saw an NP functioning adjectivally or adverbially: the form of the phrase makes it look like an NP, but in this case, as soon as we add the *'s*, the form of the phrase changes to possessive determiner. Just as any NP can be replaced by a third-person personal pronoun, as in the pronoun replacement test, any NP + *'s* can be replaced by a third-person possessive determiner, suggesting a:

> **Possessive determiner replacement test**: Any complete possessive NP—that is, NP + *'s*—can be replaced by a single-word third-person possessive determiner (i.e. *his, her, its, their*).

This test is illustrated by the following examples:

> That is *Franz's* ball. That is *his* ball.
> *The goalie's* gloves were bright yellow. *Her* gloves were bright yellow.
> Things got a little wild in *the winning team's* clubhouse after the game.
> Things got a little wild in *their* clubhouse after the game.

> **Non-Standard POSSESSIVE NPs**: In varieties of AAVE, the possessive suffix *'s* may be absent (indicated by Ø):

> The *manØ* hat is on the chair.
> *JohnØ* coat is here.[34]
> The Brotha be lookin good; that's what got the *SistaØ* nose open![35]

According to Smitherman, it is grammatical in AAVE to mark possession by adjacency or context.[36] Rickford and Rickford state that marking possession by juxtaposing two nouns, placing the possessor directly before the possession, is a common feature of pidgins and creoles: languages that arise from the contact of two different languages.[37] There is a strong argument that AAVE arises as a blending of various West African languages with English and that a number of the grammatical features that mark AAVE as different from SE can be explained in terms of features of West African languages. However, as with most features of non-SEs, the frequency of the deletion of the possessive suffix *'s* varies with social class. Citing studies by Labov and Harris, Rickford and Rickford observe that:

> Blacks who had the least contact with Whites and were most involved with other Blacks in the culture and values of the street used . . . possessive *'s* ('*John's* hat') least frequently, less than 25 percent of the time, and sometimes not at all. Blacks who had the most contact with Whites (for instance, musicians) and/or were relatively isolated from street culture, had much higher frequencies of these SE features, using them between 60 and 100 percent of the time.[38]

Labov and Harris[39] conclude that this, along with other differences between White SE and AAVE, have emerged since 1915 and the Great Migration, when large numbers of Southern Blacks moved into Northern cities and Blacks became increasingly segregated from Whites in all aspects of their daily lives.[40] As contact between the two groups declined, it seems inevitable that various features of White and Black language would diverge from each other. The greater the degree of interaction between groups, the more likely that language features will converge toward a common Standard.

Note (3): A number of determiners in the list include the word *of*: We find it in most of the Pre-determiner categories as part of multi-word determiners. In these determiners, *of* is called a "link" because it links or connects the Pre-determiner to the Central determiner. When *of* functions as a link, it is <u>not</u> a preposition.

Note (4): Some determiners consist of more than one word: In the version of English grammar we are studying, we propose the existence of multi-word determiners because of how determiners function—what words can go in what slots—and because of our notions of what the topic of a sentence or NP is. Let's consider the sentence *None of the balls is/are green*. This sort of sentence presents a grammatical and stylistic problem: traditionally, *none* is understood to be singular, a shortening of *no one*. Should the verb agree in number with the singular *none* or the plural *balls*? In traditional grammar, the subject of this sentence would be the NP *none of the balls*; its head is the word *none*, which is modified by the PP *of the balls*. Since *none* is the head noun, the number of the verb (singular or plural) must agree with the number of *none*.

Since *none* is singular, the verb must be in the singular form. For traditional grammar, the proper form of this sentence is *None of the balls is green.* But is this sentence about *none*, or is it about *balls*? Our sense might reasonably be that *balls* is the topic, so we ought to regard *balls* as the head noun of the NP *none of the balls*. This idea becomes even more reasonable when we note that many single-word determiners in English can fill the same slot as *none of*: *all*, *half*, and a good number of other words on the Pre-determiner list above. These other single-word determiners serve as a precedent for the idea that multiword phrases with meanings related to the meanings of single-word Pre-determiners could also be analyzed as Pre-determiners. More recent grammatical theory has adopted this notion of the multi-word determiner and so would argue that, since *balls* is the head noun of the NP:Subj, the verb must be plural in form to agree with the number of the subject noun. By this analysis the proper form of the sentence is, *None of the balls are green.*

Now you're wondering (perhaps with some dismay), "But which one is right?" The answer involves nothing to do with grammar: if you are writing for an audience that tends to be more conservative, curmudgeonly, or "old school," then the traditional grammar version is "right": *None of the balls is green.* If you are writing for an audience that is less likely to notice details of traditional grammar—because they don't know or don't care—or an audience that will just accept something written because it "sounds OK," then the newer version will be "right": *None of the balls are green.* If you listen to how people speak, you'll hear many use the newer version, rather than the traditional one. Some will point to the way people speak as indicating a lack of or decline in literacy; some will point to the way people speak and say that traditionalists are just being snobs.

A Further Determiner Dilemma: Allowing that the particle *of* serves as a link in multi-word determiners creates another interesting problem: on the one hand, it helps us explain some pretty complex DPs, as in a sentence like *Posey did sit for two of the first seven games.*[41] In the NP:PComp, *two of the first seven games*, there are four distinct determiners: the Pre-determiner *two of*, the Central determiner *the*, and two Post-determiners: *first* and *seven*. We could argue that *first* is specifying *seven* and that *two of the* is then specifying *first seven*; we have an intermediate structure between the individual determiner and the DP: a D′, akin to the N′ presented above. But what happens when the determiner phrase gets longer?

> It is a source of great pride for Zenith to work with Adelsheim Vineyard and Ponzi Vineyard—*two of the first five of the* Oregon Pinot noir pioneers.[42]
> *Two of the first fifteen of the last group of all of the* new entrants are Franz's brothers.

Is there a point where the weight of the determiner string becomes so great that somehow the head of the NP shifts back and the topic of the sentence becomes one of the substantive words in the determiner string that could function as a nominal? Likely, the answer depends on context. Try to create a context in which the simple subjects of these last two sentences would be *five* or *fifteen* or *group* rather than *pioneers or entrants*.

Non-Standard use of the third-person plural pronoun *them* as a demonstrative determiner: In most vernacular varieties of American English, we find the pronoun *them* used as a demonstrative determiner: ***Them** books are on the shelf. She didn't like **them** there boys.*[43] In this usage, *them* and *them there* have the same sort of distancing/pointing function as the SE determiner *those*.

4.2.2 Determiner Phrases: Forms and Functions

Determiners—or, more properly, determiner phrases—fill the initial slot in an NP—and that's <u>all</u> they do. When we see a word that only functions as a determiner, such as *the* (the most common word in formal written English), then we know we have found the beginning of an NP. Beware, however, of over-generalizing this idea: not all words that function as determiners—or Central determiners—<u>only</u> function as determiners. For example, when we see the word *that*, which has a number of distinctly different functions in English, we should beware of just assuming it is a determiner. The articles *a, an*, and *the* can <u>only</u> be determiners—so they are good words to think of when we are trying to identify determiners.

A DP most often comprises a single determiner, but as we have seen, a DP may also have a Pre-determiner and/or a Post-determiner (or two). When we have a possessive noun phrase (NP + *'s*), a DP may be quite long. As a term, "determiner phrase" is not really accurate: a phrase typically has a head and dependents. But there isn't really a head in a DP, and the relationship among the determiners within a phrase is often highly idiomatic.

A DP appears in an NP in the initial slot; if there is an ADJP in the NP, the DP appears before the ADJP; if there is no ADJP, the DP appears right before the noun. In general, only common nouns take determiners, and we cannot place a determiner in front of a proper noun. But for almost all general claims in grammar, there are exceptions, and there are contexts where a proper noun does take a <u>determiner</u>:

> The idea that history matters and that old New York is at least as interesting as <u>today's</u> New York is a recent development, Mr. Burns said.[44]
> When I was growing up in a vintage brick building overlooking the dignified curve of the Hudson River, <u>the</u> New York I knew was divided between west and east.[45]

4.3 What Makes Determiners Different From Adjectives? And Why Are Numbers Determiners?

Adjectives are content words; determiners are function words. Content words are nouns, verbs, adjectives, and adverbs; they convey substantive meaning, referring to objects and events in the world. Function words join content words to each other and mark relationships between them. Function words name or refer to more abstract qualities and relationships, such as (in the case of determiners) definiteness and specificity. Determiners, prepositions, pronouns, and conjunctions are function words.

Adjectives are an open class; determiners are, for the most part, a closed class. New nouns, verbs, adjectives, and adverbs are created and enter usage every day, while others fall out of use just as frequently. Function words are, generally speaking, closed classes: we do not create new pronouns or conjunctions at all, and, for the most part, we do not create new determiners or prepositions. Nor do we stop using existing pronouns, determiners, prepositions or conjunctions. With determiners, the exceptions are, as we have seen, partitives with *of* and possessives with *'s*, which are open sub-classes of determiners.

Adjectives can be gradable (e.g. *lean/leaner/leanest; abominable/more abominable/most abominable*); **determiners are not gradable.** We cannot say **two-er* or **more the*. There are four exceptions: *few, less, little*, and *much*, each of which can function as a determiner but can also take degree markers: *few/fewer/fewest, less/the lesser/the least, little/less/least,* and *much/more/most*.[46] *Little* has both a determiner meaning, as in *a little fresh water* (an amount), and an adjective meaning, as in *a little book* or *The book is little* (meaning "small").

Adjectives can be modified by an intensifying adverb (e.g. *very lean*); **determiners cannot be modified by an intensifying adverb.** We can't say **very the* or **very two*. The same three exceptions apply: *very few/little/much; much less*.

When an NP includes both a DP and a descriptive adjective, the DP always precedes the descriptive ADJ; the ADJ cannot precede the DP. We can say *the furry blue monster*; we cannot say, **furry the blue monster* or **furry blue the monster*.[47]

ADJPs may function as constituents of NPs or as verb complements (subject complements [SC] or object complements [OC]); DPs can only function as constituents within NPs. A DP can only function as a specifier of a noun, as in the NP *the monster*. An ADJP can modify a noun (*the blue monster*) or complement a verb (*The monster is blue*; *The potion turned the monster blue*).

ADJPs are modifiers and are therefore always optional; DPs are not modifiers and are not always optional. With or without an ADJP, the same NP will be well formed. But a singular common count noun requires a DP.

Possessives and numbers are only determiners when they precede nouns in NPs. Otherwise, possessives and numbers are pronouns, and possessive NPs (NP + *'s*) are "pronominals": constituents that function like NPs:

Possessive pronoun: <u>Hers</u> is a Mustang.
Possessive pronominal: <u>The second woman's</u> is a Chevy.
Cardinal as pronoun: <u>One</u> is a doctor and the other is an artist.
                         <u>Two</u> can live as cheaply as <u>one</u>.
Ordinal as pronoun: <u>First</u> is better than <u>last</u>.

As indefinite pronouns (see 5.1), cardinal and ordinal numbers can both function as the head of an <u>NP</u>:

Cardinal: *Arugula is <u>the green **one** with jagged edges</u>.*[48]
         *I bought <u>the last **two** in the store</u>.*
Ordinal: *Prime Minister Zapatero's government was <u>the **first** with a gender-balanced Cabinet</u>.*[49]
         *When you make pancakes, <u>the **second** off the griddle</u> is always <u>the **first** that anyone should eat</u>.*

Cardinal and ordinal numbers are not adjectives for the same reasons that other determiners are not adjectives. However, compare the use of *the first* and *the second* in the preceding sentences with the superlative degree of adjectives like *best, worst, most*, and *least*, which commonly must be preceded by *the* and which may function as adjectives (e.g. *The <u>best</u> restaurant is The Grill*) or as nouns, or perhaps pronominals, since they stand in for the complete NP (e.g. *The <u>best</u> is The Grill*). *First, next*, and *last* are more closely related to the superlative adjectives than the other ordinals: they can all take an intensifying adverb as in *the very first/ last/next car* (like *the very best car*); other ordinals cannot: **the very second car*.

Key Points

- **Adjectives** are content words that may be gradable (e.g. *big, bigger, biggest*) or non-gradable (e.g. *main; stone*).
- Four tests for identifying adjectives are the adjective slot test (function); the predicate adjective test (function); the *very* test (function); and the adjectival question test (meaning).
- An adjective functions as the head of an adjective phrase (A~DJ~P). An A~DJ~P may include an adverb phrase as a pre-modifier and/or a post-modifying PP:A~DVERBIAL~.
- Adjective phrases may function as modifiers of nouns or as verb complements.

- When they modify nouns, adjective phrases tell *which* or *what kind of* and are placed immediately before the noun.
- **Determiners** are a closed class of function words that only function as specifiers of nouns and only appear in the first slot in an NP (before an ADJP, if there is one).
- A determiner phrase (DP) may comprise one or more words. The most common determiner (and the most common word in written English) is *the*.
- Like adjectives, determiners provide information about the noun.
- However, unlike adjectives, determiners are almost never gradable; determiners can almost never be modified by an intensifying adverb; and unlike an ADJP:MOD OF N, determiners are not always optional.

4.4 Exercises

A. Adjective Phrases: made-up sentences:[50]   ↱ADjectival Phrase

For each sentence 1–10, identify all adjectives and complete ADJPs. For each ADJP, **try** to identify its function.

1. Bicycles became much more popular in 1815, after a large volcano, Mt. Tambora, erupted in present-day Indonesia.
2. Phenomenal amounts of debris were ejected into the earth's atmosphere.
3. As global temperatures cooled, crops around the world were ruined, leading to widespread famine and starvation for horses and livestock.
4. In this pre-automobile era, this immense disaster raised the question of how to transport people without horses.
5. A German inventor named Karl Drais decided he would build a propulsion device that could replace horse riding.
6. Two years later he presented his new invention: a two-wheeled contraption that came to be called a velocipede.
7. This early bicycle had a simple saddle atop two large wheels, with no pedals or propulsion.
8. More sophisticated designs soon followed, including the awkwardly humorous and accident-prone penny-farthing, with its one giant wheel and one small wheel.

B. Adjective Phrases: a real text: Same instructions as in A. Use the passage from Exercise 1.3B on pages 27–28, "Dog Belonging to Princess Anne Attacks Royal Maid."

C. Determiner Phrases: made-up sentences: ↱Determiner phrase

- For each sentence, identify each complete DP and its function.
- For each determiner, label the type of determiner (article, demonstrative, possessive, quantifier, partitive, multiplier, fraction, cardinal, ordinal).

1. We waited in the rain for three hours for the president's motorcade to arrive.
2. When the first shipment arrived, none of the staff were prepared to handle so many boxes.
3. Your mint chocolate chip cookies are our favorite!
4. A bowl of cherries sat on a bright green cloth.
5. Many of the last group of paintings, almost half of the collection, were unfinished.
6. Franz's teammates were some of the best players in the state.
7. A few of these plants survived through the winter.
8. She found her algebra book under a pile of her brother's clean clothes.
9. Every year, all of the soccer players' parents make the team a steak dinner.
10. Half a wit is better than no wit at all.

D. Determiner Phrases: a real text: Same instructions as in Exercise C. Use the passage from Exercise 1.3B on pages 27–28, "Dog Belonging to Princess Anne Attacks Royal Maid."

Notes

1. Walt Wolfram and Natalie Schilling-Estes. *American English*. 2nd ed. Malden, MA: Blackwell, 2006. 378.
2. Jim Croce, "Bad, Bad Leroy Brown."1972.
3. Brad Chacos. "Nvidia GeForce GTX Titan X: Hail to the New GPU King." *PC World* 33.5 (May 2015): 82.
4. Bonnie Azab Powell. "Mirror, Mirror on the Wall, Who's the Goodest, Cleanest, and Fairest of Them All?" *ethicurean.com*. 14 May 2007.
5. Wolfram and Schilling-Estes, op. cit. 378.
6. David Crystal. *The Stories of English*. Woodstock, NY: The Overlook Press, 2004. 464.
7. Herman Melville. *Pierre, or, The Ambiguities*. New York: Harper & Brothers, 1852. 487.
8. Eugene Field. "The Duel." *Love Songs of Childhood*. New York: Charles Scribner's Sons, 1894. 33.
9. Mark Twain. *The Adventures of Huckleberry Finn (Tom Sawyer's Comrade)*. New York: Charles L. Webster, 1885. 357.
10. Ibid. 120.
11. US Senator James Risch. Qtd. in David Keyes. "Get Risch Quick, 'less awfuller,' Sand Creek Byway Tour." *Bonner County Daily Bee*. 3 Sep 2009.
12. Keely Carroll. "Get to Know the World Around You! Biology 14: Natural History, Ecology and Conservation." *Journal of the Sierra College Natural History Museum* 3.1 (Spring 2010). <www.sierracollege.edu/>.
13. Keith Murray. "The Most Beautifullest Thing in This World." 1994.
14. Charles Carpenter Fries. *American English Grammar: The Grammatical Structure of Present-Day English with Especial Reference to Social Differences or Class Dialects*. English Monograph No. 10, National Council of Teachers of English. New York: D. Appleton-Century Co., 1940. 96–97.
15. Crystal, op. cit. 376.
16. William Shakespeare, *The Life and Death of Julius Caesar*. 1599. III.i.121–122.

17. Ibid. III.ii.182.
18. William Shakespeare. *As You Like It*. 1600. III.iii.59.
19. Acts 26:5. *King James Bible*. 1611.
20. Ben Jonson. *Every Man out of His Humour*. 1600. I.i.50–53.
21. Crystal, op. cit. 376.
22. Fries, op. cit. 97–98.
23. Ibid.
24. Op. cit. 378.
25. Daniel Malloy and Katie Leslie. "Georgians Swarm Swing States for Final Election Push." *The Atlanta Journal Constitution*. 5 Nov 2012.
26. Richard N. Haass and Martin Indyk. "Beyond Iraq: A New U.S. Strategy for the Middle East." *Foreign Affairs* 88.1 (Jan/Feb 2009): 58.
27. "All the Best Looks from the 2018 Cannes Film Festival." *PureWow*. 9 May 2019. <www.yahoo.com/>.
28. "Hot Topics." *The View*. ABC. 20 Jun 2017.
29. Julie Mason. "Political Smackdown Captivates N.Y. Voters." *Houston Chronicle*. 17 Sep 2000.
30. Tom Vanden Brook. "Recruits Hungry." *USA Today*. 15 Feb 2006.
31. XFWAGON. "Re: XHII XR8 Ute Build—'FTR 008'- The FULL LENGTH Story!!" Online posting. *FordMods: The Ford Modification Website*. 31 Aug 2012.
32. Once we accept this pattern of PARTITIVE, as *a ___ of* and *the ___ of*, it raises an interesting problem. The clearest examples of such determiners are those in which the word in the slot is a commonly used quantifier (e.g. *few, little, lot*) or a common unit of measure (e.g. *quart, pound*). But we can create an endless list of phrases using this pattern, phrases that look like PARTITIVES and may be parsed as determiners, such as *a good deal of, a/the bowl of, a/the bunch of, a/the jar of, a/the piece of, a/the slice of, a/the small quantity of, a/the kind of*, etc. But is it better to parse them as DPs or to treat them as NPs so that in a phrase like "a bunch of carrots," *bunch* is the head noun, *a* is a DP:SPECIFIER of *bunch*, and *of carrots* is a PP:ADJECTIVAL:MOD OF "bunch"? In a context where the noun is a common unit of measure (say among produce farmers), it might be more reasonable to parse *a bunch of* as a PARTITIVE DP, while in more everyday circumstances, it might be more reasonable to parse *bunch* as the head noun of the NP *a bunch of carrots*. Grammar is a mode of interpretation, and real-world context affects how we assign grammatical labels.
33. Jeremy Gottlieb and Jake Russell. "Goggles, Cigars and Plenty of Bubbly as Nationals Celebrate NL East Crown." *Washington Post Blogs DC Sports Bog*. 25 Sep 2016.
34. Wolfram and Schilling-Estes, op. cit. 382.
35. Geneva Smitherman. *Talkin that Talk: Language, Culture and Education in African America*. New York: Routledge, 2000. 21.
36. Ibid. 22. See also J. L. Dillard. *Black English: Its History and Usage in the United States*. New York: Vintage Books, 1972. 57.
37. John Russell Rickford and Russell John Rickford. *Spoken Soul: The Story of Black English*. New York: John Wiley, 2000. 112.
38. Ibid. 158; William Labov and Wendell Harris. "De facto Segregation of Black and White Vernaculars." *Diversity and Diachrony*. Ed. David Sankoff. Philadelphia: John Benjamins, 1986. 12–13.
39. Labov and Harris, op. cit. 20–22.
40. Rickford and Rickford, op. cit. 157–15.
41. Alex Pavlovic. "Giants Takeaways: What We Learned from First Road Trip of Season." *NBCSports.com*. 4 Apr 2019.
42. Zenith Vineyard. "Meet Our Vineyard Partners." Website. 10 May 2019. <www.zenithvineyard.com/>.

43. Wolfram and Schilling-Estes, op. cit. 382.

44. Barbara Stewart. "New York Yearns for an Institution of Historic Proportions." *The New York Times*. 25 Aug 2001. <www.nytimes.com >.

45. Edward Lewine. "The Great Divide: East Side, West Side, Does It Matter Anymore?" *The New York Times*. 19 Oct 1997. <www.nytimes.com>.

46. I am indebted to spring 2005 students Melissa Smith and Chris Douglas for pointing out these exceptions.

47. We <u>can</u> make up contexts where a particular shift in emphasis allows us to put AdjPs ahead of DPs. Consider this: the "normal" order for the following set of words would be *the three young French girls*. But say we had several groups of three girls, one Russian, one American, one French, and we wanted to select the group of French girls out of the crowd. Then we might say *the French three young girls*, apparently placing the adjective *French* ahead of the determiner *three*. However, this could easily be explained in terms of an N′: the apparent NP *three young girls* is being modified by the adjective *French* (which tells *which three young girls*), creating a N′ that, combined with the determiner *the*, makes a complete NP.

48. Meaghan Winter. "Shame Story." *Kenyon Review* 35.4 (Fall 2013): 143.

49. "Global | SHORT TAKES." *Ms.* 17.3 (Summer 2007): 32.

50. Sentences based on Andy Jacobs. "History of the Bicycle—The Evolution of Biking." *Backroads.com*. 23 Mar 2017.

Chapter 5

Pronouns (PRoN) and Pronoun Phrases (PRoNP)

Pronouns are a category of function words. In traditional grammar, a PRoN is often defined as a word that stands in for or replaces a noun. In fact, a PRoN stands in the place of an entire NP or other nominal (see 11.1). We have already seen this concept in the pronoun replacement test for identifying complete NPs. Consider the following sentences:

> *Franz bought* **the <u>ball</u> with the green spots**.
> *Franz bought* **it**.
> **Franz bought* **the it with the green spots**.

In the second sentence, the PRoN *it* replaces the entire NP *the ball with the green spots*. In the third sentence, when we try to replace <u>only</u> the noun—the head of the NP—with the pronoun, we get nonsense. Remember that an NP consists of a noun and all its dependents, including DPs and modifiers (both ADJPs and adjectival post-modifiers, such as PPs).

A PRoN is traditionally understood as referring back to an NP that appeared earlier in the discourse. The earlier NP is called the antecedent of the pronoun. Sometimes, a PRoN precedes the NP to which it refers, in which case the NP is a <u>post</u>cedent, rather than an <u>ante</u>cedent.

> **PRoN** and <u>antecedent</u>: <u>The wizard</u> startled everyone when **he** suddenly appeared in a puff of smoke.
> **PRoN** and <u>postcedent</u>: When **he** suddenly appeared in a puff of smoke, <u>the wizard</u> startled everyone.

Although pronouns usually refer to NPs or other nominals, a PRoN may also refer to an entire sentence: *So I dropped the objectivity and told them that I was shot when I was around their age.* **That** *got their attention!*[1] In this example the PRoN *that* refers not just to the preceding NP *their age* or *I* but the entire action described in the clause *I told them . . . age.* Arguably, in this context, *that* might be labeled as a "pro-clause," rather than a pronoun, since its antecedent is an entire independent clause (a.k.a. a sentence) rather than an NP. However, in the second sentence of the example, *That got their attention*, the word *that* functions as the subject, a role that is always filled by a nominal. It is also reasonable to label *that* as a pronoun or a "pronominal" (which would probably be a better name for the whole category).

In writing, PRONs can sometimes have no antecedent or postcedent, as when they are used to refer to generic or indefinite persons or objects:

> *If possible, **one** should always remove themselves from public places when making/taking cell phone calls.*[2]
> ***Someone** should pass the ball to Franz!*
> ***Few** remember how the suburbanization of the country was accomplished.*[3]

In conversation, rather than referring to an NP in the discourse, pronouns are commonly used to refer to objects in the physical context of the speakers: one could point to a sunset and say, ***That** is beautiful!*

5.1 Pronoun Forms

Pronouns come in six types:

1   Personal:

- Nominative (Subject) case: *I, you, he, she, it, we, they*.
- Objective case: *me, you, him, her, it, us, them*.
- Possessive case: *mine, yours, his, hers, its, ours, theirs*.

2   Reflexive: *myself, yourself, himself, herself, itself, ourselves, yourselves, themselves*.
3   Indefinite: *anyone, all, few, somebody*, etc.
4   Demonstrative: *this, that, these, those*.
5   Interrogative: *what, which, who, whom* (objective), *whose* (possessive).
6   Relative: *that, which, who, whom* (objective), *whose* (possessive).

As we saw with determiners, some of the form labels for pronouns are based on their function: among the personal pronouns, the nominative or subject case pronouns are so called because they only function as the subject of a clause; the objective case pronouns only function as verb complements (such as the direct <u>object</u> of a verb) and PCOMPS (called the "<u>object</u> of the preposition" in traditional grammar).

Three notes about pronouns: Note (1): **The distinction between possessive pronouns and possessive determiners**: The one thing that all PRONs have in common is that they all can stand alone as constituents of sentences: all PRONs can function by themselves as nominals. Thus, possessive <u>pronouns</u> can stand by themselves as sentence constituents; possessive <u>determiners</u> cannot, and possessive determiners will always be found as constituents within NPs:

<u>Possessive Pronouns</u>: *mine, yours, his, hers, its, ours, theirs, whose*

> *Mine is the yellow ball. The yellow ball is mine.*
> **Mine ball is yellow*

<u>Possessive Determiners</u>: *my, your, his, her, its, our, their, whose*

> **My is the yellow ball.* **The yellow ball is my.*
> *My ball is yellow.*

Despite the similarity between possessive pronouns and determiners, we have to remember that possessive determiners are <u>not</u> pronouns—although we must be careful with those words that have the same forms in the two categories: *his, its*, and *whose*.

There is a related issue with nouns and NPs marked as possessive by the addition of *'s*: either such possessive NPs can be possessive determiners, or they can stand alone and function as NPs:

Possessive DP:

Ed's bag was heavier than Franz's bag.
Ed's bags were heavier than Franz's bags.

Possessive NP:

Ed's was heavier than Franz's.
Ed's were heavier than Franz's.

Grammatically, the possessive NPs function like any other NPs. Semantically, however, the second pair of sentences both involve the elision or deletion of the nouns *bag* and *bags*: despite their absence, we know those nouns are still implied because the possessive NPs may take a singular or a plural verb (*was* or *were*), even though the possessive *Ed's* is not marked as singular or plural. Grammatically, the possessive NPs are NPs, but semantically, they seem to still be determiners, with the nouns they specify implied.

Note (2): Indefinite pronouns are a large category in English, although not an open class. And indefinite pronouns are the only subclass of pronouns that routinely can take both <u>modifiers</u> and <u>determiners</u>:

> *<u>Not just</u> **anyone** can handle a camel.*[4]
> *<u>Very</u> **few** see that dream through to reality.*[5]
> *"Bob Michel keeps no little black book in his desk drawer," he said. "Mine*
> *is <u>a large green</u> **one** <u>with a lot of names and plans for the future that will</u>*
> *<u>include each and every one of you.</u>"*[6]

In each of these sentences, the indefinite PRON functions as the head of a pronoun phrase (PRONP) that functions as a nominal within the sentence. Despite taking modifiers, we still know that the words in bold type are PRONs because:

- They do not name specific objects or categories of objects (as nouns do).
- The indefinite pronoun in each case replaces a more specific NP: *Not just anyone* replaces something like *not just any one person*; *Very few* replaces *very few people*; and *a large, green one . . . you* replaces *a large, green book . . . you.*
- We can drop the modifiers and determiners and have the bold-faced words stand alone:

   Anyone *can handle a camel.*
   Few *see that dream through to reality.*
   Mine is **one**.

Because of the size of the category and the complexities of the kinds of modifiers they can take, indefinite PRONs are the most complicated subclass of pronouns. Here is a fuller list:

Indefinite Pronouns

all	both	everything	less	neither	others
another	each	few	little	no one	several
any	either	fewer	many	nobody	some
anybody	enough	fewest	more	none	somebody
anyone	everybody	half	most	nothing	someone
anything	everyone	least	much	one	something

Many of these words can function not only as indefinite pronouns but as other parts of speech. Half of them can also be determiners (though <u>not</u> *others* and those ending in *-one, -body, -thing*). Be careful!

Note (3): Demonstrative pronouns, especially *those,* **can take** <u>adjectival post-modifiers</u>:

   For I say unto you, that **this** *that is written, must yet be accomplished in me.*[7]
   What's in a name? **that** *which we call a rose / By any other word would smell as sweet.*[8]
   Give me **that** *which I want, and you shall have* **this** *which you want.*[9]
   What passing bells for **these** *who die as cattle?*[10]
   Those *who cannot remember the past are condemned to repeat it.*[11]
   Microbes in the neonatal intensive care unit resemble **those** *found in the gut of premature infants.*[12]

Non-Standard pronoun forms: Possessives: In AAVE, we typically find "regularization of the possessive pronoun *mines* by analogy with *yours, his, hers*, etc.," as in ***Mines** is here. It's **mines**.*[13] And "in vernacular Appalachian English and other rural varieties characterized by the retention of relic forms," we typically find:

> the use of possessive [pronoun] forms ending in *-n*, as in *hisn, ourn*, or *yourn*. Such forms can be found in phrase- or sentence-final position (called absolute position), as in *It is **hisn*** or *It was **yourn** that I was talking about*; *-n* forms do not usually occur in structures such as *It is **hern** book*.
>
> *Is it **yourn**? I think it's **hisn**.*[14]

Wolfram and Schilling-Estes put both of these non-Standard variants (*mines*; *yourn*) down to attempts by speakers to regularize the irregular PRON system, either by changing *mine* to match the *-s* ending of all the other possessive PRON forms or by changing all of the *-s* endings to match the ending of *mine*. However, according to Fries, the historical context is more complicated. Until the fourteenth century, there was no distinction between the possessive Ds and the possessive PRONs, though there were fewer forms. *Her* was used as the third-person <u>plural</u> possessive PRON until the fifteenth century, when it was replaced by *their*. The neuter third-person singular possessive *its* appears near the end of the sixteenth century. *Our, your*, and *their* continued to be used as PRONs until the seventeenth century. But from the fourteenth century on, new forms were increasingly used to distinguish between the D and PRON uses of the possessives. *Mine* and *thine*—formerly used as both Ds and PRONs—continued to be used as PRONs after *my* and *thy* were in common use as Ds.[15] "It was natural, therefore, that *ourn, yourn, hern*, etc., after the pattern of *mine* and *thine* should be created and for a time compete with *ours, yours, hers*, etc., formed on the pattern" of the possessive PRONs ending in *-s*. In his fourteenth-century translation of the bible, John Wycliffe uses both *ourn* and *yourn*; "*hern* appeared earlier in the fourteenth century; and *hisn* appeared in the fifteenth century."[16] People from England who settled in Appalachia brought these PRON forms with them, and their descendants have maintained them, even as the dominant SE of the wealthy and powerful in the cities shifted away from those forms.

Other non-Standard pronouns: Other non-Standard pronoun forms "typically involve regularization by analogy and rule extension."[17] We routinely find several categories of non-Standard PRON usage:

Reflexives: The reflexive PRONs all take the possessive PRONs and add *-self* (***myself, yourself, herself, ourselves, yourselves***) except for *himself* and *themselves*, which use the object case personal pronouns as their base. Many American English vernaculars regularize these exceptions by creating the non-Standard forms *hisself* and *theirselves*, which are more consistent with the rest of the paradigm.

> *He hit **hisself** on the head.* (AAVE)[18]
> *They had to start supporting **theirselves** at early ages.* (Chicano English)[19]

Again, Fries observes that the current system of reflexive PRONs with its irregularities evolved over several centuries. In Middle English, the objective case forms of PRONs (*me, him, her, us, them*) "were most frequent with *self*. From the fourteenth century on, the tendency has been to regard *self* as a noun and therefore to use the [possessive] form of a preceding pronoun, thus *myself, ourselves, (thyself), yourself, yourselves.*" Fries notes that "*meself* occurs in literature as late as the sixteenth century" and that Chaucer (in the fourteenth century) uses *us selven* (with the older plural marker—*en* as in *oxen* and *children*). The plural *yourselves* didn't develop until the sixteenth century.[20] According to the *Oxford English Dictionary* (*OED*), *hisself* was in use in writing as far back as 1325, although by the nineteenth century, in works by authors like Stevenson, Dickens, and Twain, its use is limited to dialect—that is, lower class and "ethnic"—characters. Likewise, the *OED* offers examples of *theirselves* from 1525 on; but by the late nineteenth century, it is also chiefly used to mark the speech of dialect characters. Arguably, the non-Standard reflexives *hisself* and *theirselves* are simply evidence that, at least in the spoken language, these PRON forms are still in flux. The *OED* does note that even in SE, we find *his self* but only with an intervening ADJ. Actually, in SE we find this construction with both *his self* and *their selves*, as well as *their self*:

> *Most people give no thought to the everyday enormity of what Miller must face beyond <u>his very self</u>.*[21] (not **him very self*)
> *He was not <u>his usual happy self</u>.*[22] (not **him usual happy self*)
> *For men shall be lovers of <u>their own selves</u>, covetous, boasters, proud, blasphemers, disobedient to parents, unthankful, unholy.*[23] (not **them own selves*)
> *<u>Their outward self is different from</u> their inner self.*[24] (not **them outward self; *them inner self*)

It is common in many spoken varieties of American English to use *myself* as the last item in a conjoined series of names, in both subject and object positions:

> <u>Subject</u>: *The president of Mexico and <u>myself</u> have agreed to cancel our planned meeting scheduled for next week.*[25]
> <u>Object</u>: *He asked Faith, Keith and <u>myself</u> for our names.*[26]
> <u>Both</u>: *He asked Tommy and <u>myself</u>[OBJECT] had we seen Bernard Bennett. And as Tommy and <u>myself</u>[SUBJECT] was telling him, no, we hadn't seen Bernard, Kelvin Peters came off the elevator.*[27]

I suspect that people use the reflexive form to create a little more distance or formality. In each of these examples, the use of *myself* may put the speaker on a more equal footing with the other people named. While both uses of *myself* are arguably non-Standard, according to the *OED*, they have appeared in the written language since at least Chaucer's time.

Object PRoN forms in subject position: In many varieties of English, it is common to use the objective forms of personal pronouns in the subject position with subjects conjoined by *and* or *or*:

> *John and them will be home soon.*[28]
> *Him and me's lifted a beer, time to time.*[29]
> *Me or him will post updates on this thread as soon as it is fixed.*[30]

The *OED* offers examples of this usage from before 1400 to the present. Wolfram and Schilling-Estes state that no variety of English exhibits the routine use of objective case personal pronouns by themselves as subjects; we almost never find *Him will do it* or *Them will be home soon.*[31] However, Dillard reported that, "Washington inner-city children say things like:

> *Me help you?*
> *Her paintin' wif a spoon.*"[32]

Dillard ascribes this pattern of using object pronouns in subject position to the roots of AAVE in English pidgin and creole languages, where it is commonplace for pronouns to be leveled to objective case forms.[33]

Plural form of *you*: Wolfram and Schilling-Estes explain that "to fill out the person-number paradigm (*I, you, he/she/it, we, you, they*)," many varieties of English have added a plural form of *you*. The use of some versions remains markedly non-Standard, as in *Youse won the game. I'm going to leave youse now*, which occurs primarily in the North, and *You'uns won the game. I'm going to leave you'uns now*, which occurs primarily "in an area extending from Southern Appalachia to Pittsburgh," where it becomes *yinz*. However, the Southern form *y'all*, as in *Y'all won the game. I'm going to leave y'all now*,[34] has become essentially a SE (though still informal) usage throughout the Southeast. Interestingly, both *y'all* and *youse* are sometimes used as singulars, as noted by Fries,[35] leading to the development of a Southern plural form, *all y'all*.

Personal dative use of object pronoun forms: The "dative" is a grammatical term for the indirect object (IO), a variety of verb complement (see 7.1.3.1). In the sentence, *I got John a new car*, *a new car* is the direct object (DO); *John* is the IO. In some English varieties, the object case forms of personal pronouns are used as IOs: *I got **me** a new car. We had **us** a little old dog.* "The so-called personal dative illustrated in [these sentences] is a Southern feature that indicates that the subject of the sentence (*e.g we*) benefited in some way from the object (e.g. *little old dog*)."[36]

Associative plurals: Rickford, citing Mufwene, states that speakers of AAVE and some Southern White varieties use "*and (th)em* or *nem*, usually after a proper name to mark associative plurals, as in *Felicia an' (th)em* or *Felicia nem* for 'Felicia and her friends or family or associates.'"[37]

Appositive pronouns: Citing Fasold and Wolfram, Rickford also notes as an AAVE construction, "'That teacher, *she* yells at the kids' for SE 'That teacher Ø yells at the kids.'"[38]

5.2 Pronoun Attributes: Case, Number, Person, Gender, Animateness

Case: Personal PRONs give us the largest remnant of English case inflections. In English, for the most part, we use the word order of sentences to tell us how an NP is functioning. In many other languages, nouns and adjectives take different endings to mark whether the NP is the subject, the DO, or indicating a location (which we usually mark in English with prepositions appearing before an NP). In many languages, the nominative or subject case is unmarked, and other sentence roles require that nouns, modifying adjectives, and pronouns be marked with special endings or "inflections." In modern English we mark the possessive case of all NPs with *'s* (or *-s'* with plural NPs). In the personal PRONs, we actually still have different forms to mark the objective and possessive cases:

Case Forms of Personal Pronouns

Nominative	Objective	Possessive
I	me	mine
you	you	yours
he	him	his
she	her	hers
it	it	its
we	us	ours
you	you	yours
they	them	theirs

Nominative case personal PRONs only function as the subject of a sentence (PRON:SUBJ) and as the complement of the verb *be* (see 7.1.2.2). Objective case personal PRONs only function as PCOMPs (PRON:PCOMP) or as the objective complement of a verb (PRON:DO; PRON:IO; see Chapter 7). Possessive case personal PRONs may function in all of the same roles as nominative and objective case PRONs.

Objective case personal PRONs can take determiners but only partitives with *of* and cardinal numbers with *of* (which are also partitives in their meaning):

> *Several of **us** have been discussing this.*[39]
> *And part of **me** thought, maybe I'll just stay here.*[40]

> *Two of* **them** *were recently vacated by the D.C. Circuit Court of Appeals.*[41]

Just as when we use determiners and/or modifiers with indefinite pronouns, when an objective case personal PRON takes a determiner, the combination forms a PRONP that functions like other nominals.[42]

Also, in SE varieties, reflexive PRONs do not function in nominative case roles (e.g. **Himself went to the store*) or take a possessive form (e.g. **Myself's is on the table*). They only function in objective case roles (e.g. *She hurt herself; You only have yourself to blame; They saved it for themselves*) and as nominal appositives modifying nouns (*I myself was unaware of the problem*).

Number: Personal PRONs in all three cases are also marked for number. In English, we have two numbers: singular (SG) and plural (PL):

Case and Number of Personal Pronouns

Number	Nominative	Objective	Possessive
SG	I	me	mine
	you	you	yours
	he	him	his
	she	her	hers
	it	it	its
PL	we	us	ours
	you	you	yours
	they	them	theirs

Number becomes significant when we are looking for the right personal PRON form to use with a singular or plural antecedent. Number also matters when we are trying to match a nominative personal PRON with the singular or plural forms of the verb *be* and when we are trying to match the singular third-person form of a verb (the one that ends in *-s*) with the correct SE PRON (*he, she,* or *it*; see the next paragraph on "person").

Person: In English, we use different personal PRON forms (and different forms of the reflexive pronouns and possessive personal determiners) to indicate what person the speaker is talking about, relative to the speaker:

- The **first**-person form refers to the speaker (SG) or a group of which the speaker is a member (PL).
- The **second-person** form refers to the person spoken to (SG) or a group whom the speaker is addressing (PL).
- The **third-person** form refers to the person spoken about (SG) or a group whom the speaker is speaking about (PL).

All of the preceding information about case, number, and person in personal pronouns (and personal possessive determiners) is presented in the following table:

Person	#	Nominative	Objective	Possessive	
				Determiner	Pronoun
FIRST	SG	I	me	my	mine
	PL	we	us	our	ours
SECOND	SG	you	you	your	yours
	PL	you	you	your	yours
THIRD	SG	he, she, it	him, her, it	his, her, its	his, hers, its
	PL	they	them	their	theirs

Gender: In English, only the third-person singular personal pronouns (*he/him/his, she/her/hers, it/its*), the third-person singular reflexive pronouns (*himself, herself, itself*), and the third-person singular possessive determiners (*his, her, its*) are marked for three genders: masculine (M), feminine (F), and neuter (NEU). We use the appropriately gendered personal PRON to refer to NPs that name objects, or to refer to objects themselves, that possess apparent gender (e.g. *man* [M], *woman* [F], *desk* [NEU]) or conventional gender (e.g. a ship is referred to as *she*).

Animateness: One final attribute of PRONs in general, and personal pronouns in particular, is animateness. Most personal and reflexive pronouns refer to animate objects, typically people or animals and sometimes conventionally to ships, cars, and countries (e.g. *I love my car—she's a real beauty.*). The third-person plural personal and reflexive pronouns *they/them/theirs/themselves* may refer to animate or inanimate objects:

Animate:

I watched Franz and his team today. They played really well.
Children themselves may be eager to hear accounts of family formation.[43]

Inanimate:

I bought three balls today. They are all green.
The rooms themselves are modest in size and decoration.[44]

The third-person singular neuter pronouns *it/its/itself* only properly refer to inanimate objects:

*Animate: I watched Franz play today. It played really well.
Inanimate: *I bought a ball today. It is green.*

Since the late eighteenth century, there has been no singular neuter animate personal—or "epicene"—PRON in English that is accepted by conservative authorities, which creates a gap in the language: how should we refer pronominally to an animate object or antecedent of uncertain gender? For example, in

When a person comes to the office, _____ should expect . . . , how should we refer back to the NP *a person*? From the late eighteenth century until the 1970s, the masculine *he* was commonly accepted as the generic animate singular: *When a person comes to the office, he should expect.* . . . But use of the generic *he* is no longer acceptable since to refer to all people as though they were male has become socially unacceptable. A solution is emerging—a solution that simply hearkens back to a usage that was well established from the fourteenth century until the end of the eighteenth century: use *they* as the non-gendered animate singular pronoun: *When a person comes to the office, they should expect.* . . . This usage, which was common for 400 years among all levels of speakers and writers of English, was stomped upon by a series of pedagogical grammarians who tried to regularize many structures in English that they saw as irregular (Google the phrase "singular they" for a variety of academic and popular discussions of the topic).[45] Singular *they* has already regained wide acceptance in spoken English, and it is spreading in published writing. For conservative language users and authorities, the use of *they* as a singular may be grating, and such folks may harshly judge those who use singular *they*. If you know your audience will judge such matters strongly, avoid using singular *they*; but know that in most contexts, it is now fairly safe to speak or even to write *they* with reference to a singular, animate object or nominal.[46]

5.3 Pronoun Functions

Pronouns fulfill the same functions as NPs and other nominals, although PRONs must agree with their referent (antecedent, postcedent, common knowledge object, or object in the physical context of discourse) in the attributes of number, person, gender, and animateness, and personal pronouns must have the appropriate case form (nominative, objective, possessive) for their role in a sentence. We will consider the functions of each category of pronoun in turn.

Nominative (Subject) case PRONs can function as the subject of a sentence or as the complement of copular *be*: forms of the verb *be* used as the main verb in a sentence or clause:

> Subject: *I went home. She found the treasure.*
> Subject Complement of copular *be*: *It is I. I am she.*

The term "nominative" comes from the same root as the word "noun," and both relate to "naming." The "rule" that we use the nominative form of the personal PRON after *be* was created by the same late eighteenth-century grammarians who said we should not use *they* as a singular PRON. In most contexts, saying, "It is I" or "It is she," sounds overly formal. If we say "It's me," in many contexts, no one will notice, although we may offend the sensibilities of those who subscribe to the older version.

An **objective case personal PRON** can function as a PCOMP or as the complement of a verb, participles or infinitive:

> PComp: *Stand by me. We like being with them. For him, the village was the soul of India.*[47]
>
> Complement of V: *Franz kicked me. We gave them the ball. Harried motorists have silently thanked him ever since.*[48]
>
> Complement of Participle: *Finding them was easy. Finding her was easy.*
>
> Complement of Infinitive: *To know her was to love her.*[49] *Are politicians too rich to understand us?*[50]

Possessive case personal PRONs can function in nominative and objective roles, as can **indefinite** and **demonstrative pronouns.**

Reflexive PRONs often function in the same roles as objective personal pronouns: as a PCOMP or complement of a verb, participle, or infinitive. They may also function emphatically, as a nominal appositive, repeating the reference of an earlier or immediately preceding NP. In all roles, the **reflexive PRON** must have an antecedent in the same sentence:

> PComp: *I did it all by myself.*
> *We must learn to laugh at ourselves, and move on.*[51]
>
> Complement of a Verb: *I could have kicked myself.*
> *We got ourselves into this mess.*
>
> Emphatic (nominal appositive): *I did it myself.*
> *The President himself brought that issue up.*[52]

Emphatics are adjectival in that they tell *which* person: *which Franz? Franz himself.* We also sometimes find reflexives with a **postcedent**, as in *As for myself, I was never Beat.*[53]

Some **interrogative PRONs** function like nominative personal PRONs, some like objective personal PRONs, and some like both:

- *What* can function in both the nominative and objective slots:

  Nominative: *What*[PRON:SUBJ] *went wrong?*
  Objective: *What*[PRON:DO] *do you want? You do want what*[PRON:DO]?

- *Which*, as a pronoun, can function in both the nominative and objective slots (though *which* is more commonly a determiner):

  Nominative: *Which*[PRON:SUBJ] *is right?*
  Objective: *Which*[PRON:DO] *do you want? You want which*[PRON:DO]?
  (Determiner: *Which book do you want?*)

- *Who* is always nominative: *Who is right?*
- *Whom* is always objective: *Whom do you love? You do love* **whom***?*

Relative PRONs, like interrogative PRONs, also vary in function:

- *That* *and* *which* can function in both the nominative and objective slots:

Nominative:

This is the book that *made me love books.*[54] (*that* is the SUBJ of *made.*)
I was a around a lot of people, which *made me feel uncomfortable.*[55]
(*which* is the SUBJ of *made.*)

Objective:

The book that *she wanted most was* The Da Vinci Code. (*that* is the DO of
wanted: *she wanted* that.)
The book, which *she had wanted for years, was* The Da Vinci Code. (*which*
is the DO of *wanted*: *she wanted* which.)

- *Who* is always nominative:

These are the people **who** *saw you shuffle around in your pajamas, knew
your favorite bands, drank your milk.*[56] (*who* is the Subj of *saw*: **Who**
saw you—like **They** *saw you.*)

- *Whom* is always objective:

These are the people **whom** *you saw shuffle around in their pajamas.*
(*whom* is the DO of *saw*: *You saw* **whom**—like *You saw* **them**.)

There are categories of words that should best be called interrogative and relative pro-adverbs, interrogative and relative pro-determiners, and even interrogative pro-adjectives:

- Pro-adverbs: *where, when, why, how, how often, how long, how much, how many.*
- Pro-determiners: *whose, which, what, how much, how many.*
- Pro-adjectives: *which, what.*

In Chapter 10, we will examine all of these *wh*-pro-words more thoroughly.

5.4 Identifying Pronouns

Pronouns are a closed class, and the simplest way to identify them is to know them by memory (and to understand that possessive determiners are not pronouns). Given our fuller knowledge of PRONs and the attributes of personal PRONs, it is now useful to give the full version of Lester's statement of

> **The pronoun replacement test for NPs**: Any noun phrase can be replaced by an appropriate third-person pronoun. The pronoun will replace the complete noun phrase. Whichever word within the noun phrase determines the form (person, number, case, gender, animateness) of the pronoun is the head noun of the noun phrase.[57]

To make this test work, you have to trust your ear for identifying the head noun within the NP; it also helps knowing what person, number, case, gender, and animateness are, especially, as with some complex determiners, it becomes unclear what the head of the NP may be. For example, in the sentence *I saw Franz today*, native speakers know by ear that the appropriate PRON to replace *Franz* is *him*, not *he*: *I saw him today*, not, **I saw he today*. However, we can also know which PRON is correct because *Franz* names a masculine (gender), animate thing, and *Franz* is in the third person (he is the person being spoken about), and he is singular (number—there is only one of him). Case is the one concept here that may still be fuzzy, but *Franz* names the DO of the verb *saw*; the DO takes the objective case form. So the PRON that agrees with *Franz* needs to be in the objective case.

Now, consider these two sentences: which is correct?

> *I saw the crowd and they were not happy.*
> *I saw the crowd and it was not happy.*

Is *the crowd* plural and animate (*they*) or singular and inanimate (*it*)? That depends on the context: are we talking about the crowd as a bunch of human individuals (*they*) or as a single mass (*it*)? Whether they are aware of the concepts of number and animateness or not, our audience will still hear the implications of the different pronouns.

The pronoun replacement test for NPs will be extremely useful when we are working on identifying NPs (and nominals and their functions within sentences) since some NP:VCOMPS (DO; IO) will be replaced by pronouns in the objective case, while subjects and NP:SCs will be replaced by pronouns in the nominative case (see Chapter 7).

Key Points

- Pronouns (PRON) are a closed class of function words that stand in the place of a complete NP or other nominal. PRONs may function in all the ways that NPs and other nominals do.
- A pronoun must have a referent within the discourse or within the shared knowledge, experience, or physical context of speakers or writers and their audience.

- There are six types of PRoNs: personal, reflexive, indefinite, demonstrative, interrogative, and relative.
- Some pronouns are marked for case (nominative; objective; possessive), number (singular; plural), person (first; second; third), gender (masculine; feminine; neuter), and animateness (animate; inanimate).
- Indefinite pronouns are the only subclass of pronouns that routinely can take both modifiers and determiners.
- Despite their similarities, possessive PRoNs should not be confused with possessive determiners.
- Because there are so many irregularities in the SE PRoN system, it is one of the portions of English grammar with the most diverse and distinctive range of non-Standard forms, as speakers of different varieties strive to regularize the system (e.g. *mines*; *hisself*).

5.5 Exercises: Pronouns

A. Made-up sentences: for each sentence, identify all pronouns and label the type of pronoun. For each personal pronoun, identify the person (first; second; third), number (SG; PL), case (NOM; OBJ; POSS), gender (M; F; NEU), and animateness (animate; inanimate). Finally, identify the function of the PRON within the sentence.

Example: *I found the book on a different shelf.*

I—first person, singular, nominative, animate; PRON:NP:SUBJ of "found"

1. Everybody in my family, including my brother, enjoys playing board games, but few of us enjoy them as much as he does.
2. Whenever we have an evening at home, everyone gathers around the dining room table; even the dog joins us.
3. We choose games, and each selects a different one.
4. Some games take too long for us to play, but some are short enough.
5. My brother himself then chooses whose will be the first game played.
6. His is always the last game of the evening.
7. These are special evenings and I always enjoy them.
8. A family game night is something that anyone can enjoy.
9. If you don't like board games, you just haven't played the right one yet.
10. Nobody in my family would decline an opportunity to play.

B. A real text:[58] same instructions as in A:

(1) My mum died in 1980 at the age of 25. (2) I was 3. (3) I am trying to find out as much about her as I can. (4) Google is useless for anything

like this, and I'm not sure of the best way to get public records; is there somewhere you can get them for free?

(5) None of my family know much about her. (6) Her death certificate says she died of a heart attack. (7) I know it was due to drug abuse, but was recently told (from a friend of a friend's mum) that it was from a heroin overdose—something my Dad didn't know.

(8) She may have had some criminal records and it's been mentioned she spent some time in Morocco.

(9) If anyone has any ideas on the best way to start going about this or knows of her, or if anyone who knows her would contact me, all information would be much appreciated.

Notes

1. Joseph Sakran. "I'm a Trauma Surgeon and a Shooting Victim. I Have Every Right to Speak Out on Gun Violence." *theatlantic.com*. 15 Dec 2018.
2. Barbara Rosenfeld and Sharon A. O'Connor-Petruso. "East vs. West: A Comparison of Mobile Phone Use by Chinese and American College Students." *College Student Journal* 48.2 (Summer 2014): 320.
3. Jake Blumgart. "Housing Is Shamefully Segregated. Who Segregated It?" *Slate.com*. 2 Jun 2017.
4. Elizabeth Cobb. "The Camel Broker." *Atlanta Journal-Constitution*. 17 Dec 2006.
5. Kaitlin Wright. "Young Musicians Get Serious in Tustin." *Orange County Register*. 7 Jan 2016.
6. US Rep. Bob Michel. Qtd. in Margot Hornblower and Richard L. Lyons. "House GOP Picks Michel as Leader." *The Washington Post*. 9 Dec 1980.
7. Luke 22:37. *King James Bible*. 1611.
8. William Shakespeare. *Romeo and Juliet*. 1597. II.ii.47–48.
9. Adam Smith. *The Wealth of Nations*. Vol. I. Everyman's Library 412. New York: Dutton, 1964 (1776). 13.
10. Wilfred Owen, "Anthem for Doomed Youth." 1917. <https://en.wikisource.org/>.
11. George Santayana, *The Life of Reason: Or, the Phases of Human Progress*. New York: Charles Scibner's Sons, 1905. 284.
12. Brandon Brooks, et al. "Microbes in the Neonatal Intensive Care Unit Resemble Those Found in the Gut of Premature Infants." *Microbiome* 2.1 (28 Jan 2014).
13. Walt Wolfram and Natalie Schilling-Estes. *American English*. 2nd ed. Malden, MA: Blackwell, 2006. 382.
14. Ibid.
15. However, because of the popularity of the King James Bible, which uses *mine* and *thine* as both pronouns and determiners, we continue to find *mine* used as a determiner to evoke the feeling of biblical language, even long after both *mine* and *thine* had fallen out of common use. An excellent example is Julia Ward Howe's "Battle Hymn of the Republic" (1861): "**Mine** eyes have seen the glory of the coming of the Lord," as well as the enduring use of phrases like "know thine enemy," as in the article title, "Column One: Know **Thine** Enemy" (Caroline B. Glick, *The Jerusalem Post*. 16 Mar 2017). This last example is a translation from Sun Tzu's *The Art of War* and is also translated as "know thy enemy."
16. Charles Carpenter Fries. *American English Grammar: The Grammatical Structure of Present-Day English with Especial Reference to Social Differences or Class*

Dialects. English Monograph No. 10, National Council of Teachers of English. New York: D. Appleton-Century Co., 1940. 80.

17. Wolfram and Schilling-Estes, op. cit. 382.
18. Ibid.
19. Carmen Fought. *Chicano English in Context.* New York: Palgrave MacMillan, 2003. 95.
20. Fries, op. cit. 82.
21. Joe Kita. "Living Large." *Mens Health* 14.10 (Dec 1999): 134.
22. Estes Thompson. "Ashby Squadron Mates Say He Was Good Pilot." The Associated Press State & Local Wire. 20 Feb 1999.
23. 2 Timothy 3:2. *King James Bible.* 1611.
24. Marian Liebmann, ed. *Arts Approaches to Conflict.* New York: Jessica Kingsley. 11.
25. President Donald Trump. "U.S. & Mexico Cancel Meeting Over Border Wall Feud." *The First Hundred Days.* Fox. 26 Jan 2017.
26. Megan Reynolds. "Audio: Montana GOP Candidate Greg Gianforte 'Body-Slams' Reporter on Eve of Special Election." *Jezebel.* 24 May 2017. <https://theslot.jezebel.com>.
27. Chester Hicks. *Decisions and Orders of the National Labor Relations Board.* Vol. 306. Washington, DC: United States. National Labor Relations Board, 1992. 366.
28. Wolfram and Schilling-Estes, op. cit. 382.
29. Stephen King. "The Gingerbread Girl." *Just After Sunset: Stories.* New York: Scribner, 2008. 62.
30. Oge_user. "Re: Money sent but no product." Online post. *Commodore 64 Forum.* 10 Jan 2017. <www.lemon64.com/>.
31. Wolfram and Schilling-Estes, op. cit. 383.
32. J. L. Dillard. *Black English: Its History and Usage in the United States.* New York: Vintage Books, 1972. 57.
33. Ibid. 57–58.
34. Wolfram and Schilling-Estes, op. cit. 382.
35. Op. cit. 44.
36. Wolfram and Schilling-Estes, op. cit. 383.
37. John R. Rickford. *African American Vernacular English: Features, Evolution, Educational Implications.* Malden, MA: Blackwell, 1999. 7; Salikoko S. Mufwene. "The Structure of the Noun Phrase in African American Vernacular English." *African American English: Structure, History and Use.* Eds. Salikoko S. Mufwene, et al. New York: Routledge, 1998. 73.
38. Rickford, op. cit. 7.
39. Julie Rovner, et al. "Country Profile: United States of America." *The Lancet* 348.9033 (12 Oct 1996): 1001.
40. Seth Meyers. "For Our 30th Anniversary, *Fresh Air* Tapes Live with Seth Meyers of *Late Night.*" *Fresh Air.* 14 June 2017.
41. Jess Bravin. *PBS NewsHour* 8 Mar 2013.
42. Traditional grammar would argue that in *several of us* or *part of me* or *two of them*, we have to use the objective case form of the PRON (*us; me; them*) because *of* is a preposition and *of us*, *of me*, and *of them* are PPs modifying *several*, *part*, and *two*, respectively. My only recourse is to fall back on my explanation of determiners and the argument that these NPs and sentences are about, respectively, *us*, *me*, and *them*, not *several*, *part*, and *two*. At the same time, we can drop OF + PRON from each sentence (turning *several, part*, and *two* into PRONs) and still have a grammatically well-formed sentence. However, we could also paraphrase each PRONP with the appropriate subject case personal PRONs (*several of us→we; part of me→I; two of them→they*), which seems to indicate

that the heads of the phrases are *us*, *me*, and *them*, not *several, part,* and *two*, respectively. Which parse works better for you?

43. Patricia Sawin. "'Every Kid Is Where They're Supposed to Be, and It's a Miracle': Family Formation Stories among Adoptive Families." *Journal of American Folklore* 130.518 (Fall 2017): 395.
44. Cathleen McGuigan. "FDR in NYC." *Newsweek* 154.25 (21 Dec 2009): 75.
45. The strongest argument against using singular *they* has been the claim that *he, she,* and *it* are singular and *they* is properly plural and so should not be used with a singular antecedent. This argument ignores the fact that *you* serves as the singular and plural second-person nominative and objective case pronouns. If *you* can do quadruple duty, why can't *they* do double duty?
46. Dennis Baron offers a comprehensive list of proposed epicene pronouns from 1850 to 1992 in "The Words that Failed: A Chronology of Early Nonbinary Pronouns." N.d. <www.english.illinois.edu/-people-/faculty/debaron/essays/epicene.htm>. The online article is based on his "The Epicene Pronoun: The Word That Failed." *American Speech* 56 (1981): 83–97, and material from his book, *Grammar and Gender* (New Haven, CT: Yale University Press, 1986).
47. Tom O'Neill. "In the Footsteps of Gandhi." *National Geographic* 228.1 (Jul 2015): 90+.
48. Timothy Bryers. "Perfect Timing." *chicagotribune.com*. 30 Apr. 1989.
49. Samuel Rogers. *Jacqueline: A Tale*. London: J. Murray, 1814. I.67–70. p. 101.
50. Timothy Stanley. "Are Politicians Too Rich to Understand Us?" *CNN.com* 12 Jun 2012.
51. Mal Vincent. "Mark Twain Is Coming to Newport News, in the Form of Actor Hal Holbrook." *The Virginian-Pilot* (Norfolk, VA). 13 Mar 2017. <pilotonline.com>.
52. "Press Briefing by Ari Fleischer." *White House Press Releases*. 5 Feb 2001.
53. Lawrence Ferlinghetti. In Tristram Fane Saunders. "A Hundred Years Old—and Still Not Beat." *The Daily Telegraph* (London). 23 Mar 2019
54. Isaac Fitzgerald. *The Today Show*. NBC. 12 Jan 2017.
55. Eric Holder. *Fox on the Record with Greta Van Susteren*. 14 July 2014.
56. Shawn DuBravac. *Digital Destiny: How the New Age of Data Will Transform the Way We Work, Live, and Communicate*. Washington, DC: Regnery Publishing, 2015. 280.
57. Mark Lester. *Grammar and Usage in the Classroom*. 2nd ed. New York: Longman, 2000. 39.
58. jodietrew. "Any Ideas on Finding Out About a Deceased Person's Life?" Online posting. *able2know*. 31 Jan 2006. 15 Sep 2018 <http://able2know.org/topic/68317-1>.

Chapter 6

Verbs (V)

Verbs are a category of content words that, in traditional grammar, are defined as words that name actions. There are also several subcategories of verb forms, the largest two being finite and non-finite verbs. In this chapter, we will deal primarily with finite verbs: verbs that can function as the head of a verb phrase (VP) that, in turn, functions as the predicate of a sentence or dependent clause (VP:PRED). We will discuss non-finite verbs at length in Chapter 12. Finite verbs have a number of features, including tense (present, past), modality (e.g. indicative, modal, imperative, subjunctive), aspect (progressive, perfect, imperfect), and voice (active, passive). Verbs also take different kinds of complements: words or phrases that *complete* the meaning of the verb (e.g. direct object, indirect object, subject complement). We will examine verb complements in Chapter 7.

6.1 Verb Forms

In discussing finite verbs, we must talk about further sub-categories: lexical verbs, auxiliary verbs (AUX; also called "helping verbs"), and semi-auxiliaries (semi-modal and imperfect aspectual verbs).

Lexical verbs are any verb that can function alone (or with auxiliary and/or semi-auxiliary verbs) as the main verb (MV) in a clause. Lexical verbs are also inflected: they change form

- To mark tense (present, past; we will discuss tense below).
- In the present tense forms, to mark the person referred to (think back to the discussion of personal pronouns in 5.2). All verbs in English (except *be*) have one form for all persons and numbers except third-person singular, where all add -*s*.
- To mark the present participle by adding -*ing* (this is true for all verbs in English).
- To mark the past participle.

Kick, sing, run, drive, and *be* are examples of familiar lexical verbs: all name "actions" (though *be* may not seem very "active"), and all add suffixes or change spelling for tense, person, and participle forms. We will also talk about one other form: the infinitive, which is the base or "dictionary" form of the verb, commonly preceded by the particle *to* (see also 12.2):

Tensed or Finite Forms		Un-tensed or Non-finite Forms		
Present	Past	Present (-ing) Participle	Past (-ed) Participle	Infinitive
kick/kicks	kicked	kicking	kicked	to kick
sing/sings	sang	singing	sung	to sing
run/runs	ran	running	run	to run
drive/drives	drove	driving	driven	to drive
am/are/is	was/were	being	been	to be

Kick is a <u>regular</u> verb, and all new verbs that enter English will follow this paradigm, really taking only four distinct forms, with the past and past participle both ending in -*ed* (*kick/s, kicked, kicking*). We saw this back in 1.2 with the made-up verb *kadow*. *Sing, run,* and *drive* are all <u>irregular</u> verbs. In English, we still have over 400 irregular verbs that, rather than inflecting just by adding endings to indicate changes in form and function, change their spelling.[1] The only lexical verb in English that has <u>more</u> than six forms is the highly irregular *be*. *Be* has eight distinct forms (including three in the present and two in the past).[2]

Auxiliary verbs (Aux) are a limited subset of verbs in English that serve to mark three kinds of meaning: modality, aspect, and voice (we will discuss each of these features of verb meaning in detail below). In terms of form and function, true Aux verbs can:

1. Occur in front of the subject in interrogatives.
2. Serve as what the negative -*n't* attaches to.
3. Occur in tag questions.

Modal auxiliary verbs: "Modality" is the speaker's attitude toward the action named in the verb, in terms of whether the speaker regards the action as real or hypothetical. In English, hypothetical action, or "irrealis modality," is marked by the addition of modal Aux verbs (the unmarked modality in English—"realis modality"—is the default modality; in traditional grammar, a verb without a modal Aux is said to be in the "indicative mood"). Modal Aux verbs mark the action named by the main verb as involving possibility, necessity, permission, obligation, ability, volition, or desire: in short, as hypothetical, not actual. All of the modal auxiliaries in current American English are as follows:

Present/Past

can/could
shall/should

will/would
may/might
must/—

All only have present and past tense forms, except for *must*, which is always in the present tense.[3] Note that the modal AUX verbs exhibit the three features of auxiliaries:

1. Occur in front of the subject in interrogatives: *Franz <u>could</u> kick the ball. <u>Could</u> Franz kick the ball?*
2. Serve as what the negative *-n't* attaches to: *Franz <u>couldn't</u> kick the ball.*
3. Occur in tag questions: *Franz couldn't kick the ball, <u>could he?</u>*

Aspectual auxiliary verbs mark the location or duration of an action in time. Standard American English has just two aspectual auxiliaries: *have*, which marks the <u>perfective aspect</u>, indicating that the action is completed (e.g. *Franz <u>has kicked</u> the ball*), and *be*, which marks the <u>progressive aspect</u>, indicating that the action is ongoing (e.g. *Franz <u>is kicking</u> the ball*). The aspectual AUX verbs also exhibit the three features of auxiliaries:

1. Occur in front of the subject in interrogatives:

    Franz <u>has</u> kicked the ball. <u>Has</u> Franz kicked the ball?
    Franz <u>is</u> kicking the ball. <u>Is</u> Franz kicking the ball?

2. Serve as what the negative *-n't* attaches to:

    Franz <u>hasn't</u> kicked the ball.
    Franz <u>isn't</u> kicking the ball.

3. Occur in tag questions:

    Franz hasn't kicked the ball, <u>has he?</u>
    Franz isn't kicking the ball, <u>is he?</u>

   Passive voice AUX ***be*** marks that the verb is in the passive, as versus the active voice:

    Active voice: *Franz kicked the ball.*
    Passive voice: *The ball <u>was</u> kicked by Franz.*

The passive AUX *be* also exhibits the three features of auxiliaries:

1. Occurs in front of the subject in interrogatives:

    The ball <u>was</u> kicked by Franz. <u>Was</u> the ball kicked by Franz?

2. Serves as what the negative *-n't* attaches to:

    The ball <u>wasn't</u> kicked by Franz.

3. Occurs in tag questions:

    The ball wasn't kicked by Franz, <u>was</u> it?

Auxiliary *do* can be used for emphasis (e.g. *I dó love a good soccer game*; 6.1.6) or, more commonly, as a filler or dummy Aux to fulfill the three defining functions of auxiliaries when there is no auxiliary already present:

1. Occurs in front of the subject in interrogatives:

    Franz kicked the ball. <u>Did</u> Franz kick the ball?

2. Serves as what the negative *-n't* attaches to:

    Franz kicked the ball. Franz <u>didn't</u> kick the ball.

3. Occurs in tag questions:

    Franz kicked the ball, <u>didn't he?</u>

Semi-auxiliary verbs add the same kinds of meaning to the verb as do auxiliary verbs but do not have the three features that define the form of Aux verbs. As one example, the semi-modal verb *want to*, often pronounced as *wanna*, conveys modality (desire); it conveys that the action is hypothetical (i.e. just because I *want to* do something doesn't mean it will happen); and *want to* can be paraphrased by the modal Aux *may* (i.e. *I want to do it* implies *I may do it*). But we cannot put *want to* or *want* in front of the subject in an interrogative, attach negative *-n't* to it, or use it in a tag question. I will defer more detailed discussion of Standard and non-Standard semi-Aux verbs to the sections on modality and aspect below, as well as to separate discussions of the passive voice Aux *be*; the subjunctive mood partial-Aux *be*; Aux *do*; the generic past semi-Aux *used to*; and non-Standard absent *be*. However, I will note here that my treatment of semi-Aux verbs is not the one usually found in the literature on English syntax or grammar. It emerged from my own observations of the ways in which we use English finite and non-finite verb constructions to express or assert the degree to which an action is real, partially realized, or not real, and from my frustrations with the conventional ways of discussing English verbs. There is more than one spectrum or cline that connects the well-established modal and aspectual Aux verbs both with what I am calling semi-modal verbs and imperfect aspectual verbs, and with participle and infinitive phrases. As I address each of these word and phrases classes, I will return repeatedly to the relationships among them.

The complete verb in a sentence or dependent clause is a finite verb functioning as the head of a VP:PRED. The finite complete verb may comprise a finite-form MV alone, but often the complete verb comprises the MV preceded by one or more auxiliaries and/or semi-auxiliaries. When we talk about "the verb in a sentence or dependent clause," we will usually mean the complete verb, not just the MV.

As sketched above, tense, modality, aspect, and voice are the four significant features of complete verbs. We study them in the order listed because, typically, the elements in the complete verb that mark these features appear in that order.

6.1.1 Tense

We commonly think of "tense" as having something to do with time. It does, although not in a simple way. For example, we generally don't use the "present tense" form of a verb to refer to present action: the sentence *I run to the store*, doesn't usually mean "I am currently running to the store." We are more likely to use a present-tense verb to talk about

> **Habitual action**: *Every day, I run to the store.*
> **Past action**: *So yesterday, I run to the store, then to class, and then I come home; and only then I realize that I've lost my wallet.*
> **Future action**: *Tomorrow, I run to the store at eight, then class at nine, and then I come home. . . .*

We often use the past tense to refer to past action. However, its use is more complex than that. The sentence *I ran to the store*, usually means that the event occurred in the past, but it may refer to

> **A one-time event**: *I ran to the store this morning.*
> **Past habitual action**: *In the month after the baby was born, I ran to the store every day.*

Rather than thinking of tense as related to time, we will mostly talk about tense in terms of the forms of verbs. Each verb has two, and only two, inflected tensed forms: the present and the past. The present and past forms of verbs are traditionally referred to as finite or tensed verbs. Finite or tensed verbs can serve, by themselves, as the MV in a well-formed sentence:

Present tense V:

She walks to the store.
She goes to the store.

Past tense V:

She walked to the store.
She went to the store.

When we begin talking about complete verbs that comprise more than one word, we will repeatedly note that the tense of the complete verb is carried by the <u>first verb</u> in the string, whether it is an Aux, a semi-Aux, or the MV. In each of the following sentences, the complete verb is in the present tense:

> She ***goes*** *to the store.*
> She ***has*** ***gone*** *to the store.*
> She ***will*** ***have to go*** *to the store later.*

Your gut sense about these sentences will tell you that the first sentence might be about action occurring at the present time; the second about action that has already occurred in the past; and the third about future action. However, each of the verbs is in the present tense because the <u>form</u> of the first word in the complete verb is the present tense form.

In addition, all verbs in English have three other non-finite or non-tensed forms: the *-ing* or present participle form; the past participle form; and the infinitive form (which commonly comprises the particle *to* plus the base form of the verb). These non-finite forms cannot stand by themselves as the MV of a well-formed SE sentence:

> Present participle: **She <u>going</u> to the store. *She <u>walking</u> to the store.*
> Past participle: **She <u>gone</u> to the store.*
> Infinitive: **She <u>to go</u> to the store. *She <u>to walk</u> to the store.*

The present participle form of a verb <u>always</u> ends in *-ing* (a rare "always" in English grammar). Past participles of regular verbs—the vast majority of verbs in English, and the paradigm of all new verbs that enter English—end in *-ed* (as does the past form of a regular verb), but as we already noted, there are several hundred irregular verbs, many of them among the most common verbs in the language. A simple way to find the past participle of any verb is to identify the verb form that usually follows the *have* Aux: *have <u>walked</u>, have <u>driven</u>, have <u>run</u>, have <u>swum</u>, have <u>made</u>.* Along with their role in finite verbs, the present and past participles and the infinitive all form the basis for a versatile set of non-finite verb phrases that are an important feature of written and spoken communication (see Chapter 12).

Non-Standard tense forms: regularizing irregular forms: Note that in the present tense paradigm for all verbs in English except *be*, the only form that is not the base form is the third-person singular, which always ends in *-s*. Many varieties of English, including AAVE, frequently regularize the deviant form by dropping the *-s* (or *-es*). In those varieties, the non-Standard sentences *She go to the store* and *She walk to the store* are perfectly acceptable.[4]

In the past tense, English verbs, whether regular or irregular, all (except *be*) take a single form, regardless of person or number. For example, the past tense form of the regular verb *talk* is *talked*; the past tense form of the irregular verb *sing* is *sang*. Again, the only exception is *be*, which has two forms in the past tense:

Singular	first person	I	was
	second person	you	were
	third person	he/she/it	was
Plural	first person	we	were
	second person	you	were
	third person	they	were

However, Wolfram and Schilling-Estes note that in vernacular varieties we find some degree of "leveling to *is* for present tense forms of *be*" and "leveling to *was* for past tense forms of *be*," in sentences like:

> *The dogs is in the house. We is doing it right now.*
> *The cars was on the street. Most of the kids was younger up there.*[5]

These moves to regularize irregularities in the verb are part and parcel with similar leveling in the third-person singular in other verbs and regularization of irregular past and past participle forms, as in Fought's examples from Chicano English:

> *Otherwise, she <u>don't</u> know Brenda.* (third SG *does* leveled to *do*)
> *Somebody else just <u>come</u> and <u>take</u> your life.* (third SG *comes* and *takes* leveled to *come* and *take*)
> *It <u>spinned</u>.* (irregular past *spun* regularized)
> *I had, like three weeks that I had <u>came</u> out the hospital before I got shot.* (irregular past participle *come* leveled to past *came*).[6]

While none of these forms are currently part of any SE variety, all are part of the general trend in English toward the regularization of irregular verb forms.

In some non-Standard varieties of American English, we find this process of regularization taken even further, with the deletion of the past-tense marker *-ed*. "Such cases are particularly likely to be found in varieties influenced by other languages in the recent past," and they are notably "prominent in varieties such as Vietnamese English and Native American Indian English in the Southwest." In such varieties of English, we may find sentences like *Yesterday he mess up* and *He play a new song last night*. "Grammatically based tense unmarking tends to be more frequent on regular verbs than irregular ones, so that a structure such as *Yesterday he play a new song* is more likely than *Yesterday he is in a new store*, although both may occur."[7] Arguably, if the sentence is prefaced by the adverb *yesterday*, then the action is already framed as taking place in the past, and the past tense marker on the verb is redundant and so unnecessary. AAVE relies heavily on sentence or physical context "to signal conditions of time,"[8] as in the following example from Dillard: *The boy carried the dog dish to the house and put some dog food in it and put some water in and bring it out and called his dog. . . .*[9] Notice that, aside from *bring*, all of the other verbs are in the past tense, so marking the tense on *bring* is unnecessary and would simply be redundant since "the surrounding clauses or sentences give the needed time cues."[10] SE often uses adverbials "to signal conditions of time" as well but needs them less as tense is more regularly marked in the inflection of the verb.

Unmarking tense for habitual action: In Native American Indian English in the Southwest, "unmarking is favored in habitual contexts (e.g. *In those days, we play a different kind of game*) as opposed to simple past time (e.g. *Yesterday, we play at a friend's house*)."[11] This way of marking habitual action by deleting the past tense marker from the verb is akin to the use of *BE* + VERB-*ING* to mark habitual action in certain varieties of American English (see habitual *be* in the section on aspect below).

Another non-Standard verb tense form is the **historical present**:

> In the dramatic recounting of past time events, speakers may use present tense verb forms rather than past tense forms, as in *I go down there and this guy comes up to me. . . .* In some cases an -*s* suffix may be added to non-third-person forms, particularly with the first-person form of *say* (e.g. *so I says to him . . .*). This structure is more prominent in European American vernaculars than in AAVE.[12]

AAVE also has a **use of *had* to mark the complicating action in a narrative**, where SE would use the simple past:

> *This is a story that happened to me Monday, not too long ago. I was on my way to school and I <u>had</u> slipped and fell and I ran back in to change my clothes.*
> *I was riding home from school, and on my way home I was, when I was up in the driveway a car <u>had</u> backed up and it ran over my bike and I tried to run. . . . Yeah, that's when I woke up.*[13]

McWhorter identifies this usage as a **narrative tense**,[14] and Rickford and Rafal[15] cite its use among African Americans in California and Texas, as well as Puerto Rican Americans in New York City.

6.1.2 Modality, Aspect, and Voice

For regular verbs in English, the past and past participle forms are identical, both ending in -*ed*. To distinguish them, we have to look at the system of how we identify and label the constituents of complete verbs. This requires us to explore three features of complete verbs—modality, aspect, and voice—and the Aux and semi-Aux verbs that mark those features.

We will continue to discuss tense, modality, aspect and voice in terms of their meanings, but modality, aspect, and voice can be understood simply as labels for forms of verbs. For example, if there is no modal Aux or semi-Aux in a complete verb, then the mood of the verb is indicative; the presence of the modal Aux or semi-Aux marks the verb as modal—as indicating the speaker's belief or assertion that the action named is hypothetical. If there is a perfect aspect Aux (a form of *have* functioning as an Aux) in a complete verb, then that Aux *have* marks that the verb has the perfect aspect; the progressive aspect Aux *be* marks that the verb has progressive aspect; and the imperfect semi-auxiliaries mark that the verb has imperfect aspect. If there is no aspectual verb in a complete verb, then the verb has "zero aspect." If there is a passive voice Aux *be* in a complete verb, then the presence of the passive Aux marks that the verb is in the passive voice. If there is no passive voice Aux, then the verb is active. Thus, the default English verb is in the indicative mood, has zero aspect, and is in active voice.

That's a short explanation. Now, for the details.

6.1.2.1 Modality

Simply put, modality is the feature of the verb that indicates whether the action named by the verb is actual or hypothetical. Note the difference between the actions named in the following sentences: *I go to the store. I may go to the store.* In the first sentence, the MV, *go*, is in the present tense and, without other context, indicates an actual event. This verb is thus said to be in the indicative mood: it <u>indicates</u> an actual event and asserts the existence of that action as a fact. By contrast, in the second sentence, the addition of the modal Aux *may* changes the meaning of the verb: now we are not talking about an <u>actual</u> action but about a possible or <u>hypothetical</u> action. The sentence *I may go to the store* implies that I have not yet gone to the store, and I may or may not.

We can sometimes use the present indicative form of the verb to refer to future or otherwise hypothetical action: *Tomorrow, I <u>run</u> to the store, then to class, and then I <u>come</u> home. . . .* We could express the same meaning by saying:

> *Tomorrow, I <u>will run</u> to the store, then to class, and then I <u>will come</u> home. . . .*
> *Tomorrow, I <u>may run</u> to the store, then to class, and then I <u>can come</u> home. . . .*

However, when we use the present indicative to name future or hypothetical action, we are presenting that hypothetical action as though it were already a fact. That is, the speaker is expressing the attitude that they have no doubt that the named event will happen. The speaker's choice of an indicative or a modal verb presents the speaker's belief or attitude about the action.

Three Important Notes Before We Go On: **(1) In a complete verb, the first word in the verb carries the tense of the whole verb**, whether the first word is an Aux, a semi-Aux, or the MV. The past tense form of *I go to the store* is *I went to the store*. *Went* is the past tense form of *go*. The past tense form of *I may go to the store* is *I might go to the store*. *Might* is the past tense form of *may*; *might go* is the past tense form of *may go*.

(2) The verb following the modal Aux takes the base form. After the modal Aux *may*, the MV *go* is in the base or dictionary form. That is, MODAL AUX + BASE FORM OF V = modal verb. In the complete verb each Aux or semi-Aux dictates the form of the verb that immediately follows it.

(3) There is no inflected "future tense" in English. Included among the modal auxiliaries are *will* and *shall*, auxiliaries that we typically think of as marking the "future tense." But by the word tense, while we mean something about time, we also mean different inflected forms of a single base form of a verb: forms altered by spelling or the addition of a suffix. A tensed verb can stand alone as the MV in a sentence or dependent clause. For no verb in English do we simply change spelling to mark a "future tense." Instead, future action is commonly indicated in the same way as other hypothetical actions: by the use of a particular modal Aux.[16] Future action, like any hypothetical action, is simply action that hasn't happened yet and therefore may not happen at all. *Will* and *shall* are merely stronger assertions than are *may* and *can* about the likelihood of the occurrence of an event.

Modal Auxiliaries and Semi-modal Verbs: As we have already noted, there are nine modal auxiliaries in English: *will/would, can/could, shall/ should, may/might, must*. Each is only an Aux, appearing alone only in elliptical constructions with an implied MV: a speaker might respond to the question, *Will you do it?* by saying, *I will*, an elliptical sentence that implies, *I will do it*.

Like modal auxiliaries, semi-modal verbs all mark modality in the complete verb by expressing hypothetical action. Each semi-modal can be paraphrased by a modal Aux. But unlike modal auxiliaries, semi-modals comprise more than one word. All of the semi-modals (except *be about to*) are composed of a verb (V) plus the particle *to* (V + TO) or V + TO preceded by a present or past tense form of the verb *be* (BE + V + TO). Here is a list of some common semi-modals and their modal Aux paraphrases:

Semi-Modal	Modal Aux Paraphrase	Semi-Modal	Modal Aux Paraphrase
agree to	may	hope to	may
aim to	will	intend to	may
aspire to	will	long to	may

(Continued)

(Continued)

Semi-Modal	Modal Aux Paraphrase	Semi-Modal	Modal Aux Paraphrase
be about to	shall	mean to	may
be going to (gonna)	will	need to	must
be supposed to (supposeta)	should	offer to	may
be to	(see below)	ought to (oughta)	should
choose to	may	plan to	may
commit to	will	promise to	will
consent to	may	propose to	may
conspire to	may	resolve to	will
decide to	will	swear to	will
desire to	may	threaten to	will
expect to	may	want to (wanna)	may
have got to (gotta)	must	wish to	may
have to (hafta)	must	yearn to	may

The most common of the semi-modals—*gonna, gotta, supposeta, hafta, oughta,* and *wanna*—are regularly pronounced as if they were single words and are the ones most commonly recognized by linguists and grammarians; they will sometimes also mention *be able to*, which can be paraphrased by the modal Aux *can*. However, *be able to* is really just an elaboration of the semi-modal *be to*, as in *I am to report for duty on Monday*. We can put many adjectives between *be* and the particle *to*, as in *She is able to help you* (compare *She can help you*) or *I am likely to be there* (compare *I should/may be there*).[17]

The semi-modals can occupy two kinds of slots in the complete verb. First, they can fill the same slot as a modal Aux, appearing at the beginning of the complete verb and marking not only modality but tense: *I ought to go to the store* is the past modal of "go"; *I am going to go to the store* is the present modal of "go."

Second, and very much unlike modal auxiliaries, semi-modals allow us to have more than one modal-marking verb in a single complete verb:

> *To transform the world you might have to stand alone.*[18]
> *You have to want to make a difference.*[19]

In the verb *might have to stand*, *might* and *have to* both express modal meaning. We would label this verb as the "past modal modal of *stand*." In the verb *have to want to learn*, *have to* and *want to* are each semi-modals, and we would label *have to want to learn* as the 'present modal modal of "learn." This may sound a little silly: how can an action be "modal modal"? It just shows that we have nuanced ways of naming actions so as to hedge about our intentions as a politeness gesture, not insisting too directly and thereby leaving open the speaker's and listener's options for action and interpretation.

In traditional grammar, what we are calling semi-modals are analyzed as V + Infinitive. In the sentence *By then, I had to have been heading to the store*, traditional grammar would treat *had* as the main verb and *to have been heading to the store* as an infinitive phrase functioning as a nominal functioning as the direct object of "had" (InfP:Nominal:DO). But many contemporary grammarians have already recognized the most common semi-modals as a legitimate extension of the category of words that mark modality in the verb and therefore would analyze the complete verb as *had to have been heading*; part of that interpretation hinges on the pronunciation of *have to* and *had to* as *hafta* and *hadda*. The pronunciation shows that we conceptualize these as essentially being single words.

Also, by analyzing *to have been heading to the store* as an InfP:Nominal:DO of the verb "had," traditional grammar understands the InfP as answering the question "What did I have?" This assumes that *to have been heading to the store* is a thing or state that can be <u>had</u> in the same way that one might <u>have</u> an object, such as a book. It seems to me to make more sense—and to be truer to the meaning of the sentence—to treat these V + TO + V combinations as SEMI-MODAL + V.

When a V + TO combination immediately precedes a verb and expresses hypothetical action in the same way as a modal Aux, we will treat the V + TO combination as a semi-modal. In semi-modals, the word *to* is a particle: a small word that functions as a connector between the semi-modal and the following verb.

Two partial modal auxiliaries: In some English varieties, *ought to* (*oughta*) and *need* function as incomplete or partial modal auxiliaries since they convey modal meaning and exhibit two of the three defining features of auxiliaries: they (1) occur in front of the subject in interrogatives; (2) serve as what the negative *-n't* attaches to; but (3) they do not usually occur in tag questions:

ought to (oughta)

1. *You <u>ought to</u> let them in. <u>Ought</u> you to let them in?*
2. *You <u>oughtn't</u> to let them in.*[20]
3. *?You ought to let them in, <u>oughtn't you?</u> You ought to let them in, shouldn't you?*[21]

need

1. **You need ask. You need to ask. <u>Need</u> you ask? *<u>Need</u> you to ask?*
2. *You <u>needn't</u> ask.*
3. **You need to ask, <u>needn't you?</u> You need to ask, don't you?*

Denison[22] notes what might be called the brief half-life of other partial modals— *durs(t)n't* (from *durst*, a past-tense form of *dare*) and *usedn't*—which started as non-Standard usages in British English but never crossed over even into

Standard informal usage. He also makes note of *oughtn't, needn't*, and *mayn't*, all of which now "seem old-fashioned, and therefore formal." Denison also mentions *daren't*, which I will treat below as a possible partial imperfect Aux.

Non-Standard semi-modal verbs: future *be*: In AAVE, *be* has a variety of non-Standard uses, including as a semi-modal verb to mark future action, and even as a stand-alone verb with the same meaning as SE *will be*. The particular meaning of *be* is indicated by sentence context, particularly by the use of adverbials to indicate the time frame of the action. In *She be goin' there later*, *be* implies future action, as indicated by the adverb *later*. Contrast this *be* with that in the sentence *She be goin' there every day*. Here, *be* marks not a future, hypothetical action but a habitual action, one that occurs routinely, as indicated by the adverbial phrase *every day*.[23] We will discuss the aspectual semi-Aux habitual *be* below. As we shall see, *be* has developed a complex variety of uses and meanings in AAVE, uses and meanings that are often unavailable in SE. Invariant *be* is also consistent with the tendency of all varieties of English to regularize irregular forms. Thus, instead of having the SE hodge-podge conjugation of *be*, AAVE overwhelmingly uses *be* for all persons and numbers. At the same time, AAVE is influenced by the forms of SE, and AAVE forms tend to converge with SE forms. Smitherman notes that some AAVE speakers will tend to say, *She'll be goin' there later*, or *She-ah be goin' there later*, although not the full SE pronunciation, *She will be going there later*.[24]

Be fixin' to: Southern varieties of American English employ a non-Standard semi-modal, *be fixin' to*, with the specific meaning that an event is or was imminent but has not yet or did not actually happen. A more SE version of *fixin' to* would be "about to" or "planning to"[25] or "be going to" (and its more colloquial pronunciation, "gonna"). *I'm fixin' to go to the store* means I am about to do so. *It's fixin' to rain* means the rain will start soon. The construction can also be used in the past tense, as in *I was fixin' to come but I got held up*, meaning that the speaker had intended to come, and in fact was about to, when other events intervened.[26] Like the semi-modal *be going to*, *be fixin' to* includes a *be* Aux followed by the -*ing* form of the verb and might be mistaken for a verb with the progressive aspect. In AAVE, this Aux may be pronounced as *finna, fidna* or *fitna*,[27] with *is* and *are* routinely deleted (though not *am, 'm, was*, or *were*, consistent with the AAVE rules for the deletion of copular *be*[28] [see 6.1.8]).

Imma: Another AAVE variation on the SE semi-modal *be going to* is *Imma* (also spelled *I'mma* and *I'ma*), which rolls the first-person singular pronoun in with the verb, contracting *I am going to* into a single word. We find strong examples of *Imma* in the lyrics of a number of recent popular songs:

> *Imma be on the next level;*
> *Imma be rockin' that bass treble;*
> *Imma be chillin' with my mutha mutha crew;*
> *Imma be makin' all them deals you wanna do.*[29]

Don't stop, make it pop,
DJ blow my speakers up,
*Tonight **imma** fight till we see the sunlight.*[30]

Note that *Imma* only has a first-person singular form.

(su)poseta: In some varieties of American English, the SE semi-modal *be supposed to* is reduced in its pronunciation to *suposeta*, or even *poseta* (much like *be fixin' to* is reduced to *fixin' ta* or *finna*), and may be used with a following MV in the past form, as in *You suposeta went there*. In this sentence, Wolfram and Schilling-Estes interpret *suposeta* as a reduction of *supposed to have*, blending the semi-modal and the perfect aspect Aux.[31]

Need + **Past Participle**: Across the North Midlands dialect region of American English (ranging westward across the central regions of New Jersey and Pennsylvania, out to Nebraska and Kansas), it is common for speakers to reduce the semi-modal + passive construction *need to be* + past participle to *need* + past participle. Thus, it is common to hear *The car needs washed* where SE speakers would say, *The car needs <u>to be</u> washed*. Across the region, this usage may even appear in published writing. A headline in *The Pitt News*, the student newspaper of the University of Pittsburgh, read "Without popular sports, fans <u>need entertained</u> during the summer."[32] Similarly, the *Macomb* (Illinois) *Journal* printed the headline, "Zoning Changes <u>Need Stopped</u>."[33]

Double modals: According to Wolfram and Schilling-Estes, double modals— the use of two modal auxiliaries together—are a typical feature of Southern vernacular varieties and appear in a range of possible combinations, the most common of which is *might could*. Southern vernacular varieties pair modal auxiliaries with semi-modal verbs in regionally distinctive combinations, such as *might oughta*, and will also distinctively combine modal auxiliaries with the generic past semi-Aux *useta* (see below), as in *useta could*. In Northern varieties, double modals with two modal auxiliaries do not occur, although some Northern vernacular varieties will pair *useta* with a modal, as in *He useta couldn't do it*. Some double-modal constructions with at least one semi-modal verb are ubiquitous in American English varieties (e.g. *You <u>might want to</u> reconsider your investment strategy*).[34] "Double modals tend to lessen the force of the attitude or obligation conveyed by single modals, so that *She might could do it* is less forceful than *She might do it* or *She could do it*. In some Southern regions, double modals are quite widespread and not particularly stigmatized,"[35] and, as a result, double modals comprising two modal auxiliaries mark Southern varieties as particularly distinct from other regional varieties.

6.1.2.2 Aspect

Traditionally, aspect is distinct from tense and modality: tense tells when in time an action occurs (past, present); modality tells whether the action is actual or hypothetical; and aspect is understood as the feature of the verb that tells whether the action named by the verb is perfect (completed), progressive (ongoing), or imperfect (initiated, intermittent, flawed, or somehow incomplete). Since English has no inflected future tense, we have to add an Aux or semi-Aux marking future action in the same way that we mark hypothetical action. The way we place an action in time (tense) and how we mark whether an action is real or hypothetical (modality) overlap. When we discuss the imperfect aspect below, we will find that, in form and meaning, it has some kinship with the kinds of modal meaning expressed by semi-modal verbs: hypothetical action (marked by a modal Aux or semi-modal verb) is related to incomplete action (marked by an imperfect aspectual verb).

We will start with the simpler matters of the more common perfect and progressive aspects. In the complete verb, the perfect aspect is marked by the presence of the *have* Aux followed by the past-participle form of the following verb (not to be confused with the semi-modal verb *have to* or the lexical verb *have*). The progressive aspect is marked by the presence of a *be* Aux followed by the present participle form of the following verb. That is:

HAVE + Past Participle of V = V with perfect aspect

   (e.g. *have baked; have gone*)

BE + Present Participle of V = V with progressive aspect

   (e.g. *am baking; am going*)

A verb can have both the perfect and the progressive aspects. The *have* Aux comes first, followed by the *be* Aux (which has to take the past participle form *been*), followed by the present participle of a verb:

HAVE + *been* + Present Participle of V = V with perfect progressive aspect

   (e.g. *have been baking; have been going*)

A verb can also be modal and have the perfect aspect, the progressive aspect, or both aspects:

MODAL + *HAVE* + Past Participle of V = modal V with perfect aspect

   (e.g. *will have baked; will have gone*)

MODAL + *be* + Present Participle of V = modal V with progressive aspect

   (e.g. *will be baking; will be going*)

MODAL + *have* + *been* + Present Participle of V = modal V with perfect progressive aspect

   (e.g. *will have been baking; will have been going*)

Here is a paradigm for the verb *go* in the first-person singular (*I*), in the present and past tenses, with modality, and perfect and progressive aspect:

> *I go to the store.* (PRES tense; IND mood; Ø aspect)
> *I went to the store.* (PAST tense; IND mood; Ø aspect)
> *I have gone to the store.* (PRES tense; IND mood; PERF aspect)
> *I had gone to the store.* (PAST tense; IND mood; PERF aspect)
> *I am going to the store.* (PRES tense; IND mood; PROG aspect)
> *I was going to the store.* (PAST tense; IND mood; PROG aspect)
> *I have been going to the store.* (PRES tense; IND mood; PERF PROG aspect)
> *I had been going to the store.* (PAST tense; IND mood; PERF PROG aspect)
> *I may go to the store.* (PRES tense; modal; Ø aspect)
> *I might go to the store.* (PAST tense; modal; Ø aspect)
> *I may have gone to the store.* (PRES tense; modal; PERF aspect)
> *I might have gone to the store.* (PAST tense; modal; PERF aspect)
> *I may be going to the store.* (PRES tense; modal; PROG aspect)
> *I might be going to the store.* (PAST tense; modal; PROG aspect)
> *I may have been going . . .* (PRES tense; modal; PERF PROG aspect)
> *I might have been going . . .* (PAST tense; modal; PERF PROG aspect)

Imperfect aspectual verbs: Imperfect aspectual verbs are a large and complicated category of English verbs that is unrecognized by traditional grammar and rarely discussed, even by linguists. While the perfect AUX *have* marks the action as completed or "perfected" at some time, and the progressive AUX *be* marks the action as ongoing or "in progress" at some time, the imperfect aspectual verbs mark the action named by the MV as having a mushier sort of status. Imperfect aspectual verbs characterize action as being realized to some degree:[36]

> *He starts/begins to get free.*
> *He starts/begins getting free.*
> *He attempts to get free.*
> *He manages/contrives/dares to get free.*

In the first three sentences, the verbs express that the action was actually initiated (*started, begun, attempted*), but we do not know whether it is completed. In the fourth sentence, the verbs express that the action actually occurred but that it was somehow flawed, so it is not a true or adequate example of the action, as though something about the event of *getting free* isn't quite right.

These imperfect aspectual verbs exhibit another quality that marks the aspect auxiliaries. Conrad discusses how verbs like *begin, continue, cease, get* [as in *get going*], *start*, etc.

> are sometimes called aspectual verbs, because they do not refer to actions, processes, etc. which are independent of the actions, processes

etc. denoted by the complement [that is, the following verb]. For instance, *I began walking* does not refer to two actions, one of which might be talked about as "beginning," and the other as "walking." The whole of the predicate refers to just one action. The function of the finite verb is only to emphasize a particular aspect of this action.[37]

So, Conrad argues, in *I began walking*, the finite verb *began* relates to the participle *walking* in much the same way that *am* relates to *walking* in *I am walking*: *am walking* doesn't refer to two actions, an act of "being" and an act of "walking." Rather, *am walking* indicates that the action of walking is in progress, so AM + V-*ING* marks the progressive aspect; BEGAN + V-*ING* also marks some kind of aspectual character in the action named by the MV.

Imperfect aspectual verbs can also show what Conrad calls a "disposition" toward performing an action. *He began to sneeze* and *He began sneezing* do not mean he continuously sneezed but that there was a sporadic series of sneezes. Likewise, *She began studying Greek* and *She continued to study Greek* do not necessarily mark that it was an ongoing event, or a singular event, but an event that she had a disposition for, which she was disposed to do sporadically during this period.

We begin to see the mushiness of the category of imperfect aspectual verbs: they may mark

- Action that is initiated but incomplete—but not in progress at the moment.
- Action that actually occurred, but that was somehow flawed, and so not a true or adequate example of the action.
- Action that the actor has a disposition toward performing but is not performing constantly.
- A variety of other hedges or qualifications to action.

Imperfect aspectual verbs come in two forms:

- **Single-word verbs**, which take the form of the imperfect aspectual verb followed by the present participle form of a verb:

  Rogen's mom <u>starts driving</u> him to comedy clubs.[38]
  Rogen's mom <u>enjoys driving</u> him to comedy clubs.
  Rogen's mom <u>stops driving</u> him to comedy clubs.
  Rogen's mom <u>likes driving</u> him to comedy clubs.

- **Multi-word verbs**, which take the form of the imperfect aspectual verb followed by the particle *to* and the base form of the following verb:

  Rogen's mom <u>starts to drive</u> him to comedy clubs.
  Rogen's mom <u>manages to drive</u> him to comedy clubs.
  Rogen's mom <u>dares to drive</u> him to comedy clubs.
  Rogen's mom <u>likes to drive</u> him to comedy clubs.

Here is a larger (though by no means exhaustive) list of examples of each type of imperfect aspectual verb:

Single-Word Imperfect Aspectual Verbs

adore	discontinue	go	love
begin	dislike	hate	prefer
cease	enjoy	imagine	start
come	envision	keep	stop
continue	finish	like	undertake

Multi-Word Imperfect Aspectual Verbs

arrange to	contrive to	manage to	seek to
attempt to	dare to	prefer to	seem to
begin to	hate to	pretend to	start to
cease to	like to	scramble to	undertake to
continue to	love to		

There are many more, and you can easily identify them from your own experience of English and the definitions we are working with.

Notice that the form of these imperfect aspectual verbs is highly idiomatic. While the verbs *keep* and *continue* are basically synonyms, we can say *continue talking/to talk* but only *keep talking*. Then there are verbs like *arrange* and *pretend* that, as imperfect aspectual verbs, can only take *TO* + V: one can *arrange/pretend to talk*, but one cannot **arrange/pretend talking*. Also, the single- and multi-word versions of an imperfect aspectual verb sometimes have distinctly different idiomatic meanings: notice the difference in meaning between *get going*, meaning "leave," and *get to go*, which means "be permitted to go."

There is further mushiness in the category of imperfect aspectual verbs in that some carry the same sort of meaning as modal auxiliaries. The following verbs all have a meaning similar to the modal AUX *may*:

---

agree to	expect to	propose to	tend to
aim to	hope to	scramble to	threaten to
appear to	intend to	seem to	train to
choose to	offer to	strive to	try to
claim to	practice to	struggle to	undertake to
decide to	prepare to	swear to	venture to
desire to	promise to		

That is, if I *agree to go*, or *seem to go*, or *strive to go*, I may or may not actually go. This makes sense since incomplete action, or not entirely true or actual action, is, to some degree, also hypothetical action. When and whether these verbs mark modality or the imperfect aspect is a matter of interpretation, and that interpretation needs to be based on form, function, and meaning within the actual context of use.

There is one more dimension of mushiness in the category of imperfect aspectual verbs. Sometimes, it is not clear whether it is appropriate to interpret the sequence 'VERB + TO + VERB' or 'VERB + PRESENT PARTICIPLE' as part of a single complete verb, or whether it would be better to interpret it as a verb followed by a direct object, where the form of the direct object is an infinitive phrase or participle phrase, functioning as a nominal, functioning as the direct object (INFP:NOMINAL:DO or PARTP:NOMINAL:DO). Clearly, following Conrad's discussion, sentences like

> *Rogen's mom begins driving him to comedy clubs.*
> *Rogen's mom begins to drive him to comedy clubs.*
> *Rogen's mom keeps driving him to comedy clubs.*

all involve imperfect aspectual verbs, as the actions of the two verbs are inseparable. But when we move to sentences like

> *Rogen's mom loves driving him to comedy clubs.*
> *Rogen's mom loves to drive him to comedy clubs.*
> *Rogen's mom enjoys driving him to comedy clubs.*

it becomes less clear how *driving him to comedy clubs* and *to drive him to comedy clubs* differ from NP direct objects (NP:DO), as in sentences like

> *Rogen's mom loves the act of driving him to comedy clubs.*
> *Rogen's mom enjoys the act of driving him to comedy clubs.*

We will wrestle further with how to interpret V + TO + V and V + PRESENT PARTICIPLE sequences when we discuss non-finite verb phrases in Chapter 12.

A possible imperfect auxiliary? The verb *dare* permits two of the three functions that define an AUX in English: it can 1) occur in front of the subject in interrogatives; 2) serve as what the negative *-n't* attaches to; but 3) it cannot occur in tag questions

dare

1. *They <u>dare</u> (to) use the map they stole from us.*
   <u>Dare</u> they use the map they stole from us?
2. *They <u>daren't</u> use the map they stole from us.*[39]
3. **They dare use the map they stole from us, <u>dare they</u>?*
   They dare use the map they stole from us, do they?

Non-Standard aspectual verbs: Many varieties of American English commonly use a number of non-Standard aspectual verbs including completive *done*, habitual *be*, remote time stressed *been*, and unstressed *been*. A less common non-Standard aspectual verb is the use of *be*, rather than *have*, to mark the perfect aspect.

Completive *done*: In Southern European American varieties and AAVE, *done* is used as an aspectual verb with a meaning similar to the SE Aux *have*. However, while SE Aux *have* is followed by the past participle form of a verb, the non-Standard aspectual *done* is typically followed by the past tense form of a verb:

> *There was one in there that <u>done rotted</u> away.*
> *I <u>done forgot</u> what you wanted.*[40]

Smitherman also offers an example of completive *done* followed by the base form of an MV: *I <u>done finish</u> my homework today.*[41] Both constructions mark that the action has been completed in the recent past, much as does the SE Aux *have*, leading Dillard to dub this the "immediate perfect aspect."[42] Wolfram and Schilling-Estes note that "[t]he *done* form may also add intensification to the activity, as in *I done told you not to mess up*,"[43] much as *have* does in SE, as in *I have told you not to mess up*. But *done* is different from *have*: AAVE speakers note that *done* feels more intense and forceful.[44] Gee states that the completive *done* stresses that the action is "finished, complete, and done with."[45] And, perhaps more significantly, while the perfect aspect Aux *have* can be negated, completive *done* cannot:

Perfect Aux *have*:

He has gone.
He hasn't gone.

Completive semi-Aux *done*:

He done gone.
*He ain't done gone.
*He donen't gone.[46]

Completive *done* can combine with other verbs, including habitual *be* (see below), to create other mood-and-aspect forms, as in the following examples cited by Rickford and Rickford:

> *Another few weeks, the Puerto Ricans <u>be done took over</u>.* (Future or modal completive; compare SE *will have taken*)
> *If the dog wasn't spayed, she<u>'d be done got</u> pregnant cause she gets out.* (Modal completive; compare SE *would have gotten*)
> *The children <u>be done ate</u> by the time I get there.* (Habitual completive; compare SE *have usually eaten*).[47]

Be done is most common in the future or modal completive, particularly in sentences of the form *I be done _____ before you know it*:

> *I be done did this lil' spot a hair fo' you know it.*
> *If you ain mighty particular, yo' luck be done run out fo' you know it.*
> *I'll be done bought my own CB waitin' on him to buy me one.*[48]

Labov argues that this use of *be done* in AAVE has continued to evolve. In the following sentences, the implication of *be done* is that the succeeding event is a sure result of the preceding event:

> *If you love your enemy, they be done ate you alive in this society.* (SE equivalent, roughly, *In this society, if you love your enemy, it will follow as surely as night the day that they will eat you alive.*)
> *Don't do that 'cause you be done messed up your clothes.* (SE equivalent, *If you keep behaving that way, you will certainly mess up your clothes.*)

Labov identifies this modal usage as "resultative" since, rather than just indicating completion or "a simple ordering of events, it indicates that the second event will inevitably follow the first."[49]

Imperfect aspect with completive *done*: McWhorter offers an analysis of completive *done* that may actually cover all of these examples under a single umbrella. He agrees that in AAVE, *done* may commonly mark that the action occurred in the recent past, as when you find that your friend just chugged your soda and you say, *You done drunk it*. But it may also apply to action that occurred years ago, as when your father says to the forty-year-old whom he hasn't seen since she was two, *You done growed up!* "even though presumably the growing up happened years ago." In both examples, the use of *done* "marks counterexpectation. That is, . . . a sentence with *done* is always about something the speaker finds somewhat surprising, contrary to what was expected."[50] This would help explain all of the examples of completive *done* given above: when I say, *There was one in there that done rotted away*, it indicates that I did not expect there to have been one that rotted. And if I say, *The children be done ate by the time I get there*, although it was usually the case that the children have finished eating by the time I get there, it is still not the state of affairs I hope for or expect. Completive *done* can't be negated, as it is already the assertion of a counterexpectation; understood as marking a counterexpectation, verbs with completive *done* could be understood as conveying imperfect aspect, in that the action described is "flawed"—not what the speaker expected—and so isn't quite right.

Imperfect aspect with reinforcing *like*: McWhorter makes a similar argument in relation to the ubiquitous use of *like* in the speech of younger Americans:

that it, too, serves to mark counterexpectation. He offers the following example from a conversation he overheard between a sixteen-year-old and a friend:

> *So we got there and we thought we were going to have the room to ourselves and it turned out that <u>like</u> a family had booked it already. So we're standing there and there were <u>like</u> grandparents and <u>like</u> grandkids and aunts and uncles all over the place.*[51]

As with the examples of *done* above, these uses of *like* indicate the speaker's surprise that the situation was not as expected. The speaker and his colleagues assumed they "were going to have the room to themselves" but instead "a family had booked it already" (*like a family had booked it already*)—not just a couple of parents and a kid, but a whole extended family (*like grandparents and like grandkids and aunts and uncles*). This "reinforcing like," as McWhorter calls it, thus helps to mark the imperfect aspect in the verb.[52] The second sentence could have been stated more formally with the imperfect aspectual verb *seem to*: *So we're standing there and there <u>seemed to be</u> grandparents and grandkids and aunts and uncles all over the place.*

Habitual *be*: Perhaps one of the most distinctive features of AAVE, at least in the view of speakers of SE, is the use (or absence) of *be*. Most often, *be*, "sometimes written and pronounced *bees* or *be's*,"[53] is an aspectual verb used in AAVE and "in some rural European American varieties"[54] to mark action that occurs routinely, intermittently, or habitually over a period of time (c.f. Conrad's idea of imperfect aspectual verbs showing a "disposition" toward an action). *The coffee be cold* means that *Every day the coffee is cold*. If *be* is deleted, as in *The coffee cold*, that means *Today the coffee is cold*.[55] The adverbial expressions (*every day, today*) may be included for emphasis or clarity, as in *Every day the coffee be cold* and *The coffee cold today*. However, it would be grammatically incorrect to say, **Every day the coffee cold*, or **The coffee be cold today*.[56] Rickford explains that, in varieties of English that use habitual *be*, the Aux *do* is added to form questions, negatives, and tag questions:

> *<u>Do</u> he <u>be</u> walking every day?*
> *She <u>don't be</u> sick, <u>do</u> she?*[57]
> *That man <u>be</u> here every night; he <u>don't</u> want no girl.*[58]

Green[59] provides a particularly rich and detailed discussion of habitual *be*.

Intensified stative *be*: Wolfram and Schilling-Estes note a recent extension of the use of habitual *be* in hip-hop culture, where the meaning of *be* "has been extended to refer to intensified stativity or super-real status,"[60] as in the lyric of Grant, Nash, and West's "The Truth":

> *N**** the truth, every time I step in the booth*
> *I speak the truth, y'all know what I'm bringing to you*

I bring the truth, you m*****f***** know what I be
I be the truth, when I speak cell set you free
N**** the truth[61]

This "intensified stativity" is aspectual in that it describes the action as going beyond the perfect (*I have been the truth*) and the progressive (*I am being the truth*) to having unending duration.

Remote time stressed *béen*: According to Wolfram and Schilling-Estes, in AAVE, "When stressed, *béen* can serve to mark a special aspectual function, indicating that the event or activity took place in the 'distant past' but is still relevant."[62] The state indicated by stressed *béen* begins in the remote past and extends up to the moment of utterance.[63] Dillard refers to this use as the "remote perfect aspect"[64] compare the sense of the SE sentence, *I háve done my homework* or *I finished it áges ago*. Rickford adds that stressed *béen* can also indicate just that the event was initiated in the past, but may not extend to the present, as in *He béen ate it*, meaning *He ate it a long time ago*.[65] An AAVE speaker who says *I béen know that guy* means *I have known that guy for a long time*.[66] Remote time *béen* can be used ironically, as in this example cited by Rickford and Rickford, spoken by a seventy-two-year-old Black woman in Philadelphia: *He* [the dentist] *finish so quick. I ask him was he finished, and he say, 'I béen finished!'* The implication here is that the dentist was so thoroughly finished, it was as though his work were completed years ago and was still completed.[67]

As in this ironic example, Rickford and Rickford note that "the 'remoteness' of the time involved is a subjective matter: if you compliment someone on a new outfit, they might say, *I béen had this*, as a mid-twentieth-century SE speaker might have said, 'Oh, that old thing?' as a way of deflecting or downplaying the compliment".[68] Also, stressed *béen* can be used with auxiliaries "to create complex constructions in which the period designated by *béen* remains in effect until a time earlier than the moment of speech":

We had béen married when this lil' one came along. (spoken by a seventy-one-year-old Philadelphian. The SE rendering would be *We had been married awhile. . . .*)
They coulda béen ended that war. (spoken by a twenty-nine-year-old Philadelphian. The SE rendering would be *They could have ended that war much earlier.*)

(119)[69]

Remote time *been*, in common use in AAVE, is, in some contexts, readily misunderstood by SE speakers. The sentence *She been married* is typically interpreted by AAVE speakers to mean that she got married a long time ago and is still married (the correct AAVE reading). SE speakers commonly misunderstand this sentence, assuming it means she had been but is no longer married.

Unstressed *been*: According to Rickford, this usage contrasts with the preceding stressed remote time *been*. Unstressed *been* occurs in AAVE variants with the meaning of SE *has/have been*, as in *He been sick* for *He has been sick*. "Unlike remote time *been*, unstressed *been* can co-occur with time adverbials (e.g. *He been sick since last week*) and does not connote remoteness".[70] *Been* can also occur with the completive *done*:

> *By the time I got there, he been done gone.*
> *They done been sitting there an hour.*
>
> (Rickford 6)[71]

Perfective *be*: According to Fries, in Old English, the perfect aspect was marked by both *have* and *be*. *Have* "was used only with the past participles of transitive verbs"—verbs that take a direct object as their complement. *Be* was used to mark the perfect aspect with the past participles of intransitive verbs—verbs that do not take a direct object as their complement. In Old English, *be* was especially used to mark the perfect aspect with verbs of motion. These usages of *be* were very old fashioned and conservative when they appeared in the King James Bible:[72]

> *The kingdoms of this world are become the kingdoms of our Lord.*[73]
> *Babylon is fallen, is fallen; and all the graven images of her gods he hath broken unto the ground.*[74]
> *He is not here: for he is risen, as he said.*[75]

Fries notes further that in early Middle English, we find *have* with both intransitive verbs (including the main verb *be*) and with verbs of motion; however, *be* long continued to be commonly used to mark the perfect aspect.[76] And the perfective *be* persists in present perfect verbs in "some isolated varieties of American English":

> *I'm been there before.* (SE *I've been there before.*)
> *You're taken the best medicine.* (SE *You have taken the best medicine.*).

This construction occurs most frequently in first-person singular contexts (e.g. *I'm forgot*) but can also occur in the first-person plural and in second-person contexts as well (e.g. *we're forgot, you're been there*). Occasionally, the perfect can even be formed with invariant *be*, as in *We be come here for nothing* or *I'll be went to the post office.*[77]

But Fries points out that the perfective *be* lingers in contemporary SE in such constructions as *He is gone* and *He was gone*, which are in use along with *He has gone* and *He had gone.*[78]

Indignant *come*: In informal varieties of spoken English, *come*, *go*, and *start* followed by the present participle form of a verb are used as imperfect aspectual semi-AUX verbs to mark the speaker's indignation about a behavior. Spears notes examples such as the following as peculiar to AAVE: *He come walking in here like he owned the damn place.*[79] But other varieties use the same construction to mark counterexpectation through indignation:

> *You can't come barging in here.*[80]
> *The net effect of the hard-hat war on drugs approach is that we go crashing into poor neighborhoods with undercover officers looking to make arrests.*[81]
> *I'm not going to quit my job and start lording it around like I'm the king of the world.*[82]

6.1.2.3 Voice

There are two "voices" in English: active and passive. For simplicity's sake, we are treating active voice as the default since it is unmarked in the English verb. The concept of passive voice only applies to transitive verbs: verbs that take as their complement a nominal functioning as a direct object (DO). In active voice sentences, the AGENT performing the action is named in the subject of the sentence; a transitive verb follows in the predicate; and the person or thing being acted upon—the PATIENT—is named after the verb, in the NOMINAL:DO. In passive voice sentences, the order is reversed: the patient is named by the subject; the verb that follows changes to a *be* AUX followed by the past participle of the transitive MV; and the agent is either named after the verb or is not mentioned explicitly in the sentence. Compare the following examples:

> **Active voice**: *I kick the ball.*
> **Passive voice**: *The ball is kicked by me. The ball is kicked.*

In each sentence, the action is named by a form of the verb *kick*, and *I* or *me* names the agent, the one who does the kicking.

- In the <u>active voice</u> sentence, the AGENT—*I*—is named in the NP:SUBJ. The PATIENT—*the ball*—is named after the verb, in the DO position in the predicate.
- In the first passive voice sentence, the PATIENT—*the ball*—is named in the NP:SUBJ; the verb changes form from the active voice *kick* to the passive voice *is kicked*; and the AGENT—*I/me*—is named in the predicate, as the PCOMP of "by."
- In the second passive voice sentence, the PATIENT—*the ball*—is named in the NP:SUBJ; the verb—*is kicked*—is in the passive voice form; and the AGENT—*I/me*—is deleted completely.

One advantage of the passive voice is that it allows us to talk about actions that have no agents (e.g. chemical reactions); if, for some reason, we don't want to talk about the agent of an action (e.g. we want to avoid taking or giving blame), the passive voice allows us to do so. The passive voice construction also allows us to reorder the information in a sentence so that the patient becomes the topic by being mentioned first.

Note that intransitive verbs—verbs that don't take a DO—can't take passive voice. In the sentence *I fell*, there is no patient, no DO, and therefore no passive voice form. We will discuss various sorts of transitive verbs in 7.1; in 10.1.5, we will again discuss passive voice in the context of rearranging sentences and dependent clauses.

The passive voice verb takes the form of a *be* Aux followed by the past participle of a verb, unlike the progressive aspect, in which the *be* Aux is followed by the present participle:

> Active voice V: *I kick the mule.*
> Passive voice V: *The mule is kicked by me.*
> Progressive aspect V: *The mule is kicking me.*

A single complete verb can be in both the progressive aspect and the passive voice, in which case it will have two *be* auxiliaries. The first *be* Aux (BE Aux1) followed by the present participle marks the progressive aspect, while the second *be* Aux (BE Aux2) followed by the past participle marks the passive voice:

BE Aux1 + Present Participle = V with the progressive aspect

> *I am*[BE Aux1] *kicking the ball.*

BE Aux2 + PAST PARTICIPLE = V with the passive voice

> *The ball is*[BE Aux2] *kicked by me.*

BE Aux1 + *BEING* (*be* Aux2 in the present participle form) + PAST PARTICIPLE = V with the progressive aspect and the passive voice

> *The ball is*[BE Aux1] *being*[BE Aux2] *kicked by me.*

Is passive voice wrong? You have probably been told that passive voice is bad, weak, or otherwise a no-no. In itself, there's nothing wrong with passive voice: all speakers and writers of English use it, whether ordinary folks or highly regarded prose stylists. Passive voice is one of a variety of devices we have for rearranging the order of constituents in sentences to improve the flow of information in discourse (see 10.1). The problems with passive voice are, first, when we overuse it: a passage with a lot of verbs in the passive voice becomes hard to follow because it becomes hard to keep agents and patients clear, hard to identify the kernel sentence, hard to know who is doing what to whom. However, passive voice is a mainstay of much writing in the experimental sciences, in which, for example, chemical reactions are treated as having no actor who causes them.

Second, passive voice can create an ethical problem when it allows the writer to inappropriately avoid ascribing responsibility for an action: after all, passive voice lets the writer completely delete any mention of the agent who performed the action and to say *The ball was kicked* instead of *Franz kicked the ball*, *The window was broken* instead of *I broke the window*, and *Mistakes were made* instead of *The mayor made mistakes*. Nonetheless, there are situations in which no one is responsible for an action or in which it is more tactful not to lay blame; in those cases, the passive voice is appropriate.[83]

Non-Standard passive *get*: In a broad range of vernacular American English varieties, we find the verb *get* used as a semi-Aux to mark passive voice. This usage also shows up in published writing and quoted speech:

> *Mites eat, and get eaten by, other arthropods.*
> *If you're that stupid, you deserve to get eaten.*[84]

In each example, the appropriate form of the SE passive Aux *be* can be substituted directly for the passive semi-Aux *get*:

> *Mites eat, and are eaten by, other arthropods.*[85]
> *If you're that stupid, you deserve to be eaten.*

6.1.3 Tense, Mood, Aspect, Voice: Putting Them All Together

Complete verbs in English must always include an MV and, in actual usage, about ninety percent of English verbs comprise a lone MV, in the past or present tense form, unaccompanied by an Aux or other Aux-like verb.[86] Of the remainder, most complete verbs comprise an MV preceded by some combination of the most common Aux verbs: a modal, perfect aspect *have*, progressive aspect *be*, and/or passive voice *be*. A verb with one Aux is more common than a verb with two. Least common are the more complicated verbs that we can create using semi-modal verbs and/or imperfect aspectual verbs; those Aux-like verbs allow us to create complete verbs comprising more than four verbs. Though unusual, they are common enough that if we want to parse real language, we have to know about them and the forms that these complete verbs might take.

As we did above, with just modal auxiliaries and the aspect auxiliaries *have* and *be*, we can now add the passive voice Aux *be* and work through a whole verb paradigm for the tense, modality, aspect, and voice of the most common multi-word verbs:

> *I kick the ball.* (PRES tense; IND mood; Ø aspect; ACT voice)
> *The ball is kicked by me.* (PRES tense; IND mood; Ø aspect; PASS voice)

I kicked the ball. (PAST tense; IND mood; Ø aspect; ACT voice)

The ball was kicked by me. (PAST tense; IND mood; Ø aspect; PASS voice)

I may kick the ball (PRES tense; modal; Ø aspect; ACT voice)

The ball may be kicked by me. (PRES tense; modal; Ø aspect; PASS voice)

I might kick the ball. (PAST tense; modal; Ø aspect; ACT voice)

The ball might be kicked by me. (PAST tense; modal; Ø aspect; PASS voice)

I have kicked the ball. (PRES tense; IND mood; PERF aspect; ACT voice)

The ball has been kicked by me. (PRES tense; IND mood; PERF aspect; PASS voice)

I had kicked the ball. (PAST tense; IND mood; PERF aspect; ACT voice)

The ball had been kicked by me (PAST tense; IND mood; PERF aspect; PASS voice)

I am kicking the ball. (PRES tense; IND mood; PROG aspect; ACT voice)

The ball is being kicked by me. (PRES tense; IND mood; PROG aspect; PASS voice)

I was kicking the ball. (PAST tense; IND mood; PROG aspect; ACT voice)

The ball was being kicked by me. (PAST tense; IND mood; PROG aspect; PASS voice)

I have been kicking the ball. (PRES tense; IND mood; PERF PROG aspect; ACT voice)

The ball has been being kicked. (PRES tense; IND mood; PERF PROG aspect; PASS voice)

I had been kicking the ball. (PAST tense; IND mood; PERF PROG aspect; ACT voice)

The ball had been being kicked. (PAST tense; IND mood; PERF PROG aspect; PASS voice)

I may have kicked the ball. (PRES tense; modal; PERF aspect; ACT voice)

The ball may have been kicked. (PRES tense; modal; PERF aspect; PASS voice)

I might have kicked the ball. (PAST tense; modal; PERF aspect; ACT voice)

The ball might have been kicked. (PAST tense; modal; PERF aspect; PASS voice)

I may be kicking the ball. (PRES tense; modal; PROG aspect; ACT voice)

The ball may be being kicked. (PRES tense; modal; PROG aspect; PASS voice)

I might be kicking the ball. (PAST tense; modal; PROG aspect; ACT voice)

The ball might be being kicked. (PAST tense; modal; PROG aspect; PASS voice)

I may have been kicking the ball. (PRES tense; modal; PERF PROG aspect; ACT voice)

The ball may have been being kicked. (PRES tense; modal; PERF PROG aspect; PASS voice)

I might have been kicking the ball. (PAST tense; modal; PERF PROG aspect; ACT voice)

The ball might have been being kicked. (PAST tense; modal; PERF PROG aspect; PASS voice)

When we add semi-modal and imperfect aspectual verbs to our analysis, we get greater complications and subtler nuances in the English verb. The resulting verb constructions are highly idiomatic—which makes them easy for native speakers to understand and vexing for non-native speakers to learn. Consider the following sentence: *He had wanted to be leading the pack as the race entered the mountains.*[87] The complete verb is *had wanted to be leading*. The first word in the verb—*had*—is the past tense form of *have*, so the complete verb is in the past tense. And we know that *had* is the perfect aspect AUX because it is followed by the past participle of the next word in the verb, *wanted*. Thus far, we have the past perfect. *Wanted* is followed by *to* and then the verb *be*, which is the base form of that verb; *wanted to* is a semi-modal, marking modality in the complete verb. So we have past perfect modal. *Be* is followed by the present participle *heading*, which means that this *be* marks the progressive aspect and *leading* is the MV. So *had wanted to be leading* is the past perfect modal progressive of *leading*. In most verbs the modal AUX would precede the perfect AUX. But semi-modal and imperfect aspectual verbs allow us to rearrange the most common order in the complete verb.

When we use semi-modals, we can easily have more than one modal-marking verb in a single complete verb: *I was hoping to be able to attend.*[88] *Was* followed by the present participle *hoping* gives us the past progressive. *Hoping to* and *be able to* are both semi-modal verbs, and *attend* is the MV. So we have the past progressive modal modal of "attend." This sort of "double modal" is acceptable in all English varieties and marks greater distance from the action named in the verb, indicating it is even less likely that I will get to attend than if I *was hoping to attend* or *able to attend*.

Let's go a step further: *As a communication scholar, I might have been hoping to be able to put on my communication hat and think through Christian acts in terms of what they communicate verbally and nonverbally to the world.*[89] *Might* is a past tense modal AUX. *Have*, followed by the past participle *been*, is the perfect aspect AUX. *Been*, followed by the present participle *hoping*, is the progressive aspect AUX. *Hoping to* and *be able to* are both semi-modals, and *put* is the MV. So we have the past modal perfect progressive modal modal of "put."

I expect you get the point: such elaborate verbs are unusual in English, but they are possible. And we use them to carefully express very particular relationships among actors and events. The more elaborate the verb, the more speakers are trying to distance themselves from the action or event named, a linguistic politeness gesture by which the speaker is being less assertive, thus providing space and options for the listener and for the characters in the story being told.

We get similar variations in the verb when we add the imperfect aspectual verbs. Consider the following examples of various combinations of aspect-marking verbs:

- **Perfect imperfect**: *Several members of the legislature have begun working on school safety measures.*[90]

- **Progressive imperfect**: *New training protocols <u>are beginning to work</u>.*[91]
- **Imperfect perfect**: *He <u>pretended to have cured</u> patients who showed little improvement or actually got worse.*[92]
- **Imperfect progressive**: *More and more voters <u>seem to be coming</u> around to a logical conclusion.*[93]
- **Imperfect perfect progressive**: *I <u>seem to have been dancing</u> in the rain a lot lately.*[94]
- **Perfect imperfect progressive**: *All too often, the Astros <u>have seemed to be waiting</u> for their slugging first baseman to put a couple of runs on the board with one swing of his bat.*[95]
- **Perfect progressive imperfect**: *Governors <u>have been trying to fix</u> the State Police for decades.*[96]

We can also have more than one of the same aspect marked in a single verb, as in:

- **Progressive imperfect progressive**: *Norman <u>is beginning to be seeing</u> different incarnations of Norma.*[97]
- **Imperfect progressive imperfect**: *Broadcasters <u>seem to be beginning to find</u> a solution.*[98]
- **Progressive imperfect imperfect**: *The market <u>is beginning to start to levitate</u> again.*[99]

When we have semi-modal verbs and imperfect aspectual verbs together in the complete verb, the possibilities are mind-boggling:

> *I've had a lot of trouble getting motivated this morning. But if all goes according to plan, by noon I <u>might be hoping to have begun to want to work</u> on the project.*

The Aux *might* is in the past tense and marks the verb as modal. *Be* followed by the present participle *hoping*, marks the progressive aspect. *Hoping to*, followed by the base form *have*, is a semi-modal, marking the verb again as modal. *Have*, followed by the past participle *begun*, marks the perfect aspect, giving us, so far, the <u>past modal progressive modal perfect</u>. *Begun to*, followed by the base form of the verb *want*, is a multi-word imperfect aspectual verb. *Want to*, followed by the base form of the MV *work*, is a semi-modal verb marking modality for the third time. So this verb is the <u>past modal progressive modal perfect imperfect modal</u> of *work*. And notice that, with the odd glue provided by the semi-modal *hoping to*, we can put the perfect Aux *have* later in the complete verb than the progressive Aux *be*. Admittedly, I have manufactured this example. But although a complete verb of this length and complexity is highly unusual, it is <u>possible</u> as a means for the speaker to express a particular stance on or relationship to the action named.

To summarize tense, modality, aspect, and voice:

Tense	A finite verb always has a tense. A verb may have only one tense: <u>present</u> or <u>past</u>. The tense of a complete finite verb is the tense of the first word in the verb.
Modality	A finite verb always has a modality. A finite verb is, usually, either in the <u>indicative</u> mood or it is <u>modal</u>.
	Indicative mood: a complete verb is in the indicative mood when it has no modal Aux or semi-modal verb. The unmarked indicative mood asserts the speaker's belief that the action is real and actual.
	Modal: a complete verb is modal when it has a <u>modal</u> Aux or <u>semi-modal</u> verb followed by the base form of a verb. With the use of semi-modal and imperfect aspectual verbs, a complete SE verb may have more than one modal-marking verb, each of which marks a separate instance of the verb being modal. A verb may therefore be multiply modal. Marking the verb as modal indicates the speaker's assertion or belief that the action is irreal or hypothetical.
Aspect	A finite verb may have <u>no aspect</u> (∅-aspect), or a finite verb may have any combination of the <u>perfect</u>, <u>progressive</u>, and <u>imperfect</u> aspects. With the use of semi-modals and imperfect aspectual verbs, a complete verb may even have more than one instance of the same aspect. Each aspectual verb marks a separate aspect.
	No aspect (∅-aspect): a complete verb has no aspect if it includes no aspect-marking verb.
	Perfect aspect: a complete verb has the perfect aspect if it includes a *have* Aux followed by the past participle of a verb.
	Progressive aspect: a complete verb has the progressive aspect when it includes a *be* Aux followed by the present participle of a verb.
	Imperfect aspect: a complete verb has the imperfect aspect when it includes a single-word imperfect aspectual verb followed by the present participle form of a verb, or a multi-word imperfect aspectual verb followed by the base form of a verb.
Voice	A finite verb may have <u>active</u> or <u>passive</u> voice.
	Active voice is the default voice in English verbs and is unmarked. In an active voice sentence, the Agent (the entity performing the action named by the V) is named by the Nominal:Subj.
	Passive voice: a complete verb is in the passive voice when it has a *be* Aux followed by the past participle of a verb. The Patient is named by the Nominal:Subj. The Agent may be named in a PP with *by* or *with* or may be deleted. All passive-voice verbs are transitive.

6.1.4 Imperative Mood

Moods are grammatical forms that signal modality. Grammarians and linguists have identified other moods in English. The most commonly discussed is the imperative mood. Sentences in the imperative mood are used to deliver orders or commands: *Take this to the kitchen. Write it down.* The verbs in such sentences are regarded as modal because the action they name is not actual: just because the speaker commands the hearer to perform an action, it does not mean that the hearer will actually do so. Such commands are closely related to politer requests, except that the request would take the form of a question and include a modal Aux:

> *Would you take this to the kitchen?* (that is, *You would take this to the kitchen.*)
> *Would you write it down?* (that is, *You would write it down.*)

So imperative sentences are a modal construction but express a different mood from that indicated by the modal auxiliaries and semi-modal verbs.

In the imperative there is no explicit subject for the verb: the subject seems to be deleted. We will further examine the imperative mood construction when we look at different ways we can rearrange sentences and dependent clauses (10.1.2).

6.1.5 Subjunctive Mood

Traditional grammar also identifies the subjunctive mood in English. When we express a wish or desire for some state of affairs or propose a state of affairs that is counter to fact, we may use verbs in the subjunctive mood:

> *Finally, brethren, whatsoever things are true, whatsoever things are honest, whatsoever things are just, whatsoever things are pure, whatsoever things are lovely, whatsoever things are of good report; if there be any virtue, and if there be any praise, think on these things.*[100]
> *Political commentators greeted with derision the proposal that armed guards be posted in all U.S. schools.*[101]
> *Whether you be trans, whether you be black, whether you be Latino, whether you be disabled—we're here to be a platform for you.*[102]
> *If I were to read her book, I'd learn something about myself.*[103]
> *We suggest that the interested reader seek more detailed coverage of the foundations.*[104]
> *I assume the governor will insist that his appointee run as a Republican.*[105]

Verbs in the subjunctive mood usually appear in clauses marked by the expletives *if*, *whether*, or *that*. In English, the subjunctive mood is marked in the verb in one of three ways:

1. By using the base form of the verb with any subject, regardless of person or number (including the third-person singular).
2. By using *be* (present) or *were* (past) as the MV with a subject of any person or number.

3. By using, with a subject of any person or number, *be* as a semi-Aux or *were* as an Aux followed by the present or past participle form of the MV or a semi-Aux.

There are a number of verbs that are regularly followed by a clause beginning with *that* and including the subjunctive *be*; among them are:

advise (that)	demand (that)	propose (that)	suggest (that)
ask (that)	desire (that)	recommend (that)	urge (that)
command (that)	insist (that)	request (that)	

Note that several of these verbs can also function as semi-modal verbs: *I demand to/desire to/propose to see the president.* Several can also take as their complement an NP:DO followed by an infinitive phrase: *I advise/ask/command/desire/urge you to see the president.* These overlapping usages point to the overlapping function of all three forms (subjunctives; semi-modals; V + NP:DO + INFP) in naming hypothetical actions.

There are also a number of common idioms in English that take a clause beginning with *that* and a verb in the subjunctive mood; some examples include:

It is best (that)	It is imperative (that)	It is urgent (that)
It is crucial (that)	It is important (that)	It is vital (that)
It is desirable (that)	It is recommended (that)	It is a good/bad idea (that)
It is essential (that)		

The subjunctive *were* is a partial Aux in that, while it cannot occur in front of the subject in interrogatives[106] and it cannot occur in tag questions, it can serve as what the negative -*n't* attaches to: *I'm swamped, and even if I weren't, you know I won't work for the CIA.*[107] While serving to mark the subjunctive mood, both subjunctive *be* and *were* can also serve to mark either the progressive aspect or the passive voice, depending on the form of the following MV:

Present Subjunctive Progressive:

It is recommended that you be waiting at the stop a few minutes early.[108]

Past Subjunctive Progressive:

I hate waiting. I hate waiting more than burnt pizza, cold weather, and wearing wet socks combined. Of course, if I were waiting for burnt pizza in cold weather with wet socks, that'd be much worse than just waiting. But I still hate waiting.[109] (also, *if I weren't waiting*)

Present Subjunctive Passive:

Provost Rogers recommended that a new major <u>be created</u> for a B.S. degree in Environmental & Natural Resources.[110]

Past Subjunctive Passive:

If a new major <u>were created</u>, it would serve 40 students in its first year.

Past Subjunctive Progressive Imperfect:

If I <u>were starting to teach</u>, I would want to feel that I was undertaking a job which warranted my abilities and enthusiastic efforts.[111]

The subjunctive *be* occurs in the stereotypical dialect of movie pirates (*Yar, if that scallywag <u>be</u> skulkin' around here . . .*) and in the familiar rhyme of the giant in "Jack and the Beanstalk":

Fee, fi, fo, fum,
I smell the blood of an Englishman!
<u>Be</u> he live or <u>be</u> he dead
I'll grind his bones to make my bread.

The use of *be* here is a present subjunctive; the relevant clauses might be paraphrased as *Whether he be alive, or whether he be dead. . . .*

This all being said, the oddity of the subjunctive *were* is being leveled to *was* with first- and third-person singular subjects in all varieties of spoken American English and increasingly in writing:

If I <u>was</u> able to track the shuttle's position, whoever's been using it will as well.[112] (compare *If I <u>were</u> able to track . . .*)
If she <u>wasn't</u> released on her own recognizance soon, the infant would have to be turned over to a relative.[113] (compare *If she <u>weren't</u> released . . .*)

6.1.6 Auxiliary dó

The verb *dó*, spoken with stress, is used as an Aux that adds emphasis to verbs in declarative sentences (sentences typically used to make statements or claims):

I dó believe in spooks![114] *I díd eat my peas!*

Notice that Aux *dó* is followed by the base form of a verb and that, as with any first Aux in a verb string, *dó* carries the tense of the whole verb: in the second example above, *díd* marks the past tense. Aux *dó* never appears in combination with other auxiliaries but does appear with semi-modals and imperfect aspectual verbs:

> DÓ + SEMI-MODAL VERB: *They dó want to meet and kind of talk this out.*[115] (emphatic modal active of "meet")
>
> DÓ + IMPERFECT ASPECTUAL VERB: *I have gotten to the point where sometimes I dó try to employ mindfulness.*[116] (emphatic imperfect active of "employ")
>
> DÓ + SEMI-MODAL VERB + IMPERFECT ASPECTUAL VERB: *I really díd want to start sewing again.*[117] (emphatic modal imperfect active of "sewing")
>
> DÓ + IMPERFECT ASPECTUAL VERB + SEMI-MODAL VERB: *Though I díd manage to be able to connect via wifi and use their app to view and download as expected, transferring video to my phone was a bit clunky.*[118] (emphatic imperfect modal active of "connect")

The sense of emphatic *dó* is very different from the non-Standard aspectual semi-AUX completive *done* in a sentence like *I done forgot what you wanted*, discussed above.

Note that, just as with *have* and *be*, *do* can function as both an AUX and as a lexical, as in *I did my homework*. And, like other lexical verbs, *do* as a lexical verb can take auxiliaries:

> *I will do my homework. I have done my homework. I am doing my homework. I did do my homework.*

6.1.7 Generic Past Semi-Auxiliary used to

Another commonly used verb is the semi-AUX *used to* (*useta*), which marks a special tense called the "generic past." It is always followed by the base form of a verb and can appear with just an MV (*I used to buy books at garage sales.*)[119] or followed by certain semi-modals (*Black parents used to have to buy books about white children and color in the faces.*)[120] and imperfect aspectual verbs (*I used to try to write lyrics when I drove around in my work truck.*).[121] *Used to* is understood as marking the *generic* past because it "indicates something that generally and habitually occurred."[122] It is thus related to the present and past tenses, which can convey a sense of habitual action:

> Present: *I buy books at garage sales every day.*
> Past: *I bought books at garage sales every day.*
> Generic Past: *I used to buy books at garage sales every day.*

Useta is also related to habitual *be*; *useta* is habitual and completive, indicating action performed habitually in the past but that is no longer done.

6.1.8 Non-Standard Absent be

Another notable feature of AAVE and Southern American English varieties is the absence of forms of *be*, also called "zero copula." Tensed forms of *be* are called "copular" because they couple, or join together, the subject and the complement that follows the *be* form. Gee contrasts the absent *be* with invariant *be*, stating that absent *be* is used to mark events that are ongoing or repeated but of limited duration, while invariant *be* is used to mark events that are ongoing or repeated but of extended duration.[123] Dillard argues persuasively that this sort of marking of aspect in the verb is obligatory in AAVE, while tense marking is optional, whereas in SE, tense marking is obligatory, while it is possible to have Ø aspect. Thus, an AAVE sentence like *He sleepin'* is not merely or always the equivalent of SE *He is sleeping*. Rather, it may simply be saying that "he usually or routinely or frequently sleeps," without any necessary implication about whether he is sleeping now.[124]

Not all *be* forms can be deleted: only present tense contractible forms of *be*, specifically *is* and *are*, can be absent.[125] Thus, in these varieties, the final versions of the following sentences are appropriate:

> *You are ugly→You're ugly→You ugly.*
> *She is taking the dog out→She's taking the dog out→She taking the dog out.*[126]

Notice that the form of *be* can be deleted when it is functioning as the MV (*You are ugly*) and when it is functioning as the progressive aspect Aux (*She is taking the dog out*). In most American informal varieties, both uses of *be* can be deleted from questions: *(Are) you in there? (Is) she taking the dog out?* However, in SE, we cannot contract past tense forms of *be* (*was, were*): *You were ugly→*You're ugly* (with past tense meaning), and therefore we cannot delete those past forms, so we do not find **Yesterday you ugly* or **Last night she taking the dog out*. And in American varieties, *am* and *'m* are never deleted, even though the contraction *I'm* occurs routinely in both AAVE and Southern American English. According to Rickford and Rickford, both *am* and *'m* can be deleted in Caribbean Creole English, as in the example they cite of a Barbadian fisherman explaining *I cutting off de heads*. Base form *be* also cannot be deleted from infinitive constructions (after *to*) and after modal auxiliaries.[127]

Rickford and Rickford also describe several restrictions on the zero copula. Only *is* and *are* can be deleted, but they cannot be deleted from the end of a sentence ("*That's what he is*," but not **That's what he*") or when they are stressed for emphasis. Neither can negative *is* or *are*—as *ain't*—be deleted. And generally, the *be* forms can't be deleted from other contractions, such as *what's/what're, it's,* and *that's,* although some greetings allow for *be* deletion, as in *Wa'apnin* for *What's happenin* and *What up?* for *What's up?*[128]

Wolfram and Schilling-Estes conclude by noting that "A more general version of *be* absence—that includes *am* and past tense—is sometimes found in varieties developed in the process of learning English as a second language."[129]

6.1.9 How Many bes Are There?

We have thus far encountered a large number of ways in which *be* functions in Standard and non-Standard varieties of English, and we will encounter a few more in the remainder of the book:

- Finite lexical verb *be* in the present (*am, are, is*) and past (*was, were*) tenses.
- Non-finite base form *be*, present participle *being*, and past participle *been* used as part of finite verbs (e.g. *will be, am being, have been*).
- As part of Standard semi-modal verbs: *be about to, be going to (be gonna), be supposed to (be supposeta), be to.*
- As part of non-Standard semi-modal verbs (future *be*; *be fixin' to*; *Imma*; *poseta*).
- Progressive aspect AUX *be.*
- Non-Standard aspectual verbs (habitual *be*; intensified stative *be*; remote time stressed *béen*; unstressed *been*; perfective *be*).
- Passive voice AUX *be.*
- Subjunctive MV *be* and *were* and subjunctive AUX *be.*
- Copular *be* (7.1.2.2) and the non-Standard zero copula (6.1.8).
- Existential *be* (10.1.3) in expletive *there* sentences (e.g. *There is a book on the table*).
- Present participle *being* as the head of nominal, adjectival, and adverbial participle phrases.
- Infinitive *to be* as the head of nominal, adjectival, and adverbial infinitive phrases.

The question must be raised: how many *bes* are there in English? As we saw in 1.2, there are words like *play*_{VERB} and *play*_{NOUN} that may be regarded as variants of the same word but may more productively be regarded as homonyms. As a general rule, I will try to treat each of these *bes* as separate forms that simply resemble each other and that are, of course, historically related.

6.2 Identifying Verbs

Many words in English may be used as more than one part of speech without changing their form. In the sentences *I play piano* and *They went to see a play*, how do we determine whether either use of *play* is a verb? We can use

> **The tense or mood shift test for verbs**: Change the word in question into the past-tense verb form, or put the auxiliary verb *will* in front of the word. If the sentence is still grammatically well formed, then the word is a verb.[130]

Applying this test to the first sentence, we get: *I play the piano→I played the piano; I will play the piano.* But if we apply it to the second sentence, we get:

> *They went to see a play→*They went to see a played;*
> **They went to see a will play.*

This test only works for finite verbs functioning as the MV of a sentence or dependent clause.

Key Points

- Verbs (V) are an open class of content words that name actions (meaning) and function as the head of a verb phrase (VP) that functions as the predicate in a sentence or dependent clause.
- Verbs are commonly divided into several subcategories, including finite and non-finite, lexical verbs, and auxiliary verbs (AUX).
- Finite verbs are marked for several features, including tense (present, past); modality (indicative, modal, imperative, subjunctive); aspect (perfect, progressive, imperfect); and voice (active, passive).
- Present tense, indicative mood, Ø-aspect, and active voice are the default or unmarked features of verbs. All other features are marked by changes in spelling (e.g. *swim, swam, swum*); inflectional suffixes (e.g. *baking, baked*); or the addition of AUX or semi-AUX verbs (for modal and subjunctive modality; perfect, progressive, and imperfect aspect; and passive voice).
- Speakers use "tense" to locate an action in time but more broadly to place an event in relation to other events in the discourse.
- Speakers use "modality" to express their attitude or understanding about whether an event is actual or hypothetical.
- Speakers use "aspect" to express their attitude or understanding about the duration of an event in time in relation to other events in the discourse.
- Speakers use "voice" to shift the focus of a sentence between the AGENT (the doer of the action) and the PATIENT (the recipient of the action).
- Because there are so many irregularities in the SE verb system, especially in the realization and use of marking for tense, mood, and aspect, it is one of the portions of English grammar with the most diverse and distinctive range of non-Standard forms, as speakers of different varieties strive to regularize the system and to shape it to match their groups' perceptions and understanding of how the world works.

6.3 Exercises: Verbs: Tense, Mood, Aspect, Voice

A. Made-up sentences: in the following sentences, identify each complete finite verb and, for each, identify the tense (present; past), modality (indicative indicative mood; modal; subjunctive mood; imperative mood), aspect (progressive; perfect; imperfect), and voice (active; passive). **ALSO**: identify the person (first; second; third) and number (singular; plural).

Example: They were running for office.
>>They <u>were running</u> for office. Third-person pl. indicative past progressive active

1. They are taking the train to town.
2. The Marxes have been agitating for workers' rights again.
3. The demonstrators broke the windows.
4. We had alerted the police.
5. Our equipment has been delivered.
6. The workers are starting to unpack the boxes
7. That unfinished house has been being built for years.
8. I may have to leave the office early today.
9. The committee will try to be finished with the report by Friday.
10. They be studying grammar.
11. I enjoy a good demonstration.
12. You might like it too.
13. The demonstrators done been arrested.
14. He is gone.
15. You may have to start thinking about a new candidate.
16. He crazy.
17. We are going to have to be going.
18. Despite all the noise, she managed to start thinking about the project.
19. Today, the artist is supposed to decide to finish polishing the marble.
20. If I were going to begin considering at least exploring the possibility of downsizing and consolidating government, I would first examine the United States Custom Service.[131]

B.   More made-up examples: for each of the following, provide a correct kernel sentence as directed (some answers may vary).

Example: First-person singular indicative present progressive active of *sleep*.
>>*I am sleeping.*

1. Third-person singular feminine present indicative perfect progressive active of *study*.
2. Second-person plural present modal perfect passive of *expect*.
3. Third-person singular feminine past modal active of *run*.
4. First-person singular past indicative active of *look*.
5. First-person plural present indicative progressive passive of *deceive*.
6. Second-person singular past indicative perfect active of *eat*.
7. Third-person plural present modal perfect progressive passive of *convince*.
8. Third-person singular masculine past indicative passive of *know*.
9. First-person plural past modal perfect modal active of *practice*
10. Third-person plural present modal modal active of *leave*.
11. Second-person singular present modal perfect imperfect active of *eat*

12. First-person plural past indicative imperfect imperfect active of *escape*
13. Third-person singular past indicative imperfect modal passive of *appreciate*

C. A real text: identify each complete finite verb that is functioning as a main verb in a clause and, for each, identify its person, number, (gender), tense, modality, aspect, and voice. Use the passage from Exercise 1.3B on pages 27–28, "Dog Belonging to Princess Anne Attacks Royal Maid."

Example: (1) *attacked*: third-person singular past indicative active

Notes

1. For an extensive list of 470 irregular verbs in English (as of 25 Apr 2019), see <www.englishpage.com/irregularverbs/irregularverbs.html>. See also the extensive list and discussion of irregular verbs at <https://en.wikipedia.org/wiki/List_of_English_irregular_verbs>.
2. *Be* historically involves the collapsing together of several verb paradigms. The only other verb in English that exhibits this sort of blending is *go/goes, went, going, gone*.
3. *Must* is regarded as being in the present tense because, if we paraphrase it, we have to use a present tense modal semi-Aux in its place: *I must go home* is paraphrased by *I have to go home* rather than *I had to go home*. Similarly, the partial modal *ought to* is regarded as being in the past tense because, if we paraphrase it, we have to use a past tense modal semi-Aux in its place: *I ought to go home* is paraphrased by *I should go home* rather than *I shall go home*. The question of whether modal auxiliaries have tense remains quite controversial, hinging on whether "tense" relates primarily to "time" or to the physical, temporal, or social distance of the action from the speaker.
4. J. L. Dillard. *Black English: Its History and Usage in the United States.* New York: Vintage Books, 1972. 40–41.
5. Walt Wolfram and Natalie Schilling-Estes. *American English.* 2nd ed. Malden, MA: Blackwell, 2006. 375–376.
6. Carmen Fought. *Chicano English in Context.* New York: Palgrave MacMillan, 2003. 94.
7. Wolfram and Schilling-Estes, op. cit. 376.
8. Geneva Smitherman. *Talkin' and Testifyin': The Language of Black America.* Boston: Houghton Mifflin, 1977. 26.
9. Dillard, op. cit. 41.
10. Ibid.
11. Wolfram and Schilling-Estes, op. cit. 376.
12. Ibid. 377.
13. John R. Rickford and Christine Théberge Rafal. "Preterite Had + V-*ed* in the Narratives of African-American Preadolescents." *American Speech* 71 (Autumn 1996): 229–230.
14. John McWhorter. *Talking Back, Talking Black: Truths about America's Lingua Franca.* New York: Bellvue Literary Press, 2017. 42–44; see also Lisa J. Green. *African American English: A Linguistic Introduction.* New York: Cambridge University Press, 2002. 91–93.
15. Op. cit.
16. Of course, other features of language mark the timing of the action. In the sentence *Tomorrow, I run to the store at eight, then the office by nine, and then I come home*, it is the adverb *tomorrow* that indicates the timing of the action as being in

the future. It is thus reasonable to argue that there are modal nouns (e.g. *decree, demand, necessity, requirement, request*), modal adjectives (e.g. *advisable, crucial, imperative, likely, necessary, probable, possible*), and modal adverbs (e.g. *arguably, maybe, perhaps, probably, possibly, surely*), all of which help mark the hypothetical nature of the action in the sentence. Such structural redundancies are a common feature in all languages, as they help to make sure the audience gets the speaker or writer's meaning.

17. There is one hitch in this analysis of semi-modals with the form *BE* + ADJP + *TO*: it is unclear whether it is best to analyze them as part of the complete finite verb or as *BE* + ADJP + an infinitive phrase, where the infinitive phrase might be functioning as an adverbial post-modifier of the ADJ, or as a second complement of the verb *be*. We will come back to these two interpretations in 12.2 and later in this chapter, respectively.

18. Dan Koeppel. "Joe Breeze Wants to Change the World." *Bicycling* 44.8 (Sep 2003): 32.

19. "Interview with Cristina Saralegui." *The Crier Report*. Fox. 27 Mar 1998.

20. Dashiell Hammett. *Red Harvest*. *Novels*. New York: Knopf, 1977. 44.

21. Jan Svartvik and David Wright. "The Use of ought in Teenage English." *Acceptability in Language*. Ed. Sidney Greenbaum. New York: Mouton, 1977. 179–201. This detailed study of "the use of *ought* in teenage English" found a split among speaker opinions about the positive tag question "ought you?" and the negative tag question "oughtn't you?" About half of their subjects found these usages old fashioned; half found them ungrammatical.

22. Daniel Denison. Chapter 3: "Syntax." *The Cambridge History of the English Language. Vol. IV: 1776–1997*. Ed. Suzanne Romaine. New York: Cambridge University Press, 1998. 197.

23. Smitherman, op. cit. 20.

24. Ibid.

25. Wolfram and Schilling-Estes, op. cit. 373.

26. Ibid.

27. Green, op. cit. 70–71.

28. John Russell Rickford and Russell John Rickford. *Spoken Soul: The Story of Black English*. New York: John Wiley, 2000. 121.

29. The Black Eyed Peas. "Imma Be." 2009.

30. Kesha Sebert, Lukasz Sebastian Gottwald, and Benjamin Levin. "Tik Tok." 2009.

31. Wolfram and Schilling-Estes, op. cit. 374.

32. Tony Jovenitti. "Without Popular Sports, Fans Need Entertained During the Summer." *The Pitt News* (12 Apr 2011): 12.

33. mftcf[@UXA.ECN.BGU.EDU. "Re: Some U.S. 'Midland' Regionalisms?" Online posting. *ADS-L* (American Dialect Society). 5 Dec 1993. <www.americandialect.org>. Qtd. in Thomas E. Murray, Timothy Frazer, and Beth Lee Simon. "*NEED* + Past Participle in American English." *American Speech* 71 (Autumn 1996): 256; for a thorough survey of the research on this construction, see Zach Maher and Jim Wood. "Needs washed." *Yale Grammatical Diversity Project: English in North America*. 2011. Updated by Tom McCoy (2015) and Katie Martin (2018). <http://ygdp.yale.edu/phenomena/needs-washed>.

34. Susan O'Mara. "In the Aftermath of the Brexit Vote." *Construction* (Jul/Aug 2016): 47.

35. Wolfram and Schilling-Estes, op. cit. 374.

36. Patrick J. Duffley. *The English Infinitive*. New York: Longman, 1992. 19–20.

37. Bent Conrad. *Referring and Non-referring Phrases: A Study in the Use of the Gerund and the Infinitive*. Copenhagen, Denmark: Akademisk Forlag, 1982. 146.

38. Claire Hoffman. "Seth Rogen's Wonder Years." *Rolling Stone* 1034 (6 Sep 2007): 77.

39. Victor Appleton (pseud.). *Tom Swift in the Land of Wonders.* "Chapter XIX: Poisoned Arrows." New York: Grosset and Dunlap, 1917.
40. Wolfram and Schilling-Estes, op. cit. 374.
41. Smitherman, op. cit. 24.
42. Dillard, op. cit. 47; see also McWhorter, *Talking,* op. cit. 34.
43. Wolfram and Schilling-Estes, op. cit. 372.
44. Rickford and Rickford, op. cit. 120.
45. James Paul Gee. *Social Linguistics and Literacies.* 3rd ed. New York: Routledge, 2008. 18; see also Green, op. cit. 54–63.
46. Rickford and Rickford, op. cit. 120.
47. Ibid. 120; see also Green, op. cit. 64–65.
48. Smitherman, op. cit. 25–26; Rickford and Rickford, op. cit. 120; see also Green, op. cit. 65–67.
49. William Labov. *Dialect Diversity in America: The Politics of Language Change.* Charlottesville, VA: University of Virginia Press, 2012. 63–64.
50. McWhorter, op. cit. 40–41.
51. John McWhorter. *Words of the Move: Why English Won't—and Can't—Sit Still (Like, Literally).* New York: Henry Holt and Co., 2016. 215.
52. McWhorter (Ibid. 217–218) also discusses quotative *like* (see 7.1.2.5), and a third contemporary use of *like* among younger American speakers, "easing *like*," which serves as a hedge to "cushion a blow," as in *This is, like, the only way to make it work.* Taken altogether, these three distinct-yet-common uses of *like*, along with the older prepositional use, can make it sound like young people are, like, using this one word all the time.
53. Smitherman, op. cit. 19; see also John R. Rickford. *African American Vernacular English: Features, Evolution, Educational Implications.* Malden, MA: Blackwell, 1999. 6.
54. Wolfram and Schilling-Estes, op. cit. 372.
55. Smitherman, op. cit. 19.
56. See also Dillard, op. cit. 45.
57. Rickford, op. cit. 6.
58. Dillard, op. cit. 45. These sentences imply that, because the man is habitually *here every night* (in the bar; hanging out with his male friends), he also routinely or habitually doesn't really want a girlfriend.
59. Op. cit. 47–54.
60. Op. cit. 372–373.
61. Dwight Grant, Graham Nash, Kanye West. "The Truth." 1999.
62. Op. cit. 373.
63. Rickford and Rickford, op. cit. 18.
64. Dillard, op. cit. 47.
65. Rickford, op. cit. 6; see also Green, op. cit. 54–60; McWhorter, *Talking,* op. cit. 34.
66. Rickford and Rickford, op. cit. 118.
67. Ibid.
68. Ibid. 119.
69. Ibid.
70. Rickford, op. cit. 6.
71. Ibid.
72. Charles Carpenter Fries. *American English Grammar: The Grammatical Structure of Present-Day English with Especial Reference to Social Differences or Class Dialects.* English Monograph No. 10, National Council of Teachers of English. New York: D. Appleton-Century Co., 1940. 194.
73. Revelation 11:15. *King James Bible.* 1611.

74. Isaiah 21:9. *King James Bible.* 1611.
75. Matthew 28:6. *King James Bible.* 1611.
76. Fries, op. cit. 194.
77. Wolfram and Schilling-Estes, op. cit. 377.
78. Fries, op. cit. 194.
79. Spears, Arthur K. "The Black English Semi-Auxiliary *Come.*" *Language* 58 (Dec 1982): 852; see also Green, op. cit. 73–74.
80. Sara Paretsky. *Burn Marks.* New York: Delacorte Press, 1999. 145.
81. George M. Anderson. "The Crisis in Drug Treatment." *America* 174.9 (Mar 1996): 10.
82. Jim Mullen. "I'm Dreaming of a Lottery Windfall." *The Evening Sun* (Norwich, NY). 11 Dec 2012.
83. To learn more about how to appropriately—and responsibly—use passive voice to improve your writing, you should consult Joseph M. Williams and Joseph Bizup. "Lesson Four: Characters." *Style: Lessons in Clarity and Grace.* 12th ed. New York: Pearson, 2017. See especially 54–59.
84. Walidah Imarisha. "Portrait of a Young Zombie in Crisis." *Obsidian* 42.1/2 (2016): 94+.
85. Peter Garnham. "The Visible Life." *Horticulture* 111.5 (Sep/Oct 2014): 23.
86. David Crystal. *Making Sense of Grammar.* Harlow, Essex, UK: Pearson/Longman, 2004. 158.
87. Jamey Keaten. "Colombia's Botero Wins Ninth Stage of Tour; Armstrong Looks Less Invincible." *The Canadian Press.* 15 July 2002.
88. "Sean Payton on March for Our Lives Protests: 'I was hoping to be able to attend.'" *University Wire.* 27 Mar 2018.
89. Deborah S. Leiter. "Healthy Acts of Resistance: A Book Review." *Assertive Spirituality.* 2 Feb 2019. <http://assertivespirituality.com>.
90. Tennessee Office of the Governor. "Gov. Bill Lee Announces New Investment in School Safety." 21 Feb 2019. <www.tn.gov/>.
91. Michael Schwirtz. "Report to Criticize City on Pace of Rikers Reforms." *The New York Times* (16 Oct 2015): A28.
92. Laura Miller. "Cutting 'Em Down to Size." *Slate.com.* 5 Sept 2017.
93. Ted Berg. "FTW: Barry Bonds and Roger Clemens Will Make Hall, So Deal with It." *For the Win. USA Today.* 18 Jan 2017.
94. "The Hot Spot: Onto Every Dance a Little Rain Must Fall." *The Daily Courier* (Prescott, AZ). 26 July 2012.
95. Carlton Thompson. "Astros Summary." *Houston Chronicle.* 18 June 1997.
96. Nestor Ramos. "Governors Have Been Trying to Fix the State Police for Decades." *The Boston Globe.* 6 Apr 2018.
97. Carlton Cuse. Qtd. in Amber Dowling. "*Bates Motel*'s Carlton Cuse Breaks Down Shocking Season-Finale Death." *The Hollywood Reporter.* 15 May 2011.
98. Bruce Reese, President and CEO, Hubbard Radio. "Committee Hearing, House Committee on the Judiciary, Subcommittee on Intellectual Property, Competition and the Internet." Washington, DC. *CQ Transcriptions.* 28 Nov 2012.
99. Sam Donaldson. "The Roundtable: The Week's Politics." *This Week.* ABC. 7 Jul 2010.
100. Philippians 4:8. *King James Bible.* 1611.
101. Aaron Kupchik. "The NRA's Faulty School-security Proposal." *washingtonpost.com.* 30 Dec 2012.
102. Keegan-Michael Key. Qtd. in Maxwell Strachan. "Hollywood Talent Agency Ditches Usual Oscar Party in Favor of Anti-Trump Rally." *Huffington Post.* 26 Feb 2017.
103. Chris McCormick. "Mother, Godfather, Baby, Priest." *Desert Boys.* New York: Picador/Macmillan, 2017. 9.

104. Katie Atkinson. "Toward Artificial Argumentation." *AI Magazine* 38.3 (Fall 2017): 26.

105. Milwaukee County Judge John Siefert. Qtd. in Don Behm. "Milwaukee County Sheriff David Clarke Accepts Department of Homeland Security Job." *USA Today.* 17 May 2017.

106. However, the subjunctive *be* and *were* can be inverted with their subject, as in, "Were she a man, Solo probably would have been excused for being passionate." ("Hope Solo Spearheaded the USWNT Lawsuit for Equal Pay." *washingtonpost. com.* 12 Jul 2019), and "Be he alive or be he dead," which we will see below. Note how this usage feels very formal and old fashioned.

107. Iris Johansen. *Chasing the Night.* New York: St. Martin's, 2010. 4.

108. "Medlink." Ft. Wayne, IN Citilink. 2018. <www.fwcitilink.com>.

109. Steve Hofstetter. "The Waiting Is the Hardest Part." *collegehumor.com.* 15 Dec 2002.

110. "Minutes of the Clemson University Board of Trustees." Clemson University. 21 Apr 2000. <http://media.clemson.edu/>.

111. Samuel M. Brownell. "If I Were Starting to Teach." *National Association of Secondary School Principals (NASSP) Bulletin* 52.330 (1 Oct 1968): 1.

112. G. David Nordley. "To Climb a Flat Mountain." *Analog Science Fiction & Fact* 129.12 (Dec 2009). 73.

113. Megan Crepeau. "Judge, Top Prosecutor Engage in Shouting Match over Jailing of Pregnant Woman." *chicagotribune.com.* 15 Aug 2017.

114. Noel Langley, Florence Ryerson and Edgar Allen Woolf. *The Wizard of Oz.* Film. MGM, 1939.

115. Bob Schieffer. *CBS Evening News.* 26 Jul 2009.

116. Robert Wright. "Can Buddhist Practices Help Us Overcome the Biological Pull of Dissatisfaction?" *Fresh Air.* NPR. 7 Aug 2017.

117. Nicoleao. "Look at Me! I'm Sewing My Own Skirt!" Online posting. 9 Mar 2014 <https://en.paperblog.com/>.

118. John Loyd. "Overall Satisfied—App Improvements Needed." Customer Review of "Andoer HDV-Z20 Portable 1080P Full HD Digital Video Camera." *Amazon. com.* 5 Feb 2017.

119. Shane Kuhn. Qtd. in John Wenzel. "Colorado's Shane Kuhn Writes His Second Act with *Intern's Handbook.*" *The Denver Post* (7 May 2014): 1C.

120. Glenderlyn Johnson. Qtd. in Marjorie Coeyman. "Black Books: The Word on the Street." *Christian Science Monitor.* 28 Aug 2001.

121. "Alabama Shakes' Brittany Howard on Small-Town Life, Big-Time Music." *Fresh Air.* NPR. 28 Jan 2016.

122. Hopper, Paul J. *A Short Course in Grammar: A Course in the Grammar of Standard Written English.* New York: Norton, 1999. 109.

123. Gee, op. cit. 19.

124. Dillard, op. cit. 43–44.

125. Rickford, op. cit. 6.

126. Wolfram and Schilling-Estes, op. cit. 375.

127. Rickford and Rickford, op. cit. 115.

128. Ibid.

129. Op. cit. 375.

130. Mark Lester. *Grammar and Usage in the Classroom.* 2nd ed. New York: Longman, 2000. 54.

131. Based on Salvatore R. Martoche. "Hearing of the Crime Subcommittee of the House Judiciary Committee. Subject: Role of Federal Law Enforcement." *Federal News Service,* 15 Nov 1995.

Chapter 7

Verb Phrases (VP)

A finite verb functions as the head of a verb phrase (VP); the VP, in turn, functions as a predicate (VP:PRED). A VP <u>always</u> contains a complete finite verb (with or without AUX and/or semi-AUX verbs) and may include complements and/or modifiers. The <u>modifiers</u> of a verb are all adverbial, whether adverb phrases, adverbial PPs, or other adverbial constituents. <u>Adverbial modifiers</u> of a verb may appear before or after or even in the middle of the **complete verb**: *I <u>hardly</u> **slept**. I **slept** <u>in my own bed</u>. I **have** <u>not</u> **slept**.*

Adverbial modifiers of verbs always occur near the verb. Adverbial constituents further removed from the verb typically have some other function in the sentence or dependent clause, the most common being sentence modifier. We will examine adverbs and adverb phrases in Chapter 8, and we will more fully examine adverbials (including sentence modifiers) and their functions in 11.3.

Verb complements generally appear after the verb and come in a range of patterns. Verbs are often categorized by the kinds of complements they can take.

7.1 Verb Complements

Remember that a complement is a constituent that *completes* the sense of another constituent, such that, without the complement, the first constituent would not be grammatically well formed or clearly convey the same essential meaning. While modifiers are optional constituents, complements are obligatory constituents. In the sentence *Townshend threw his guitar*, the NP *his guitar* completes the sense of the verb *threw* by telling what *Townshend* (the subject of the verb) *threw*. Without the NP complement *his guitar*, the sentence would make little sense. Certainly, we can contrive contexts in which the sentence ?*Townshend threw* would make sense. But in most contexts, the verb *threw* requires an NP or other nominal as a complement. In this case, that nominal complement is called a direct object (DO) because it names the thing upon which the subject (*Townshend*) directly performs the action named by the verb (*threw*).

As a native speaker of English, you don't have to think very much about what kinds of complements or patterns of complement can accompany a particular verb: you just know what "sounds right." In this part of our discussion of grammar, we will spend most of our energy focusing on the most common kinds and patterns of verb complementation in English. In her book *English Verb Classes and Alternations*, linguist Beth Levin identifies over 300 different verb complement patterns in English, grouping verbs by both meaning and the patterns of their complements. If you're curious, once you've learned the terminology and concepts in this chapter, you should be ready (with some patience) to take on Levin's discussion.[1] We will have some reference below to verbs related by meaning (for example, quotative verbs, which take people's quoted words as their complements), but mostly we will focus on broader categories of complement pattern characterized by form and function, rather than meaning.

A good way to identify the complement of the verb is to start by analyzing the basic structure of the whole sentence. Once you have identified the verb and its subject, you want to ask a question that will lead you to identify the complement of the verb. For most sentence patterns, particularly the most common verb complement patterns, there will be a common-sense question, based on the subject and the verb, a question that will lead you to identify the verb complement(s)—and so their pattern.

Some of the terms for verb complement patterns (intransitive, transitive, and ditransitive) may be familiar, and you will regularly see them in dictionary entries.

7.1.1 Verbs with No Complements: Intransitive Verbs

Some verbs in English take no complement at all. Such verbs are called intransitive verbs since they don't take an NP:DO:

> I *am shopping*.
> I *slept*.
> She's *talking*.
> My back *aches*.
> The old willow tree *fell*.

In the first sentence, the verb *am shopping* needs no complement: in SE, we do not "shop something" the way we "throw something." An even better example is the verb *sleep* in the second sentence: after all, we don't "sleep something"; we just *sleep*. When you are looking for an example to serve as a benchmark for intransitive verbs, I recommend using the verb *sleep* as your point of comparison: we almost always use the verb *sleep* intransitively. But sometimes, a verb that is usually intransitive can be used transitively: that is, it can be used with a following nominal that completes a particular sense or meaning of the verb, as in, *I slept*[V] *a deep, refreshing sleep*[DO]. In this sentence, *slept* is followed by a complement, an NP:DO. *Sleeping* becomes something I did to something, and *slept* is now transitive.

When we label a verb by its complement pattern, we need to remember that, while a verb may commonly be used without a complement, the verb is not, itself, intransitive. The appropriate complement pattern label depends on the context of actual use. *Slept* without a complement is intransitive; *slept* + NP:DO is <u>transitive</u>.

Also, do not be confused by an adverb or adverbial phrase following the intransitive verb and modifying it, as in *I slept **well**. I slept **in a ditch**. Well* and *in a ditch* are each adverbial; both answer adverbial questions about the verb, telling *how* the *sleeping* went (*well*) and *where* the *sleeping* took place (*in a ditch*). By contrast, in *I slept a deep, refreshing sleep*, the NP *a deep, refreshing sleep* does not tell something adverbial about the *sleeping*: it doesn't answer *how, where, when*, or any of the other adverbial questions (see Chapter 8). Also, *well* and *in a ditch* are modifiers of the verb *slept*, both by providing adverbial information about the act of *sleeping* and by being optional constituents: if we drop them from the sentence, the sentence is still well formed. Arguably, when we drop *a deep, refreshing sleep* from its sentence, the sense of the verb *slept* changes. Also, neither *well* nor *in a ditch* is functioning as a sentence modifier since we cannot move either to the front of the sentence without sounding like Yoda (though, as usual, we could imagine a context where at least the second sentence would be well formed; try to make one up): ***Well** *I slept*. ?***In a ditch*** *I slept*. Because we can drop them without changing the sense of the verb, we know they are modifiers, but because we can't move them, we know that these modifiers are attached to the verb.

7.1.2 Verbs with One Complement

7.1.2.1 Monotransitive Verbs

Monotransitive verbs are those that take a single NP or other nominal (for simplicity, we'll just talk about NPs) as a complement when that NP is functioning as a direct object (DO) of the verb. The NP:DO names the PATIENT: the person, place, or thing that is directly receiving the action or that is being acted upon by the AGENT, who is the doer of the action named by the verb. Monotransitive verbs are very common in English usage, and transitive verbs—those verbs that take a direct object as a complement (even when they take other complements as well)—are generally regarded as the strongest and clearest verbs because they can express most directly who is doing what to whom.

> *Franz*[NP:SUBJ] *kicks*[V] <u>*the ball*</u>[NP:DO].
> *Orville*[NP:SUBJ] *chased*[V] <u>*Wilbur*</u>[NP:DO].
> *Edison*[NP:SUBJ] *has developed*[V] <u>*a light bulb*</u>[NP:DO].
> *The Bronte sisters*[NP:SUBJ] *wrote*[V] <u>*several novels about human passions*</u>[NP:DO].

In each sentence, the verb is followed by an NP. Each of these NPs completes the sense of the verb by telling what or who received the action or on what or whom the action was performed. Thus, *the ball* was the thing *kicked*, and *Wilbur* was the person Orville *chased*.

To identify the NP:DO, and to determine whether the NP following the verb is functioning as a DO, you need to ask, "What did S V?" That is, what did *Franz kick*? The answer to this question determines that there is a DO and identifies what it is: *the ball*. If, for a given sentence, you get an answer to the question "What did S V?" then you know you have a transitive verb and possibly a monotransitive verb.

The passivization test: An even better test for whether a verb is transitive, a test that we will use frequently, is the passivization test. Above, we looked at the passive voice as simply involving the placement of a *be* AUX before the past participle form of the MV within the complete verb. But we can also think about the passive voice as a rearrangement of the order of constituents in an active voice sentence. Only sentences with transitive verbs—verbs that take an NP:DO as one of their complements—can be rearranged from active to passive voice. That fact will prove very useful for identifying verbs and for understanding the relationships among constituents in a sentence.

Here's how to transform a sentence with an active voice transitive verb into a sentence with a passive voice verb (note: even in a passive voice construction, the verb is still being used transitively):

$$\underline{\text{ACTIVE}}: \text{NP}_{[\text{AGENT}]}:\text{SUBJ} + \text{MV} + \text{NP}_{[\text{PATIENT}]}:\text{DO} \rightarrow$$
$$\underline{\text{PASSIVE}}: \text{NP}_{[\text{PATIENT}]}:\text{SUBJ} + \textit{BE}\ \text{AUX} + \text{MV}_{[\text{PAST PARTICIPLE}]} + \{\textit{BY} + \text{NP}_{[\text{AGENT}]}:\text{PCOMP}\}$$

That looks too much like algebra, doesn't it? But it's not so bad, really. It translates like this: in the active voice sentence, we have a first NP that names the AGENT: the character performing the action named by the verb. That first NP is functioning as the subject of the sentence ($\text{NP}_{[\text{AGENT}]}:\text{SUBJ}$), followed by a complete verb ending in the main verb (MV), followed by a second NP that names the PATIENT: the person or thing being acted upon or receiving the action. That second NP is functioning as the direct object ($\text{NP}_{[\text{PATIENT}]}:\text{DO}$). The complete verb in an active voice sentence may, of course, have more constituents than just the MV, but the MV is the crucial constituent for the shift from active to passive voice.

There might also be sentence modifiers, or modifiers of the verb, but since they are modifiers, and therefore optional, we do not need to worry about them here: we're just dealing with <u>obligatory</u> constituents of the sentence.

When we convert the complete verb from active to passive voice, the structure of the whole sentence changes: the $\text{NP}_{[\text{PATIENT}]}$ in the active voice sentence becomes the subject of the passive voice sentence, followed now by the complete verb, which is changed into the passive form by adding an appropriate form of the *be* AUX (the AUX that marks the passive voice) right before the MV and changing the form of the MV to the past participle. We then make the $\text{NP}_{[\text{AGENT}]}$ the complement of the preposition *by* (or much more rarely *with*) in a prepositional phrase at the end of the sentence. Note that the PP that comprises BY + NP[AGENT] is often deleted from the passive voice version of the sentence. The function of this PP is labeled as AGENTIVE since the NP that is the complement of the PP names the agent performing the action named by the verb. In traditional grammar, the agentive phrase is understood as modifying the verb; more recent work in grammar treats the agentive phrase as having a greater role in the sentence because the *by* phrase includes the NP naming the actual AGENT in the sentence. We'll discuss agentive PPs more fully in 11.3.3.

In the following examples note the shifting of the NP:SUBJ and the NP:DO, as well as the changes in the <u>complete verb</u> with the addition of the ***be* AUX**:

Active: *Franz <u>kicks</u> the ball.*
Passive: *The ball **is** <u>kicked</u> by Franz.*
Passive, agentive PP deleted: *The ball **is** <u>kicked</u>.*

Active: *Orville <u>chased</u> Wilbur.*
Passive: *Wilbur **was** <u>chased</u> by Orville.*
Passive, agentive PP deleted: *Wilbur **was** <u>chased</u>.*

Active: *Edison <u>has developed</u> a light bulb.*
Passive: *A light bulb <u>has **been** developed</u> by Edison.*
Passive, agentive PP deleted: *A light bulb <u>has **been** developed</u>.*

Active: *The Bronte sisters <u>wrote</u> several novels about human passions.*
Passive: *Several novels about human passions **<u>were</u>** <u>written</u> by the Bronte sisters.*
Passive, agentive PP deleted: *Several novels about human passions **<u>were</u>** <u>written</u>.*

Active: *Henry <u>was watching</u> Edsel.*
Passive: *Edsel <u>was **being** watched</u> by Henry.*
Passive, agentive PP deleted: *Edsel <u>was **being** watched</u>.*

Active: *This gun <u>shot</u> the victim.*
Passive: *The victim **<u>was shot</u>** with this gun.*
Passive, agentive PP deleted: *The victim **<u>was shot</u>**.*

In the transformation of a sentence from active to passive voice, the tense stays the same and remains marked on the first word (AUX or MV) of the verb.

The final sentence, about the gun, is an example of the less common PP using *with* instead of *by*. In such sentences, the function of the PP (e.g. *with this gun*) is said to be "instrumental" rather than agentive since the PCOMP (here, *this gun*) is the <u>instrument</u> by which someone performed the action named by the verb, rather than the actor or agent who used the instrument to perform the action (we're putting responsibility for the action on the instrument, rather than the actor). We can use such instrumental passives when we don't know or are avoiding saying who the agent is. Note that *This gun shot the victim* sounds a little strange, while the passive voice sentence with the instrumental PP sounds more normal, since the passive version seems to imply that <u>someone</u> used the gun to perform the action of shooting.

When analyzing the complement of a verb that is in the passive voice, you must first convert the verb—and the whole sentence—to its active voice order.[2] Linguists commonly think of the passive voice construction as a rearrangement or transformation of the default active voice construction.

Though we may think of a verb as typically monotransitive, we sometimes use such verbs intransitively. For example:

Monotransitive: *I broke the vase.*
Intransitive: *The vase <u>broke</u>.*

Monotransitive: *Franz kicked the ball.*
Intransitive: *Franz played in a grueling slug fest today. He just <u>kicked</u> and <u>kicked</u>.*

Monotransitive: *I wrote a novel.*
Intransitive: *What did you do this summer? I <u>wrote</u>.*

In each of these pairs of examples, the verb (*broke, kicked, wrote*) in the second version is <u>intransitive</u> because, although it is commonly monotransitive (as in the first version), it is here being <u>used</u> intransitively.

7.1.2.2 Intransitive Linking Verbs and Copular *be* with a Nominal or Adjectival Subject Complement

Linking verbs take a single nominal (most often an NP) or ADJP as a complement when that nominal or ADJP is functioning as a subject complement (SC). When a form of *be* appears as the MV in a clause, this is the copular use of *be*; it, too, takes an SC. The NOMINAL:SC (called in traditional grammar a "predicate nominative") or ADJP:SC (called in traditional grammar a "predicate adjective") either renames the subject or names a quality that is being ascribed or joined to the subject. Copular *be* is the most commonly used verb form in English.

*Shopping **is**$_{[V]}$ my favorite activity$_{[NP:SC]}$.*
*We **were being**$_{[V]}$ foolish$_{[ADJP:SC]}$.*
*Franz **seems**$_{[V]}$ sluggish$_{[ADJP:SC]}$.*
*She **has become**$_{[V]}$ the most well-traveled woman in the world$_{[NP:SC]}$.*[3]
*The crowd **grew**$_{[V]}$ restless$_{[ADJP:SC]}$.*
*Dinner **smells**$_{[V]}$ delicious$_{[ADJP:SC]}$.*

Here is a fairly complete list of linking verbs; they can be broadly divided into two subcategories:

> **Linking verbs that indicate a state**: *act, appear, be, fall, feel, look, prove, remain, seem, smell, sound, stay, taste*
> **Linking verbs that indicate a result**: *become, get, grow, run, turn*

Linking verbs of state can all be paraphrased by copular *be*:

> *Imelda acts/appears/feels/looks/seems/sounds/<u>is</u> happy.*
> *The stew smells/tastes/<u>is</u> delicious.*
> *We all remained/stayed/<u>were</u> calm.*
> *First-quarter earnings fell/<u>were</u> short of estimates.*[4]
> *Wiretaps and bugs proved/<u>were</u> effective in garnering intelligence about gangsters.*[5]

Linking verbs of result can all be paraphrased by *become*:

> *After hours of waiting, the crowd got/grew/turned/<u>became</u> restless.*
> *When the teacher left the room, the children ran/<u>became</u> wild.*

Linking verbs are intransitive. They do not take a DO as a complement and cannot be put in the passive voice. Given a sentence in which the MV is a form of *be* and the complement of the verb is a nominal, you may be tempted to identify that nominal as a DO. Consider the difference between *Franz kicked the goalie*, and *Franz is the goalie*. In the first sentence, as we try to parse it into its major constituents, we will first identify the verb as *kicked*. To find the subject, we ask, *Who kicked?* The answer, *Franz*, identifies the NP:SUBJ. *Franz kicked <u>whom</u> or <u>what</u>?* then identifies the DO as *the goalie*, the person or thing immediately affected by *Franz kicking*. If we proceed through the same questions for the second sentence, we seem to get the same result: *is* is the verb; *Who is?* gives us the subject, *Franz*; and *Franz is <u>who</u> or <u>what</u>?* gives us *the goalie*, which then appears to be an NP:DO. How do we know that, in the second sentence, this is not the case and that, instead, *the goalie* is an NP:SC?

There are two things we have to remember: first, when the MV is some form of *be*, and the complement of the verb is a nominal, the NOMINAL:SUBJ and the NOMINAL:SC name <u>the same</u> person or thing. When the MV is transitive, the NOMINAL:SUBJ and the NOMINAL:DO do not usually name the same thing: in a sentence like *Franz kicked the goalie*, part of the meaning is usually not that "Franz is the goalie." Except in the context of a joke or a science fiction story about human cloning, the only time that the NOMINAL:SUBJ and the NOMINAL:DO name the same thing in a single sentence is when we use a reflexive pronoun for the DO, as in *Franz kicked <u>himself</u>*.

Second, you just have to remember that when the main verb is a form of *be*, the complement of the verb will be a NOMINAL:SC; an ADJP:SC; or, as we will see in a moment, an adverbial functioning as an SC. Since *be* is the most common MV in the language, you will see plenty of examples of it, and that should help you learn to recognize it and its complements. When you are reading for this and other classes and you need a little brain-break, look for forms of *be* as an MV and try to identify their complements.

Some linking verbs do have alternate transitive meanings. Consider the difference between *Imelda felt happy* and *Imelda felt the wind*. In the former sentence, *felt* is an intransitive linking verb that can be paraphrased by a form of *be* (*Imelda was happy*), and it cannot be put in the passive voice (**Happy was felt by Imelda.*). In the latter sentence, *felt* cannot be paraphrased by a form of *be* (**Imelda was the wind.*), the NPs *Imelda* and *the wind* name two different objects, and the sentence can be put in the passive voice (*The wind was felt by Imelda.*). Look at the list of linking verbs, and see which ones also have transitive uses.

Copular *be* is not the auxiliary verb *be*. Consider the difference between *Imelda is driving my '65 Mustang* and *Imelda is caring and kind*. In the first sentence, the complete verb, *is driving*, includes the AUX *be* marking the progressive aspect. We know this because we can drop the AUX and change the MV to its finite form and have a sentence with much the same meaning as the original: *Imelda drives my '65 Mustang*. By contrast, in the second sentence, the complete verb is just *is*—that is, copular *be*; if we drop that verb and try to change *caring* into a finite verb, we do not get a comparable sentence: **Imelda cares and kind*. Many words ending in *-ing* have developed into full-on adjectives that are simply homophones of the present participle; some, such as *interesting*, are much more common as adjectives than as verbs. We can show the difference between these two sentences' verbs another way. Because *caring* is an adjective, it is gradable: *Imelda is more caring and kind than Franz*. The adjective can also take an intensifying adverb as a modifier: *Imelda is very caring and kind*. By contrast, *driving* is not gradable and cannot take an intensifying adverb as a modifier: **Imelda is more driving my '65 Mustang than Franz. *Imelda is very driving my '65 Mustang.*

7.1.2.3 Intransitive Copular be with an Adverbial Subject Complement

Copular *be* can also take adverbial complements. These adverbials are always locative complements (LC, naming a location—a *where*) or temporal complements (TC, naming a time—a *when*):

Copular *be* with an LC:

You[NP:SUBJ] *are*[V] *here*[AdvP:LC].
They[NP:SUBJ] *were*[V] *home*[NP:ADVERBIAL:LC].
Edsel[NP:SUBJ] *is*[V] *up the creek*[PP:ADVERBIAL:LC].

Copular *be* with a TC:

The party[NP:Subj] *was <u>yesterday</u>*[NP:Adverbial:TC].
The deadline[NP:Subj] *is <u>right now</u>*[AdvP:TC]!

In each of these sentences, the copular *be* works just as it does with a nominal or adjectival subject complement, connecting the location or time named in the complement back to the subject NP. We will also call this kind of complement a subject-complement (SC).

A few other linking verbs, including *fall, remain,* and *stay,* can also take adverbial SCs; and the verbs *lie* and *live* can function as linking verbs that only take adverbial SCs:

Next year July 4th falls/<u>is</u> on a Tuesday.
We remained/stayed/lay/lived/<u>were</u> there.

In each sentence, the adverbial following the verb is a complement and not a modifier; it cannot be moved or deleted and leave a well-formed sentence:

The party was yesterday.
*The party was. *Yesterday the party was. *The party yesterday was.

Next year July 4th falls on a Tuesday.
*Next year July 4th falls. *Next year on a Tuesday July 4th falls. *Next year July 4th on a Tuesday falls.

7.1.2.4 Intransitive Verbs with an Adverbial Complement

There are a number of verbs that are not linking verbs but routinely take adverbial complements. These verbs break down into three large groups, based on the kinds of meaning conveyed by the complements (we have just seen two of them):

- Locative complements (LC), which tell *where* an action takes place or the goal of an action: where the action is directed or where it ends.
- Manner complements (MC), which tell *how* an action is performed.
- Temporal complements (TC), which tell *when,* or the time during which an action was performed.

LC: *They*[NP:Subj] *went*[V] ***home***[NP:Adverbial:LC].
Edsel[NP:Subj] *drives*[V] ***up the street***[PP:Adverbial:LC].
Tiresias[NP:Subj] *the prophet sees*[V] ***into the future***[PP:Adverbial:LC].
Peary[NP:Subj] *gazed*[V] ***northwards***[AdvP:LC].

MC: *They*[NP:Subj] *went*[V] ***by train***[PP:Adverbial:MC].
Edsel[NP:Subj] *drives*[V] ***well***[AdvP:MC].

> *Tiresias the prophet*[NP:Subj] *sees*[V] **without using his**
> **eyes**[PP:Adverbial:MC].

TC: *They*[NP:Subj] *went*[V] **on Tuesday**[PP:Adverbial:TC].
   Edsel[NP:Subj] *drives*[V] **daily**[AdvP:TC].
   Tiresias the prophet[NP:Subj] *sees*[V] **all of the time**[NP:Adverbial:TC].
   I[NP:Subj] *looked*[V] **at three o'clock**[PP:Adverbial:TC].

We know that the adverbials in the predicate are complements and not modifiers because we can neither drop them, nor move them without changing their meaning. And we know that these verbs are not linking verbs because they do not simply rename or ascribe a quality to the subject but name an action for which the adverbial in the predicate is the location or goal.

We can identify the complement in each type of sentence by using questions. Once we have found the verb and subject, to identify the verb type and to find the verb complement, we need to use an adverbial question.

- For an LC, the question needs to be related to location, such as "Where V S?" or "Where does/did S V?" *Where does Edsel drive? Edsel drives up the street*.
- For an MC, the question needs to be related to manner, such as "How does/did S V?" or "In what manner did S V?" or "By what means did S V?" *How did they go? They went by train. In what manner does Tiresias see? Tiresias sees without using his eyes*.
- For a TC, the question needs to be related to time, such as "When do/does/did S V?" or "At what time do/does/did S V?" *When did they go? They went on Tuesday. At what time did you look? I looked at three o'clock*.

In each case, the verb itself suggests the question: one *goes/went* somewhere, or by means of some vehicle, at some time or on some day. One *drives/drove* somewhere; one *sees* somehow or in some particular manner; one *looks* at some particular time. The answer to the question will be the verb complement.

These verbs are intransitive because they do not take a Nominal:DO as a complement; even when the complement appears to be a nominal, as in *They went home*, it is functioning adverbially. Try putting these verbs in the passive voice. Unfortunately, we have a number of phrases that are nominal in form but typically adverbial in function, all related to time, including *all of the time, today, yesterday, tomorrow, Monday/s* (as in *I work Mondays*, which implies *on Monday*), *every day, someday, some days*, etc.

7.1.2.5 Intransitive Quotative Verbs

Quotatives are verbs that are used to mark a complement as being reported speech, writing, or thought, where the words or thought are commonly placed in quotation marks. In the sentence *Nancy said, "He'll be happy to do it,"* the verb *said* is a quotative, and the quoted speech, "*He'll be happy to do it,*" is the verb complement. The form of that complement is a sentence (Sent), and that Sent is functioning as a quotation (Sent:Quot). Quoted language can take the widest possible variety of forms. Consider this sentence: *I asked Imelda where the Mustang was and she replied, "In the garage."* Here, the quotative verb is *replied*, and its complement, "*in the garage,*" is a PP:Adverbial:Quot.

We also commonly use quotative verbs with indirectly quoted speech, writing, and thought, placing the quoted material in a noun clause: *I asked Imelda where the Mustang was. Imelda knew where the Mustang was.*

SE quotative verbs include *say, reply, state, utter, ask, mumble, write, think, wonder,* and the whole range of verbs that can be used to introduce a quotation in speech or writing. In written English, especially in fictional narrative, we find a broad range of verbs used as quotatives. In spoken SE the most common quotative is *say*; however, the non-Standard quotatives *be like; go;* and, to a lesser degree, *be all* are growing in usage.

Since about 1980, **quotative *be like*** has spread swiftly across the English-speaking world. We often see this usage in reported dialogue:

> *He was like, "Where do you wanna go?"*
> *I was like, "I dunno."*
> *He was like, "Okay."*
> *I was like, "Where are we going?"*
> *He was like, "Don't worry about it."* (qtd. in Singler)[6]

While predominantly associated with the speech of White middle-class teenagers, by 2005 *be like* was being used at least some of the time by "virtually all native speakers of American English under the age of forty."[7]

The older SE quotatives *go* and *say* are limited in their use to marking the speaker's rendering of what someone might literally have said. Likewise, studies of the use of *be like* have found that the third-person forms are used with direct, expressed speech, but unlike *go* and *say*, the first-person forms are most frequently used to introduce inner speech (e.g. *I was like, "I am so screwed"*). Quotative *like* is also commonly used with descriptions of gestures (*So I'm like* [speaker shrugs]).[8] Yet, although quotative *be like* has spread among American English users, there are some constructions in which its use is not yet fully integrated; specifically, while it is possible, it is still unusual to hear *be like* used in negative constructions and interrogatives where the use of *say* still sounds perfectly normal: among adult speakers of American English, one is more likely to hear:

> *When people ask what I do, I don't say, "I own a store."*
> *Did he say, "You're cute"?*

than

> *When people ask what I do, I'm not like, "I own a store."*
> *Was he like, "You're cute"?*[9]

However, the use of *be like* in both negative and interrogative constructions is significantly more common among American English speakers born after 1980. As with many changes in a language, the use of quotative *be like* seems to have originated with younger speakers and to be "trickling up" and spreading as those speakers age. It seems likely that, within a generation or so, quotative *be like* will be as completely integrated into common usage as quotative *say*.

According to Singler, **quotative *go*** came into common use in American English in the 1940s. We still find it in sentences like:

> *He goes, "Do you know the make and model of your phone?"*
> *She goes to me, "By the way, do you have the tickets?"*[10]

However, as a quotative verb, *go* seems to be giving way to *be like*; that the usage is in transition can be illustrated by utterances like the following, taken from an interview of pro wrestler The Miz: *She <u>goes</u> to me, "We're doing a photo shoot." I'm <u>like</u>, "Okay. Great."*[11]

Quotative *be all* is a still later addition to non-Standard American English. Originating in California, its use still seems to be limited to younger speakers in California and the immediately surrounding states. Singler offers the following examples:

> *Then, after a while, I was all, "See you later, good luck!"*
> *And my sister's all, "It's soooooooo weird. The teachers are actually talking to us."*
> *He was all, "I don't know."*

Singler posits that, just as *be like* seems to be superseding *go* as a non-Standard quotative, *be all* may be poised to supersede *be like*.[12]

Some speakers of AAVE also use a **non-Standard quotative *say***, as in *I told him, say, "Where you going?"* Wolfram and Schilling-Estes note that this usage "is rapidly receding. In fact, quotative *be like* is taking over in [AAVE], as it is in other dialects."[13]

7.1.3 Verbs with Two Complements

7.1.3.1 Ditransitive Verbs

The next three verb complement patterns each include two complements. They therefore require more care if we are to identify them consistently. In each case, the key is finding the borders between the constituent phrases that make up the predicate and correctly identifying the form of each constituent.

Of these three complement patterns, you are probably most familiar with ditransitive verbs: those that take two NPs or other nominals as complements, where each complement functions as an object of the verb. The first nominal functions as the indirect object (IO), while the second functions as the DO. Remember that the DO is the person, place, or thing acted upon by the subject. In *Martina hit the ball*, the NP *the ball* is functioning as the DO, naming the thing *Martina hit*. In a sentence with two NPs after the verb, the first functioning as the IO and the second as the DO, the second NP names the person, place or thing acted upon, while the first, the NP:IO, names the recipient or beneficiary of the act. In the sentence *The judge gave Martina*[NP:IO] *the point*[NP:DO], *the point* is the thing acted upon, the thing that *the judge gave*; *Martina* names the recipient or beneficiary of the act (of the judge's giving). So, once again, to find the DO, we have to ask, "What did the S V?" In this case, "What did *the judge give?*" And the answer, *the point*, is the DO. To find the IO, we must ask, "To or for whom did the S V DO?" In this case, "To whom did *the judge give the point?*" The answer, *Martina*, is the IO. Note that *Martina* cannot be the DO since *Martina* was not the thing *given*. That is, *Martina* is not the thing acted upon directly by the subject. Also note that the two NPs, *Martina* and *the point*, name two distinct and different objects.

The preceding discussion suggests the first of two ways to identify this type of verb and its complements. That first way is the "*to/for*" test: the IO always names the person or thing *to* or *for* whom the action was done; to find the IO and DO, we can revise the sentence by putting the nominal that we think is functioning as the DO right after the verb and the nominal that we think is functioning as the IO at the end of the sentence in a PP beginning with *to* or *for*:

> *The judge gave Martina*[NP:IO] *the point*[NP:DO].
> *The judge gave the point*[NP:DO] *to Martina*.
>
> *Chef Antoine made me*[NP:IO] *a peanut butter sandwich*[NP:DO].
> *Chef Antoine made a peanut butter sandwich*[NP:DO] *for me*.

We encounter the ditransitive construction as both V + IO + DO and V + DO + PP. When we encounter the latter form of the ditransitive construction, we will say that the PP:IO.

The second test for identifying ditransitive verbs is to passivize the sentence. If the nominals following the verb are, in fact, the IO and DO, respectively, they both name objects that are being acted upon (albeit in different ways: one <u>directly</u> and one <u>indirectly</u>). We can change the sentence from active to passive voice in either of two ways: by moving either the NOMINAL:DO or the NOMINAL:IO to the subject slot:

> *The judge gave Martina*[NP:IO] *the point*[NP:DO].
> NOMINAL:**DO**→SUBJ: *The point*[NP:SUBJ] *was given (to) Martina (by the judge)*.
> NOMINAL:**IO**→SUBJ: *Martina*[NP:SUBJ] *was given the point (by the judge)*.
>
> *Chef Antoine made me*[NP:IO] *a peanut butter sandwich*[NP:DO].
> NOMINAL:**DO**→SUBJ: *A peanut butter sandwich*[NP:SUBJ] *was made for me (by Chef Antoine)*.

NOMINAL:IO→SUBJ: $I_{[NP:SUBJ]}$ *was made a peanut butter sandwich* (*by Chef Antoine*).

This class of verbs are called "ditransitive" precisely for this reason: they are transitive in two ways, with respect to two different objects.

All three versions of each example sentence have the same basic meaning, but each has a different focus or emphasis. In 10.1.5, we will discuss how passivizing a sentence allows us to alter the order of information for the purpose of controlling information flow.

7.1.3.2 Complex Transitive Verbs with a Direct Object and a Nominal or Adjectival Object Complement

In this verb complementation pattern, the NP:DO follows the verb directly. The second complement is called an object complement (OC) because, just as an SC refers back to or renames the subject of a linking verb or copular *be*, so an OC refers back to or renames the DO. Thus, in *Nancy considered Ron*$_{[NP:DO]}$ *an excellent husband*$_{[NP:OC]}$, *Ron* is the DO—the person whom *Nancy considered. An excellent husband* is the OC: it refers back to or renames the DO, *Ron*. As with linking verbs and their SCs, we can paraphrase the relationship between the DO and the OC by putting an appropriate form of *be* between them. Thus, *Nancy considered Ron an excellent husband* implies that, in Nancy's consideration, *Ron <u>was</u> an excellent husband*. Inserting *be* between the DO and the OC is the surest test for identifying verbs that take a DO and an OC.

However, object complements come in two flavors: although the DO is always a nominal, the OC may be either a nominal <u>or</u> an ADJP. Thus the verb complementation pattern may be either V + NP:DO + <u>NP:OC</u> or V + NP:DO + <u>ADJP:OC</u>:

> *He considered the investment*$_{[NP:DO]}$ *safe*$_{[ADJP:OC]}$.[14]
> *He considered the investment*$_{[NP:DO]}$ *a safe one*$_{[PRONP:OC]}$.[15]
> *Nancy found rock climbing*$_{[NP:DO]}$ *exciting*$_{[ADJP:OC]}$.
> *We elected him*$_{[NP:DO]}$ *president*$_{[NP:OC]}$.
> *The magician waved his wand and made his assistant*$_{[NP:DO]}$ *a peanut butter sandwich*$_{[NP:OC]}$. (meaning 'the magician turned the assistant into a peanut butter sandwich')

We now have two verb complement patterns in which the complement consists of two NPs: NP:IO + NP:DO and NP:DO + NP:OC—and even an example of a verb, *make*, that can take <u>both</u> complement patterns. There are two ways to distinguish between them: first, while the DO and OC name the same thing, the IO and DO must name different—or at least distinct—things. The *be* insertion test helps us here. The test will work for the DO + OC complement but not for the IO + DO complement: *The judge gave Martina*[NP:IO] *the point*[NP:DO] does not imply that *Martina was the point*. But *We elected him*[NP:DO] *president*[NP:OC] implies that *he was president*. Likewise, the *to/for* test, which works for identifying the IO and DO, will not work with DO + OC verbs: *The judge gave Martina*[NP:IO] *the point*[NP:DO] means *The judge gave the point to Martina*. But you cannot turn *We elected him*[NP:DO] *president*[NP:OC] into **We elected president to/for him*.

Further, because it includes a NOMINAL:DO in its complement, we can put DO + OC verbs in active or passive voice:

Active: *We elected him*[NP:DO] *president*[NP:OC].
Passive: *He was elected president by us*.

However, we cannot make the OC the subject of a passive voice sentence: **President was elected him by us*.

7.1.3.3 Complex Transitive Verbs with a Direct Object and an Adverbial Object Complement

Verbs that take a <u>DO</u> and an adverbial object complement (OC) look—and are analyzed—much like verbs that take a DO + NOMINAL:OC or ADJECTIVAL:OC.

Martina put the racket[NP:DO] ***there***[AdvP:OC].
Orville found the propeller[NP:DO] ***in the sand***[PP:ADVERBIAL:OC].
We left the boxes[NP:DO] ***on the living room rug***[PP:ADVERBIAL:OC].
We hung the plants[NP:DO] ***near the window***[PP:ADVERBIAL:OC].

As with verbs that take a DO and a nominal or adjectival OC, we can easily check that the adverbial OC is related to the DO by the *be* insertion test: if we can put an appropriate form of *be* between the DO and the following adverbial (AdvP or PP:ADVERBIAL) and have a reasonable paraphrase of the relationship between those two phrases, then the adverbial is functioning as an OC—that is, it is related to the DO. So, *Martina put the racket*[NP:DO] ***there***[Adv:OC] implies that *the racket was there*; *Orville found the propeller*[NP:DO] ***in the sand***[PP:OC] implies that *The propeller was in the sand*. Also, unlike sentence modifiers, these adverbials are not easily moved.

?There, Martina put the racket. *Martina, there, put the racket.
?In the sand Orville found the propeller. *Orville, in the sand, found the propeller.
*In the living room we left the boxes. *We, in the living room, left the boxes.
?Near the window we hung the plants. *We, near the window, hung the plants.

Another clue to identifying this verb complement pattern is that these verbs take locative adverbials—adverbials that answer the question, "Where did S V DO?" "Where did *Martina put the racket?*" There.

Finally, like all verbs that take a NOMINAL:DO as part of their complement, DO + ADVERBIAL:OC verbs can be passivized:

> *The racket was put there (by Martina).*
> *The propeller was found in the sand (by Orville).*
> *The boxes were left on the living room rug (by us).*
> *The plants were hung above the entry (by us).*

7.1.3.4 Complex Transitive Verbs with a Direct Object and a Participle Phrase

A number of verbs in English take as complements a <u>NOMINAL:DO</u> followed by a participle phrase functioning as a verb complement (PARTP:VC). Included among the verbs that take this complement pattern are verbs of sensation (*see, smell, hear, feel*) and observation (*discover, observe, admire, catch, find*).

> *We found <u>Fred</u>[NP:DO] **playing pinball**[PARTP:VC].*
> *I see <u>Fred</u>[NP:DO] **seated in the front row**[PARTP:VC].*
> *I left <u>the kids</u>[NP:DO] **watching Lilo and Stich**[PARTP:VC].*
> *They heard <u>the choir</u>[NP:DO] **singing "Scarborough Fair."**[PARTP:VC]*

At first blush, these verbs look like DO + OC verbs; we can passivize them and the NOMINAL:DO moves to the front while the PARTP stays after the verb:

> <u>Active Voice</u>: *We found Fred playing pinball.*
> <u>Passive Voice</u>: *Fred was found (by us) playing pinball.*

Also, as with the DO + OC verbs, we can paraphrase the relationship between the NP:DO and and PARTP:OC by putting a form of *be* between them: *We found Fred playing pinball* implies *Fred <u>was</u> playing pinball.* But the relationship between the NOMINAL:DO and the PARTP is different from that between the DO and OC. Unlike the DO + OC verbs, the NOMINAL:DO is also the agent of the participle in the PARTP:VC. The form of *be* we insert between the NOMINAL:DO and the PARTP is not copular *be*; rather, it is a *be* AUX, the progressive auxiliary, which turns the non-finite *playing* into the finite verb *was playing* and casts the agent *Fred* into the role of subject.

Addionally, with the NOMINAL:DO + PARTP:VC verbs, we know the PARTP is a complement because, if we move the PARTP, its reference changes:

> *Maizie saw <u>Alex</u> **sitting at the bar**.*
> ***Sitting at the bar**, Maizie saw Alex.*
> *Maizie, **sitting at the bar**, saw Alex.*

When we move the PARTP to the beginning or middle of the sentence, we understand it as referring to the nearest noun: in the first version, it is *Alex* who is sitting at the bar. In the other two versions, it is *Maizie* who is *sitting at the bar*. These PARTPs are not sentence modifiers but are clearly tied to their role and location as complements of the verb and as incomplete predicates attached to their agent. Even these non-finite verbs must always have a stated or implied agent (see 12.1.4). This sort of sentence can be paraphrased in two different ways:

> *Maizie saw Alex sitting at the bar.*
> *Maizie saw Alex, who was sitting at the bar* (*who was sitting at the bar* is an adjective clause modifying *Alex*); or,
> *Maizie saw Alex while he was sitting at the bar* (*while he was sitting at the bar* is an adverb clause, describing an action that was concurrent with the action of *Maizie saw Alex*).

These NOMINAL:DO + PARTP:VC constructions express both kinds of meaning at the same time. In 12.1, we will look at this complementation pattern again.

7.1.3.5 Complex Transitive Verbs with Direct Object and Infinitive Phrase

A number of verbs in English take as complements an <u>NP:DO</u> followed by an infinitive phrase functioning as a verb complement (INFP:VC). There are many verbs in English that take this complement pattern, particularly verbs of persuasion or obligation:

> *Walt told <u>him</u>[NP:DO] **to go and do it**[INFP:VC].*[16]
> *Maizie persuaded <u>Fred</u>[NP:DO] **to play pinball with us**[INFP:VC].*
> *The law requires <u>the fiduciary</u>[NP:DO] **to be other-regarding**[INFP:VC].*[17]
> *I convinced <u>a prosecutor</u>[NP:DO] **to consent to DNA testing**[INFP:VC].*[18]
> *The injury forced <u>him</u>[NP:DO] **to miss the opener**[INFP:VC].*[19]

As with the NOMINAL:DO + PARTP:VC verbs, these verbs can be passivized, although the agentive PP can go directly after the verb or at the end of the sentence:

> <u>Active</u>: *Walt told him to go and do it.*
> <u>Passive</u>: *He was told (by Walt) to go and do it. He was told to go and do it (by Walt).*

We can paraphrase the relationship between the NP:DO and and INFP:OC by putting a form of *be* between them: *Walt told him to go and do it* does imply that *He <u>is</u> to go and do it*. But once again, this *be* is not the copular: we are not renaming the PRON *he* by the INFP *to go and do it*. Nor is the form of *be* here the progressive AUX. Rather, *be to*, as we saw above, is a semi-modal verb, meaning *must* or *should*. As with the NOMINAL:DO + PARTP:VC verbs above, the NOMINAL:DO is the agent of the INFP, the doer of the action named by the infinitive. Finally, as with the NOMINAL:DO + PARTP:VC, we cannot move the INFP from its complement slot without, at best, altering the reference of the INFP and, at worst, sounding like Yoda:

> *Walt told <u>him</u> **to go and do it**.*
> **To go and do it Walt told <u>him</u>*
> **Walt **to go and do it** told <u>him</u>.*

We will examine this verb complement pattern further in 12.2.

7.1.3.6 Transitive Quotative Verbs

Some quotative verbs take two complements: a DO (naming the person being spoken to) and the quotation:

> Active Voice: *The caption accompanying the Shearer layout asked the reader*[NP:DO]*, "Can This Be the Same Girl?"*[SENT:QUOT][20]
> Passive Voice: *The reader was asked (by the caption accompanying the Shearer layout), "Can This Be the Same Girl?"*

> Active Voice: *Nancy told me*[NP:DO] *there was a remote possibility that she could be transferred from Houston to Atlanta.*[NCL:QUOT][21]
> Passive Voice: *I was told (by Nancy) there was a remote possibility that she could be transferred from Houston to Atlanta.*

> Active Voice: *No one had informed him*[NP:DO] *when his client would be extradited.*[NCL:QUOT][22]
> Passive Voice: *He had not been informed (by anyone) when his client would be extradited.*

As with intransitive quotative verbs, the quotation may be direct (taking quotation marks) or indirect, and the quote may take a variety of grammatical forms.

Non-Standard quotatives: When the quote is an embedded question in the form of a noun clause, as in SE *I asked him if he could go with me*, AAVE speakers may instead use inversion of the subject with the AUX to form the embedded question: *I asked him <u>could he</u> go with me* see (10.1.1).[23]

7.1.4 Phrasal Verbs (PV)

"Grammar books" almost never discuss phrasal verbs (PV), a huge set of remarkably common, highly idiomatic constructions that are notoriously difficult for non-native speakers to master. PVs combine a verb with a particle (a little word that, in other contexts, would function as a preposition or adverb) to create a compound that behaves like a single word. The meaning of a PV is not simply the sum of the literal meanings of the verb and the particle, and the meaning of a PV can always be paraphrased by a single word.

> *In Kansas, a breeder had to <u>put down</u> 1,200 dogs after failing to inoculate them for distemper.*[24] (*put + down* ≠ "euthanize")
> *Saddam Hussein's troops <u>put down</u> the rebellion.*[25] (*put + down* ≠ "quelled")
> *He tried to <u>beat up</u> his lawyer right before jury selection.*[26] (*beat + up* ≠ "pummel")
> *Everything will <u>turn out</u> for the best in the long run.*[27] (*turn + out* ≠ "conclude")

English dictionaries list many of these idioms and their meanings. *The Longman Dictionary of Phrasal Verbs in English* lists over 12,000 of them, in a variety of patterns, including PVs that take more than one particle; PVs that take one or more particles and a NOMINAL:DO; and even PVs that take PPs as part of their complement.[28]

On the one hand, PVs have patterns of form much like other compounds and categories of words. On the other hand, those patterns affect what comes after and completes the meaning of verbs. I have chosen to treat PVs along with verb complements. Sometimes, the particle can be separated from the verb and placed after a NOMINAL:DO (which leads to the notorious "ending a sentence with a preposition"; more on that below) so that the PV and the verb complement seem to be tangled together. Often the particle stays close to the verb, even when the verb is moved under passivization.

7.1.4.1 Intransitive PVs

Of the most common varieties of PVs, the first we will examine are intransitive, comprising only a verb and a particle and needing no complement:

> *When I asked about it, he <u>blew up</u> at me.*[29]
> *After the Cuban missile crisis, Khrushchev <u>backed down</u> once. He couldn't <u>back down</u> a second time.*[30]
> *The truck <u>broke down</u>.*[31]
> *We all <u>sat around</u> and wondered, wow, who did this?*[32]
> *I tend to let things just <u>blow over</u>.*[33]

In some of these examples, an adverbial phrase follows the PV (*at me; once*), but in each case, the adverbial is just a modifier and not a complement. In each example, the particle cannot be dropped or moved: if we try to move the particle away from the verb, we get some of our best examples yet of Yoda-speak—or plain nonsense:

*Up he blew. *He up blew.
*Down he couldn't back. *He down couldn't back.
*Down the truck broke. *The truck down broke.
*Around we all sat. *We all around sat.
*Over I tend to let things just blow. *I over tend to let things just blow.

The simplest way to think about these intransitive PVs is as if they were just one word. But this puts us up against the pseudo-rule about not ending a sentence with a preposition. The first thing to get over is that these particles are not functioning as prepositions. The words that look like prepositions here are post-posed particles, each a part of a phrasal idiom (the term "preposition" applies to these words when they are "pre-posed," appearing before an NP). To avoid ending some of these sentences with a "preposition," you would have to change the wording: *He just blew up* would have to become *He just exploded*; *He couldn't back down* would have to become *He couldn't retreat.* In each case, the change to avoid the pseudo-rule results in a change of tone: the one-word paraphrase of a PV is typically a Latinate word and therefore sounds more formal than the commonly Germanic PV idioms. Sometimes there is simply no way to avoid ending a sentence with a particle.

7.1.4.2 PVs with One Particle and One Complement

7.1.4.2.1 TRANSITIVE SEPARABLE PVs

Many PVs take a NOMINAL:DO. These verbs fall into two subclasses: in the first, the NOMINAL:DO may precede or follow the particle: that is, the **particle** may be *separated* from the verb by the NOMINAL:DO.

I can let **down** my hair with you.[34] I can let my hair **down** with you.
McCullum knocked **over** a cocktail table.[35] McCullum knocked a cocktail table **over**.
Saddam Hussein's troops put **down** the rebellion. Saddam Hussein's troops put the rebellion **down**.
He tried to beat **up** his lawyer. He tried to beat his lawyer **up**.

With transitive separable PVs, when we substitute a PRON for the NOMINAL:DO, the particle must follow the NP:

I can let **down** my hair with you. I can let my hair **down** with you.
*I can let **down** it with you. I can let it **down** with you.

> *McCullum knocked **over** <u>a cocktail table</u>. McCullum knocked <u>a cocktail table</u> **over**.*
> **McCullum knocked **over** <u>it</u>. McCullum knocked <u>it</u> **over**.*

Because of this restriction on particle movement, we can use the pronoun replacement test to distinguish transitive <u>separable</u> PVs from transitive <u>inseparable</u> PVs, which we will look at below.

Also, the transitive separable PVs can be easily confused with a verb followed by a PP. For example, the sentence *McCullum knocked over a coffee table* might be parsed in two ways:

> *McCullum*[NP:SUBJ] *knocked*[V] *over a coffee table*[PP:ADVERBIAL:VC].
> *McCullum*[NP:SUBJ] *knocked over*[PV] *a coffee table*[NP:DO].

There is a simple test to tell which parse is correct: if the sentence includes a NOMINAL:DO, then it can be passivized:

> <u>Active voice</u>: *McCullum knocked over a cocktail table. McCullum knocked a cocktail table over.*
> <u>Passive voice</u>: *A coffee table was knocked over (by McCullum).*

No matter which active voice version of the sentence we start with, the passive voice version keeps the particle with the verb, showing that the combination of V + PARTICLE works as a compound. By contrast, if the constituent following the verb actually were a PP:ADVERBIAL:VC, it would sound odd if the sentence were passivized:

> <u>Active</u>: *He slept*[V] *in a sleeping bag at his office*[PP:ADVERBIAL:VC].[36]
> *"<u>Passive</u>": **A sleeping bag at his office was slept in by him.*

Since there is no actual NOMINAL:DO in this sentence, the sentence cannot be put into the passive voice.

7.1.4.2.2 TRANSITIVE INSEPARABLE PVs

In the second type of transitive PV, the particle cannot be separated from the verb (e.g. *We <u>toyed</u> **with** the idea*; **We <u>toyed</u> the idea **with**)*. Rather, although it <u>appears</u> that we have an idiomatic expression in which a verb must be followed by a PP that begins with a particular preposition, instead we have a PV whose complement consists of a particle followed by a NOMINAL:DO. We know that the combination of PARTICLE + NOMINAL that follows the verb is not simply a PP since, when we passivize the sentence, the particle stays with the verb when the nominal shifts to the subject position:

Active: *We <u>toyed with</u> the idea of tackling all 30 miles of the Hong Kong Trail in one day.*[37]

Passive: *The idea of tackling all 30 miles of the Hong Kong Trail in one day was <u>toyed with</u> (by us).*

Active: *Farmers in the tropics <u>rely on</u> this breed.*

Passive: *This breed is <u>relied on</u> (by farmers in the tropics).*[38]

Active: *Baby-yoghurt-loving bears <u>broke into</u> Brooklyn Decker's cars.*

Passive: *Brooklyn Decker's cars were <u>broken into</u> (by baby-yoghurt-loving bears).*[39]

Passivization shows that the nominal is functioning as a DO; because the particle stays with the verb after passivization, we know we have a PV.

7.1.4.3 Transitive PV with a Second NP Verb Complement

These PVs are also transitive: the nominal after the verb functions as a DO, and the sentence can be passivized. But rather than a single particle being tied to the verb, both the particle and a following second NOMINAL:VC are tied to the verb so that they stay together in the passive voice version of the sentence. As with other PVs, the combination of the verb and the particle has a particular idiomatic meaning.

Active voice: *Pat Boone's agent talked him$_{[NP:DO]}$ into$_{[PARTICLE]}$ making this film$_{[NOMINAL:VC]}$.*

Passive voice: *Pat Boone was talked into making this film (by his agent).*[40]

Active voice: *We asked the waiter$_{[NP:DO]}$ about$_{[PARTICLE]}$ our order$_{[NP:VC]}$.*[41]

Passive voice: *The waiter was asked about our order (by us).*

Active voice: *The 200 people that didn't want me in the job stacked the odds$_{[NP:DO]}$ against$_{[PARTICLE]}$ me$_{[NP:VC]}$.*

Passive voice: *There were probably 200 people that didn't want me in that job. And so you know Washington as well as I know Washington. The odds were stacked against me in the job (by the 200 people that didn't want me in it).*[42]

In some verbs in this category, the relationship between the NOMINAL:DO and the following PARTICLE + NOMINAL is like that between a DO and an OC: *They stacked the odds against me* means *The odds <u>were</u> against me.* In some cases, the NOMINAL:DO can be deleted: we can say, *We asked the waiter about our order*, or we can delete the NP:DO *the waiter* and just say, *We asked about our order.* In the latter sentence, the verb is *asked about* (V + PARTICLE), an inseparable PV, and *our order* is the NP:DO; we can passivize the sentence, and the particle stays with the verb: *Our order was asked about (by us).*

7.1.4.4 Transitive PV with Two Inseparable Particles

We will not exhaust the number and variety of PV patterns, but we will look at just a couple more that suggest some of their range. Some transitive PVs take two inseparable particles:

Active Voice: *Since we have a job, we put*[V] *up*[PARTICLE1] *with*[PARTICLE2] *those conditions*[NP:DO].[43]
Passive Voice: *Since we have a job, those conditions are put up with (by us).*

Active Voice: *I think they'd look*[V] *down*[PARTICLE1] *on*[PARTICLE2] *me*[NP:DO].[44]
Passive Voice: *I think I would be looked down on (by them).*

Active Voice: *Obama barged*[V] *in*[PARTICLE1] *on*[PARTICLE2] *a private meeting of the developing countries*[NP:DO].[45]
Passive Voice: *A private meeting of the developing countries was barged in on (by Obama).*

Active Voice: *The faithful look*[V] *forward*[PARTICLE1] *to*[PARTICLE2] *the great day of the Lord*[NP:DO] *as a time of triumphant celebration.*
Passive Voice: *Among the faithful, the great Day of the Lord is looked forward to as a time of triumphant celebration.*[46]

7.1.4.5 PVs with Two Particles and Two Complements

7.1.4.5.1 TRANSITIVE PV WITH TWO SEPARABLE PARTICLES AND AN NP:VC

Just when you thought verb complementation couldn't get any wackier, we have an idiomatic pattern in which a separable PV also takes a second particle and a nominal as a complement. When we shift the verb to passive voice, the first particle stays with the verb, although the second particle and the attached NOMINAL:VC may appear before or after the PP:AGENTIVE. And we know that the nominal after the second particle functions as a VC and that the combination of the second particle and the following nominal is not some kind of PP functioning as a modifier because we can neither drop nor move it without creating an inversion that sounds like Yoda:

Active Voice:

The Beast may have rage issues, but he mostly takes[V] *his anger*[NP:DO] *out*[PARTICLE1] *on*[PARTICLE2] *the inanimate furniture*[NP:VC].[47]
The Beast may have rage issues, but he mostly takes[V] *out*[PARTICLE1] *his anger*[NP:DO] *on*[PARTICLE2] *the inanimate furniture*[NP:VC].

Passive Voice:

The Beast's anger is mostly taken out on the inanimate furniture (by him).
The Beast's anger is mostly taken out (by him) on the inanimate furniture.

*Deletion; *Movement:

*The Beast takes his anger out. ?On the inanimate furniture the Beast takes his anger out.

Active Voice:

What business had a small-grain farmer such as he was with all those books? Books were fine for a rich man. But Sully would fill[V] *up*[PARTICLE1] *his head*[NP:DO] *with*[PARTICLE2] *whatever was in them*[NP:VC].[48]
Sully would fill[V] *his head*[NP:DO] *up*[PARTICLE1] *with*[PARTICLE2] *whatever was in them*[NP:VC].

Passive Voice:

Sully's head would be filled up with whatever was in the books (by Sully reading them).
Sully's head would be filled up (by Sully reading the books) with whatever was in them.

*Deletion; *Movement:

*Sully would fill his head up. ?With whatever was in them Sully would fill his head up.

7.1.4.5.2 TRANSITIVE PV WITH TWO INSEPARABLE PARTICLES AND AN NP:VC

Here's an example of one last PV pattern: *Clark talked him*[NP:DO] *out*[PARTICLE1] *of*[PARTICLE2] *it*[NP:VC]. It is transitive, and as in the preceding pattern, the two particles and the NOMINAL:VC move with the verb:

Active voice: *Clark talked him*[NP:DO] *out*[PARTICLE1] *of*[PARTICLE2] *it*[NP:VC].[49]
Passive voice: *He was talked out of it (by Clark).*

7.2 Summary of Verb Complement and Phrasal Verb Patterns

7.1.1 No Complement (Intransitive)
7.1.2 One Complement:

   7.1.2.1 V + NP:DO (Transitive or Monotransitive Verbs)
   7.1.2.2 V + NP/ADJP:SC (Intransitive Linking Verbs and Copular *be* with Nominal or Adjectival Subject Complement [SC])
   7.1.2.3 BE + ADVP:SC/PP:ADVERBIAL:SC (Intransitive Copular *be* with Adverbial Subject Complement [SC])

7.1.2.4 V + ADVERBIAL:AdvC (Intransitive Verbs with Adverbial Complement [AdvC])

7.1.2.5 V + QUOT (Intransitive Quotative Verbs)

7.1.3 Two Complements:

7.1.3.1 V + NP$_1$:IO + NP$_2$:DO (Ditransitive Verbs)

7.1.3.2 V + NP:DO + NP/AdjP (Complex Transitive Verbs with Direct Object [DO] and Object Complement [OC])

7.1.3.3 V + NP:DO + AdvP/PP:ADVERBIAL:OC (Complex Transitive Verbs with Direct Object [DO] and Adverbial Object Complement [OC])

7.1.3.4 V + NP:DO + PartP (Complex Transitive Verbs with Direct Object [DO] and Participle Phrase [PartP])

7.1.3.5 V + NP:DO + InfP (Complex Transitive Verbs with Direct Object [DO] and Infinitive Phrase [InfP])

7.1.3.6 V + NP:DO + QUOT (Transitive Quotative Verbs)

7.1.4 Phrasal Verbs

7.1.4.1 Phrasal Verbs with One Particle and No Complement: V + PARTICLE (Intransitive Phrasal Verbs)

7.1.4.2 Phrasal Verbs with One Particle and One Complement:

7.1.4.2.1 V + PARTICLE + NP:DO (Transitive Separable Phrasal Verbs)

7.1.4.2.2 V + PARTICLE + NP:DO (Transitive Inseparable Phrasal Verbs)

7.1.4.3 Phrasal Verbs with One Particle and Two Complements: V + NP:DO + PARTICLE + NP:VC (Transitive Phrasal Verbs with a Second NP Verb Complement)

7.1.4.4 Phrasal Verbs with Two Particles and One Complement: V + PARTICLE$_1$ + PARTICLE$_2$ + NP:DO (Transitive Phrasal Verbs with Two Inseparable Particles)

7.1.4.5 Phrasal Verbs with Two Particles and Two Complements:

7.1.4.5.1 V + NP:DO + PARTICLE$_1$ + PARTICLE$_2$ + NP:VC (Transitive Phrasal Verbs with Two Separable Particles and an NP:VC)

7.1.4.5.2 V + NP:DO + PARTICLE$_1$ + PARTICLE$_2$ + NP:VC (Transitive Phrasal Verbs with Two Inseparable Particles and an NP:VC)

While this list includes all of the most common patterns of verb complementation and PVs, it is by no means complete. In fact, it would be impossible to construct a perfectly complete list of verb complement patterns and PVs in

English because the language keeps changing. But this list and the accompanying discussion should help you have some confidence about trying to identify patterns you haven't seen before.

Key Points

- A finite verb functions as the head of a verb phrase (VP); the VP, in turn, functions as a predicate (VP:PRED) in a sentence or dependent clause. A VP comprises a V, its modifiers (adverbials), and complement(s).
- There are hundreds of verb complementation patterns in English.
- The most common complementation patterns involve copular *be* (the most common MV in English), which takes a subject complement (SC); the SC may be nominal, adjectival, or adverbial.
- Also common are verbs whose complement includes an NP or other nominal functioning as a direct object (NOMINAL:DO). A verb with a DO as its complement is transitive and may be arranged in active or passive voice.
- Phrasal verbs (PV) comprise a verb and, at a minimum, one particle. Together, the V + PARTICLE combination forms a compound idiom whose meaning is not simply the sum of its parts. There are thousands of PVs in English, appearing in numerous patterns.

7.3 Exercises: Verb Complements and Phrasal Verbs

A. Made-up sentences: identify the verb complement pattern in each of the following sentences.

1. I went to the movies.
2. My brother bought me some popcorn.
3. He and I watched a Harrison Ford movie.
4. Of course, Ford played the hero.
5. The hero seemed unsure of himself.
6. The hero put down the treasure.
7. We found the character hard to tolerate
8. When the film was over, we had had enough of the dark.
9. We went out into the blinding daylight.
10. Movies are good on a rainy day.
11. We heard birds singing in the trees.
12. I wanted us to walk home.
13. Suddenly, it rained.
14. We played in the puddles.
15. That night, I slept well.

B. Real sentences: for each finite verb, identify the complete verb phrase; identify any modifiers of the verb; identify the complete complement of the verb; and identify the verb complementation pattern. Use the passage from Exercise 1.3B on pages 27–28, "Dog Belonging to Princess Anne Attacks Royal Maid."

Example:

(1) VP: *attacked a royal maid*
       Modifiers of V: none
       V: *attacked*
       Verb Complement: *a royal maid*
       Complementation Pattern: V + NP:DO (Monotransitive)

Figure 7.1

Notes

1. Beth Levin. *English Verb Classes and Alternations*. Chicago: University of Chicago Press, 1993.
2. I am indebted to fall 2007 student Brian Hyken for this observation.
3. Tom Junod. "Hillary Happy." *Esquire* 153.5 (May 2010): 82.
4. Ciara Linane. "Lowe's Earnings Are Still 'Some of the Best' in Retail: Credit Suisse." *MarketWatch* 24 May 2017.
5. Jack Kelly. "The Most Dangerous Institution." *American Heritage* 53.4 (Aug/Sep 2002): 30–40.
6. John Singler. "Like, Quote Me." *Do You Speak American? Sez Who?* New York: PBS, 2005. <www.pbs.org/speak/words/sezwho/like/> 27 Apr 2019. This article is a beautiful discussion of the complexities of this oft-maligned usage. Also see the discussion in 6.1.2.2 of *like* as it reinforces the imperfect aspect of a verb.
7. Ibid.
8. Federica Barbieri. "Quotative Use in American English: A Corpus-Based, Cross-Register Comparison." *Journal of English Linguistics* 33 (2005): 249.
9. Singler, op. cit.
10. Ibid.
11. Chuck Carroll. "WWE's The Miz and Maryse on Parenthood, Daniel Bryan, Her Return." *Sports. CBS.* 19 Jul 2018 <https://sports.cbslocal.com/>.
12. Singler, op. cit.
13. Walt Wolfram and Natalie Schilling-Estes. *American English*. 2nd ed. Malden, MA: Blackwell, 2006. 375.
14. Mary Earhart Dillon. *Wendell Willkie 1892–1944*. New York: J. B. Lippincott, 1952. 114.
15. William H. Brooks. *Holyoke Water Power Company, Petitioner, V. City of Holyoke*. Vol. XIX: 25 Feb to 6 Mar 1902. Boston: George H. Ellis, 1902. 267.
16. Bob Weis. Qtd. in Matt Novak. "X Atencio, Disney Animator and Co-Writer of the *Pirates of the Caribbean* Theme Music, Dies at 98." *Gizmodo.com*. 12 Sep 2017.
17. Robert H. Sitkoff. "The Fiduciary Obligations of Financial Advisers under the Law of Agency." *Journal of Financial Planning* 27.2 (Feb 2014): 42–49.
18. Molly Triffin. "Their Year of Living Fearlessly." *Cosmopolitan* 250.1 (Jan 2011): 118.
19. Jordan Raanan. "Odell Beckham Jr. Sustains Dislocated Finger, Slight Ankle Sprain." *ESPN.com*. 1 Oct 2017.
20. Patrick Keating. "Artifice and Atmosphere: The Visual Culture of Hollywood Glamour Photography, 1930–1935." *Film History* 29.3 (Fall 2017): 107.
21. "Commuter Couples." *Ebony* 8.10 (Aug 1993): 56.
22. Jake Halpern. "Bank of the Underworld." *The Atlantic* 315.4 (May 2015): 115.
23. William Labov, et al. *A Study of the Non-Standard English of Negro and Puerto-Rican Speakers in New York City. Final Report, Cooperative Research Project 3228*. Philadelphia: US Regional Survey, 1968. 296–300; see also John R. Rickford. *African American Vernacular English: Features, Evolution, Educational Implications*. Malden, MA: Blackwell, 1999. 8.
24. Paul Solotaroff. "The Dog Factory: Inside the Sickening World of Puppy Mills." *Rolling Stone* 1278/1279 (12 Jan 2017): 42+.
25. Elizabeth Farnsworth. "Protesting Kurds." *PBS Newshour* 17 Feb 1999.
26. Tresa Baldas. "Kwame Kilpatrick: I Tried to Beat Up My Lawyer Before Trial." *Detroit Free Press* 13 July 17.
27. Lyle Hurd. "Kathy Smith." *Total Health* 28.2 (Jun/Jul 2006): 17.
28. Rosemary Courtney. *The Longman Dictionary of Phrasal Verbs*. New York: Longman, 1983.

29. C. Stuart Hardwick. "Dreams of the Rocket Men." *Analog Science Fiction & Fact* 136.9 (Sep 2016): 83+.
30. Robert Groden. "Who Really Killed JFK?" *Larry King Live*. 27 Nov 1990.
31. Chhun Sun. "Early Risers Rewarded at Annual Bighorn Sheep Day at Garden of the Gods." *Colorado Springs Gazette*. 11 Feb 2017.
32. Gary Henderson. "Live to Tell: Sole Survivor." *48 Hours*. CBS. 5 Mar 2016.
33. Vanessa M. Villate. "Yoga for College Students: An Empowering Form of Movement and Connection." *Physical Educator* 72.1 (Late Winter 2015): 54.
34. Gordon Lish. "Jelly Apple." *Salamagundi* 194 (Spring 2017): 106+.
35. "Many NC Inmates Legally 'Innocent,' Still Jailed." *USA Today*; WFMY. 14 Jun 2012. <www.wfmynews2.com>.
36. Stephanie Clifford and Colin Moynihan. "Guilty of Fraud, Shkreli Grins and Shrugs It Off." *The New York Times*. 5 Aug 2017.
37. Lori Rackl. "Sense of Wander: The 30-Mile-Long Hong Kong Trail Gives Nature Lovers a Green Getaway from the Hustle and Bustle of the Big City." *The Chicago Sun-Times*. 26 Aug 2009.
38. Charles Siebert. "Food Ark." *National Geographic* 220.1 (Jul 2011): 108+.
39. Robyn Merrett. "Brooklyn Decker's Cars Were Broken into by Baby Yoghurt-Loving Bears." *People.com*. 28 Sept 2018.
40. "Trivia." *Journey to the Center of the Earth*. IMDb.com. N.d.
41. Todd Kliman. "Tuesday, September 25 at 11 AM." *Washingtonian.com*. 18 Sep 2012.
42. "One-On-One with Anthony Scaramucci; Scaramucci Speaks Out After Short WH Stint." ABC. 13 Aug 2017.
43. Bennett Heine. "*Aguantamos*: Limits to Latino Migrant Farmworker Agency in North Carolina Labor Camps." *Human Organization* 76.3 (Fall 2017): 244.
44. Geoffrey Hunt, et al. "Asian American Youth, the Dance Scene, and Club Drugs." *Journal of Drug Issues* 35.4 (Fall 2005): 723.
45. Steven Mufson. "A Bumpy Road to U.N. Climate Summit in Paris." *The Washington Post* (4 Nov 2015): A09.
46. Mike Mason. *The Gospel According to Job: An Honest Look at Pain and Doubt from the Life of One Who Lost Everything*. Wheaton, IL: Crossway, 2002. 220.
47. Peter Keough. "Beauty Gets the Spotlight, but What of the Beast?" *The Boston Globe*. 9 Mar 2017.
48. Bonnie Nadzam. "The Lady in Bonesweep." *Tikkun.org*. 14 Nov 2013.
49. John H. Richardson. "How the Attorney General of the United States Became Saddam Hussein's Lawyer." *Esquire* 147.2 (Feb 2007): 88–124.

Chapter 8

Adverbs (Adv) and Adverb Phrases (AdvP)

Adverbs are a mixed category, primarily comprising content words (e.g. *slowly, here, now, frequently*) but also including function words (e.g. *very, just, not*). In traditional grammar, the term "adverb" refers to words that modify a verb, adjective, or another adverb, telling *when, where, why, how, how much, how often, how long*, and other versions of those sorts of information. In reality, adverbs and AdvPs also modify whole sentences, dependent clauses, infinitive phrases, and participle phrases; and we have seen that AdvPs can function as several different types of verb complement. In 11.3, we will talk more generally about adverbial constituents, but for now, we start out by looking at garden variety adverbs.

Adverbs often end in *-ly*, and we can easily convert many adjectives to adverbs by adding *-ly*: for example, the Adj *light* becomes the Adv *lightly*. Of course, some local spelling conventions apply: *happy* becomes *happily*, not **happyly*. However, not all words that end in *-ly* are adverbs: *costly, crumbly, deadly, friendly, lovely, slatternly, slovenly*, etc. are all adjectives; these adjectives do not form adverbs by adding *-ly*. And many common adverbs do not end in *-ly* and are not derived from adjectives, including *far, fast, just, never, not, often, only, quite, rather, so, soon, too, very*, etc. *Not* (and its contracted form *n't*) is the most common Adv.

Also, like adjectives, adverbs come in two forms: gradable and absolute (or non-gradable). Gradable adverbs have three forms or degrees: the base, the comparative, and the superlative:

Base: *fast, happily, well*
Comparative: *faster, more happily, better*
Superlative: *fastest, most happily, best*

The three ways in which we conventionally form the different degrees of adverbs are much like the three ways in which we form the three degrees of adjectives. Gradable adverbs of one syllable generally take the endings *-er* and *-est* to mark degree. Gradable adverbs of two or more syllables typically take the words *more* and *most* to mark the comparative and superlative. *Well* is one of a small set of irregular exceptions: *well/better/best; badly/worse/worst; a* *little/less/the least; much/more/most.* Absolute or non-gradable adverbs do not show degree. Examples include the negative adverbs *not* and *never* and intensifying adverbs like *just, only, quite, rather, so, too,* and *very.*

Non-Standard adverbs: *-ly* absence: Wolfram and Schilling-Estes note that even in contemporary SE, "some adverbs that formerly ended in an *-ly* suffix no longer take *-ly.* Thus, in informal contexts, most general American English speakers say *They answered wrong* instead of *They answered wrongly.*" Likewise, American English speakers commonly say *I feel bad* rather than *I feel badly*; even street signs say *Go Slow,* not *Go Slowly.* In Southern varieties, "particularly Southern mountain varieties such as Appalachian and Ozark English," *-ly* absence extends to more words. "These items may be relatively unobtrusive (e.g. *She enjoyed life **awful** well*) or quite obtrusive (e.g. *I come from Virginia **original***)."[1]

> *Y'know a cold, cold heart sleeps **awful** well.*[2]
> "*As many times as they talk about me losing three Super Bowls, it would be **awful** nice to go because one win would erase all those losses.*"[3]
> "*But, you know, it's a **real** simple program.*"[4]
> *I could hear the owls and the wolves away off in the woods, and it seemed **terrible** still.*[5]

8.1 Adverb Phrases

Adverbs often appear alone, although they may appear with modifiers as the head of an adverb phrase (ADVP). In general, an ADVP takes the form [ADVP:MOD OF ADV] + ADV + [PP:ADVERBIAL: MOD OF ADV]. That is, an ADVP always has an adverb as its head, and it may take an ADVP as a pre-modifier and/or a post-modifying adverbial PP. ADVPs can function in five roles.

Complement of verb: Just as we saw with adverbial PPs, an ADVP can function as the complement of a verb:

> **SC**: *Winter is here.*[6]
> **LC**: *Imelda walked inside.*
> **TC**: *Secretary of State Madeleine Albright will go soon after.*[7]
> **MC**: *Machado has played well.*[8]
> **OC**: *Franz left the ball here.*

Modifier of verb: As a modifier of a verb (ADVP:MOD OF V), an ADVP will appear very close to the verb that it modifies. It can appear immediately after the verb, immediately before the verb, or even between an AUX and the MV:

> *She slept **well**.*
> *She slept **very** well.*
> *He **hardly** ate his dinner.*

*He <u>has</u> **hardly** <u>eaten</u> his dinner.*
*He **just barely** <u>beat</u> the storm.*
*I <u>do</u> **not** <u>like</u> green eggs and ham.[9]*
*We <u>did</u> **not quite** <u>make</u> it home.*

We know these ADVPs are modifiers because, if we drop them, the sentences are still well formed. Below, we will look at how we know that they are adverbial.

Sentence modifier: ADVPs commonly appear as sentence modifiers. As we've already seen, as sentence modifiers, ADVPs can be moved to three locations in the sentence: the beginning, the end, and between the subject and the verb.

<u>Very frequently</u>, my husband's work takes him away from home.
My husband's work takes him away from home <u>very frequently</u>.[10]
My husband's work <u>very frequently</u> takes him away from home.

Modifier of ADJ: ADVPs that modify adjectives are mostly intensifiers such as *very, so, too, extremely, hardly, terribly*, etc.

This is <u>very</u> good.
Charmin's <u>so squeezably</u> soft, it's irresistible![11]

Modifier of ADV: ADVPs that modify adverbs are also mostly intensifiers:

We have <u>hardly</u> ever seen anything of the kind.[12]
Cats were <u>so</u> well regarded in Ancient Egypt, because they kept homes free of dangerous creatures.[13]

Just as we did with adverbial PPs, we can sum up the features that define each of the functions of ADVPs:

	In this function is AdvP required or optional?		In this function is ADVP movable?	In this function, where is the ADVP located?
	required	optional		
VC	X		No	Usually after the verb
MOD OF V		X	Not usually	Usually immediately before or after the verb, or between AUX and V
SENTMOD		X	Yes	At the beginning or end of the clause, or between the SUBJ and PRED
MOD OF ADJ		X	Not usually	Before the ADJ
MOD OF ADV		X	Not usually	Before the ADV

8.2 Identifying Adverbs

There are three tests for identifying ADVs. The most general, which we have already encountered, is:

> **The adverb question test**: If we are testing whether a word or phrase complements a verb or modifies a verb, a clause, an adjective, or an adverb, if the word or phrase answers an adverb question about the verb, clause, adjective, or adverb, then the word or phrase is an adverbial that modifies or complements the verb, clause, adjective, or adverb. Adverb questions include *when, where, why, how, how much, how often, how long*, etc.

Adverbs provide particular kinds of information about qualities (named by adjectives and adverbials) and actions (named by verbs, clauses, and non-finite verb phrases). Those kinds of information include location in space (*where*) or time (*when*); reason (*why*); manner (*how; to what degree*); frequency (*how often*); amount (*how much*); and duration (*how long*). If you can bend one of those ADV questions around a word, then the word is an ADV. In the sentence *He hardly ate his dinner*, we know that *hardly* is an ADVP modifying the verb *ate* because it answers the ADV question, "How (in what manner; to what degree) did he eat his dinner?"

Note that ADVPs modifying verbs, adjectives, or adverbs are like adjectives that modify nouns in that they cannot be moved to a different position relative to the word they modify:

> *He hardly ate his dinner.* **He ate hardly his dinner.*
> *This is very good.* **This is good very.*
> *We have hardly ever seen anything of the kind.* **We have ever <u>hardly</u> seen anything of the kind.*

And they cannot be separated from the word they modify: **Hardly he ate his dinner.* **He ate his dinner hardly.*

The close connection between the ADVP and the verb, ADJ, or ADV it modifies provides us with a simple test for whether or not an ADVP is functioning as a sentence modifier or clause modifier: the movability test.

> **The movability test for ADVP:SENTMOD and ADVP:CLAUSEMOD**: Given a word or phrase before the subject, after the predicate, or in the slot between the subject and the verb of a clause, if you can move that word or phrase from its position to one or both of the other clause modifier positions without changing the meaning of the clause, then the word or phrase you have moved is a clause-modifying adverbial—which we refer to as a sentence modifier (SENTMOD) or clause modifier (CLAUSEMOD).

In *My husband's work takes him away from home very frequently*, we know that *very frequently* is an ADVP because it answers the question, "How often does my husband's work take him away from home?" We know that it is a modifier because it is <u>optional</u>: if we drop it from the sentence, the sentence is still well formed: *My husband's work takes him away from home*. And we know that it is a sentence modifier because we can <u>move</u> it, as we saw above.

We <u>can</u> use the adverb question test to identify ADVPs modifying adjectives—although the question those ADVPs answer will almost always be *how*. In the sentence *We may get a completely unreliable story*,[14] the ADVP *completely* answers the question of *how unreliable* or *to what degree unreliable*.

ADVPs can modify adjectives, but ADVPs cannot modify nouns. Sometimes, however, in an NP like *a completely unreliable story*, we may be unsure as to which words are adjectives, which are adverbs, and what is modifying what. To determine which words are adverbs, first find the head noun of the NP—in this case, *story*. Then apply

> **The pair test for adverbs modifying adjectives**: Generally, if a substantive word in an NP *cannot* be paired up with the head noun but can be paired with a nearby adjective, then that word is an adverb modifying an adjective.[15]

Let's start at the beginning of the NP *a completely unreliable story*, and pair each modifier with the head noun *story*: the determiner *a* pairs with *story* in *a story*, so *a* is specifying the noun *story*. However, *completely* does not pair with *story*: **completely story*, while it might be poetic, is not a well-formed phrase in any variety of English. The ADJ *unreliable* pairs with *story*: *unreliable story* sounds right, so *unreliable* is an ADJ. We can pair *completely* with *unreliable* to make a well-formed ADJP, *completely unreliable*. Therefore, *completely* is an ADVP modifying the adjective *unreliable*.

Non-Standard adverbs: There are a number of non-Standard adverbs that appear in (and often help to mark) particular vernacular varieties of English.

Liketa: Common in Appalachian English, the non-Standard ADV *liketa* is used to indicate that some event was narrowly avoided or averted. It is often used in a figurative "rather than literal sense; for example, in a sentence such as *It was so cold, I* **liketa** *froze to death*, the speaker may never have been in any real danger of freezing, but the use of *liketa* underscores the intensity of the condition."[16]

A number of non-Standard intensifying adverbs are common in some Southern vernaculars. The SE ADV *right*, as in *He lives right around the corner*, "is currently limited to contexts involving location or time."

> However, in Southern-based vernaculars, *right* may be used to intensify the degree of other types of attributes, as in *She is* **right** *nice*. Other adverbs, such as *plumb*, serve to indicate intensity to the point of totality,

as in *The students fell **plumb** asleep*. In some parts of the South, *slam* is used to indicate "totality" rather than *plumb*, as in *The students fell **slam** asleep; clean* may be used in the same way in other areas, including some Northern dialects (e.g. *The hole went **clean** through the wall*). The use of *big* in *big old dog, little* in *little old dog*, and *right* in *It hurts right much* also function as intensifiers in these varieties.[17]

In AAVE, *steady* is often used as an intensifier after habitual *be* but before a present participle[18] "to refer to an intense, ongoing activity," as in *They be steady messing with you*.[19] This use of *steady* may also imply that action is occurring right now.[20]

And although it looks like a negation, in AAVE we find *"ain't but* and *don't but* for 'only,'* as in 'He ain't but fourteen years old' for SE 'He's only fourteen years old' or 'They didn't take but three dollars' for 'They only took three dollars.'"[21]

The word *fucking* is a non-Standard adverbial intensifier, common in American vernaculars. It is used with adjectives (*That's fucking stupid*) and verbs (*You can do whatever you fucking like*), as well as with adverbs (*Why are you driving so fucking slowly?*). Of course, *fuck* (and its inflected forms *fucking, fucked*, and *fucker*) can be used in various contexts as a noun, adjective, verb, and interjection. Unusually for English morphology, *fucking* can also be used as an infix (e.g. *abso-fucking-lutely*).[22]

8.3 Negation

Negation is a complex topic in English grammar. English has a great variety of ways to express negative meaning, including determiners (e.g. *neither, no, none of, not, nothing of*); indefinite pronouns (*neither, no one, nobody, none, nothing, nowhere*); conjunctions (*neither ... nor*); adverbs (*never, not, nowhere* [which can be a pronoun or a pro-adverb]); and prefixes (e.g. *de-, dis-, in-, mis-, non-*, and *un-*). The most common negator is the adverb *not* (sometimes contracted to *n't*), which is used to negate verbs.

In SE varieties, verb negation occurs in a limited number of constructions.

1. In a verb consisting only of an MV with no Aux, we must add an Aux *do*; the negative marker *not* is then attached to the Aux *do*, and the MV takes its base form:

Present tense:

Affirmative: *I go to the store.*
Negative: *I do not/don't go to the store.*

Past tense:

Affirmative: *I went to the store.*
Negative: *I did not/didn't go to the store.*

We say that the negative marker *not* "is attached" to the Aux because, when we contract *not*, it joins the preceding Aux.

2. However, if the MV is copular *be* without an Aux, the negative marker *not* is attached directly to the *be* form:

Present tense:

Affirmative: *She is at the store.*
Negative: *She is not/isn't at the store.*

Past tense:

Affirmative: *She was at the store.*
Negative: *She was not/wasn't at the store.*

3. In a multi-word complete verb, if the first Aux is a modal, the perfect aspect Aux *have*, the progressive aspect Aux *be*, or the passive voice Aux *be*, the negative marker *not* is attached directly to the first Aux in the verb:[23]

Modal Aux: *She can/cannot/can't go to the store.*
Perfect Aux *have*: *She has/has not/hasn't gone to the store.*
Progressive Aux *be*: *She is/is not/isn't going to the store.*
Passive Aux *be*: *The ball was/was not/wasn't kicked by Franz.*

4. In a multi-word complete verb, if the first word in the verb is a semi-modal, or an imperfect aspectual verb, then we must add an Aux *do* at the beginning of the complete verb, attach the negative marker *not* to the Aux *do*, and change the following verb to its base form:

Semi-modal:

Affirmative: *I have to go to the store.*
Negative: *I do not have to/don't have to go to the store.*

Imperfect aspectual verb:

Affirmative: *I started going to the store.*
Negative: *I did not start/didn't start going to the store.*

In the system of verb negation in English, there is a problem with negation of present-tense *be* in the first-person singular, as it doesn't follow the rest of the paradigm:

		Affirmative	Negative
Sg	first person	I am	I am not/I'm not/?I amn't ?I ain't
	second person	you are	you are not/you're not/you aren't
	third person	he, she, it is	he, she, it is not/he's, she's, it's not/he, she, it isn't

(Continued)

(Continued)

		Affirmative	Negative
Pl	first person	we are	we are not/we're not/we aren't
	second person	you are	you are not/you're not/we aren't
	third person	they are	they are not/thet're not/we aren't

SE varieties have no way to contract *am not* so that the *n't* attaches to *am*. This gap leads us to the most prominent form of non-Standard negation in English: the use of *ain't*.

Non-Standard negation: When people learn English as a second language, they may exhibit forms of non-Standard negation like *He no like the man*, but such forms do not seem to persist in "the vernacular English variety of such speakers once they have completed their transition to English." A possible exception is that, in some Hispanic English varieties, *no* is used as a tag question, as in *They're going to the store, no?*[24] However, this use of *no* is not a full negative: its SE version would be something like, *They're going to the store, aren't they?* The question has the force of undercutting the negation.

Ain't does not originate in American English; rather, it entered the language along with other still-common contractions in seventeenth-century British English. During the twentieth century, the use of contractions in formal writing was generally disapproved of by teachers and other language authorities. But while the number of language authorities who still disapprove of the use of other contractions has declined, those authorities never attacked the use of words like *can't* and *don't* with the bitter revulsion they would still heap on the merest whiff of *ain't*. And yet, *ain't* appears at some point in the usage of most speakers of American English, even if only when safely cradled in real or imagined quotation marks, as when a speaker of otherwise formal SE says jauntily, "You *ain't* seen nothing yet!"[25]

Although it is typically regarded as a "bad English" contraction of *am not*, in actual usage, *ain't* is used not only to mean *am not* but also where SE would use other forms of:

> *be + not*—including *aren't*, and *isn't*;
> *have + not*—including *haven't* and *hasn't*; and
> *do + not*—including both the present tense *don't* and *doesn't*, and the past tense *didn't*.

All of these uses of *ain't* are found in most non-Standard varieties of American English, with the exception of the use of *ain't* in place of the SE *didn't*, which has only been observed in AAVE.[26]

Here are some examples of each use of *ain't*, with SE versions:

Ain't for forms of *be + not*:

I ain't trying to hide nothing now.[27] [compare *I am not/I'm not*]

The hell you say! You ain't a day over forty.[28] [compare *you are not/you're not/you aren't*]

Julia Roberts, she ain't a backup date either.[29] [compare *she is not/she's not/she isn't*]

Ain't for forms of *have + not*:

I ain't never seen nothing like that in my life.[30] [compare *I have not/I haven't*]

You ain't heard nothing yet![31] [compare *you have not/you haven't*]

He ain't had nothing to eat.[32] [compare *he has not/he hasn't*]

Ain't for forms of *do + not*:

He thinks I ain't got no more aces.[33]

I ain't go to school yesterday. [compare *I did not/I didn't*]

He ain't tell him he was sorry. [compare *he did not/he didn't*][34]

Interestingly the non-Standard aspectual verb, habitual *be*, commonly found in AAVE, does not take *ain't* in the negative—nor, for that matter, in the interrogative form. Rather, with habitual *be*, AAVE uses *do* and *don't*. The negative of *John be walkin'* (which means that *John habitually or usually walks*) is *John don't be walkin'*. **John ain't be walkin'* is simply ungrammatical. The interrogative version of the same sentence would be *Do John be walkin'?* "This is also true of so-called tag questions, in which the speaker assumes a positive response, as in *John be listenin', don't he?* or a negative response, as in *John don't be listenin', do he?*[35] Remember: even though a form is non-Standard, it is still rule-governed.

Multiple negation or negative concord: Throughout the first several hundred years of the life of the English language, "double negatives" or multiple negation, more formally called "negative concord" (where "concord" means "agreement"), was a common device in all English varieties, as it still is in many languages. Indeed, we find it in Chaucer's *Canterbury Tales* in his description of the Friar: *Ther nas no man nowher so vertuous.*[36] And in Shakespeare's *As You Like It*, Celia says, *I pray you, bear with me; I cannot go no further.*[37] In negative concord languages and varieties of English, typically, everything that can be negated in a sentence must be, as in, "*Don't nobody want no bossy woman.*"[38] Each major constituent of the sentence is negated: the NP:SUBJ, *nobody*; the Verb *don't want*; and the NP:DO, *no bossy woman*. Negative concord sentences with two negations are quite common (hence the use of the phrase "double negative" to describe this construction). Sentences with three or more negations are less common, but they occur and are rule-governed, according to the conventions of the variety of English.

In the eighteenth century, prescriptive grammarians declared that negative concord was improper and illogical: after all, in math, if we multiply two negative numbers, we get a positive number. By this reasoning, in a double negative, one negative term negates the other, creating an affirmative. In actual usage, this logic fails: in the many vernacular varieties of English where negative concord is used, the negatives have an additive function, creating greater emphasis on the negation.

According to Wolfram and Schilling-Estes, negative concord appears in four different patterns in non-Standard varieties of American English. The most common form of negative concord, which appears in nearly all American vernacular varieties, marks the negative on an Aux verb and on one or more indefinite pronouns or determiners after the verb, as in:

I *wasn't* doing *nothing*.[39] [compare *I was doing nothing* or *I wasn't doing anything.*]

I *didn't* say *nothing* to *nobody*.[40] [compare *I said nothing to anybody* or *I didn't say anything to anybody.*]

In some Northern vernaculars and in most Southern vernaculars, we find a negative indefinite ProN in the subject position, and the negative marked on the Aux verb, as in:

I *was really surprised why* nobody *didn't* come up with *nothing*.[41] [compare *nobody came up with something* or *somebody didn't come up with something.*]

The ancestors, when they sit down in banquet and finish their deliberations, they pick him. They say, "That one." They say so long before he born, and nothing can't *change that.*[42] [compare *Nothing can change that.*]

In most Southern vernaculars, we also find the negative Aux verb and the indefinite subject inverted:

Didn't nobody *know who I was.*[43] [compare *Nobody knew who I was* or *Somebody didn't know who I was.*]

Can't nothing *be the same after a day like today.*[44] [compare *Nothing can be the same after a day like today.*]

Green and Sistrunk[45] note that in AAVE these negative Aux-inversion constructions can also occur in a dependent clause, specifically a noun clause, as in:

She didn't say [*that* **didn't nobody** *want to ride the bus*]$_{[Noun Clause]}$ [compare *She didn't say that nobody wanted to ride the bus.*]

Finally, in some Southern varieties and AAVEs, we find multiple negations marked in different clauses within the same sentence, as in:

There **wasn't** *much that I* **couldn't** *do.* [compare *There was little that I couldn't do* or *I could do most things.*]

I wasn't sure that nothing wasn't going to come up. [compare *I wasn't sure that something wasn't going to come up* or *I thought something might come up.*][46]

Smitherman[47] points out that while double negation has been a feature of most English vernacular varieties, and even of the literary language historically, sentences with three and four negatives have been exclusively a feature of AAVE. However, in this last category of negation, where multiple terms are negated in more than one clause within the same sentence, an interesting condition holds: if a sentence consists of only one clause, negating all negatable terms creates a negative meaning, but if a sentence contains two or more clauses, negating all negatable terms creates a positive meaning, while having all negatives with one positive term indicates negative meaning. She offers the following examples:

It ain't nobody I can trust [compare *I can trust no one.*]
It ain't nobody I can't trust [compare *I can trust everyone.*]

Wasn't no girls could go with us [compare *None of the girls could go with us.*]
Wasn't no girls couldn't go with us [compare *All the girls could go with us.*]

Ain't none of these dudes can beat me [compare *None of these dudes can beat me.*]
Ain't none of these dudes can't beat me [compare *All of these dudes can beat me.*][48]

Kimmika Williams discusses the rhetorical effect of multiple negation in AAVE and how it reflects on an event's location in time. The double negative, "Ain't got none" implies that the speaker doesn't have any *now*. However, the triple negative, "Ain't <u>never</u> got none" can be understood as meaning that the speaker "hardly *ever* has any of whatever the desired 'thing' is," neither in the past nor the present nor the future. And in the quadruple negative, "Ain't never had none neither," the speaker is saying that they have "never had (and quite probably never will) have any of the desired 'thing.'"[49] The 'logic' of negative concord is clearly not simply mathematical. Rather, multiple negations have significant implications for the speaker's state and attitude.[50]

Leveling to *were* with negative past tense *be*: As we have seen, the regular past tense of verbs in English takes a single form for all persons and numbers—except for the verb *be*, which has two past-tense forms: *was* and *were*. In a move that regularizes the irregularity of *be*, some varieties of American English "level" the past tense form of *be* so that it is *were* for all persons and numbers—but only when the verb is negated:

It weren't me that was there last night.
She weren't at the creek.[51]

Wolfram and Schilling-Estes observe that, "The leveling of past *be* to *weren't* appears to be regionally restricted to some coastal dialect areas of the Southeast such as the Eastern Shore of Virginia and Maryland, and the Outer Banks of North Carolina."[52] This usage is sometimes presented in fictional representations of Southern speech as *warn't*:

> *I never said nothing, because I warn't expecting nothing different.*[53]
> *Jim warn't on his island, so I tramped off in a hurry for the crick.*[54]
> *We said there warn't no home like a raft, after all.*[55]
> *Only to be real honest, we warn't really like the Three Musketeers; it was more like three fellas that two of 'em warn't talking with one of 'em any more'n they could help.*[56]

Agreement with the form *don't*: A final irregularity in the negation of verbs in English has to do with the leveling of the present tense form of *do* when it is negated. SE would have the third-person singular as *doesn't*, but one will often hear

> *She <u>don't</u> like the scarves I've been wearing on my head.*[57]
> *You've got certain teammates who are like, "Man, it <u>don't</u> matter what I eat, I can't gain weight."*[58]

According to Wolfram and Schilling-Estes,[59] "Virtually all vernacular varieties show this pattern, but in different degrees."

Key Points

- Adverbs are a mixed category of both content words (e.g. *slowly, here, now, frequently*) and common function words (e.g. *very, just, not*).
- Like adjectives, adverbs may be gradable (e.g. *happily, more happily, most happily*) or non-gradable (e.g. *too; so; very*).
- An adverb functions as the head of an adverb phrase (AdvP). An AdvP may itself include an adverb phrase as a pre-modifier and/or post-modifying PP:Adverbial.
- AdvPs tell *when, where, why, how, how much, how often, how long*, and other versions of those sorts of information.
- According to traditional grammar, an AdvP may modify a verb, adjective, or another adverb. AdvPs also modify whole sentences, dependent clauses, infinitive phrases, and participle phrases, and AdvPs can function as several different types of verb complement.
- AdvPs functioning as sentence or clause modifiers are movable to the beginning or end of the clause and often to the slot between the Subj and Pred.
- The most common forms of negation involve placing the Adv *not*, or its contracted forms, with a V. Some of the most highly marked features of non-Standard varieties involve negation, most notable among them being the non-Standard but common *ain't*.

8.4 Exercises: Adverb Phrases

A. Made-up sentences: there are 28 adverb phrases in the following paragraphs. List all of them in order and, for each one, identify its function in its sentence. A dictionary may prove helpful.

Example: (a) *today* NP:AdvP:SentMod

(a) Today my brother Jim and I shopped for dictionaries. (b) The large ones were much too expensive for us. (c) Also, we knew that unabridged dictionaries are nearly always intended for libraries. (d) They are not used easily at home for conveniently quick reference.

(e) Suddenly, Jim had a brainstorm. (f) "Let's buy two very different dictionaries and use them simultaneously. (g) That way, we can compare rather different styles of definition, and the differences will automatically give us a better understanding of the meanings of the words."

(h) At the book store the owner, Mr. Baker, welcomed us cheerfully. (i) We told him we wanted two distinctly different abridged dictionaries. (j) We mentioned that our teachers often tell us to look words up, but that a single definition rarely helps us. (k) "I know exactly what you need," Mr. Baker replied. (l) "The *American Heritage Dictionary* and the *Oxford American Dictionary* take different approaches to language. (m) If you have both, you will readily learn how to use words more precisely."

(n) At home we carefully examined the dictionaries, comparing the definitions of individual words. (o) Then we discussed what we had found. (p) Soon, we began to notice distinct differences between the two books' definitions. (q) To our surprise, we discovered that many definitions seemed deliberately crafted to capture different senses of words. (r) This would prove one of the most valuable lessons we would ever learn!

B. Real Sentences: for each of the following passages, list all of the adverb phrases in order and, for each one, identify its function in its sentence.

(1) The river was way down behind the house and there warnt nothing in front but a road, and not much of a road at that, only some weeds with ruts on either side, and he had sense enough to know that no boat would be coming down that way; so he was right puzzled about it all right.[60]

(2) "I aint getting smart, and why does it worry you if I dont go on KP because they gonna get the dishes washed if I aint there just like they are if I am, and it dont make any difference to me whether they do or not, as far as that goes. (3) And if they want to send me on back home, that's all right with me too. I never wanted no trouble about it."[61]

(4) And he kind of grinned around at the others again, settling down some more, and then he chuckled and said, "He thought if you went on sick call, you had to go on KP anyhow." (5) Then he laughed some and said, "You ever heard anything like that before?" and laughed some more like it was real funny and like he hadnt heered nothing more comical

in his life, but none of the others did, they only looked at him; and then he chuckled some more and wiped the tears out of his eyes and stopped and said right quick, "Well, you better be sure to get your name on the sick book in the morning then, understand?"[62]

(6) Then she told me all about the bad place, and I said I wished I was there. (7) She got mad then, but I didn't mean no harm. (8) All I wanted was to go somewheres; all I wanted was a change, I warn't particular.[63]

Figure 8.1

Notes

1. Walt Wolfram and Natalie Schilling-Estes. *American English*. 2nd ed. Malden, MA: Blackwell, 2006. 378.
2. Gary Louris. "Poor Little Fish." 1997.
3. John Elway. Qtd. in Jay Mariotti. "Elway Drives, Denver Thrives; Old Spark Back for Broncos QB." *Chicago Sun-Times* (12 Jan 1992): 3.
4. Kirstie Alley. *The Today Show*. NBC-TV. 12 Jan 2017.
5. Written in the voice of the narrator, Huck. In Mark Twain, *Huckleberry Finn*. New York: Charles L. Webster & Co., 1884. 52.
6. Josh Wigler. "*Game of Thrones*: What That Destructive Ending Means for the Final Season." *The Hollywood Reporter*. 28 Aug 2017.
7. *The PBS Newshour*. PBS. 5 Aug 1997.
8. Anthony Fenech. "Midseason Grades for Tigers Infield: Several Falling Short of Star Status." *The Detroit Free Press*. 12 Jul 2017.
9. Dr. Seuss. *Green Eggs and Ham*. New York: Random House, 1960.
10. Mary Cleary Kiely. "I Brake for Family." *U.S. Catholic* 72.6 (Jun 2007): 31.
11. "Charmin Tissues So Just Don't Squeeze the Video." *TVdays.com*. YouTube. 10 Nov 2008. <www.youtube.com/watch?v=8m62J3Q8Ng0>.
12. Alexis de Tocqueville. Qtd. in William Murchison. "Lead Us Not into Temptation." *The American Spectator* 46.2 (Mar 2013): 17.
13. Cumberland Valley Veterinary Clinic. "International Hug Your Cat Day." Online posting. 1 Jun 2017. <https://cumberlandvalleyvets.com>.
14. "Interview with Congresswoman Jane Harman." *The Big Story*. Fox News. 8 Nov 2005.
15. An important exception is determiners that include the linking particle *of* (e.g. *one of*, *all of*).
16. Wolfram and Schilling-Estes, op. cit. 374.
17. Ibid. 378.
18. John R. Rickford. *African American Vernacular English: Features, Evolution, Educational Implications*. Malden, MA: Blackwell, 1999. 6.
19. Wolfram and Schilling-Estes, op. cit. 378; see also Lisa J. Green. *African American English: A Linguistic Introduction*. New York: Cambridge University Press, 2002. 71–73.
20. John McWhorter. *Talking Back, Talking Black: Truths about America's Lingua Franca*. New York: Bellvue Literary Press, 2017. 34.
21. Walt Wolfram, cited in Rickford, op. cit. 8.
22. Melissa Blevins. "Where the F-word Comes From." *Gizmodo.com*. 28 Mar 2014.
23. Remember that "serving as what the negative *-n't* attaches to" is one of the defining features of an auxiliary verb.
24. Wolfram and Schilling-Estes, op. cit. 379.
25. For the most thorough available treatment of *ain't*, see Patricia Donaher and Seth Katz, eds. *Ain'thology: The History and Life of a Taboo Word*. Newcastle-upon-Tyne, UK: Cambridge Scholars Press, 2015.
26. John Russell Rickford and Russell John Rickford. *Spoken Soul: The Story of Black English*. New York: John Wiley, 2000. 123; Wolfram and Schilling-Estes, op. cit. 380.
27. "I Planned No Harm, Says Man Accused of Wisconsin Gun Shop Theft, Sending Manifesto to Trump." *chicagotribune.com*. 12 May 2017.
28. Thom Hartmann. *Death in the Pines: An Oakley Tyler Novel*. Chicago: Chicago Review Press, 2015. 9.
29. Gayle King. *CBS This Morning*. CBS. 6 Apr 2017.

30. Dominique Rodgers-Cromartie. Qtd. in "DRC, Landon Collins Dispute Two Teammates Saying Ben McAdoo Has Lost Giants." *ESPN.com*. 8 Nov 2017.
31. Alfred A. Cohn. *The Jazz Singer*. Film. Warner Brothers, 1927.
32. John Carlisle. "The Breakfast Club." *The Detroit Free Press*. 30 Dec 2018. <www.freep.com/>.
33. Rickford and Rickford analyze this example as showing a double use of non-Standard verbs: they read the *ain't* as equivalent to SE *don't*, giving us a gloss of this sentence as *He thinks I don't got no more aces*. This use of *got* is the equivalent of SE *have*, and the use of *no* is part of a "double negative"; their SE version of this sentence would be *He thinks I don't have any more aces*. I'm willing to buy this reading because the intermediate step—*He thinks I don't got no more aces*—would be an acceptable sentence in the regional vernacular around Paterson, NJ, where I grew up (think of the speech patterns of *The Sopranos* or other stereotypical Italian Americans).
34. Rickford and Rickford, op. cit. 123; Wolfram and Schilling-Estes, op. cit. 380.
35. Rickford and Rickford, op. cit. 114; J. L. Dillard. *Black English: Its History and Usage in the United States*. New York: Vintage Books, 1972. 45; 53.
36. Geoffrey Chaucer. "The Prologue." *The Canterbury Tales*. ln. 251.
37. William Shakespeare. *As You Like It*. II.iv.8.
38. Janine Zeitlin. "Against Odds, Man's Marriage to Former Nanny Endures." *The News-Press* (Fort Myers, FL). 14 Feb 2014.
39. Muhammad Ali. "New Muhammad Ali Biography Reveals a Flawed Rebel Who Loved Attention." *Fresh Air*. NPR. 4 Oct 2017.
40. Gerald Duff. "The Way a Blind Man Tracks Light." *The Kenyon Review* 29.3 (Summer 2007): 94.
41. "Tent Girl; DNA Testing Helps Family Discover That an Unidentified Murder Victim Found 30 Years Ago Was Actually Their Lost Sister." *48 Hours*. CBS. 26 Nov 1998.
42. John Stewart. "Ancestry." *TriQuarterly*. Fall 1995: 212+.
43. Scott Spencer. "Buddy Guy." *Rolling Stone* 618 (28 Nov 1991): 72+.
44. Aimee E. Liu. "Cloud Mountain." *Good Housekeeping* 224.5 (1997 May): 179+.
45. Lisa J. Green and Walter Sistrunk. "Syntax and Semantics in African American English." Ed. Sonja Lanehart. *The Oxford Handbook of African American Language*. New York: Oxford University Press, 2015. 367.
46. Wolfram and Schilling-Estes, op. cit. 379–380; see also Green, op. cit. 77–80; Green and Sistrunk, op. cit. 366.
47. Geneva Smitherman. *Talkin' and Testifyin': The Language of Black America*. Boston: Houghton Mifflin, 1977. 30.
48. Ibid. 31.
49. Kimmika L. H. Williams. "Ties that Bind: A Comparative Analysis of Zora Neale Hurston's and Geneva Smitherman's Work." *African American Rhetoric(s): Interdisciplinary Perspectives*. Eds. Elaine B. Richardson and Ronald L. Jackson, II. Carbondale, IL: Southern Illinois University Press, 2004. 94.
50. See William Labov. *Language in the Inner City: Studies in Black English Vernacular*. Philadelphia: University of Pennsylvania Press, 1972. 130–196.
51. Wolfram and Schilling-Estes, op. cit. 375.
52. Ibid. 376.
53. Mark Twain. *The Adventures of Huckleberry Finn*. New York: Harper Brothers, 1899. 302.
54. Ibid. 159.
55. Ibid. 160.
56. Ira Levin and Mac Hyman. *No Time for Sergeants*. Act II. New York: Dramatists Play Service, 1955. 50.

57. Snoop Dogg. "Lady Antebellum Just Kicked off the North American Leg of Their Tour Wheels Up." *The Today Show*. NBC. 13 May 2015.
58. Eddie Lacy. Qtd. in Kevin Van Valkenburg. "'You Just Can't Shake It': For the First Time, Seahawks Running Back Eddie Lacy Opens Up about His Agonizingly Public Struggle with Weight." *ESPN.com*. 20 Sep 2017.
59. Wolfram and Schilling-Estes, op. cit. 376.
60. Mac Hyman. *No Time for Sergeants*. New York: Random House, 1954. 4.
61. Ibid. 85.
62. Ibid. 86.
63. Mark Twain. *The Adventures of Huckleberry Finn*. New York: Harper and Brothers, 1923. 3.

Chapter 9

Conjunctions (CONJ)

Conjunctions are a category of function words and an extremely stable closed class; indeed, according to the *Oxford English Dictionary*, *and* and *but* are among the very oldest words in the language; *or*, though a relative latecomer, has been in the language for nearly 800 years. In traditional grammar conjunctions are divided into two classes: coordinating conjunctions (CCONJ) and subordinating conjunctions (SCONJ). CCONJs are used to join together and separate or mark the boundaries of words, phrases, and clauses that have the same function within a clause. CCONJs include *for, and, or, but, nor, yet, so*—easily remembered by the acronym *fanboys*.[1] CCONJs also include the paired correlative conjunctions (CORRELCONJ) *either . . . or, neither . . . nor, not only . . . but also, both . . . and,* and *whether . . . or*. Although grammar books don't typically treat them as such, several punctuation marks also often function as CCONJs, including commas, colons, semicolons, parentheses, dashes, hyphens, and virgules (slashes).

SCONJs are used to join an adverb clause (ADVCL or "subordinate clause") to its super-ordinate container clause. The list of SCONJs is significantly longer than the list of CCONJs, and we will examine them in detail with the discussion of adverb clauses in 10.2.3.1. However, among the most common SCONJs are words like *after, although, as, because, if,*[2] *since, though, unless, until, when, whenever, where, wherever,* and *while*. Note that some of these words can also be prepositions (*after, as, since, though, until*). The difference between prepositions and SCONJs is that, to form a complete phrase, the preposition needs no more than a following NP or other nominal as a complement (making a PP), while an SCONJ must be followed by a complete independent clause (forming an adverb clause [ADVCL]):

> PP = P + [NP]: *Since* [*the game*] *we haven't seen Franz.*
> ADVCL = SCONJ + [CLAUSE]: *Since* [*the game ended*], *we haven't seen Franz.*

9.1 Coordinating Conjunctions

CCONJs most frequently join together sentence constituents that have the same form and the same function. CCONJs can also join complete clauses, including sentences.

[Betty][NP:Subj] *and* [Alvin]*[NP:Subj] *went to the store.*
[Betty ran][Sent]*, but* [Alvin walked]*[Sent]*.
Ed likes [red]*[Adj:Mod of "suspenders"] *or* [blue]*[Adj:Mod of "suspenders"] *suspenders.*

Also, constituents of different forms can be joined by a CConj so long as those constituents are performing the same function in the sentence:

In Ollantaytambo I think it's *either* [pizza]*[NP:SC] *or* [eating at your hotel]
[PartP:Nominal:SC].[3]
But this man was entirely [at home]*[PP:SC] *and* [happy]*[AdjP:SC] *in his century and the world.*[4]

9.2 Conjoining Punctuation

Sometimes we conjoin more than two constituents with CConjs or Correl-Conjs alone, but more often we use commas. And for long lists of constituents, each of which may have a different constituent structure, we may use semicolons. We also often use semicolons or colons to conjoin large clause elements or entire clauses; we can use hyphens, dashes, parentheses, and virgules for similar conjoining roles. The following discussion of the uses of conjoining punctuation is adapted from Warriner's *English Grammar and Composition*[5] and the article on "Punctuation" in Lovinger's *The Penguin Dictionary of American Usage and Style*.[6] Both are solid, conservative sources on the topic, full of the blend of rigid clarity and mushy edicts that characterize all the style-guide treatments of punctuation I've ever seen. My discussion combines matters of grammar with matters of conventional style and offers some guide rules for formal usage of conjoining punctuation. Along the way, I attempt to pull back some curtains and debunk some myths. Commas, the most commonly used punctuation mark, will form the base of our discussion, with side trips to conjoining functions of other punctuation marks.

9.2.1 Commas

Like conjunctions, commas and other conjoining punctuation both conjoin and separate: they typically mark the end of one constituent and the beginning of another while serving as the glue between them. Lovinger notes that commas "set off attributions, definitions, explanations, elaborations, and identifications."[7] That is, commas mark the barrier between, but connect together, the quote or other borrowed material and its author (attributions), and explanatory asides such as non-essential modifiers and parenthetical utterances (definitions, explanations, elaborations, and identifications). Commas are also used "to separate three or more items in a series."[8]

A **brief commentary on the "Oxford" or serial comma**: According to the Oxford University Press style manual,[9] when you have a series of three or more constituents that function in the same way in a sentence, they should be punctuated as follows: *We like apples, peaches, and grapes.* However, in many cases, the second comma is not required to avoid ambiguity. One might just as well have written the sentence without the second comma, without changing meaning or sacrificing clarity: *We like apples, peaches and grapes.* However, in some cases, without the Oxford comma, ambiguity will arise—or meaning will be distinctly different. In the following two sentences, crucial meaning hinges on the second comma:

> We invited the comedians, Stalin, and Churchill to the party.
> We invited the comedians, Stalin and Churchill, to the party.

In this case, the second comma is required to make clear that we have three entities (1. The comedians; 2. Stalin; and 3. Churchill) as opposed to a second constituent—an appositive—that renames the first entity (i.e. the comedians are a team named "Stalin and Churchill"). The simple answer is that you will <u>never</u> be wrong if you use the second ("Oxford") comma, but you <u>don't always</u> need it.

Warriner[10] states as a rule that, "If all items in a series are joined by *and* or *or* (*nor*), do not use commas to separate them," since the conjunctions are fulfilling that function and the punctuation would be redundant. The exception is sentences in a series: according to Warriner, short sentences may be conjoined (or separated) with a conjunction alone (e.g. *The stage was set, the guests were seated.*);[11] longer sentences should be conjoined with a semicolon or with a comma followed by a CConj. Lovinger[12] concurs.

> *Results are properly objects of celebration and regret*$_{[Sent]}$, *only actions should be objects of moral praise and blame*$_{[Sent]}$.
> Results are properly objects of celebration and regret, **but** only actions should be objects of moral praise and blame.[13]
> Results are properly objects of celebration and regret; only actions should be objects of moral praise and blame.

Using the comma alone to conjoin the two longer sentences is generally regarded as a stylistic error called a "comma splice."

9.2.2 An Aside About Semicolons

When you conjoin two sentences with a semicolon, the semicolon is only used without a CConj:[14] **Results are properly objects of celebration and regret; but only actions should be objects of moral praise and blame.*[15] However, a semicolon may be used to conjoin clauses when the second clause begins with a conjunctive adverb such as *however, therefore,* or *consequently*[16] (see 11.3.5 for more on conjunctive adverbs):

> **The relative success of both processes cannot be denied, **however**, they failed to reach their ultimate goal of a long-term cease-fire.

> *The relative success of both processes cannot be denied; **however**, they failed to reach their ultimate goal of a long-term cease-fire.*[17]

Warriner states that when conjoining two clauses, if there are commas within the clauses, then "a semicolon (rather than a comma) may be needed to separate [or conjoin] the independent clauses," functioning as a sort of higher-order comma:

> *Speedo might recall (dimly) that he had hidden a bone somewhere, five minutes ago; beyond that, his past was blank.*[18]

Similarly, Lovinger and Warriner both point out that semicolons should be used between items in a series when those items already contain commas.[19] Lovinger gives an unclear example then offers a clarifying correction:

> **John Major greeted me, my executive assistant, Colonel Dick Chilcoat, the British secretary of state for defense, Tom King, and my counterpart, British chief of defense staff, Marshal of the Royal Air Force Sir David Craig, in a sitting room at 10 Downing Street.*[20]
> *John Major greeted me; my executive assistant, Colonel Dick Chilcoat; the British secretary of state for defense, Tom King; and my counterpart, **the** British chief of defense staff, Marshal of the Royal Air Force Sir David Craig, in a sitting room at 10 Downing Street.*

Lovinger states that a semicolon can be used in place of a period, or the combination of a comma and CConj, to conjoin two or more sentences, as in *He came; he saw; he conquered*, which might also be written in any of the following ways:

> *He came, he saw, and he conquered.*
> *He came and he saw and he conquered.*
> *He came. He saw. He conquered.*[21]

Similarly, the sentence *Money is not the root of all evil; the love of money is*, could be written: *Money is not the root of all evil **but** the love of money is*, <u>or</u> with a comma before the word *but*. Lovinger concludes that, in this way, "the semicolon performs the linking function of a conjunction like *and* or *but*."[22]

Now, back to commas: As another comma rule, Warriner offers that we should, "Use commas to separate two or more adjectives preceding a noun."[23] Lovinger offers a test: if you can put the word *and* between each ADJP before a noun, then you should put a comma there.[24] Thus, the commas are appropriately placed in the following sentence: *There were several large, intensely blue, very hairy monsters on Sesame Street.* In the following sentence, however, the final comma is wrong: **Franz bought a new, yellow, soccer ball.*

After all, it is not a *new and yellow and soccer ball*. Rather, the words "soccer ball" form a compound noun, rather than an adjective-noun combination.[25]

Lovinger and Warriner both note that commas can also set off—and conjoin—part of a sentence.[26] Warriner particularly notes the use of commas to set off non-essential modifiers, whether they are clauses, phrases, or single words[27] (see 10.2.1, 12.1.2, and 12.2.2 for more on the distinction between essential and non-essential modifiers). We have already seen one type of non-essential modifier: nominal (2.2) and adjectival (4.1) appositives:

Nominal appositive:

My older brother, <u>Thomas</u>, is twenty-one.
My aunt and uncle, <u>the Giovannis</u>, own a store, <u>the Empire Shoe Shop on Main Street</u>.
<u>A good all-around athlete</u>, Roland is a promising candidate for the decathlon.

Adjectival appositive:

Franz, <u>happy with his new purchase</u>, left the store.

Arguably, the commas around these non-essential modifiers do more separating than conjoining; they mark that the non-essential modifiers express separate or expendable information. A brief one- or two-word appositive phrase may not need to be separated by commas: *My older brother Thomas is twenty-one* would be mechanically acceptable. However, Lovinger is quick to add that "when the set-off matter comes amid this sentence, as in this very sentence, a pair of commas is needed."[28] Incautious writers often leave out the second comma of the pair, which is only appropriate when the set-off material is at the end of the sentence.

Lovinger and Warriner both note that we should "use commas after certain introductory elements"[29] such as AdvPs, adverb clauses, a succession of introductory PPs (though not a single PP alone, unless there is potential ambiguity without the comma),[30] and introductory PartPs and InfPs.[31] When these elements are used to interrupt a sentence, bracket them with commas.

As a matter of fact, the quantum world is like a parallel universe.[32]
The quantum world, as a matter of fact, is like a parallel universe.
The quantum world is, as a matter of fact, like a parallel universe.
The quantum world is like a parallel universe, as a matter of fact.

Such interrupting elements, including PPs, PartPs, and InfPs, are most often adverbial and are, as we shall see in 11.3 and Chapter 12, related to non-essential modifiers.

9.2.3 An Aside About Dashes and Parentheses

Lovinger points out that dashes and parentheses are like commas: all can be used to set off—and conjoin—part of a sentence, as I just did with the dashes. Dashes tend to raise the prominence of the offset words, while commas typically downplay the offset words, "and parentheses play them down even further." Parentheses always come in pairs, while dashes, like commas, come in pairs unless the offset words are at the end of a sentence.[33]

Both Lovinger and Warriner state that dashes may be used to "set off an explanation or expansion of the preceding thought";[34] Warriner elaborates this idea by saying that the initial dash means something like *namely*, *that is*, or *in other words*.[35] That is (hah!), the dash seems to have the force of a conjunctive adverbial (e.g. *however, therefore, moreover, in other words*; see 11.3.5). The dash also seems to have the force of an SCONJ (e.g. *because, although, since, as though*; see 10.2.3.1). Warriner notes further that "the dash and the colon are frequently interchangeable in this type of construction."[36] We could write the same sentence several different ways:

With a dash:

Anna has been more than steady for us—she's been outstanding.

With a comma and a coordinating conjunction:

Anna has been more than steady for us, **for** *she's been outstanding.*

With a colon:

Anna has been more than steady for us: she's been outstanding.[37]

With a semicolon, a conjunctive adverb, and a comma:

Anna has been more than steady for us; **indeed,** *she's been outstanding.*

With a comma and a subordinating conjunction:

Anna has been more than steady for us, **because** *she's been outstanding.*

Among these sentences, meaning varies mostly in terms of emphasis, so the choice is a matter of stylistic preference. But in each case, the words and/or punctuation placed between the two sentences have the force of a CONJ: marking the boundary between constituents but, at the same time, joining them together.

A dash can be used just as a comma can to separate and conjoin an introductory constituent of a clause, such as an introductory adverb clause. Clearly, parentheses would not be an option for an introductory constituent. In the following example, the comma might be a better choice:

When you consider a recent national survey showing 21 percent of men say they're on the lookout for a better relationship while they're in a relationship—then it's all the more important that women know the signs of a guy who's looking for the exit before he's even in the room.[38]

Or a dash might be used after an introductory series to set off and conjoin a summary: *Rare, medium, or well done—these are such personal preferences.*[39] In this example, a colon could replace the dash and have much the same meaning and effect.

A dash or parentheses can be used like a comma to set off a constituent at the end of the sentence, especially an adverb clause or other adverbial constituent (such as a sentence modifier or, in the case of this remark, a non-essential adjectival modifier of the word *constituent*). The original version of the following sentence reads, *A man who clams up during a fight or a discussion isn't necessarily just trying to make you mad (though some are).*[40] But it could just as well have been written with a dash or a comma:

A man who clams up during a fight or a discussion isn't necessarily just trying to make you mad—though some are.

A man who clams up during a fight or a discussion isn't necessarily just trying to make you mad, though some are.

This is purely a stylistic choice; the meaning is the same. A dash can also be used to mark a concluding contrast or contradiction:[41] *People wanted to laugh, and weep—and could do neither.*[42] A comma could be used in place of the dash, but the dash directs the reader to pause longer and so gives more dramatic impact to the final phrase.

Dashes and parentheses can also be used to conjoin and set off matter in the middle of a sentence. Warriner makes particular note of the use of dashes to mark "an abrupt change in thought,"[43] as in the sentence *The dog skidded on the floor—his nails acted like ice skates—and crashed into the kitchen table.* Arguably, "a concluding contrast or contradiction" and "an abrupt change of thought" are similar. These sorts of mushy descriptive phrases are commonplace in discussions of "proper" punctuation use.

We come full circle in our discussion of dashes with a final example from Lovinger, where paired dashes are used to set off a list in the middle of a sentence, a list that "explains or expands the preceding thought," which seems to be the main function of dashes when they are used for conjunctive purposes:[44] *Tchaikovsky omitted the bass instruments—cellos, double basses, trombones, tuba—as well as the trumpets.* Parentheses would also work for the same purpose.

This brings us to the subject of parentheses as conjoining punctuation. Warriner directs us to "use parentheses to enclose matter which is added to a sentence but is not considered of major importance."[45] Lovinger elaborates further:

the offset material should be "an explanatory or incidental word, phrase, notation, figure, or abbreviation."[46] Both Warriner and Lovinger state that commas and dashes may be used for the same purpose as parentheses, but both use impressionistic descriptions to distinguish among their effects: Lovinger again asserts that each sort of punctuation ascribes a different level of prominence to the inserted material, with dashes giving the greatest prominence, commas intermediate prominence, and parentheses drawing the least attention.[47] Warriner describes the contrast among dashes, commas, and parentheses in a different way: he claims that commas indicate "a slight pause," dashes "a stronger break in the sentence," and parentheses "a strong interruption,"[48] and he offers the following examples in support; I offer my own comments in parentheses after each sentence:

Comma: "a slight pause":
We fished in the muddy stream, a brown torrent after the downpour.
(This sentence could also have used a colon or possibly a dash.)

Dash: "a stronger break in the sentence":
We fished in the muddy stream—a waste of time!
(This sentence could also have used a comma, a semicolon, or a colon.)

Parentheses: "a strong interruption":
We fished (or should I say drowned worms?) in the muddy stream.
(This sentence could also have used dashes or commas if it were re-written
   as *We fished, or I should say drowned worms, in the muddy stream.*)

Given that each parenthetical comment could be punctuated in more than one way, I do not think that either Warriner or Lovinger's mushy generalizations about the relative differences in the effect of commas, dashes, and parentheses work. Rather, I think the effect of each depends on both the content of the comment (what is between the commas, dashes, or parentheses) and the larger context. There are few firm rules, little science, and much <u>art</u> to the proper use of conjoining punctuation.

9.2.4 A Further Aside on Hyphens

First, to clarify: the hyphen is the shorter line, the dash the longer one. Conventionally, a dash equals two hyphens; Microsoft Word, which I am using to write this book, automatically turns two consecutive hyphens into a dash so long as there are no spaces between the hyphens and the preceding and following words. There should not be spaces before or after a hyphen or dash.[49]

Hyphens conjoin in two distinct ways. Before computer-based text editing programs, a hyphen was most commonly used to divide—and join together—a word across a line break, placing one or more syllables of the word on the next line. With word processing, proportional fonts (typefaces with different widths for the letters), and automatic text-wrapping (that is, when you get to the end of a line, the cursor just moves to a new line), word hyphenation across line breaks has, for most people, a thing of the past. A major exception is newspaper and magazine writing, where the constraints of column widths often force writers and editors to hyphenate words so as to make maximal use of minimal space. If you find yourself handwriting, typing on a typewriter, or constrained by space, and so must hyphenate word breaks, use a dictionary as a guide for where to break syllables across a line break.

Hyphens also conjoin compound words and are used with certain prefixes, especially when, without the hyphen, there might be some ambiguity or confusion.

Lovinger's discussion of hyphens and compounding is quite extensive, and I commend it to you. Briefly, he urges readers to consult not one but two dictionaries to check on whether or not to hyphenate a compound since dictionaries will sometimes disagree (e.g. *coworker* versus *co-worker*; *vice-president* versus *vice president*). Then he offers several categories of hyphenation.

Compound adjectives: Warriner states this well, as a rule: "Hyphenate a compound adjective when it precedes the noun it modifies. Do not use a hyphen if one of the modifiers is an adverb ending in *-ly*." As examples Warriner gives us *an after-school job* but *a heavily laden burro*.[50]

Both Lovinger and Warriner point out that a phrase which appears as a hyphenated adjective before a noun will not be hyphenated after the noun,[51] as in Warriner's example: *a well-planned campaign* (but: *The campaign was well planned*).[52]

Established hyphenated compound adjectives: Lovinger offers several examples, including "*cold-blooded, law-abiding, one-horse* (town), and *ten-gallon* (hat). Such expressions may have multiple hyphens: *out-and-out, dyed-in-the-wool, will-o'-the-wisp*."[53] Add to this group another rule from Warriner: a hyphen should be used with compound numbers from *twenty-one* to *ninety-nine* and with fractions used as determiners.[54] He offers the examples *seventy-six trombones* and *a two-thirds majority*.

Certain prefixes and suffixes: Both Warriner[55] and Lovinger[56] note that certain prefixes and suffixes normally appear with hyphens, such as *ex-mayor, great-grandson, all-encompassing, post-Reformation, president-elect, mother-in-law, and show-off*.

Certain potentially ambiguous words and phrases: Lovinger[57] notes that we must hyphenate "*re-form*, meaning to form again, to distinguish it from *reform*, meaning to correct defects." The same goes for *re-creation* and *recreation*. Note also the difference between a *big business opportunity* (a chance to make a lot of money) and a *big-business opportunity* (a chance to work with large corporations).[58] And there is the potential ambiguity of leaving the hyphen out of a phrase like *man-eating*, as in a newspaper headline that Lovinger quotes: "Man eating piranha sold as pet fish." This headline "prompted *The New Yorker* [magazine] to ask, 'Did he *look* like a fish?'"[59]

As this last category in particular shows, hyphenation, like the use of commas, dashes, and parentheses for conjunctive purposes, is often more a matter of style, clarity, and avoiding ambiguity than it is a matter of simple rules.

9.2.5 Hey: What About Colons?

Colons can also be understood as marking the boundary between a clause and non-essential (or at least less essential) information. Warriner cites two conjunction-related uses for the colon: first, to separate a complete clause from a list of specific items, as in, *We visited four states last year: Nevada, Idaho, Montana, and Colorado*;[60] and, second, to separate a complete clause from a long quote:

> *Thomas Paine's first pamphlet in the series* The American Crisis *starts with these famous words: "These are the times that try men's souls. The summer soldier and the sunshine patriot will, in this crisis, shrink from the service of their country; but he that stands it* now *deserves the love and thanks of man and woman."*[61]

In each usage, the colon conjoins the preceding complete clause to the following list or quote, and the list or quote renames or elaborates information from the clause—*four states* and *these famous words*, respectively. As my last sentence illustrates, the dash can be used in much the same way. Note that the clause preceding the colon must be complete: it is improper to use a colon right after a verb to set off a list of NPs when those NPs are the direct objects of the verb:

> Incorrect: *In the zoo can be seen: an Indian elephant, two giraffes, four gnus, and a rare Himalayan snow leopard.*
> Correct without a colon: *In the zoo can be seen an Indian elephant, two giraffes, four gnus, and a rare Himalayan snow leopard.*[62]
> Correct with a colon: *In the zoo can be seen several exotic animals: an Indian elephant, two giraffes, four gnus, and a rare Himalayan snow leopard.*

Much like dashes, a colon can also mark that an elaboration or explanation is to follow.[63] Like the dash, the colon can have the same value as a conjunctive adverbial or a subordinating conjunction (see above under "Dashes and Parentheses"): Lovinger notes that, when used this way, the colon "substitutes for *e.g., i.e.*, or *viz.*, or the equivalent *for example, that is*, or *namely*, respectively,"[64] all of which are conjunctive adverbials.[65] Though a complete sentence must precede the colon, after the colon we may find either a complete sentence or a phrase, as in the examples Lovinger offers:[66]

> *In addition, our economy provides a much more powerful antidote to the rule of the rich: the economies of scale.*[67]

Here we have a dilemma: we must choose between pleasure at some sacri-
fice of comfort and more complete comfort at the sacrifice of pleasure.[68]

Lovinger notes that all of the preceding uses of the colon are "optional": one
could always rearrange the preceding examples so as to punctuate them without the colon. Other uses of the colon are, in Lovinger's terms, "mechanical"[69]
or, as Warriner says, "conventional."[70] In each, the colon at once both marks a
boundary and conjoins. Colons are used in several fixed ways:

- **Between hour and minute or between minute and second**, as in *8:45
  p.m.*, or a race time of *3:45* (that is, *three minutes and forty-five seconds*).
- **After the salutation on a formal letter**, as in *Dear Sir:*
- **To separate the subtitle of a book or other work**, as in *The Fight for
  English: How Language Pundits Ate, Shot, and Left.*
- **Between chapter and verse numbers in biblical references**, as in *Prov-
  erbs 15:3.*
- **In web addresses**, as in *https://www.yahoo.com.*

Of course, there are such "mechanical" or "conventional" uses for commas:

- **In dates**, as in *Wednesday, June 30, 1981.*
- **In addresses**, as in *1501 W. Bradley Ave., Peoria, IL 61625.*
- **After the salutation of a friendly letter**, as in *Dear Delia,*
- **After the closing of any letter**, as in *Sincerely yours,*
- **After a name followed by a title such as *Ph.D., Jr., Sr.,* etc.:** as in *Dr.
  Imelda Sanchez, Ph.D.* or *Marcus Welby, M.D.*[71]
- **In numbers**, as in *$4,356,281.*[72]

9.2.6 One More Conjunctive Punctuation Mark You Don't Think About: Virgules

As detailed by Lovinger,[73] virgules ("slashes") are used largely for fixed
or "mechanical" purposes, such as in fractions (e.g. 13/16); in dates (e.g.
5/16/07); to replace *per* in terms like *miles/hour*; and to indicate line breaks
when poetry is included in prose text. However, the virgule is also used to
mean *or* in the phrase *and/or*, as well as in computer programs in which an
option may be given as "Move/Rename File," meaning "move or rename."
In other computer program options, such as "Paper Size/Type," the virgule
seems to mean either *and* or *or*. And virgules (and colons, and sometimes
semicolons) also appear in web addresses, as in *https://search.yahoo.com/
search;_ylt=AwrJ61gpUuNcr6YAZRxXNyoA;_ylu=.*
Lovinger sees the virgule emerging as a more widely used and flexible punctuation mark, and he bemoans its use in contexts where "the substitution may
be no improvement: take *secretary/treasurer* instead of *secretary-treasurer*."

Worse, he says, is when the use of the virgule becomes ambiguous so that "Diners cannot be sure whether the virgule means *and* or *or* in a menu's 'steak/ lobster plate.'" And Lovinger seems simply disgusted when a writer "dispenses with commas and conjunctions to describe someone as a 'writer/painter/ photographer' and later writes, 'She has this phobia/quirk/fatal flaw. . . .'"[74] However, the virgule is already working as a conjunctive punctuation mark and may well grow in use before its meaning and function become more accepted and formalized.

9.2.7 Summary of Conjunctive Punctuation "Rules"

The following list should serve as a recap of the "rules" (both hard and mushy) of conjunctive punctuation detailed in this chapter. As the list simply repeats material already attributed in detail to Warriner and Lovinger throughout the chapter, for the sake of—well, not brevity; readability?—I will not repeat those citations here.

Commas

1. Use commas to separate three or more items in a series; however, if all items in a series are joined by *and* or *or* (*nor*), do not use commas to separate them.
2. Use commas to separate two or more adjectives preceding a noun. If you can put the word *and* between each adjective or adjective phrase, then you should put a comma there.
3. Use commas to set off non-essential modifiers, whether they are clauses, phrases, or single words (e.g. nominal and adjectival appositives; non-essential adjectival clauses with *which* or *who*).
4. Use commas to set off extra-clausal adverbials, such as adverb clauses and sentence modifiers.
5. Use commas after certain introductory elements and before certain concluding elements such as adverbs, adverb clauses, a succession of introductory PPs (though not a single PP alone, unless there is potential ambiguity without the comma), and introductory participle and infinitive phrases. When these elements are used to interrupt a sentence, bracket them with commas.
6. Use commas typically to downplay the prominence of offset words.
7. Kinds of "elements" set off by commas, in terms of their meanings, may include:

   a. Attributions (e.g. author of quoted or borrowed material).
   b. Definitions (e.g. non-essential modifiers and parenthetical utterances).
   c. Explanations and elaborations (e.g. non-essential modifiers and parenthetical utterances).
   d. Identifications (e.g. non-essential modifiers and parenthetical utterances).

8.   Use a comma followed by a coordinating conjunction to conjoin sentences unless the sentences are short, in which case they may be conjoined by a coordinating conjunction alone.

9.   Conventional uses of the comma:

   a.   Use commas in dates: *Wednesday, June 30, 1981.*
   b.   Use commas in addresses: *1501 W. Bradley Ave., Peoria, IL 61625.*
   c.   Use commas after the salutation of a friendly letter: *Dear Delia,*
   d.   Use commas after the closing of any letter: *Sincerely yours,*
   e.   Use commas after a name followed by a title such as *Ph.D., Jr., Sr.,* etc.: *Dr. Imelda Sanchez, Ph.D.* or *Marcus Welby, M.D.*
   f.   Use commas in numbers, as in *$4,356,281.*

Semicolons

1.   You may use a semicolon to conjoin two sentences but only without a coordinating conjunction.
2.   You may use a semicolon to conjoin clauses when the second clause begins with a conjunctive adverb such as *however, therefore,* or *consequently.*
3.   Use semicolons between items in a series when those items already contain commas; this includes conjoining sentences with commas in them.
4.   You may sometimes use a semicolon in place of a conjunction like *and* or *but.*
5.   Semicolons are also conventional in complex web addresses: *https:// search.yahoo.com/search;_ylt=AwrJ61gpUuNcr6YAZRxXNyoA;_ylu.*

Dashes

1.   Use dashes to raise the prominence of offset words.
2.   You may use dashes to set off an explanation or expansion of the preceding thought.

   a.   The initial dash may have the force of a **conjunctive adverbial**: words and phrases like *however, therefore, moreover, namely, that is, in other words,* etc. that connect clauses and paragraphs.
   b.   The initial dash may have the force of a **subordinating conjunction**: words and phrases like *because, although, since, as though,* etc. that mark the beginning of an adverb clause, joining it to its container clause.

3.   You may use a dash, just as you may use a comma, to separate and conjoin an introductory constituent of a clause, such as an introductory adverb clause; or you might use a dash after an introductory series to set off and conjoin a summary.
4.   You may use a dash, just as you may use a comma, to set off a constituent at the end of the sentence, especially an adverb clause or other adverbial constituent (such as a sentence modifier), or to mark a concluding contrast or contradiction.

5. You may use dashes and parentheses to conjoin and set off matter in the middle of a sentence, such as an abrupt change in thought, or a list in the middle of a sentence that explains or expands the preceding thought.

Parentheses

1. Use parentheses to enclose matter that is added to a sentence but is not considered of major importance. The offset material should be "an explanatory or incidental word, phrase, notation, figure, or abbreviation."
2. Use parentheses to downplay the prominence of offset words even further than do commas.

Hyphens

1. Use a hyphen to divide—and join together—a word across a line break.
2. Use a hyphen in compound words, and with certain prefixes, especially when, without the hyphen, there might be some ambiguity or confusion.

   a. Hyphenate a compound adjective when it precedes the noun it modifies. Do not use a hyphen if one of the modifiers is an adverb ending in *-ly*.
   b. Use hyphens with established hyphenated compound adjectives (e.g. *cold-blooded, law-abiding*).
   c. Use a hyphen with compound numbers from *twenty-one* to *ninety-nine* and with fractions used as determiners.
   d. Use a hyphen with certain prefixes and suffixes (e.g. *ex-mayor, great-grandson, all-encompassing, president-elect, mother-in-law*).
   e. Use a hyphen with potentially ambiguous words and phrases (e.g. *re-form* vs. *reform; man-eating* vs. *man eating*).

3. Hyphens are also used conventionally in complex web addresses: *https://forward.com/life/faith/434245/ira-glass-hasidim-dialogue/*.

Colons

1. Use a colon to mark the boundary between a clause and non-essential (or at least less essential) information.

   a. Use a colon to separate a complete clause from a list of specific items.
   b. Use a colon to separate a complete clause from a long quote.

2. You may use a colon, like a dash, to mark that an elaboration or explanation is to follow.
3. You may use a colon, like a dash, with the same value as a **conjunctive adverbial** or a **subordinating conjunction**; the colon substitutes for *e.g., i.e.,* or *viz.* or the equivalent *for example, that is,* or *namely,* respectively.
4. Conventional uses of the colon.

   a.   Use a colon between hour and minute or between minute and second, as in *8:45 p.m.*, or a race time of *3:45* (that is, *three minutes and forty-five seconds*).

   b.   Use a colon after the salutation on a formal letter, as in *Dear Sir:*

   c.   Use a colon to separate the subtitle of a book or other work, as in *The Fight for English: How Language Pundits Ate, Shot, and Left.*

   d.   Use a colon between chapter and verse numbers in biblical references, as in *Proverbs 15:3.*

   e.   Use a colon in web addresses, as in *https://www.yahoo.com.*

Virgules

1. Use a virgule in a fraction (e.g. 13/16).
2. Use a virgule in a date (e.g. 5/16/07).
3. Use a virgule to replace *per* in terms like *miles/hour.*
4. Use a virgule to indicate line breaks when poetry is included in prose text.
5. Use a virgule to mean *or* in the phrase *and/or* and in computer programs in which an option may be given as "Move/Rename File."
6. Use a virgule to mean either *and* or *or* in other computer program options, such as "Paper Size/Type."
7. You may see a virgule in place of a hyphen in certain compounds such as *secretary/treasurer* instead of *secretary-treasurer*).
8. Virgules are also used conventionally in web addresses: *https://search. yahoo.com/search;_ylt=AwrJ61gpUuNcr6YAZRxXNyoA;_ylu.*

A Brief Discussion of Interjections

Here at the end of our discussion of the parts of speech and their phrases, I would be remiss in not mentioning that traditional grammar generally includes one more minor part-of-speech category: interjections. As defined by Warriner, "an interjection is a word that expresses emotion and has no grammatical relation to other words in the sentence."[75] An interjection is often followed by an exclamation point to indicate the strength of the emotion expressed (e.g. *Oh dear! Ouch! Wow!*). That emotion—generally only discernible from context—is the meaning of the interjection, and that emotion may run the whole gamut of strong emotions, from pain to pleasure to surprise to anger. Unusual in writing, though common in conversation, I know of no detailed treatment of the grammar of interjections. What I offer here is a sketch of three possible subcategories (these terms are mine):

    Simple Interjections: Simple interjections appear as single words or brief phrases followed by an exclamation point. Examples include words like *Ouch! Oh! Wow!* and *Hey!* and phrases like *Oh my! Oh my God/gosh/goodness! Good grief!* and my mother's favorite, *Jiminy gee whiz!* Although simple interjections are always fragments, they are always punctuated as though they were complete sentences, beginning with a capital letter and followed by an exclamation point.

Conjunctive Interjections: Some interjections are used at the beginning of a sentence and separated from the sentence by a comma: *Oh, she'll win the race. Gosh, I didn't know you were waiting for me. Man, it's hot out here!* I call these interjections "conjunctive" in that they indicate the speaker's recognition of a preceding utterance or some larger context that is shared by the speaker and the hearer. Thus, the interjection in each of these sentences serves to conjoin the following sentence with the preceding context.

Elliptical Interjections: Some exclamations might be parsed as interjections or perhaps more properly as instances of ellipsis: sentences with parts deleted. Consider *Help!* which might be understood as a shortened version of the imperative sentence *Help me!* or even as a version of *Would you help me?* And a phrase like *Oh my God!* might be understood as an elliptical prayer, something like, *Oh my God, please protect me from whatever it is I'm exclaiming about.*

Key Points

- Conjunctions are a closed class of function words.
- Conjunctions are divided into two categories: coordinating conjunctions (CCONJ) and subordinating conjunctions (SCONJ).
- CCONJs include *for, and, or, but, nor, yet, so* (*fanboys*) and are used to join together and separate phrases and clauses that have the same function within a sentence or clause.
- CCONJs also include the paired correlative conjunctions (CORRELCONJ) *either . . . or, neither . . . nor, not only . . . but also, both . . . and,* and *whether . . . or.*
- Several punctuation marks also often function as CCONJs, including commas, colons, semicolons, parentheses, dashes, hyphens, and virgules (slashes). These punctuation marks also have fixed mechanical usages.
- SCONJs are used to join an adverb clause (a.k.a a "subordinate clause") to its super-ordinate container clause. SCONJs will be examined in detail in 10.2.3.1.

9.3 Exercises: Conjunctions and Conjoining Punctuation

A. Made-up sentences: list the coordinating (CCONJ) and correlative conjunctions (CORRELCONJ) in the following paragraphs and, for each conjunction, identify the constituents it conjoins along with their forms and functions. By my count, there are nineteen (**remember**: correlative conjunctions are two words that count as one conjunction).

(1) *and*—CCONJ; *Peoria*—NP:SUBJ; *Decatur*—NP:SUBJ

Once Peoria and Decatur were home to numerous theatrical companies. Decatur was the first town in Illinois to open a stage theatre, but Peoria's theatrical district soon became larger and more important. The theaters channeled tremendous revenue into these towns, but the golden days of small-city theater ended about the time of World War II. The members of these theatrical companies could not count on receiving regular wages or a paycheck. Both the management and the performers worked on a profit-sharing basis. All the company members received shares in the profits of a show, and the size of a share depended on the length of a member's tenure with the company. Naturally the theater owner's portion was the largest and was usually about one tenth of a season's total receipts.

In the days before modern buses, a touring season was not easy for either the company manager or the performers, for they travelled long hours on dusty roads to reach their performance venues. Maintaining order was no easy task on a long tour because the food and living conditions gave rise to discontent.

Inevitably the actors and crew had time on their hands, for they didn't perform or rehearse or travel all day, every day. To relieve the dullness and boredom on long tours, company members often would make visits to children's homes and hospitals. Not only the actors but also the whole company looked forward to such visits. All enjoyed the chance to chat with and entertain those in need.

The decline of theaters and of theatrical companies began with the rise of television. Our country no longer needed large numbers of stage theaters, for a cheaper medium of entertainment had replaced them.

B.   A real text: using the following essay, identify each colon, comma, dash, hyphen, pair of parentheses, semicolon, and virgule, and for each, identify its function. In identifying each function, use the numbers from the list above titled "Summary of Conjunctive Punctuation 'Rules.'" Note: more than one rule may apply. If you think this is the case, identify all of the rules that apply to an example.

(1) Fighting the Wrong War
(2) by Gloria Borger
(3) *U.S. News & World Report*, 11/5/2001, Vol. 131 Issue 19, p 39
(4) Before September 11, we had a whole lot more patience. (5) If Republicans and Democrats were squabbling, we'd shrug and go on with our lives. (6) No big deal—a week here, a week there. (7) In fact, most of us hardly paid any attention. (8) Nothing was a matter of life and death. (9) Now everything is a matter of life and death.
(10) Tell that to Tom DeLay, the House Republican whip. (11) DeLay, it seems, has a big, important, serious problem with a crucial and timely airport-security measure. (12) His problem is so huge, in fact, that he kept the bill from reaching the House floor for weeks—despite the fact that it passed the Senate unanimously. (13) Does DeLay worry that it's not strong enough? (14) Does he want more money for federal air

marshals and baggage X-ray machines? (15) Does he have stricter plans to reinforce cockpit doors? (16) Not a chance. (17) DeLay's concern—shared by some other House GOP leaders—is that the measure calls for federalizing airport-security workers. (18) How can we allow that to happen? he must be thinking. (19) It's not only big government; it's new union members. (20) Thousands of them!

(21) Such a prospect fills like-minded conservatives with fury. (22) "What the Democrats want is 30,000 new dues-paying contributors," grumped House Majority Leader Dick Armey. (23) So House GOP leaders went to work: First, they pounded Transportation Secretary Norman Mineta (a Democrat himself!) at a private meeting in early October, when he dared suggest that the White House might support the idea of federal screeners. (24) ("He got his ass kicked" is the way one Senate Republican describes it.) (25) Then the leaders took their grievance to the White House. (26) Fearing the wrath of conservatives, the administration caved: Make the supervisors federal employees, keep the worker bees private. (27) Armed with White House support, DeLay then began to do what he does best—pressure lobbyists, summoning a group from the airport-security industry for a chat. (28) Work with us, he said, or we're not going to be friends. (29) (It's hard to say why anyone would want to befriend this industry at this moment, considering that the Justice Department has accused it of hiring screeners with criminal records. (30) Think about it: felons confiscating tweezers at airports everywhere.)

(31) **On the cheap.** (32) For public consumption, conservatives prefer not to dwell on the political matter of unions, for obvious reasons. (33) Instead, they argue that Israel, with its good airport security, does not use the federal model. (34) But Senate Commerce Committee sources say that is not always true: Baggage and passenger screeners at El Al airlines, for instance, are government employees. (35) Private companies provide the perimeter airport security. (36) House GOP leaders rightly argue that the security has been lax at airports because the cheap airlines were paying—and they got what they paid for: screeners who were also convicted forgers, bribe takers, and felons in possession of weapons. (37) Bunglers who last week allowed a man with a loaded handgun onto a flight out of New Orleans.

(38) But here's where DeLay & Co. misses the point: Why reward incompetent security firms? (39) "They're still going to be for-profit companies," says one Senate staffer. (40) "This is not the Salvation Army." (41) But this is a matter of law enforcement. (42) "Should we start to contract out the Border Patrol and DEA [Drug Enforcement Administration]?" asks Sen. John McCain, who wants to federalize these employees. (43) And for those who worry that a new batch of civil servants

would be hard to fire, consider: The Senate bill gives the government the authority to hire and fire at will, as well as to forbid strikes.

(44) Happily, the president now believes this has gone on too long. (45) After a closed-door session with congressional leaders last week, Republicans groused that Bush sounded like he was willing to sign the Democratic version. (46) They complained to the vice president, so the president came out calling for "flexibility," backing DeLay. (47) One top White House aide says Bush still hopes for a compromise—say, federalizing half of the airport workforce. (48) But would he veto a Democratic bill? (49) Don't bet on it.

(50) After all, 77 percent of Americans want to put the government in charge of airport security. (51) They're not complaining about big government anymore; they're worried about big airports. (52) And they also remember that the firefighters and police officers and postal workers were good citizens. (53) And union members, too.

Notes

1. However, the CConj *for*, as in, *At first, she had not noticed this plaque, _for_ it was hidden beneath dark ivy and blood-red hibiscuses* (Mhani Alaoui. "Anna's House." *The Massachusetts Review* 58.1 [Spring 2017]: 103), has largely fallen out of use. These days we are more likely to read such a use of *for* as an SConj marking an adverb clause (see Chapter 10), and we are even more likely to use *because* instead of *for*: *At first, she had not noticed this plaque, _because_ it was hidden beneath dark ivy and blood-red hibiscuses. For* just sounds overly formal, stuffy, or even archaic.
2. *If* can also mark a noun clause (NCL) but only when the NCL functions as a DO: *I don't know _if I would classify Amos as consistent_* (Brad Biggs. "Bears Q&A: QB Depth Chart, State of the Offensive Line, Danny Trevathan's Progress & More." *chicagotribune.com*. 9 Aug 2017). We know this is an NCL because we can replace it with a third person ProN: *I don't know _this_* (see 10.2.2).
3. mlgb. "Please Help Me Eat Well in Peru!" Online posting. *Fodor's Travel Talk Forums. Destinations. South America*. 27 Feb 2018. 2 <www.fodors.com>.
4. Ralph Waldo Emerson. "Goethe; or, the Writer." *The Works of Ralph Waldo Emerson. Vol. IV: English Traits and Representative Men*. New York: MacMillan, 1902. 475.
5. John E. Warriner. *English Grammar and Composition*. Fourth Course. Orlando: Harcourt Brace Jovanovich, 1982 [1948]. 416; 420–424.
6. Paul M. Lovinger. *The Penguin Dictionary of American Usage and Style*. New York: Penguin, 2000. 321–348.
7. Lovinger, op. cit. 326.
8. Ibid; Warriner, op. cit. 416.
9. "Instructions for Authors: 05 House Style." Oxford University Press. 2019. <https://global.oup.com/academic/authors/author-guidelines/house-style/?lang=en&cc=ch>.
10. Op. cit. 416.
11. Heather Chick Photography. "Kelli & Gregg: Wedding at the Miraval Ballroom, East Bridgewater." 23 Jun 2015. <www.heatherchickphotography.com>.
12. Op. cit. 326–327.
13. Stephen J. Morse. "Reason, Results, and Criminal Responsibility." *University of Illinois Law Review*. 2004: 383.

14. Warriner, op. cit. 420.
15. That is, in theory, not this: *One vital guide to a court's view of material facts is its stated rules of law;* **but** *it is also true that its rule of law can best be understood in terms of the facts before it.* (Kent Greenwalt. *Statutory and Common Law Interpretation.* New York: Oxford University Press, 2012. 205–206. Qtd. in Ryan C. Williams. "Questioning Marks: Plurality Decisions and Precedential Constraint." *Stanford Law Review* 69.3 [Mar 2017]: 825 [fn. 139]). A search on the *Corpus of Contemporary American English* (*COCA*) found 1.1 million examples of the "correct" form but an additional 10.6 thousand examples of the "incorrect" form, with the "incorrect" forms appearing in a similar range of academic and popular periodicals and published fiction. However, the use of the "incorrect" form has declined steadily since 1990. Warriner's assertion of correctness remains the stronger, and clearly preferred, candidate.
16. Warriner, op. cit. 420.
17. Talha Köse. "Rise and Fall of the AK Party's Kurdish Peace Initiatives." *Insight Turkey* 19.2 (Spring 2017): 157.
18. Josephine Humphreys. *The Fireman's Fair.* New York: Viking, 1991.
19. Warriner, op. cit. 421; Lovinger, op. cit. 346–347.
20. This unclear example appears originally in exactly this form in Colin Powell, with Joseph E. Persico. *My American Journey.* New York: Ballantine, 1995. 494.
21. Though neither Warriner nor Lovinger would approve of *He came, he saw, he conquered.* (Jasmin K. Williams. "Julius Caesar: He Came, He Saw, He Conquered." *nypost.com.* 15 Oct 2007). While they condone conjoining two short sentences with a comma alone, they apparently prefer other options for three or more short sentences.
22. Lovinger, op. cit. 346.
23. Warriner, op. cit. 416.
24. Lovinger, op. cit. 347.
25. Remember, though, that compound nouns act like single-word nouns but also have an analyzable interior structure. While *soccer ball* is effectively a single noun that is modified by the adjectives *new* and *yellow*, within the compound, *soccer* modifies *ball* as an adjective, telling which or what kind of *ball*.
26. Lovinger, op. cit. 326; Warriner, op. cit. 416.
27. Warriner, op. cit. 416.
28. Lovinger, op. cit. 326.
29. Warriner, op. cit. 416.
30. Traditional British and American usage differ here. The British tend to use more commas than do Americans (yes, I've actually studied this) and will place a comma after a single PP at the beginning of a sentence, regardless of questions of clarity. British and American usage also differ as to the placement of commas in relation to the second of a pair of quotation marks. Americans put the comma inside the quotation mark; Brits put it outside.
31. Warriner, op. cit. 416; Lovinger, op. cit. 326.
32. *PBS NewsHour.* 5 Oct 2016.
33. Lovinger, op. cit. 331.
34. Ibid.
35. Warriner, op. cit. 445–446.
36. Ibid. 446.
37. Jon Nowacki. "Local Players Play a Part in Bulldog Softball Split." *duluthnewstribune.com* (Duluth, MN). 2 Apr 2010.
38. David Zinczenko. "Is It Time to Dump Him?" "Mysteries of the Sexes Explained." *Men's Health.* 20 Mar 2007.
39. Lovinger, op. cit. 331.
40. Zinczenko, op. cit.

41. Lovinger, op. cit. 331.
42. Herbert George Wells. *The Outline of History: Being a Plain History of Life and Mankind.* Vol. 2. NY: MacMillan, 1920. 532.
43. Warriner, op. cit. 445.
44. Lovinger, op. cit. 331.
45. Warriner, op. cit. 446.
46. Lovinger, op. cit. 340.
47. Ibid.
48. Warriner, op. cit. 446–447.
49. Except according to Associated Press style. See Mignon Fogarty. "Em Dash Space." *Grammar Girl.* 31 Jan 2011. <www.quickanddirtytips.com/education/grammar/em-dash-space>. Also, with a "hanging hyphen," as in "first- and second-grade students."
50. Warriner, op. cit. 445.
51. Lovinger, op. cit. 334.
52. Warriner, op. cit. 445.
53. Lovinger, op. cit. 333.
54. Warriner, op. cit. 444.
55. Ibid.
56. Lovinger, op. cit. 334.
57. Ibid.
58. Ibid.
59. Ibid. If you're bored and want to pursue such issues further, check out the discussion of hyphens in Theodore M. Bernstein. *The Careful Writer: A Modern Guide to English Usage.* New York: Atheneum, 1973. 366–367, where he points out that we commonly write *self-conscious* but *unselfconscious* (not **unself-conscious*). Also note the problem of *businessman* but *small-business men.* And he waxes on the problem of the phrase, "Hence the large number of ex-public schoolboys in every Labor Cabinet," where we have the prefix *ex-* crashing into the conflation of *public school* and *schoolboys.* Where should the hyphens go to keep everything clear?
60. Warriner, op. cit. 423.
61. Ibid. 424.
62. Ibid. 423.
63. Lovinger, op. cit. 324, 331.
64. Ibid. 324.
65. *E.g.* = *exempli gratia* in Latin, literally "for the sake of example." *I.e.* = *id est* in Latin, literally "that is." *Viz.* = *videlicet,* in Medieval Latin, a contraction of *videre licet,* literally "it is permitted to see," and so, "namely."
66. Lovinger, op. cit. 324.
67. Tibor Scitovsky. *The Joyless Economy: The Psychology of Human Satisfaction.* New York: Oxford UP, 1992. 8.
68. Ibid., 71.
69. Lovinger, op. cit. 324.
70. Warriner, op. cit. 424.
71. Warriner, op. cit. 412–413.
72. Lovinger, op. cit. 325.
73. Ibid. 347–348.
74. Ibid. 348.
75. Warriner, op. cit. 24.

Chapter 10

Clauses

"Clause" is a term that covers a whole family of constituents, all of which share the following basic features:

- A clause always contains a finite verb that acts as the head of a VP:PRED.
- The verb in a clause always has a nominal functioning as the subject of the verb (NOMINAL:SUBJ).
- The NOMINAL:SUBJ and the verb agree in number and person.
- To be formally complete, the VP:PRED in a clause must include all complements required by the verb.

In English, the order of the clause is typically Subject-Verb-Complement (SVC). The SVC clause is the unmarked or default structure; other ways of ordering these clause constituents are marked by being transformed from the SVC order. We routinely rearrange clause constituent order in English. To most easily analyze those rearranged clauses, we will first transform them back to their underlying SVC structure.

Clauses sound like sentences in that they include a NOMINAL:SUBJ and a VP:PRED; however, the reality is the other way around: sentences, also known as "independent clauses," are only one variety of clause. There are also three kinds of dependent clauses:

- Adjective Clauses (ADJCL), a.k.a. Relative Clauses.
- Noun Clauses (NCL).
- Adverb Clauses (ADVCL), a.k.a. Subordinate Clauses.

What makes independent clauses different from dependent clauses is that independent clauses can stand by themselves as well-formed sentences, while dependent clauses cannot; a dependent clause is always a constituent within another clause.[1]

Independent Clause: *I want to buy that ball.*
ADJCL: *The ball that I want to buy*[ADJCL:MOD OF "ball"] *is quite expensive.*

That I want to buy.

NCL: *You know <u>that I want to buy that ball</u>*[NCL:DO].

   **That I want to buy that ball.*

ADVCL: *I have to save my money <u>because I want to buy that ball</u>*[AdvCl:SentMod].

   **Because I want to buy that ball.*

Each dependent clause comprises an independent clause that has been altered. In the NCL and the ADVCL, an extra word—a subordinator or complementizer—has been added to the beginning of the clause, marking the clause as dependent. In the ADJCL, the order of the clause has been rearranged so that the dependent clause begins with a type of subordinator or complementizer (called a relative pro-word) that refers back to the N' in the container clause that is modified by the ADJCL.

In this chapter, we will start out by examining independent clauses and how they can be rearranged. We will then dig further into the details of the forms of dependent clauses.

10.1 Independent Clauses—a.k.a. Sentences

Typically, an independent clause is organized so that the NOMINAL:SUBJ precedes the VP:PRED. This SVC order is called a declarative sentence because it is commonly used to make a statement or declaration. However, there are several common ways in which that usual sentence order can be rearranged, including interrogative and imperative sentences, the use of expletive *there* and expletive *it*, passive voice sentences, and inversion. Each of these sentence rearrangements is further marked by the presence (or absence, in the case of the imperative mood) of particular constituents, marking those constructions as different from the default SVC construction. We commonly use these rearrangements of clause order to place familiar or topical information in the sentence initial position, unfamiliar/new or emphasized information at the end of the sentence—the positions in which we generally expect those sorts of information to appear in clauses—and to create greater cohesion among sentences in paragraphs.

10.1.1 Interrogative Sentences

Although sentences in SVC order are typically used to make a statement or declaration, in speaking we can use the declarative-order sentence to ask a question, simply by raising our pitch at the end of the sentence. Think of the difference in how you would say and use these two sentences: *He isn't going to win. He isn't going to win?*

An interrogative sentence rearranges the SVC declarative order, and, as its name implies, it is commonly used to ask a question. In an interrogative sentence, the NP:SUBJ + VP:PRED order of a declarative sentence is usually distorted according to four patterns.

Pattern 1: We may reverse the order of the subject and the first Aux of the complete verb. If the verb in the declarative sentence has one or more Aux verbs preceding the MV, to change the declarative sentence into an interrogative sentence, simply swap the positions of the NP:Subj and the first Aux:

Declarative sentence: *They*[NP:Subj] *are*[Aux] *kicking*[MV] *the ball*[NP:DO].
Interrogative sentence: *Are*[Aux] *they*[NP:Subj] *kicking*[MV] *the ball*[NP:DO]?

This pattern holds when the MV is copular *be* with one or more auxiliaries:

Declarative sentence: *Franz*[NP:Subj] *is*[Aux] *being*[MV] *a team player*[NP:DO].
Interrogative sentence: *Is*[Aux] *Franz*[NP:Subj] *being*[MV] *a team player*[NP:DO]?

Notice that if there is more than one Aux in the verb, only the first **Aux** moves:

*They **have been** kicking the ball. **Have** they **been** kicking the ball?*
*They **will have been being** beaten. **Will** they **have been being** beaten?*

If the complete verb has no Aux, we simply add an Aux *do* at the beginning of the sentence as a dummy Aux; this is called *do* support:

1. *They kick the ball. They **do** kick the ball. **Do** they kick the ball?*
2. *She kicks the ball. She **does** kick the ball. **Does** she kick the ball?*
3. *He kicked the ball. He **did** kick the ball. **Did** he kick the ball?*

However, the *do* Aux is not just a dummy term: notice that, like the first Aux in any verb, *do* marks the tense of the verb in the interrogative sentence: in sentence 1, *kick* and *do* are both in the present tense, while in 3, *kicked* and *did* are in the past tense. Also, the *do* Aux must agree with the NP:Subj in person and number: in 2, *does* is the third-person singular form so that it agrees with *she*. Also, the *do* Aux changes the form of the following main verb to the base form.

Notice that the sentence in the interrogative order can also be used to make a statement, as when one exclaims, *Have they been kicking the ball!* The labels "declarative" and "interrogative" refer primarily to the organization of the sentence and only secondarily to the speech act (making a statement; asking a question) that we perform by using that sentence.

Pattern 2: With copular *be* as the MV and no Aux, we may reverse the order of the subject and the verb, without needing *do* support:

Declarative sentence: *Franz*[NP:Subj] *is*[copular be:MV] *a star*[NP:SC].
Interrogative sentence: *Is*[MV] *Franz*[NP:Subj] *a star*[NP:SC]?

Copular *be* is the only verb in English for which it is currently conventional to form an interrogative sentence by inverting the subject and verb.[2]

Patterns 3 and 4 both involve the use of interrogative pro-words. As with pronouns and the other varieties of pro-words we have discussed so far, interrogative pro-words stand in for or replace words, phrases, or clauses. In the declarative-order clause, the interrogative pro-words usually stand in for the answer to the question. Here is a complete list of interrogative pro-words in English:

Interrogative Pro-Words:

- **Pronoun** (unmarked for case; PRON): *what, whatever, which, whichever.*
- **Nominative case pronoun:** *who, whoever.*
- **Objective case pronoun:** *whom, whomever.*
- **Pro-adjective** (PROADJ): *how, which.*
- **Pro-determiner** (PROD): *what, which.*
- **Possessive pro-determiner:** *whose.*
- **Pro-adverb** (PROADV): *how, how long, how many, how much, however, when, whenever, where, wherever, why, whyever.*

Pattern 3: We may precede sentences of patterns 1 or 2 with an interrogative PROADV. In transforming the declarative clause order to the interrogative clause order, the positions of the first AUX and SUBJ, or copular *be* and SUBJ, are swapped (as in Patterns 1 and 2), and the PROADV is simply moved from its position in the declarative order to the front of the interrogative sentence:

Declarative with AUX + MV: *They are kicking the ball.*
Interrogative with AUX + MV: *Are they kicking the ball?*
Declarative with answer: *They are kicking the ball because they want to.*
Declarative with PROADV: *They are kicking the ball why.*
Interrogative with PROADV: *Why are they kicking the ball?*

Declarative with *do* support: *They did kick the ball.*
Interrogative with *do* support: *Did they kick the ball?*
Declarative with answer: *They did kick the ball into the woods.*
Declarative with PROADV: *They did kick the ball where.*
Interrogative with PROADV: *Where did they kick the ball?*

Declarative with copular *be*: *Franz is a star.*
Interrogative with copular *be*: *Is Franz a star?*
Declarative with answer: *Franz is a star because he practices constantly.*
Declarative with PROADV: *Franz is a star why.*
Interrogative with PROADV: *Why is Franz a star?*

Pattern 4: We may replace a phrase in the declarative sentence with an interrogative pro-word of the same form and move the interrogative pro-word to the front of the interrogative sentence. Sometimes, other changes must be made to the sentence as well.

A nominative interrogative pronoun can <u>only</u> function as a subject. It simply replaces the subject of the declarative sentence to change the declaration to a question:

> <u>Declarative</u>: *Franz kicked the ball. Franz could be kicking the ball.*
> <u>Interrogative</u>: *Who kicked the ball? Whoever could be kicking the ball?*

An objective interrogative pronoun can function as a DO, IO, or PComp. However, the change from a declarative to an interrogative sentence will, in this case, require that the subject and the first Aux switch places. In the absence of an Aux, this construction will require *do* support:

> <u>Declarative</u>: *You saw Franz today.*
> <u>Interrogative with PRON:DO</u>:
> *You saw whom today?→Whom did you see today?*

> <u>Declarative</u>: *I passed Franz the ball.*
> <u>Interrogative with PRON:IO</u>:
> *I passed whom the ball?→Whom did I pass the ball?*
> *I passed the ball to whom?→ To whom did I pass the ball?*
> *Whom did I pass the ball to?*

> <u>Declarative</u>: *You bought a gift for someone.*
> <u>Interrogative with PRON:PCOMP</u>:
> *You bought a gift for whomever?→ For whomever did you buy a gift?*
> *Whomever did you buy a gift for?*

When an interrogative PRON functions as a PComp, we may just move the PRON to the front of the sentence, or we may move the whole PP.

An interrogative PROD is attached to the noun it specifies. Therefore, the whole NP of which the interrogative PROD is a constituent must move to the front of the interrogative sentence:

> <u>Declarative</u>: *These mountains were formed roughly 425 million years ago.*[3]
> <u>PROD:SPEC OF N$_{[SUBJ]}$</u>:
> *Which mountains were formed roughly 425 million years ago?*

> <u>Declarative</u>: *She wants the green ball.*
> <u>Interrogative PROD:SPEC of N$_{[DO]}$</u>:
> *She wants which ball?→Which ball does she want?*

> <u>Declarative</u>: *She wants that green ball.*
> <u>Interrogative PROD:SPEC of N$_{[DO]}$</u>:
> *She wants which green ball?→Which green ball does she want?*

Declarative: *She gave Franz my new ball.*
Interrogative PROD:SPEC of N$_{[DO]}$:
She gave Franz whose new ball? → *Whose new ball did she give Franz?*
                                   Whose new ball did she give to Franz?

Declarative: *She gave my fiancée a present.*
Interrogative PROD:SPEC of N$_{[IO]}$:
She gave whose fiancée a present? → *Whose fiancée did she give a present?*
                                      To whose fiancée did she give a present?
                                      Whose fiancée did she give a present to?

Declarative: *She paid for the present with my credit card!*
Interrogative PROD:SPEC of N$_{[IO]}$:
She paid for the present with whose credit card? →
                        With whose credit card did she pay for the present?
                        Whose credit card did she pay for the present with?

In the transition from *She wants the green ball* to *Which ball does she want?* strictly speaking, the interrogative pro-word *which* does not just substitute for the determiner *the* but for the D + ADJ, *the green.* "The green" is neither a DP nor an ADJP. Nor is it an N′ because it has no noun. I don't have a good term for labeling *which* in this context. PRO-(D + ADJ)? Pro-prenominal? This use of *which* is in the hazy turf between determiners and adjectives.

However, the problem of interrogative *which* having *the green* as its antecedent points up an interesting issue: *which* can be an interrogative PROADJ but only when its antecedent ADJP modifies a plural count noun or a singular mass noun because these nouns can be used without a determiner:

With a plural count noun:

Declarative: *You do not like green eggs.*
Interrogative PROADJ:MOD OF N:
You do not like which eggs? → *Which eggs do you not like?*

With a singular mass noun:

Declarative: *Unbleached flour is the best for this recipe.*
Interrogative PROADJ:MOD OF N: *Which flour is the best for this recipe?*

How can also be an interrogative PROADJ when it replaces an ADJP:SC:

Declarative: *The soup is delicious.*
Interrogative PROADJ:SC: *The soup is how?* → *How is the soup?*

Declarative: *He's feeling fine.*
Interrogative PROADJ:SC: *He's feeling how?* → *How's he feeling?*

To parse an interrogative sentence, start by rearranging it into declarative order. This is easy to do when the interrogative sentence has no interrogative pro-word: just reverse the order of the NP:Subj and the first Aux or copular *be*. In sentences with interrogative pro-words, identify the pro-word's function by identifying the complete verb, its subject and complements, and finally the slot where the pro-word would logically fit in the sentence.

> Interrogative sentence: *Where were they kicking the ball?*
> Declarative sentence order: *They were kicking the ball where.*
> Declarative sentence: *They were kicking the ball in the park.*

Although the second "sentence," *They were kicking the ball where*, is not grammatically well formed, the interrogative ProAdv *where* serves to hold or mark the place where the question-answering constituent would go. This approach works for parsing sentences with each of the interrogative pro-words.

Non-Standard interrogatives: interrogatives without inversion: AAVE speakers may form interrogatives "without inversion of the subject and auxiliary verb, usually with rising intonation, as in 'Why *I can't* play?' for SE 'Why can't I play?' and '*They didn't* take it?' for SE 'Didn't they take it?'"[4] While the former example is not a feature of SE varieties, the latter, without the interrogative pro-word, is quite common across SE and non-SE varieties.

Interrogatives with Aux-deletion: Also, as we saw earlier, in the section on absent *be* (6.1.8), in American informal varieties, both copular *be* and progressive Aux *be* can be deleted from the beginning of interrogative sentences, as can the perfect Aux *have*, passive Aux *be*, and Aux *do*:

Informal deletion of:

> **Copular *be***: *(Are) you in there?*
> **Progressive Aux *be***: *(Is) she taking the dog out?*
> **Perfect Aux *have***: *(Have) you gone to the store yet?*
> **Passive Aux *be***: *(Are) the downstairs lights turned off (by you)?*
> **Aux *do***: *(Does) he know how to play?*

Non-Standard quotatives: When the Quot is an embedded question in the form of a noun clause, as in SE (e.g. *I asked him if he could go with me*), AAVE speakers may instead use inversion of the Subj with the Aux to form the embedded question: *I asked him could he go with me*,[5] spoken with a declarative intonation. Saying, "I asked him" marks that what follows will be a question, so it makes sense to state the question as a question. In SE and formal written English, we find the same word order with a pause before the Quot and a rising inflection on the question: *I asked him, "Could he go with me?"* (see the related verb complementation pattern with DO + Quot verbs in 7.1.3.6).

10.1.2 Imperative Mood Sentences

As we saw in 6.1.4, the imperative mood is used to deliver directions or commands. In imperative sentences, the usual subject-predicate structure is altered in that the subject seems simply to be deleted: *Take this to the kitchen. Write it down.* Traditional grammar says that the subject is "understood" to be the second-person personal PRON *you.* But this notion is counter-intuitive: although we could create appropriate contexts for the following sentences, we do not generally say them and mean the same thing as the two imperative voice sentences above: ?*You take this to the kitchen.* ?*You write it down.* While *Take this to the kitchen* would be understood as an order to do something, *You take this to the kitchen* is an instruction or direction that would appear in a series of such instructions. Another analysis has it that the imperative sentence is more like, [*I am telling you to*] *take this to the kitchen.* [*I am telling you to*] *write it down.* In this analysis, the verb of the imperative is an infinitive functioning as part of a verb complement, where the portion of the sentence in the brackets is conventionally deleted. Yet another analysis treats the verb of the imperative as modal but with the modal AUX and subject deleted, as in, [*You should*] *take this to the kitchen.* [*You should*] *write it down.* This makes sense in that the action named in the command has not occurred yet and is therefore irreal and thus modal, hence the traditional label of imperative <u>mood</u>.

Which analysis meshes best with your sense of the meaning of the imperative voice? Take your pick. In any event, an imperative sentence, by deleting the subject, moves the verb forward in the sentence and gives the verb more emphasis.

10.1.3 Expletive there

Four types of sentences are commonly analyzed as declarative sentences that have been rearranged to present information for purposes of cohesion between sentences, for emphasis, or for some other rhetorical effect. These four types are sentences beginning with an expletive *there* or an expletive *it*, sentences in the passive voice, and inverted sentences.

The expletive *there* construction can be used to rearrange sentences in which the VP:PRED comprises a <u>copular *be*</u> followed by an adverbial **subject complement (SC)**:

> Declarative: *A package <u>is</u> on our porch.*
> Expletive *there*: *There <u>is</u> a package on our porch.*
>
> Declarative: *Forces of change <u>are</u> at work in the world.*
> Expletive *there*: *There <u>are</u> forces of change at work in the world.*[6]

In the second sentence of each pair, the word *there* is a pseudo-subject: a kind of expletive or place holder for the agent. Note that *there* is not functioning adverbially: it is not telling us <u>where</u> something is. In the expletive *there* sentence, the agent is the nominal that follows the copular *be* (e.g. *a package; forces of change*). These sentences with the expletive *there* in the subject position are sometimes called existential *there* sentences since they assert the <u>existence</u> of some person, thing, or state of affairs.

The existential *there* construction is also useful because it allows us simply to assert the existence of some person, thing, or state of affairs. In order to introduce as a topic the idea that some particular house exists, it would sound odd to say, *A house is in New Orleans*. Instead, the existential *there* sentence expresses the same idea: *There is a house in New Orleans*.[7] The existential *there* construction also shifts the stress in the sentence from *A hóuse is in New Orleans* to *There ís a house in New Orleans*, thus emphasizing the fact of the existence of the house.

Non-Standard existential *there* constructions: According to traditional and conservative ideas of style, in an existential *there* sentence, the form of *be* must agree in number with the agent: thus, *There is$_{[SG]}$ a package$_{[SG]}$ on our porch*, but *There are$_{[PL]}$ forces of change$_{[PL]}$ at work in the world*. However, in "virtually all vernacular varieties" of American English, this "rule" doesn't apply, and we find leveling to the singular form in sentences like *There was$_{[SG]}$ five people$_{[PL]}$ there* and *There's$_{[SG]}$ two women$_{[PL]}$ in the lobby* with varying degrees of frequency. "In fact, Standard dialects are moving towards this pattern" as well.[8]

Another non-Standard version of the existential *there* construction occurs in vernacular varieties of English that use *it* or *they* instead of *there*:

> ***It's*** *a dog in the yard.* ["There's a dog in the yard."]
> ***They's*** *a good show on TV.* ["There's a good show on TV."]

These constructions are a notable feature of AAVE.[9] These are, of course, what I call "spokenisms": usages that appear in particular spoken varieties of English but in no formal written variety. "*They* for *there* seems to be found only in Southern-based vernaculars; *it* is more general in vernacular varieties."[10] I'm not saying that I approve or disapprove of using these forms; I'm saying that people do, in fact, use them in speaking and in informal writing. If you wish to fit in as a member of a community, then you will speak in some passable version of how the locals speak or deal with the social consequences of being perceived as ill-spoken, different, or uppity. This holds for all communities: just as much for speakers of SE varieties trying to fit into non-Standard speech communities as for speakers of non-Standard varieties trying to fit into SE speech communities.

10.1.4 Expletive it

Another "existential construction" involves using an expletive *it* as a pseudo-subject. We can use expletive *it* in a sentence construction called "*it* extraposition" to rearrange a declarative sentence, taking the independent clause, turning it into a <u>noun clause</u> (NCL) beginning with the subordinator or complementizer *that*, and placing the NCL after *it* and a LINKING VERB or COPULAR *be* + ADJP. The NCL remains the agent of the new sentence but functions as an SC.

> *The fiction writer has a revolting attachment to the poor.*
> *It seems <u>that the fiction writer has a revolting attachment to the poor</u>.*[11]
> *It is obvious <u>that the fiction writer has a revolting attachment to the poor</u>.*
> *It is beyond any reasonable doubt true <u>that the fiction writer has a revolting attachment to the poor</u>.*

As with *there* in the existential construction just discussed, the word *it* in these sentences is also an expletive: *it* has no antecedent or postcedent nominal to which it refers; it's just a place holder. The sentence *It **seems** <u>that the fiction writer has a revolting attachment to the poor</u>* implies something like "That the fiction writer has a revolting attachment to the poor seems to be the case." *It* extraposition allows us to say the latter thought in fewer words. In general, readers of English prefer to see a clause constructed so that a short subject is followed by a longer predicate.[12] We often use *it* extraposition to rearrange a sentence in order to move a long subject into the predicate position. In the following example, the subject of the first sentence is an NCL:

> *That the galaxy is teeming with intelligent beings that voluntarily confine themselves to their home planets seems unlikely.*
> *It seems unlikely that the galaxy is teeming with intelligent beings that voluntarily confine themselves to their home planets.*[13]

While both sentences are grammatically well formed, the second sounds (to my ears) clearer.

Note that the non-Standard example above, *It's a dog in the yard*, could be understood as developing from the convergence of the two expletive sentence constructions with *there* and *it*.

10.1.5 Passive Voice

As we have seen in the earlier discussions of passive voice, the passive construction takes a sentence with a transitive verb and rearranges the order of its constituents, moving the DO (which names the patient) from the original declarative sentence order into the subject position, changing the verb by adding a passive AUX *be* followed by the past participle of a verb, and moving the original subject nominal (which names the agent) into an optional *by*/*with* PP at the end of the sentence:

<u>Active:</u>

Franz[SUBJ/AGENT] *kicked the ball*[DO/PATIENT].

Passive:

The ball[SUBJ/PATIENT]*was kicked* [*by Franz*[AGENT]][PP:AGENTIVE]
The ball[SUBJ/PATIENT] *was kicked.*

In the passive voice version of the sentence, the agent—the character who performs the action named by the verb—is now named by the nominal in the optional *by/with* PP. We label that PP with the function of "agentive" because it contains the nominal naming the agent. As we've seen (7.1.3.1), we can also create a passive voice sentence by moving an IO (sometimes called the "beneficiary," as distinct from the "patient" since the person or object named in the IO receives the benefit of the action) to the subject position:

Active:

I[SUBJ/AGENT] *gave my love*[IO/BENEFICIARY] *a cherry*[DO/PATIENT].

DO Passive:

A cherry[SUBJ/PATIENT]*was given to my love*[IO/BENEFICIARY] (*by me*[AGENT]).

IO Passive:

My love[SUBJ/BENEFICIARY] *was given a cherry*[DO/PATIENT] (*by me*[AGENT]).[14]

Passive voice allows us to rearrange the order of information in a sentence; we may choose the passive voice in order to make the patient (or the beneficiary), rather than the agent, the subject, and thereby the topic of the sentence. We may do this for purposes of emphasis, or because the patient is the topic of the current paragraph, or because the patient is familiar information and the agent is new information. Typically, readers expect familiar or old information—information that is common knowledge, or that has already been mentioned in the text—to appear at the beginning of a sentence, in the subject; readers then expect new or unfamiliar information to appear after the verb, in the predicate. Passive voice and inversion (the next type of sentence reordering) both give writers and speakers a way of reshaping sentences so they conform to the audience's expectations about information flow.[15]

10.1.6 Inversion

A common rhetorical and poetic device is sentence inversion. Arguably, the first sentence of this paragraph is itself inverted: since this section is about "sentence inversion," the topic of the sentence (*sentence inversion*) ought to come first, in the subject position, followed by the elaborating information (*a common rhetorical and poetic device*). A great many forms of inversion are commonly used in English speech and writing, including, as we have already seen, most types of interrogative sentences and *there* extraposition. Here are some more.

Sometimes the S<small>UBJ</small> and <u>MV</u> are inverted:

Negative introduction:

Unlike MacDonald, I have no ready verbal paraphrase with which to replace it, nor<small>[NEG]</small> *have*<small>[V]</small> *I*<small>[SUBJ]</small> *a ready answer to a friend of mine, a composer, who asked, "Why couldn't he just have been experimenting?"*[16] (compare *I <u>have</u> no ready answer.*)

Introductory Adverbial:

First <u>comes</u><small>[V]</small> *love*<small>[SUBJ]</small>, *then <u>comes</u>*<small>[V]</small> *marriage*<small>[SUBJ]</small>. (compare *First love <u>comes</u>, then marriage <u>comes</u>.*)

After A <u>comes</u><small>[V]</small> *B*<small>[SUBJ]</small>, *then <u>comes</u>*<small>[V]</small> *C*<small>[SUBJ]</small>, *next <u>comes</u>*<small>[V]</small> *D*<small>[SUBJ]</small>. (compare *After A B <u>comes</u>, then C <u>comes</u>, next D <u>comes</u>.*)

Down <u>came</u><small>[V]</small> *the rain*<small>[SUBJ]</small> *and washed the spider out.* (compare *The rain <u>came</u> down and washed the spider out.*)

AdvCl with *as*:

Analytical rigor is important to learn, as <u>is</u> the ability to defend an unorthodox view<small>[SUBJ]</small>.[17] (compare *Analytical rigor is important to learn, as the ability to defend an unorthodox view <u>is</u>.*)

Sometimes an A<small>UX</small> is inverted with the S<small>UBJ</small> or the MV:

Negative introduction:

Not until I heard the sound of my son's old pickup rounding the corner could<small>[AUX]</small> *I*<small>[SUBJ]</small> *drift off*<small>[MV]</small> *to sleep.*[18] (compare *I*<small>[SUBJ]</small> *could*<small>[AUX]</small> *not*<small>[NEG]</small> *drift off*<small>[MV]</small> *to sleep until....*)

Introductory Participle:

Forgotten<small>[MV]</small> *in the discussion was*<small>[AUX]</small> *the fact that President George W. Bush said virtually the same thing in Mexico two years ago*<small>[SUBJ]</small>.[19] (compare *The fact that President George W. Bush said virtually the same thing in Mexico two years ago*<small>[SUBJ]</small> *was*<small>[AUX]</small> *forgotten*<small>[MV]</small> *in the discussion.* [passive voice verb])

Coming<small>[MV]</small> *in last in the race was*<small>[AUX]</small> *Joe "Elephant Legs" Blow*<small>[SUBJ]</small>. (compare *Joe "Elephant Legs" Blow*<small>[SUBJ]</small> *was*<small>[AUX]</small> *coming*<small>[MV]</small> *in last in the race.* [progressive aspect verb])

So Adv Aux Subj MV ... :

So rarely<small>[ADV]</small> *does*<small>[AUX]</small> *a game*<small>[SUBJ]</small> *make*<small>[MV]</small> *you feel the weight of the awful things that you do.*[20] (compare *A game*<small>[SUBJ]</small> *does*<small>[AUX]</small> *make*<small>[MV]</small> *you feel the weight of the awful things that you do so rarely.*)

So ... that ... :

So rarely does[Aux] *a comet*[Subj] *appear*[MV] *visible to the naked eye that when one does, it is considered a major event.* (compare *A comet*[Subj] *does*[Aux] *appear*[MV] *visible to the naked eye so rarely that when one does, it is considered a major event.*)

Had-for-if clauses:

I gladly would have reported it had[Aux] *I*[Subj] *remembered*[MV] *it.*[21] (compare *I gladly would have reported it if I*[Subj] *had*[Aux] *remembered*[MV] *it.*)

The verb complement may also be inverted with other clause constituents:

Introductory DO: *Whose woods these are*[DO] *I think I*[Subj] *know*[MV].[22]
(compare *I think I* [Subj] *know*[MV] *whose woods these are*[DO].)
Introductory SC: *Whose woods*[SC] *these*[Subj] *are*[MV] *I think I know.*
(compare *These* [Subj] *are*[MV] *whose woods*[SC] ...)

Once again, we associate such strong inversions with poetry—so much so that Subj-V and complement inversions are sometimes called "poetic inversion."

As we shall see below, dependent clauses provide us with a further repertoire of devices for rearranging, combining, and elaborating declarative sentences and their structure.

10.2 Dependent Clauses

Dependent clauses occur as constituents within independent clauses, and an independent clause may contain several dependent clauses: *Because I made the honor roll, my mother, whom I love dearly, said she would buy me whatever I wanted.* *Because I made the honor roll* is an adverb clause (AdvCl) functioning as a sentence modifier (AdvCl:SentMod). *Whom I love dearly* is an adjective clause (AdjCl) functioning as a post-modifier of *mother* (AdjCl:Mod of "mother"). *Whatever I wanted* is a noun clause (NCl) functioning as the direct object of *buy* (NCl:DO).

Dependent clauses may also occur as constituents within other dependent clauses:

The book that the man who owned the store wanted was a novel that had what some people call a plot.
The book [that the man [who owned the store][AdjCl:Mod of "man"] *wanted]*[AdjCl:Mod of "book"] *was a novel [that had [what some people call a plot]*[NCl:DO of "had"]]*[AdjCl:Mod of "novel"].

Who owned the store is an AdjCl functioning as a post-modifier of the noun "man," while *that the man who owned the store wanted* is an AdjCl functioning as a modifier of "book." Likewise, *what some people call a plot* is an NCL functioning as the DO of "had," while *that had what some people call a plot* is an ADJCL functioning as a post-modifier of "novel." To keep these relationships clear, we will refer to a dependent clause as being a constituent within a container clause. Thus, the dependent clause that starts *that had* is a container clause for the dependent clause *what some people call a plot*, and the independent clause, *The book ... plot*, is a container clause for the dependent clause *that had ... plot*. Remember that a container clause may be either an independent or a dependent clause.

As the names of each type implies, dependent clauses function within their container clauses in many of the ways that other adjectivals, nominals, and adverbials function in clauses (see Chapter 11).

10.2.1 Adjective Clauses (ADJCL; a.k.a. Relative Clauses)

All dependent clauses are marked as different from independent, declarative clauses. Adjective clauses may be marked in three ways:

1. An ADJCL is most commonly a constituent within an NP, functioning as a post-modifier of the head noun and appearing after the noun it modifies, either immediately or very shortly.
2. An ADJCL is usually marked by the presence of a relative pronoun (REL-PRON) (although, as we'll see below, that RELPRON may be deleted when it functions as the DO or IO <u>within</u> the ADJCL) or some other relative pro-word (relative pro-determiner [RELPROD]; relative pro-adverb [REL-PROADV]); the antecedent of the relative pro-word is always an N' comprising all of the other constituents of the NP that precede the ADJCL.
3. An ADJCL is often marked by the distortion of the order of the clause: whatever the grammatical function of the relative pro-word (RELPRON, RELPROD, or RELPROADV) <u>within</u> the ADJCL, the relative pro-word will be moved to the beginning of the ADJCL (except when a RELPRON functions as a PCOMP; then the whole PP may move to the beginning of the ADJCL). In these respects, relative pro-words work very much like interrogative pro-words.

Adjective clauses most commonly function as post-modifiers of nouns within NPs. The only exception is when an ADJCL functions as a non-essential modifier of a preceding clause; we will discuss this usage below. When an ADJCL modifies a noun, it functions as an adjectival constituent of the NP, much like ADJPs and PPs. We can see this clearly when we apply the pronoun replacement test for determining which sentence constituents are part of a particular NP. In the sentence *The woman whom I met at Panera lives in Pekin*, the verb in the container clause is *lives*. We might be inclined to say that the subject of *lives* is *the woman*. We can double-check whether we have identified the whole NP:SUBJ by using the pronoun replacement test:

[*The woman*] *whom I met at Panera lives in Pekin.*
?*She whom I met at Panera lives in Pekin.*

Substituting *she* for the apparent NP *the woman* sounds odd in the context of the rest of the sentence because we have not identified the complete NP:SUBJ. The ADJCL *whom I met at Panera* functions as a post-modifier of the noun *woman* and is a constituent of the NP:SUBJ:

[*The woman whom I met at Panera*] *lives in Pekin.*
She lives in Pekin.

In everyday language, ADJCLs do not, typically, modify personal pronouns. However, we find this construction in formal ritual language, as in:

Four suns since was the word brought to me from 'She-who-must-be-obeyed.' [23]
This was the holy place, the place of He Who Walks Behind the Rows. [24]
He who can, does. He who cannot, teaches. [25]

Personal pronouns modified by ADJCLs are also quite common in biblical language. John 8:7 is translated in many different ways, several of which use this construction:

He who is without sin among you, let him be the first to throw a stone at her. [26]
Let him who is without sin among you be the first to throw a stone at her. [27]
He that is without sin among you, let him first cast a stone at her. [28]

Demonstrative and **indefinite pronouns** may take ADJCLs as modifiers in ordinary language:

Those who attended research institutions were least likely to be K-12 teachers. [29]
Anyone who attended college through the mid-1960s will recall the in loco parentis *regulations.* [30]

Then there is Woody Allen's variation on George Bernard Shaw's oft-quoted line: ***Those** who can't do, teach. **Those** who can't teach, teach gym.* [31]
As a post-modifier of a noun, an ADJCL will commonly appear directly after the noun it modifies, as in the sentence *The woman whom I met at Panera lives in Pekin.* However, just as we can have more than one ADJP as pre-modifiers of a noun, we can have more than one post-modifying adjectival:

The woman	[*in the red suit*]	[*whom I met at Panera*]	*lives in Pekin.*
	PP:MOD OF "woman"	ADJCL:MOD OF "woman"	

For purposes of clarity, though, we prefer to keep the ADJCL close to the noun that is the head of the NP so that the reference of the RELPRON remains clear. In the following sentence, it is not clear what the ADJCL modifies:

The woman	[with the tall man]	[whom I met at Panera]	lives in Pekin.
	PP:MOD OF "woman"	?ADJCL:MOD OF "woman" ?ADJCL:MOD OF "man"	

As a speaker or writer, we might <u>intend</u> *whom I met at Panera* to modify the noun *woman*; but because the ADJCL immediately follows the noun *man*, a reader or listener will assume that the ADJCL modifies the noun it is closer to.

Although I have said that the ADJCL modifies a noun, it seems more reasonable to argue that the ADJCL does not just modify the head noun of the NP but that it modifies the entire N′ that precedes it. That N′ is the antecedent of the RELPRON. In the sentence *The woman <u>whom I met at Panera</u> lives in Pekin*, the antecedent of the RELPRON *whom* is not just the noun *woman* but the whole N′ *the woman*:

> *I met <u>whom</u> at Panera.*
> **I met <u>woman</u> at Panera.*
> *I met <u>the woman</u> at Panera.*

The same is true for the sentence *The woman in the red suit <u>whom I met at Panera</u> lives in Pekin*, in which the antecedent of *whom* is not just the noun *woman* but the whole N′, *the woman in the red suit*:

> *I met <u>whom</u> at Panera.*
> *I met <u>the woman in the red suit</u> at Panera.*

ADJCL functioning as a modifier of a clause: There is one context in which an ADJCL does not function as a post-modifier of a noun: when it functions as a non-essential modifier of an entire preceding clause.

> *The problem is the plant is difficult to propagate, <u>which put a damper on efforts to try to produce stock and breed new varieties</u>.*[32]
> *Thousands of East Germans drove their Trabants over the border when the Wall fell, <u>which made it a kind of automotive liberator</u>.*[33]

In each of these sentences, we know that the ADJCL is modifying the entire preceding clause—as though that clause were an N′—because the antecedent of the relative pro-word *which* is the entire clause. *Which* functions as the subject in both adjective clauses, so its antecedent is, in the first sentence, whatever *put a damper ...* , which is the NCL [*that*] *the plant is difficult to propagate*: "That the plant is difficult to propagate put a damper ..."; in the second sentence, the antecedent of *which* is whatever *made it a kind ...* , which is [*that*] *thousands of East Germans drove their Trabants over the border when the Wall fell.* At the same time, the ADJCL tells something about *what kind of* event is named in the modified clause. Notice that these ADJCLs are not sentence modifiers: they do not provide adverbial information, and we cannot move them. Nonetheless, because they are outside the SUBJ-PRED structure of the clauses they modify, we will consider them further when we get to ADVCLs below. Finally, we know that these ADJCLs are non-essential modifiers because the reader does not need the information in them in order to know which events are being described in the sentences they modify.

10.2.1.1 Relative Pro-words

Relative pro-words—pronouns (RELPRON), pro-determiners (RELPROD), pro-adverbs (RELPROADV), and pro-clauses (RELPROCL)—perform two jobs: first, relative pro-words refer back to an antecedent, which except in the case of a RELPROCL, is an N' comprising all of the constituents within the NP that precede the ADJCL. Second, the relative pro-word has a function within the ADJCL itself. Because the ADJCL is a clause, it has an interior constituent structure like a sentence, and the relative pro-word fulfills some role within the clause structure. When we turn the default SVC declarative structure of a sentence into an ADJCL, we rearrange the order of clause constituents. Specifically, we displace the relative pro-word from whatever slot it fills in the declarative SVC clause order and move the relative pro-word to the front of the ADJCL. To most easily analyze the function of the relative pro-word and the structure of the ADJCL, we must first rearrange the ADJCL into its declarative SVC clause order.

The sentence *The woman in the red suit* <u>*whom I met at Panera*</u> *lives in Pekin* contains the ADJCL, *whom I met at Panera,* in which *whom* refers back to *the woman in the red suit.*

<u>*whom*</u> *I met at Panera*→<u>*the woman in the red suit*</u> *I met at Panera*

To parse the ADJCL, we must determine where to put *the woman in the red suit* so as to restore the clause to SVC order. Within the clause, the verb is *met,* and its subject is *I. I met whom or what?* The answer, *the woman in the red suit,* will be the DO. Thus, in the adjective clause, *whom* is a relative pronoun that functions as the DO of *met* (RELPRON:DO OF "met").

the woman in the red suit I met at Panera→

   I met [*the woman in the red suit*] *at Panera.*
   I met whom[RELPRON:DO OF "met"] *at Panera.*

Relative pro-words have a variety of forms and can fill a variety of functions. Although the relative pro-word must agree with its antecedent as to whether the pro-word is animate or inanimate, the form of the pro-word is dictated by its function within the ADJCL. Traditionally, members of this class of words are called "relative pronouns," but we will more properly speak of relative pro-words since several of them do not function as nominals within the ADJCL:

Relative Pro-Words:

- **Relative pronoun** (unmarked for case): *that, which.*
- **Relative nominative case pronoun:** *who.*
- **Relative objective case pronoun:** *whom.*
- **Relative possessive pro-determiner:** *whose.*
- **Relative pro-adverbs:** *why, when, where, that.*
- **Relative pro-clause:** *which.*

There is nothing that distinguishes or marks the case of *that* and *which*, and both can function in nominative roles (SUBJ, SC) or objective roles (DO, IO, PCOMP). And *that*, the amazing all-purpose word, can sometimes take on an adverbial function. In *That's the reason why he's on the list*,[34] the REL-PROADV *why* stands-in for a sentence modifier, such as *because he deserves to be*, but because we are dealing with an ADJCL and not a sentence, we say that *why* functions as a clause modifier. We could also use *that* to have the same meaning: *That's the reason that he's on the list.* Here, *that* fills the same role as *why* did in the preceding sentence. *That* is thus functioning here as a RELPROADV:ADJCLMOD.

Remember that the form label we put on the relative pro-word is dictated by its function within the ADJCL. This is most significant when the relative pro-word refers to a person and functions in a role that demands the objective case, as in our earlier example, *The woman whom I met at Panera lives in Pekin.* In formal English, the RELPRON in this sentence must be the objective case form *whom* because that PRON refers to a living person (*the woman*) and functions as the DO of "met."

Here are examples of the whole range of functions that relative pro-words may perform within an ADJCL. We start with **nominal functions**:

- Subject: *The reporter **who wrote the article** has since been fired.*[35]
  Who[RELPRON:SUBJ] *wrote the article.*
  *The book **that/which fell off the shelf** was* War and Peace.
  *The problem is the plant is difficult to propagate, **which put a damper on efforts to try to produce stock and breed new varieties**.*[36]

In the last sentence above, *which* functions as the subject of the ADJCL, so it would be reasonable to label it as a RELPRON. At the same time, because its antecedent is a clause, *which* can also be understood as a relative pro-clause (RELPROCL).

- DO: *The woman **whom I met at Panera** lives in Pekin.*

I met whom[RelProN:DO] *at Panera.*
*The book **that/which I dropped** was* War and Peace.

A RelProN may also function as an IO; however, the prepositions *to* or *for* must typically be included in the AdjCl (remember the *to/for* test for the IO?):

- IO: *The woman **that/whom I gave the book to** lives in Pekin.*
  *The woman **to whom** I gave the book lives in Pekin.*
  I gave whom[RelProN:IO] *the book.*
  *The woman **that/whom I made dinner for** lives in Pekin.*
  *The woman for **whom** I made dinner lives in Pekin.*
  I made whom[RelProN:IO] *dinner.*

However, it is possible in informal language to delete the preposition:

> *This is the same friend whom I gave* The Book of the Forsaken [ ] *as a birthday present.*[37]

As we just saw with the *to/for* IO, a RelProN may function as a PComp:

- PComp:
  *The woman **with whom I went dancing** lives in Pekin.*
  *The woman **that/whom I went dancing with** lives in Pekin.*
  I went dancing with whom[RelProN:PComp].
  *The ship **on which I sailed to Tahiti** was called* The Bounty.
  *The ship **that/which I sailed to Tahiti on** was called* The Bounty.
  I sailed to Tahiti on that/which[RelProN:PComp].

These last sentences show us the one situation in which an AdjCl will not begin with a relative pro-word. When a RelProN functions as a PComp, we can move the whole PP to the beginning of the AdjCl. But we also often just move the RelProN and leave the preposition at the end of the AdjCl.

A major warning: when the RelProN functions as the DO, IO or PComp, it can be, and often is, deleted:

- DO: *The woman whom I met at Panera lives in Pekin.*
  The woman I met at Panera lives in Pekin.

  The book that/which I dropped was War and Peace.
  The book I dropped was War and Peace.

- IO: *The woman whom I gave the book to lives in Pekin.*
  The woman I gave the book to lives in Pekin.

- PComp: *The ship on which I sailed to Tahiti was called* The Bounty.

The ship that/which I sailed to Tahiti on was called The Bounty.
The ship I sailed to Tahiti on was called The Bounty.

As we've already seen, when the RELPRON functions as the IO, we usually still need to include the words *to* or *for* when the RELPRON is deleted. However, in informal usage, *to* can sometimes also be deleted: *This is the same friend* [*whom*] *I gave* The Book of the Forsaken [*to*] *as a birthday present.*

When you are parsing sentences and, immediately after a noun, you encounter an NP, you must consider the possibility that what you have found after the noun is an ADJCL with the relative pro-word deleted. It's easy to test: just try to put the word *that* between the preceding noun and the following NP:

The ball[N] *Franz*[N] *bought had a leak.*
The ball[N] *that Franz*[N] *bought had a leak.*

The pronoun replacement test will also work to identify, as a constituent of an NP, the ADJCL with the relative pro-word deleted:

[*The ball Franz bought*] *had a leak.*
It had a leak.

Whose is a **relative pro-determiner** (RELPROD):

*The woman **whose book this is** lives in Pekin.*
  This is whose[RELPROD:SPEC OF "book"] *book.*
*Weldon would marry Jean, a woman **of whose background nothing was known**.*[38]
  Nothing was known of whose[RELPROD:SPEC OF "background"] *background.*

Why, when, where (and *that*) are **relative pro-adverbs** (RELPROADV), which can sometimes be deleted; in the following sentences, I indicate the possibility of deleting the RELPROADV with the number "Ø":

- ADJCLMOD: *But that, I don't think, is the reason **why/that/Ø it is at risk**.*[39]
    It is at risk why[RELPROADV:ADJCLMOD].
    *He remembers the time **when/that/Ø he and a friend carried asphalt into the street to create their own bike ramps**.*[40]
    *We returned to the place **where/that/Ø we had seen it**.*[41]

- SC: *In my native Illinois and other places **where/that/Ø I have been**, all four ferns have always been associated with crevices in limestone outcroppings.*[42]
    I have been where[RELPROADV:SC].

- **LC**: *I don't even know the name of the place **where/that/Ø** we went.*[43]
  We went where/that[RELPROADV:LC].
- **TC**: *Ideally, call before the time **when/that/Ø** you are supposed to arrive.*[44]
  You are supposed to arrive when/that[RELPROADV:TC].
- **OC**: *Go to the table **where** you put the bulletins.*[45]
  You put the bulletins where[RELPROADV:OC].

Although it is not uncommon to find non-native English speakers using *how* as a RELPROADV, it cannot function that way in SE:

> **I like the way* how you played "Hey Jude."*
> *I like the way* that you played "Hey Jude."*

However, we will see below that *how* can function as a PROADV marking an NCL:

> *I like [how you played "Hey Jude."]*[NCL:DO]

Non-Standard relative pronouns: Wolfram and Schilling-Estes[46] discuss several non-Standard constructions involving RELPRONs, such as using *what* in place of *that, who,* or *whom*:

> *Then I likes a man* what's *partial to the ladies, young or old.*[47]
> *I don't remember him scolding me or forcing me to do anything* what *I don't like to do.*[48]

Wolfram and Schilling-Estes claim that it is becoming more common to use "the relative pronoun *which* as a coordinating conjunction (c.f. *and*), as in *They gave me this cigar,* **which** *they know I don't smoke cigars*" and that this usage is "spreading into informal varieties of general American English."[49]

We have seen that a RELPRON:DO, IO, or PCOMP can be deleted from the ADJCL. Generally, when a RELPRON functions as the <u>subject</u> of the ADJCL, it cannot be deleted, as in *That's the dog* that *bit me.* However, in Southern vernaculars, and particularly in AAVE, it is possible to delete RELPRONs functioning as subjects, as in *That's the dog bit me* or *The man come in here was my father.*[50] Rickford and Rickford, as well as Fries, cite other examples:

> *He the man ____ got all the old records.*
> *Wally the teacher ___ wanna retire next year.*[51]
> *I have a son-in-law ___ has served 7 years....*[52]

Wolfram and Schilling-Estes note that "the absence of the relative pronoun is more common in existential constructions such as *There's a dog bit me* than in other constructions."[53] Rickford, citing Mufwene, notes that "many varieties of English allow for the omission of object relative pronouns, e.g. 'That's the man (whom) I saw,' but the omission of subject relatives is rarer, and more unique [sic] to AAVE."[54] Dillard cites the example, *That's the chick I keep tellin' you about got all that money*, where the object relative pronoun of the first ADJCL (*[whom] I keep tellin' you about*) may be deleted in SE but where the subject relative pronoun of the second ADJCL (*[who's] got all that money*) is obligatory in SE.[55]

10.2.2 Noun Clauses (NCL)

Like ADJCLs, NCLs are marked as different from independent, declarative clauses. NCLs are commonly classified by the two ways in which they are marked: as *that*-clauses and *wh*-clauses.

That-clauses are typically marked at their beginning by the expletive *that*. While expletive *that* is the most common marker of this type of NCL, *that*-clauses may also be marked by an expletive *whether* or an expletive *if* (when *if* is used to mean "whether"). Both traditional grammar and more recent work commonly regard the expletive (*that, whether*, or *if*) that marks the NCL as having no meaning or grammatical role in the NCL or the container clause but as only marking the beginning of the NCL.[56]

Here are some examples of NCLs:

> *That I want to be a doctor is obvious.*
> *I know that I want to be a doctor.*[57]
> *You will know if/whether/that I want to be a doctor when I tell you.*

An NCL marked by an expletive *if* can usually only be used as a DO, not in other nominal functions (such as SUBJ, IO, or PCOMP).

As with RELPRONs, the expletive *that* marking the NCL can often be deleted when the NCL functions as a DO within the container clause (NCL:DO):

> *I know that I want to be a doctor.*
> *I know I want to be a doctor.*
>
> *You will know if/whether/that I want to be a doctor when I tell you.*
> *You will know I want to be a doctor when I tell you*

However, following some verbs, the expletive cannot be deleted:

> *I love that I want to be a doctor.* **I love I want to be a doctor.*
> *I can't help that I want to be a doctor.* **I can't help I want to be a doctor.*
> *I don't care whether I want to be a doctor.* **I don't care I want to be a doctor.*[58]

Finally, the order of a *that*-clause is not distorted from the declarative sentence order. A *that*-clause is just a declarative sentence with an expletive (*that, whether*, or *if*) stuck on the front.

An alternate analysis: As we have just seen, a *that*-clause can function as the complement of a verb, specifically as a DO. Current syntactic theory treats *that*-clauses as *complement clauses* and refers to *that, whether*, and *if* (used to mean *whether*) as complementizers. According to this analysis, not only verbs but nouns, adjectives, and adverbs can also take complement clauses as, well, complements:

> V + COMPLEMENT CLAUSE (**NCL:DO**): *Schempp reported*[V] *that their collective dream for a family business was kaput.*
>
> N + COMPLEMENT CLAUSE (**NCL:APPOSITIVE:MOD OF N**): *Schempp called to break the news*[N] *that their collective dream for a family business was kaput.*[59]
>
> ADJ + COMPLEMENT CLAUSE (**NCL:ADVERBIAL MODIFIER OF ADJ**):*Schempp was sure*[ADJ] *that their collective dream for a family business was kaput.*
>
> ADV + COMPLEMENT CLAUSE (**NCL:ADVERBIAL MODIFIER OF ADV**): *Now*[ADV] *that their collective dream for a family business was kaput, Schempp could call to break the news.*

Traditional grammar would analyze the complement clause following the noun as a nominal appositive: in form, the clause looks like an NCL, but it is functioning like an adjectival, telling *which* or *what kind of news*. For traditional grammar, the complement clause following the adjective causes more trouble: in form, it looks like an NCL; but if it is modifying an adjective, it seems to be telling *how* or *in what manner Schempp was sure*—that is, it is providing adverbial information. Likewise, the *that*-clause following the adverb *now* seems to be telling *how* or *in what manner now*. The notion of the complement clause is, on the one hand, an elegant formal work around in that, rather than treating these clauses as modifiers, it treats them as complements: constituents that complete the meaning of the head constituent of their phrase. At the same time, I have chosen to define modifiers as optional constituents and complements as required. Following the noun, adjective, and adverb, the *that*-clause is not required: if you delete the *that*-clause in each case, the sentence is still well formed. Although I will mention this notion of the complement clause again in discussing adverb clauses below, I will otherwise stick with the distinction I have already established between modifiers and complements and only refer to these *that*-clauses as complements when they follow verbs.

Non-Standard *that*-clause: Dillard[60] describes how, in AAVE, it is common to find sentences of the form *I don't know can he go*. Sometimes mistakenly identified as an indirect quotation of a question, this construction is better analyzed as equivalent to the SE *I don't know whether/if/that he can go*. The inversion of the AUX *can* and the subject *he* has the same function as the SE complementizer.

Wh-noun clauses have a *wh*-word that marks the beginning of the NCL, and, in a *wh*-clause, the *wh*-word has a grammatical function within the NCL, like the function of a relative pro-word within an ADJCL or an interrogative pro-word in an interrogative sentence. Likewise, the *wh*-noun clause is marked by its distortion of the default SVC clause order. To parse a *wh*-clause, and to determine the function of the *wh*-word within the NCL, we must first restore the NCL to declarative order. For example, in the sentence *What we don't know is an ocean,*[61] *what we don't know* is an NCL functioning as the subject of the container clause. To parse the NCL, we first identify the verb (*do know*) and its subject (*we*). *Not* is an ADVP modifying *do know*. *We don't know* typically implies the question, "We don't know what?"; the verb *do know* usually takes a NOMINAL:DO. In this case, we have a possible answer in the word *what*, which appears to be a PRON functioning as the DO of *do know*. This parsing of *what* is verified by the NP *an ocean*, which appears to be the post-cedent of the PRON *what*. That is, in the NCL, *what* seems to be replacing the NP *an ocean* since, in the context of this sentence, the answer to the question, "What do we not know?" is "an ocean." *What* is the PRON:DO of "do know." Therefore, in terms of its use of a *wh*-word, the *wh*-clause seems to be behaving like an ADJCL.

However, unlike a RELPRON, the *wh*-word in an NCL may or may not refer to another word in the container clause. In the example above, *what* refers to *an ocean*; in the following example, *whoever* refers to nothing in the container clause: ***Whoever** finds the starter motor, the genetic wellspring of motivation, will have found a key to good health.*[62] In an ADJCL, the relative pro-word always has an antecedent in the container clause. By contrast, the antecedent or reference of the *wh*-word in an NCL may be in the container clause, in the surrounding text, in the immediate physical context of the discourse, part of common knowledge, or something that the speaker or writer presumes is familiar to the audience.

Also, although the expletive in a *that*-clause may be deleted, the *wh*-word in a *wh*-clause cannot ever be deleted (even if it functions as the DO within the NCL) without changing the meaning of the NCL: *I know **what** you are thinking.* **I know* you are thinking.* We normally take the starred example to mean the same thing as a *that*-clause, but, of course, *that you are thinking* does not mean the same thing as *what you are thinking*.

Finally, *wh*-NCLs are different from ADJCLs in that, when an ADJCL functions as a modifier of a noun, the RELPRON at the beginning of the ADJCL always renames a preceding N' in the container clause. But the only time an NCL follows directly after a noun, such that the *wh*-word at the beginning of the NCL names the same thing as the noun that precedes the clause, is when the NCL functions as an OC, as in, *Tom Hanks says community college made him*[NP:DO] *who he is today*[NCL:OC].[63]

Noun clause functions: NCLs can perform all of the same grammatical functions as NPs:

SUBJ: *Whoever finds the starter motor will have found a key to good health.*
AGENT: *It was then that he realized that puppetry could be an art form.*[64]
DO: *I want to meet whoever found the starter motor.*
IO: *We want to make whomever you invite a really good lunch.*[65]
SC: *You are what you eat.*
OC: *Community college made him who he is today.*
PCOMP: *You may eat when you wish with whomever you want.*[66]

Because the NCL is a clause, it has an interior constituent structure like a sentence. As with the RELPRON in an ADJCL, in a *wh*-NCL, the *wh*-word, is taken out of the slot it fills in conventional declarative clause order and moved to the front of the NCL. The list of forms and functions of *wh*-words as they are used in NCLs is very similar to the list of interrogative pro-words:[67]

Wh-words:

- **PRON** (unmarked for case): *what, whatever, which, whichever.*
- **Nominative case PRON**: *who, whoever, whosoever.*
- **Objective case PRON**: *whom, whomever, whomsoever.*
- **PROADJ**: *how, what, whatever, which, whichever.*
- **PROD**: *what, whatever, which, whichever.*
- **Possessive PROD**: *whose, whosever, whoever's.*
- **PROADV**: *why, when, whenever, where, wherever, how, how long, how much, however.*

Some notes about this list: *How* can be either a pro-adjective or a pro-adverb, depending on the context. We can see this in the following sentences:

That's how fast the world is changing.[68]
You know how I feel about Twitter.[69]

In the first sentence, *how* takes the place of a degree ADV, such as *very*, that modifies *fast*. In the second sentence, putting the NCL in SVC order, we get *I feel how about Twitter*; most commonly, we would read *how* as filling in for an ADJ such as *unhappy* or *angry.*

What, whatever, which, and whichever can be pronouns, but they can also be pro-adjectives, pro-determiners, or, as we saw with interrogative pro-words, a PRO-(D + ADJ) or a pro-prenominal:

I don't know what action we can take.

> *We can take what action.* →
> **PRODET:** *We can take this action.*
> **PROADJ:** *We can take immediate action.*
> **PRO-(D + ADJ):** *We can take the right action.*[70]

I don't know which balls I should buy.

I should buy which balls. →
PRoDET: *I should buy these balls.*
PRoADJ: *I should buy green balls.*[71]
PRo-(D + ADJ): *I should buy these green balls.*

You can readily make up similar examples for *whatever* and *whichever*.

Whoever's: According to the *Corpus of Contemporary American English* (COCA),[72] though it can appear as a possessive PRoD, *whoever's* is used much more frequently as a contraction of *whoever is*, and sometimes *whoever has*:

> Possessive PRoD: *Whoever's DNA this was would be the killer.*[73]
> **Contraction of "whoever is"**: *Whoever's patrolling the hall can see into every room.*[74]
> **Contraction of "whoever has"**: *If I was able to track the shuttle's position, whoever's been using it will as well.*[75] (c.f. *whoever has been using it*)

Whosever is a non-Standard informal conversational variant of *whoever's* that, according to COCA, is most frequently used as a possessive PRoD but that may also be used as a contraction of *whoever is* or *who has ever*:

> Possessive PRoD: *Whosever fingerprints they are, they aren't hers.*[76]
> **Contraction of "who is ever"**: *Whosever the closest will get there first and secure the scene.*[77] (c.f. *Whoever is the closest*)
> **Contraction of "who has ever"**: *There is no one that fit that type of description that would have been there that night or whosever been there with that type of hair.*[78] (c.f. *who has ever been there* or *whoever has been there*)

In an NCL, the *wh*-word functions to mark the beginning of the NCL except, as in an interrogative sentence or an ADJCL, when the *wh*-PRoN functions as a PCOMP or when a *wh*-PRoD functions within an NP:PCOMP. In those cases, we can move the entire PP to the front of the NCL, and the NCL can start with a preposition immediately followed by the *wh*-word. And, as in an ADJCL, the form of the *wh*-word is dictated by its function within the NCL:

> SUBJ:*They need to know **what makes him tick**.* $What_{[PRoN:SUBJ]}$ *makes him tick.*[79]
> *I know **who did this**.* $Who_{[PRoN:SUBJ]}$ *did this.*[80]

> AGENT:*The researcher examined **by whom** the safety references were made.*[81]
> *The researcher examined **whom the safety references were made by**.*
> *The safety references were made by* $whom_{[PRoN:AGENT]}$.

> DO:*You need to figure out **whom you want to include in your plans**.*[82]
> *You want to include* $whom_{[PRoN:DO]}$.

*You're allowed to take **whatever/whomever/what/whichever you want**.*[83]
You want whatever$_{[PRON:DO]}$.

IO:***Whom/whomever I gave the book to*** *is none of your business.*
I gave whom$_{[PRON:IO]}$*the book.*

PCOMP: *I know **for whom the bell tolls**. I know **whom the bell tolls for**.*
The bell tolls for whom$_{[PRON:PCOMP]}$.

Possessive D: *I will find out **whose woods these are**.*
These are whose$_{[PossPROD:SPEC \text{ OF "woods"}]}$ *woods.*

D: *I wake up here and wonder **what century I'm in**.*[84]
*I wake up here and wonder **in what century I am**.*
I am in what$_{[PROD:SPEC \text{ OF "century"}]}$ *century.*
***Whatever/whichever approach you choose**, keep evaluating what works and what doesn't.*[85]
You choose whatever$_{[PROD:SPEC \text{ OF "approach"}]}$ *approach.*

These next sentences are similar to the examples of ADJCLs that used the same PROADVs:

NCLMOD:[86] *That's **why he's on the list**. He's on the list why*$_{[PROADV:NCLMOD]}$.
*He remembers **when he and a friend carried asphalt into the street**.*
He and a friend carried asphalt into the street when$_{[PROADV:NCLMOD]}$.
*We returned to **where we had seen it**. We had seen it where*$_{[PROADV:NCLMOD]}$.
***However you do it** is fine with me.*[87] *You do it however*$_{[PROADV:NCLMOD]}$.

LC: *They leave a detailed digital trail of **where we went**.*[88]
We went where$_{[PROADV:LC]}$.

TC: *I remember **when we went**. We went when*$_{[PROADV:TC]}$.
MC: *Here's **how it works**.*[89] *It works how*$_{[PROADV:MC]}$.
OC: *If the hose won't stay **where you put it**, use short stakes or wire staples to hold it in place.*[90] *You put it where*$_{[PROADV:OC]}$.
*I can't recall **how you made the soup**. You made the soup how*$_{[PROADV:OC]}$.

Because of the apparent similarity between *wh*-NCLs and ADJCLs, it may seem like it would be difficult to identify NCLs or, at least, *wh*-NCLs. But an NCL functions in the same way as a complete NP or other nominal. We can use the pronoun replacement test to identify a complete NCL:

[*Whoever finds the starter motor*] *will have found a key to good health.*
She will have found a key to good health.

You know [how I feel about Twitter].
You know it.

I know [that I want to be a doctor].
I know this.

The pronoun replacement test works even if the expletive is deleted from the *that*-clause:

You know [I want to be a doctor].
You know this.

10.2.3 Adverb Clauses (ADvCL; a.k.a. Subordinate Clauses)

Like both ADjCLs and NCLs, ADvCLs are marked as different from independent, declarative clauses. An ADvCL always begins with a subordinating conjunction (SCONJ). SCONJs come in two types: those that do not play any role in the ADvCL and those that do. With the great majority of SCONJs, an ADvCL consists of the SCONJ followed by a string of words that, without the SCONJ, would be a well-formed independent clause. In the sentence *We've all been taught **since we were kids** that strangers equal danger*,[91] *since* is the SCONJ; the string of words that follow, *we were kids*, is, by itself, an independent clause. The word *since* has no role in the ADvCL. Rather, like the expletives *if* and *whether* in NCLs, the SCONJ establishes a relationship between the ADvCL and its container clause. In the case of *since*, that relationship involves time and duration: the event described in the ADvCL (*we were kids*) is an anchor in the past, and in the ensuing period up to the present, the event described in the container clause (*We've all been taught that strangers equal danger*) has been constant or frequent. SCONJs always help establish this kind of rhetorical connection and relationship between and among clauses within paragraphs and even between paragraphs.

In some cases, the SCONJ plays a role within the ADvCL, just as a *wh*-word does in an interrogative sentence, ADjCL, or NCL. For example, in the sentence ***Wherever you go***, *you will always remember this class*, *wherever* is the SCONJ, marking the beginning of the ADvCL. But *wherever* also functions within the ADvCL as an LC of the verb *go* (*You go wherever*[PROADV:LC]).

ADvCLs function in many of the roles in which other adverbials function:

* Modifier of ADj (though only as post-modifiers).
* Modifier of ADv (though, again, only as post-modifiers).
* Complement of verb (SC; OC).
* Modifier of verb.
* Sentence and clause modifier.

Modifier of ADj: We find ADvCLs modifying adjectives in a limited set of idiomatic patterns:

I was happy[ADJ] **_that I made the right decision._**[92]
We couldn't be happier[ADJ] **_that Billy Crystal is emcee of this year's extravaganza._**[93]
I'm happier[ADJ] **_than I've ever been._**[94]
It's much more difficult[ADJ] **_than I thought it would be._**[95]
I was as happy[ADJ] **_as I've ever been._**[96]

As we saw in the discussion of NCLs, contemporary syntactic theory would describe each of the *that*-clauses as a complement clause, functioning as a complement of the ADJ. However, in each of these examples, we might also parse the *that*-clause as an adverbial modifier of the preceding ADJ, telling *why I was happy/we couldn't be happier/*etc. I will therefore persist in calling these ADVCLs. Note that the adjectives in the comparative degree (*happier*; *more difficult*) require the following clause to be marked by the SCONJ *than*. And the idiomatic frame AS + ADJ + *as* + CLAUSE is so fixed that it is really a phrasal SCONJ, marking the following clause as adverbial and establishing its relationship with the container clause, a relationship that generally involves a comparison.

Modifier of ADV: As with adjectives, ADVCLs can only modify adverbs within a limited set of idiomatic patterns:

He spoke <u>so</u> slowly[ADV] **_that I was able to write down every word he said._**[97]
He spoke <u>more</u> slowly[ADV] **_than we had ever heard him speak._**
Selena Gomez disappears through the crowd <u>as</u> quickly[ADV] **_<u>as she appeared._</u>**[98]

These are not the only patterns for ADVCLs modifying adverbs, but they are representative. Notice that we only find ADVCLs modifying ADVs in these fixed idiomatic frames (e.g. *SO* + ADV + *THAT*; *LESS* + ADV + *THAN*; *AS* + ADV + *AS*, each followed by a clause) that, again, may be best analyzed as phrasal SCONJs, marking the following clause as adverbial and establishing its relationship with the container clause, a relationship that generally involves a comparison, as in the last two examples.

As the **complement of a verb**, an ADVCL can only function as an SC or OC:

<u>SC</u>: *That was <u>before he picked up an extra first-round pick in next year's draft._</u>*[99]
<u>OC</u>: *Let's put the blame **<u>where it belongs.</u>***[100]

It is sometimes hard to distinguish whether an ADVCL is limited to <u>modifying a verb</u> or if it is movable and so may be considered a <u>sentence or clause modifier</u>. In the sentence *Jim talks **as if he doesn't like me**, talks* is an intransitive verb: we could just say *Jim talks*. Therefore, if we can't move the AdvCl, then it is a modifier of the verb; if we can move it, it is a SENTMOD. To my ear, ****_As if he_** *doesn't like me, Jim talks* does not sound like a well-formed SE sentence. And so, I would judge *as if she doesn't like me* to be functioning as a modifier of *talks* or possibly as a manner complement (MC).

By contrast, in the sentence:

> *Jim talks **because** he has nothing else to do.*
> ***Because** he has nothing else to do, Jim talks.*

the AdvCl *because he has nothing else to do* can be moved and so should be regarded as a SentMod of the independent clause *Jim talks*.

We have to exercise the same judgment in determining whether an AdvCl that has a dependent clause as its container clause is functioning as a modifier of the verb in the container clause or as a modifier of the whole container clause (an AdjClMod, NClMod, or AdvClMod). I have included examples of both situations below:

- **AdvCl:Modifier of the V in an AdjCl:**

  *Anyone who talks **as if Chinese freedom hasn't grown since China went capitalist**[AdvCl:Mod of "talks"] is evincing a hazy historical memory.*[101]

- **AdvCl:AdjClMod:**

  *Australian actress Sarah Snook stars as a woman who, **after her fiance dies**[AdvCl:AdjClMod of "who moves . . . mansion"] moves into her father's decaying Louisiana mansion.*[102]
  *Australian actress Sarah Snook stars as a woman who moves into her father's decaying Louisiana mansion **after her fiance dies**[AdvCl:AdjClMod of "who moves . . . mansion"].*

- **AdvCl:Modifier of a V in an NCl:**

  *That Jim talks **as if he doesn't like me**[AdvCl:Mod of "talks"] comes as no surprise.*

- **AdvCl:NClMod:**

  *That he passed the test, **even though he had a miserable cold**[AdvCl:NClMod of "That he . . . the test"] is amazing.*
  *That, **even though he had a miserable cold**[AdvCl:NClMod of "That he . . . the test"] he passed the test, is amazing.*

- **AdvCl:Modifier of V in an AdvCl:**

  *When Jim talks **as if he doesn't like me**[AdvCl:Mod of "talks"] it comes as no surprise.*

- **AdvCl:AdvClMod:**

  *When he passed the test **even though he had a miserable cold**[AdvCl:NClMod of "When he . . . the test"] I thought it was amazing.*

When, ***even though*** *he had a miserable cold*[ADVCL:NCLMOD OF "When he ... the test"]*, he passed the test, I thought it was amazing.*

10.2.3.1 Subordinating Conjunctions (SConj)

"Subordinating conjunctions" are so called because they mark the beginning of a subordinate clause (the traditional name for ADVCLs). SCONJS also join ('conjoin') ADVCLs to their container clauses by marking the rhetorical relationship between the concepts named by the two clauses. We will examine and classify some of those rhetorical relationships when we examine SENTMODS in 11.3.6.

SCONJS are of two varieties: (1) those that play no role in the ADVCL and (2) those that do. However, (1) SCONJS that play no role in the ADVCL are more common. And (2) SCONJS that have some role in the ADVCL, unlike RELPROWORDS and *wh*-words in NCLS, are still always the first word in the ADVCL.

(1) In ADVCLs in which the SCONJ plays no role in the ADVCL, the SCONJ is followed by a clause that, without the SCONJ, would be a sentence. This type of ADVCL thus resembles a *that*-NCL. In the following examples, ***because*** and ***if*** are the SCONJS.

> ***Because*** *we were convinced that we had all the truth, we never listened to those who thought differently from us.*[103]
> ***If*** *we weren't convinced that we had all the truth, we would have listened to those who thought differently from us.*

If we remove the SCONJ from the ADVCL, then, in each example, what is left is an independent clause: *We were/n't convinced that we had all the truth.*

Here is a list of common SCONJS that have no function within the ADVCL:

after	as though	inasmuch as	provided (that)	though
although	because	in order that	rather than	till (or 'til)
as	before	lest	since	unless
as if	even if	like	so that	until
as long as	even though	now that	supposing	whereas
as much as	if	on condition that	than	whether
as soon as	if only	once	that	while

Some of these SCONJS can also function as prepositions. That list includes *after, as, before, like, since, than,* and *until*. If they are followed by just an NP, together with which they comprise a single constituent, then they are prepositions; if they are followed by a clause, together with which they comprise a single constituent, then they are SCONJS:

> **SCONJ:** *After the party ends, we load our children into the car.*[104]
> *So the dancers whirled on* ***until the sun rose.***[105]
> **P:** *After the party, Hollender began a nationwide speaking tour.*[106]
> *The partying continued* ***until sunrise.***[107]

Current syntactic theory chooses to analyze these SConjs-that-can-also-be-prepositions the other way: by arguing that these words can take either an NP or a clause as their complement. Either analysis works, and either analysis makes some things simpler and some more complicated. I leave it to you to reflect on which analysis might be better and why.

Note that *because* is only an SConj; *because of* is a preposition:

> SConj: ***Because*** *you love wolves or other predators, you have to study their food source, which is deer.*[108]
>
> P: ***Because of*** *you, I laugh, smile and I dare to dream again.*[109]

Note also that, just as when they function as prepositions, when *after* and *before* function as SConjs, they can take adverbial modifiers like *even, just, long, right, well*:

> <u>*Even before*</u> *this work was accepted for publication, rumors about it prompted prominent figures in the scientific community to urge caution, if not an outright halt, to such research.*[110]
>
> *In March 1933,* <u>*just after*</u> *he was inaugurated, FDR looked for a way to avoid a financial panic after he announced that he was closing the nation's banks.*[111]

SConjs are not only related to prepositions but also to CConjs and conjunctive adverbs (see 11.3.5). SConjs, Conjs, and conjunctive adverbs all guide the reader or listener in how to understand the relationships between clauses—and so the relationships between the concepts expressed in those clauses. When your teachers have marked on your writing, "Transition?" they have very often probably meant that you need an SConj, Conj, or conjunctive adverb.

(2) In AdvCls in which the SConj has a function, the subordinating conjunctions are ProAdvs or ProNs, and all are *wh*-words:

> ProNs: *whatever, whoever, whomever*
> ProAdvs: *however, when, whenever, where, wherever*

All of these SConjs behave just like the *wh*-words in a *wh*-type NCl in that they mark the beginning of the AdvCl, they have a function within the AdvCl, and they are displaced from their slot in a normal declarative sentence order. The ProAdvs may function within the AdvCl as complements of the verb or as modifiers of the whole AdvCl (AdvClMod):

> *Take your skateboard safely and securely with you* <u>***wherever and however***</u> <u>*you go.*</u>[112]
>
> *You go **however***[SConjProAdv:MC of "go"].

*You go **in a car**.* (MC—how you go)

*You go **wherever***[SConjProAdv:LC of "go"].
*You go **to the store**.* (LC—where you go)

When *he stands up in front of the room, everybody listens to him.*[113]

*He stands up **when***[SConjProAdv:AdvClMod].
*He stands up **during a meeting**.*
***During a meeting** he stands up.*

No matter where *I go, I always have my camera with me.*[114]

*I go **no matter where***[SConjProAdv:LC of "go"].
*I go **somewhere**.*

An SConj that functions as a ProN within the AdvCl may function as a Subj, DO, or PComp (*whomever* as a SubConj does not seem to be used as an IO; I could find no examples):

Whatever *you say, never mention the name Ilse Zhalina to Lord Kosenmark.*[115]

*You say **whatever***[SConjProN:DO of "say"].

Whatever *happens to us, we're taking you down.*[116]

Whatever[ConjProN:Subj] *happens to us.*

Whomever *you ask in the child-custody or family-abduction world, they all know—or have heard of—Yager.*[117]

*You ask **whomever***[SConjProN:DO].

Whomever *you're living with, make it a time for saving money.*[118]

*You're living with **whomever***[SConjProN:PComp].

To tell the difference between an AdvCl that starts with a *wh*-word and a *wh*-NCl, use the pronoun replacement test:

- NCl: [**Wherever** *you go*] *is fine with me.*

  It is fine with me.

- AdvCl: [**Wherever** *you go*], *I'll go with you.*

  *It I'll go with you.

To identify an AdvCl: There are two solid methods. Most AdvCls are SentMods; the movability test for SentMods is good to have in mind. The other test—a more impressionistic one, but one that you should practice—is the adverb question test. ADVCLs should answer one of the adverb questions, providing information about *how, how long, how much, when, where,* or *why.*

A final note on clauses: Like any constituent of a clause, independent clauses may be conjoined with independent clauses, and dependent clauses may be conjoined with other dependent clauses or phrases that fulfill the same function within the sentence:

Independent Clauses:

I want to buy the ball. I want to go play with it.
*I want to buy the ball **and** I want to go play with it.*

ADVCL:SENTMOD *AND* ADVCL:SENTMOD

*I want to buy the ball **not only** because I want to play with it**, but** because it's on sale.*

PP:ADVERBIAL:SENTMOD *and* ADVCL:SENTMOD

*I like to go for a run in the morning**, but only** when it's not raining*

In traditional grammar, two or more conjoined independent clauses are referred to as a "compound sentence." A sentence that consists of a container clause with one or more dependent clauses is called a "complex sentence." Two or more conjoined independent clauses that, among them, contain one or more dependent clauses are called a "compound-complex sentence."

Key Points

- A clause contains a finite verb that acts as the head of a VP:PRED and a nominal functioning as the subject of the verb (NOMINAL:SUBJ), such that the NOMINAL:SUBJ and the verb agree in number and person. In addition, to be formally complete, the VP:PRED in a clause must include all complements required by the verb.
- Clauses may be independent (a.k.a. a sentence) or dependent.
- There are three kinds of dependent clauses: adjective clauses (ADJCL), a.k.a. relative clauses; noun clauses (NCL); and, adverb clauses (ADVCL), a.k.a. subordinate clauses.
- Each type of dependent clause is marked by the use of special words, including relative pronouns (RELPRON) and other relative pro-words; expletives (*that, whether, if*); and subordinating conjunctions (SCONJS).
- In English, the default order of the clause is Subject-Verb-Complement (SVC).
- We routinely rearrange the clause constituent order of both independent and dependent clauses to create questions or otherwise rearrange the information flow of independent clauses and to mark that a clause is dependent.

- This rearrangement often involves the movement of a *wh*-pro-word (e.g. interrogative pro-word; relative pro-word) from its slot in the SVC clause to the front of the clause.

10.3 Exercises: Clauses

A. Independent Clauses: made-up sentences: for each of the following independent clauses, identify the form as one of the following: declarative, interrogative, imperative, expletive *there*, expletive *it*, passive, inverted. **Warning**: a sentence may have more than one form.

- For interrogative sentences with a pro-word, identify the interrogative pro-word and its form: pro-adverb, pro-adjective, pro-determiner, possessive pro-determiner, pronoun (nominative, objective, possessive).
- For expletive *there* and expletive *it* sentences, identify the agent.
- For inverted sentences, identify the complete subject and the complete verb.

1. When did you buy your new car?
2. I was driven to drink.
3. There is a house in New Orleans.
4. Down the hole he fell.
5. It seems that the neighbors are having a party.
6. Cry me a river.
7. Perform random acts of kindness.
8. The light is particularly beautiful today.
9. Whose woods are these?
10. It is clear that we will win.
11. There is little question in my mind.
12. Were you followed?
13. It appears that you have been swindled.
14. Eat, drink, and be merry.
15. The sun is up.
16. Had I been there, I'd have stopped her.
17. There's a party going on right here.
18. How do you do?
19. That ain't no way to treat no friend of yourn.
20. When 900 years old you reach, look as good you will not.[119]

B. Independent Clauses: for sentences 1–10 above, try to compose versions that are (1) declarative, (2) interrogative, (3) imperative, (4) expletive *there*, (5) expletive *it*, (6) passive, and (7) inverted in some way. Not all will work: for example, a sentence can only be made passive if it has a transitive verb.

C. Dependent Clauses: made-up sentences: for each sentence:

- • Identify each complete dependent clause (there may be more than one).
- • Identify whether the dependent clause is an adjective clause, a noun clause, or an adverb clause.
- • Identify the dependent clause's function in the container clause.

And finally,

- • If the dependent clause is an **adjective clause**:
  - • Identify the noun that the clause modifies.
  - • Identify the relative pro-word in the adjective clause, and, for each RELPRO-WORD:
    - • Identify its form (e.g. RELPRON, RELPROD; RELPROADV).
    - • Identify its function within the adjective clause (e.g. SUBJ, DO, SENTMOD).

- • If the dependent clause is a **noun clause**:
  - • Identify its type (*that*-clause or *wh*-clause).
  - • If it is a *wh*-clause, for each *wh*-pro-word:
    - • Identify its form (e.g. pronoun, pro-determiner, pro-adverb).
    - • identify its function within the NCL.

- • If the dependent clause is an **adverb clause**:
  - • Identify the subordinating conjunction.
  - • If the subordinating conjunction has a function in the adverb clause, identify that function.

1. When the city was new, travelers often had difficulty finding interesting entertainment.
2. The city soon had distinct ethnic neighborhoods in which immigrants opened restaurants and clubs where visitors could partake of exotic and foreign foods and amusements.
3. Adventurous visitors could choose whichever one they wanted.
4. There were many reasons why the ethnic neighborhoods developed where they did.
5. Experienced travelers, who realized they would frequently have to amuse themselves, brought musical instruments on their journeys.
6. After the subway system was opened, theaters were built in one district of town.
7. However theater-goers wanted to get to the show was, of course, fine with the locals.
8. These early theaters were what we would call a combination restaurant, dancehall, and theater.
9. Spending the evening in a downtown theater was an irritating experience for those who were used to more high-toned surroundings.

10. When the actors were performing, the audience would chatter noisily.
11. Another complaint about the theaters was that the food was poor in quality.
12. The presence of fleas, mice, and other vermin was another discomfort that annoyed the early theater goers.
13. Because the construction of some early theaters used cheap wood and fabric, fire was a great danger.
14. The construction of some early theaters, which used cheap wood and fabric, led to fire being a great danger.
15. That the construction of some early theaters used cheap wood and fabric made fire a great danger.
16. On the ground floors of many theaters were found dance palaces that resounded with noisy revelry.
17. The dance palaces that were found on the ground floors of many theaters resounded with noisy revelry.
18. Because dance palaces were often located on the ground floors of theaters, at night the buildings resounded when the revelry grew noisy.
19. As soon as the show ended, most of the audience would come down to the dance hall.
20. Visitors to the city often tried to act as though they had always lived there.

Figure 10.1

Notes

1. A dependent clause can also be a constituent within a sentence fragment. Although traditional texts on grammar and style generally attack fragments as Bad Writing, the best writers all, in fact, use them. If it begins with a capital "B" and ends with a period, *Because I said so* is not a grammatically well-formed sentence in English. However, in the right context, this ADVCL, punctuated as if it were a sentence but really just a sentence fragment, can be very stylistically effective. Really. (That was a fragment, too.) The world is still waiting for a corpus-based study of the grammar and use of English sentence fragments.

2. However, we will occasionally encounter other verbs used to form SUBJ-V inversions, as in:

> Have I checked on all possible contraindications? Have I found a clear indication? **Have I** a chance of success? Have I done premanipulative testing? Have I recalled Cyriax's advice? (Ludwig Ombregt, MD. "Treatment of the Cervical Spine." *A System of Orthopaedic Medicine*. 3rd ed. Amsterdam: Elsevier, 2013. 182.)

Here, the inversion of the MV *have* with the SUBJ *I* is hidden among a series of AUX-SUBJ inversions. Less common still is the inversion of the SUBJ with an MV that is never an AUX:

> **Lives there** a man with soul so dead
> He's never to his toaster said:
> "You are my friend; I see in you
> An object sturdy, staunch, and true;
> A fellow mettlesome and trim;
> A brightness that the years can't dim"? (Thomas Disch. *The Brave Little Toaster: A Bedtime Story for Small Appliances.* New York: Doubleday, 1986).

Here the V *lives* is inverted with the pseudo-SUBJ *there* (see 10.1.3). We will see this same inversion used in a declarative sentence in 10.1.6. This inversion is distinctly poetic, the more so as it parodies Sir Walter Scott's immortal lines, "Breathes there the man, with soul so dead, / Who never to himself hath said, / This is my own, my native land!" (*The Lay of the Last Minstrel.* 5th ed. London: Longman, Hurst, Rees, and Orme, 1806. 175).

3. Alfred Vick. "Cherokee Adaptation to the Landscape of the West and Overcoming the Loss of Culturally Significant Plants." *American Indian Quarterly* 35.3 (Summer 2011): 394.

4. William Labov, Paul Cohen, et al. *A Study of the Non-Standard English of Negro and Puerto-Rican Speakers in New York City. Final Report, Cooperative Research Project 3228.* Philadelphia: US Regional Survey, 1968. 291–296; Martin, Stefan E. and Walt Wolfram. "The Sentence in African American Vernacular English." *African American English: Structure, History and Use.* Eds. Salikoko S. Mufwene, et al. New York: Routledge, 1998. 29; John R. Rickford. *African American Vernacular English: Features, Evolution, Educational Implications.* Malden, MA: Blackwell, 1999. 8.

5. Labov, Cohen, et al. op. cit. 296–300; Rickford, op. cit. 8.

6. General Harold K. Johnson, Chief of Staff, U.S. Army. Keynote Address. *Report of the Eleventh Annual Army Human Factors Research and Development Conference, Fort Bragg, NC.* Washington, DC: Department of the Army, 1965. 85.

7. From the traditional folk song, "The House of the Rising Sun." See Robert B. Waltz and David G. Engle. "House of the Rising Sun, The." *The Ballad Index.* 2019. <www.fresnostate.edu/folklore/ballads>.

8. Walt Wolfram and Natalie Schilling-Estes. *American English.* 2nd ed. Malden, MA: Blackwell, 2006. 375–376.

9. Lisa J. Green. *African American English: A Linguistic Introduction.* New York: Cambridge University Press, 2002. 80–83.

10. Wolfram and Schilling-Estes, op. cit. 383–384.

11. Flannery O'Connor. "The Teaching of Literature." *Mystery and Manners: Occasional Prose.* Eds. Sally and Robert Fitzgerald. New York: Farrar Straus Giroux, 1969. 131.

12. See Joseph M. Williams and Joseph Bizup. "Lesson 10: Shape." *Style: Lessons in Clarity and Grace.* 12th ed. New York: Pearson, 2017. See especially 137–144.

13. Nick Bostrom. "Where Are They?" *Technology Review* 111.3 (May/Jun 2008): 72+.

14. Craig Hancock. "IO." Online posting. Assembly for the Teaching of English Grammar. 23 Sep 2004.

15. For a detailed introduction to sentence structure and information flow, I highly recommend Williams and Bizup, op. cit., "Lesson 5: Cohesion and Coherence." 64–78.

16. Richard Taruskin. "Who Was Shostakovich?" *The Atlantic* 275.2 (Feb 1995): 71.

17. Scott A. Westfahl. "The Leadership Imperative: A Collaborative Approach to Professional Development in the Global Age of More for Less." *Stanford Law Review* 69.6 (Jun 2017): 1704 [fn. 153].
18. Bonnie Henry. "Curse of the Light Sleeper." *Arizona Daily Star*. 29 Oct 2016.
19. Peter Baker. "On Foreign Policy, Obama Shifts, but Only a Bit." *The New York Times*. 17 Apr 2009.
20. Jason Sheehan. "Reading the Game: This War of Mine." *All Tech Considered*. NPR. 16 Dec 2017.
21. US Attorney General Jeff Sessions. Qtd. in Miles Parks. "'My Story Has Never Changed,' Attorney General Jeff Sessions Tells House Committee." NPR. 14 Nov 2017.
22. Robert Frost. "Stopping by Woods on a Snowy Evening." *New Hampshire: A Poem with Notes and Grace Notes*. New York: Henry Holt, 1923. 87.
23. H. Rider Haggard, *She: A History of Adventure*. London: McDonald, 1886. 95.
24. Stephen King. "Children of the Corn." *Night Shift*. New York: Doubleday, 1978. 278.
25. George Bernard Shaw, "Maxims for Revolutionists." *Man and Superman: A Comedy and a Philosophy*. Cambridge, UK: The University Press, 1903. 230.
26. *New American Standard Bible*. La Habra, CA: The Foundation Press, 1963.
27. *English Standard Version Study Bible*. Wheaton, IL: Crossway, 2008.
28. *King James Bible*. 1611.
29. David McClough. "Not All Education Is Created Equal: How Choice of Academic Major Affects the Racial Salary Gap." *The American Economist* 62.2 (Oct 2017): 193.
30. Joshua Zeitz. "Back to the Barricades." *American Heritage* 52.7 (Oct 2001): 70+.
31. Woody Allen. *Annie Hall*. MGM, 1977.
32. Amalie Adler Ascher. "Plant Notebook: Miniature Mountain Laurel." *baltimoresun.com*. 18 May 1991.
33. *Time* Staff and Dan Neil. "The Fifty Worst Cars of All Time: The 1975 Trabant." *Time.com*. 25 Apr 2017.
34. "Way-Too-Early Ranking of 2017 Heisman Trophy Candidates." *Bleacher Report*. 19 Sep 2017.
35. Craig S. Smith. "On Death Row, China's Source of Transplants." *The New York Times*. 10 Jan 2001.
36. While either *that* or *which* may be used with an ADJCL when it is an essential modifier, only *which* can be used when the ADJCL is a non-essential modifier. So this, *The book,* **which** *had lain on the table for weeks, was coated in dust*, but not this, **The book,* **that** *had lain on the table for weeks, was coated in dust*. In *Style* (12th ed., Boston: Pearson, 2010. 14–15), Williams and Bizup offer a history and appraisal of the stylistic "rule" that "requires" writers to only use *that* with essential and *which* with non-essential modifiers.
37. Tara Mcinnis. "*The Ringmaster's Gambit* (*The Game* #2) by Yannis Karatsioris." Online posting. *Goodread.com*. 22 Oct 2013.
38. Timothy Zahn. "For Love of Amanda." *Analog Science Fiction & Fact* 122.10 (Oct 2002): 62.
39. Ron Brownstein. *Face the Nation*. CBS. 3 Dec 2017.
40. Andy Rosen. "Opening of New Park in Boston Highlights Dawn of New Era for Emerald Necklace." *Bostonglobe.com*. 15 Apr 2017.
41. Christina Wood Martinez. "Overlook." *The Literary Review* 59.3 (Summer 2016): 123.
42. Robert H. Mohlenbrock. "Getting in Shape." *Natural History* 121.10 (Dec 2013/ Jan 2014): 45.

43. Paul Woody. "NFC East Preview. Washington Redskins. Snapshot with RG Randy Thomas." *The Sporting News* 230.36 (8 Sep 2006): 52.
44. Sola Onitiri. "How to Always Make Good Reservations." *Nowletsgetgoing.com*. 29 Oct 2018.
45. "Top Ten List for Ushers." St. Therese of Lisieux Catholic Church, Munhill, PA. N.d. <www.st-therese.net>.
46. Op. cit. 383.
47. Howard V. Sutherland. "Omar in the Klondyke." *Biggs's Bar, and Other Klondyke Ballads*. Philadelphia: D. Biddle, 1901. 27.
48. Priya Karjigi. "What Makes You Feel Proud about Your Father?" Online posting. *Quora.com*. 21 Sep 2016.
49. Op. cit. 383.
50. Ibid.
51. John Russell Rickford and Russell John Rickford. *Spoken Soul: The Story of Black English*. New York: John Wiley, 2000. 125.
52. Fries, Charles Carpenter. *American English Grammar: The Grammatical Structure of Present-Day English with Especial Reference to Social Differences or Class Dialects*. English Monograph No. 10, National Council of Teachers of English. New York: D. Appleton-Century Co., 1940. 232.
53. Wolfram and Schilling-Estes, op. cit. 383.
54. Rickford, op. cit. 8; see Salikoko S. Mufwene. "The Structure of the Noun Phrase in African American Vernacular English." *African American English: Structure, History and Use*. Eds. Salikoko S. Mufwene, et al. New York: Routledge, 1998. 76–77; see also Lisa J. Green and Walter Sistrunk. "Syntax and Semantics in African American English." *The Oxford Handbook of African American Language*. Ed. Sonja Lanehart. New York: Oxford University Press, 2015. 367.
55. J. L. Dillard. *Black English: Its History and Usage in the United States*. New York: Vintage Books, 1972. 59.
56. This is not strictly true. Unlike relative pro-words, the expletive has no grammatical function within the NCL. However, *that* can indicate that the clause states a presumed fact; often, *that*, like *if* and *whether*, indicates the conditional quality of the action named in the clause. Recall that after a number of verbs, an NCL may require a verb in the subjunctive mood (see 6.1.5), so expressing conditional meaning requires a change in the grammatical form of the verb. The conditional meaning is, in part, marked by the expletive. Also, *if* and *whether* clearly mark a relationship between the container clause and the NCL, much like a subordinating conjunction (SCONJ; see 10.2.3.1). Indeed, both *if* and *whether* can mark an NCL and can function as SCONJs, marking the beginning of an ADVCL. The pronoun replacement test will always identify whether a clause marked with *if* or *whether* is nominal or adverbial.
57. Andrea Sigala. *PBS NewsHour*. PBS 20 Jan 2015.
58. This last deletion can actually show up in informal usage, as in, *I don't care you want to run the government differently . . . if it ends up being demonstrably better* (Christopher Welsh. "Why do so many conservatives and conservative outlets dislike California?" Online posting. *Quora.com*. 26 Nov 2018).
59. "Brothers' Venture Taps Family Roots, Film Legacy of Colorado Springs." *Colorado Springs Gazette*. 6 Oct 2017.
60. Dillard, op. cit. 63–64.
61. Attributed to Sir Isaac Newton.
62. Michael Craig Miller, M.D. "Exercise Is a State of Mind; Researchers Are Learning More About How Physical Activity Affects Our Moods." *Newsweek* 149.12 (Mar 2007): 48.
63. Tyler Kingkade. "Tom Hanks Says Community College Made Him Who He Is Today." *Huffpost.com*. 14 Jan 2015.

64. Erica Wagner. "Inside the Secret World of *The Muppet Show*." *thedailybeast.com*. 22 July 2017.

65. The NCL:IO may seem a little forced, especially for formal writing. We would, I think, be more likely to use the alternative version of such a sentence, *We want to make a really good lunch for whomever you invite*, in which the IO is the complement of the preposition *for*.

66. Marty Leshner. "Is it true what they say about cruises? Maybe not . . ." *The Christian Science Monitor*. 25 Sep 2002.

67. Note that several of these words cannot function as relative pro-words: *what*, *how*, forms beginning with *how-*, and those ending in—*ever*.

68. Laura Miller. "Voice in the Wilderness: It's Hard to Be the Voice of a Generation When Your Generation Doesn't Need You Anymore." *Slate.com*. 15 May 2017.

69. Michelle Collins. "Hot Topics." *The View*. ABC. 19 May 2015.

70. Mark Zuckerberg. Qtd. in Don Reisinger. "Facebook Live Has Been Used to Stream Nearly 50 Acts of Violence." *Fortune.com*. 19 Jun 2017.

71. Note that with a plural count noun (e.g. *balls*), all three parses work. With most singular count nouns (e.g. *ball*), the adjective parse won't work: *I should buy which ball.→*I should buy green ball.* See the discussion of mass and count nouns in 2.1.

72. <www.english-corpora.org/coca/>.

73. Brittany Smith. "Janet's Secret." *48 Hours*. CBS-TV: Season 28, Episode 30. 16 May 2015.

74. Giulio Mozzi. "F." *Massachusetts Review* 53.3 (Aug 2012). 459.

75. Gerald David Nordley. "To Climb a Flat Mountain." *Analog Science Fiction & Fact* 129.12 (Dec 2009). 73.

76. Susan Isaacs. *Lily White*. New York: HarperCollins, 1996. 148.

77. Chris Carey. "In an Instant; He Grabbed the Wrong Girl." *20/20*. ABC-TV, 9 Jul 2016.

78. Licensing Board Minutes. New Bedford, MA. 22 Apr 2013. <www.newbedfordma.gov>.

79. Owen Gleiberman. "Three of Hearts." *Entertainment Weekly* 428 (24 Apr 1998): 51.

80. Jeff Mariotte. *Thunder Moon Rising*. New York: Tor Books, 2016. 22.

81. LeaAnn Tyson Martin. "Perceptions of High, Average and Low Performance Second Graders About Physical Education and Physical Education Teachers." *Physical Educator* 59.4 (Early Winter 2002): 204+.

82. Katharine Merlin. "Horoscopes: Gemini." *Town and Country* 165.5369 (Feb 2011): 116.

83. Daniel Sieberg. *Next@CNN*. CNN. 18 Sep 2004.

84. Don George. "Japan's Past Perfect." *National Geographic Traveler* 29.1 (Jan/Feb 2012): 67.

85. Abby Hayes/Credit.com. "Should You Combine Money When You Get Married?" *cbsnews.com*. 3 Jul 2017.

86. Compare the three NCLMOD examples with comparable sentences that include an ADJCL:

> *That's why he's on the list.→That's the reason why he's on the list.*
> *I remember when she visited.... → I remember the time when....*
> *I thought of where we can go.... → I thought of a place where we can go....*

Clearly, the meanings of the sentences in each pair are closely related. Perhaps the NCL examples are derived from the ADJCL examples by deleting the N' (i.e. *the reason, the time, a place*) that the ADJCL modifies, turning the ADJCL into an NCL.

87. Matt Fulks, et al. *If These Walls Could Talk: Kansas City Royals: Stories from the Kansas City Royals Dugout, Locker Room, and Press Box*. Chicago: Triumph Books, 2017. 171.

88. Erik Larkin. "New Privacy Threats." *PC World* 24.6 (Jun 2006): 20.
89. Eric Bolling. *The Five*. Fox News. 24 Mar 2017.
90. Barbara Pleasant. "Grow Your Best Fall Garden What, When and How." *Mother Earth News* 235 (Aug/Sep 2009): 34.
91. Joe Gebbia. "How Do You 'Design' Trust Between Strangers?" *The TED Radio Hour*. NPR. 20 May 2016.
92. Rankie. "The Wedding Guest." *Trikone Magazine* 14.1 (Jan 1999): 18.
93. Lisa Kennedy. "A Heartfelt Letter, Before the Envelope." *Denver Post*. 22 Jan 2012. 2E.
94. Valorie Burton. "Your Prime Time Is Now." *Essence* 45.5 (Sep 2014): 129.
95. Sunny Hostin. "Hot Topics." *The View*. ABC. 20 May 2016.
96. Richard C. Zimler. "Nigger Fate." *African American Review* 28.4 (Winter 1994): 557.
97. Jim Holt. "Hello Dalai." *The New Republic* 205.20 (11 Nov 1991): 22.
98. Ann Binlot. "A Play by Play of the Mark Hotel Departures Before the Met Gala." *hollywoodreporter.com*. 1 May 2017.
99. Mary Kay Cabot. "Browns and Jimmy Garoppolo: They Have Plenty of Picks to Try to Trade for Him." *cleveland.com*. 27 Apr 2017.
100. Shirley Bryan. "Letters to the Editor." *St. Louis Post-Dispatch*. 6 Jun 2015.
101. Robert Wright. "The Market Shall Set You Free." *The New York Times*. 28 Jan 2005.
102. Joe Gross. "50 Movies Coming This Fall." *Austin American-Statesman* (Austin, TX). 5 Sep 2014. T25.
103. Leonard Swidler. "The 'Dialogue of Civilizations' at the Tipping Point: The 'Dialogosphere'." *Journal of Ecumenical Studies* 50.1 (Winter 2015): 6.
104. Polly Morrice. "Just Your Average Soccer Mom." *Redbook* 195.3 (Sep 2000): 123.
105. Albert E. Cowdrey. "Queen for a Day." *Fantasy & Science Fiction* 101.4/5 (Oct/Nov 2001): 195+.
106. Jess McCuan. "It's Not Easy Being Green." *Inc.* 26.11 (Nov 2004): 112.
107. "Olé, Mexico!" *Town and Country* 159.5297 (Feb 2005): 155+.
108. Rick Bass. "Two Deer." *The Paris Review* 37.137 (Winter 195): 18.
109. Danika Fears. "This Couple Might Have the Most Improbable Love Story of All-time." *nypost.com*. 25 Oct 16.
110. Natalie Ram. "Science as Speech." *Iowa Law Review* 102.3 (Mar 2017): 1187.
111. Shirley Biagi. *Media/Impact: An Introduction to Mass Media*. 11th ed. Stamford, CT: Cengage Learning, 2015. 272.
112. "Skate Home Backpack, Shoulder Bag for 7.5 and 8.5 Inches Skateboard. Black." Advertisement. *Amazon.com*. 2019.
113. Jarrett Bell. "Bears Remember Lessons of Forgettable '04." *Sports*. USA Today. 11 Aug 2005.
114. Kathleen Z. Braun. "2008 PSA Youth Showcase." *PSA Journal* 74.9 (Sep 2008): 21.
115. Beth Bernobich. *Queen's Hunt*. New York: Tor Books, 2012.
116. David Lieberman. "Comcast Chief's Dream for Cable Stretches Far." *USA Today*. 8 May 1995.
117. Donovan Webster. "Alicia, Underground." *Men's Health* 10.8 (Oct 1995): 120+.
118. Karen Cheney and Jackie Zimmermann. "The New Grad's Guide to Money." *Money* 44.4 (May 2015): 71.
119. Yoda. *Star Wars: Return of the Jedi*. LucasFilms, 1983.

Chapter 11

Nominals, Adjectivals, and Adverbials

It is now time to elaborate on some broader functional categories. We have mentioned these categories already when we have talked not just about NPs or NCLs but about nominals in general and when we have talked not just about ADVPs, adverbial PPs, or ADVCLs but about adverbials. We have several forms—a variety of phrases and clauses—that can function in roles generally occupied by NPs, ADJPs, and ADVPs. We will, from here on, talk about these categories of functions and the constituents that fill them using the terms nominal, adjectival, and adverbial. Each of these terms labels a category of constituents that convey a particular kind of information—answer a particular kind of question—and fill a limited set of functional roles.

11.1 Nominals

A "nominal," as the name implies, is a constituent (phrase or clause) that provides noun-like information and that is functioning in a role or slot that could be filled by an NP. We defined noun-like information or noun meaning back in the discussion of nouns and NPs: an NP <u>names</u> a person, place, thing, quality, or idea; NPs generally tell *what* or *who*. Nominals may take several forms, including NP, NCL, PRON, PARTP, and INFP (see Chapter 12) and occasionally even ADJP or PP. The functions of nominals include SUBJ, AGENT, PCOMP, and several verb complement roles, including DO, SC, IO, and OC.

To be a nominal, a constituent must have both noun meaning and be functioning in a role that can be filled by an NP. For example, in the NP *the soccer ball*, the word *soccer* appears to be a noun in form and to name a thing. However, it is functioning as an ADJ—as a modifier of a noun—and it is not providing noun-like information: it is telling us *what kind of ball*. Adjectives provide information about *what kind of* thing is being named by a noun. So, in this context, the word *soccer* is not functioning as a nominal but as an adjectival.

When a phrase or clause is performing a nominal function, the complete nominal can be identified by the pronoun replacement test.

11.2 Adjectivals

An "adjectival" is a constituent (phrase or clause) that provides ADJ-like information <u>and</u> that is functioning in a role or slot that could be filled by an ADJP. We defined ADJ-like information or ADJ meaning back in the discussion of adjectives and ADJPs: an ADJP generally tells *which* or *what kind of.* Adjectivals may take several forms, including ADJP, PP, ADJCL, appositive NP, noun within a compound noun, and PROADJ in a dependent clause or question, as well as PARTP and INFP (see Chapter 12). Adjectivals only function as modifier of a noun; SC and OC; and sentence or clause modifier. Not all adjectival forms can fulfill all adjectival functions; here is a list of the possible combinations:

Form:Functions

- ADJP:MOD OF N; SC; OC.
- PP:ADJECTIVAL:MOD OF N.
- ADJCL:MOD OF N; MOD OF CLAUSE (when the relative pronoun prefers back to the entire clause, as in *The wind knocked down our tent, **which ruined our camping plans***).
- PartP:MOD OF N; SC.
- INFP:Post-modifier of N.
- NP:MOD OF N (e.g. in a compound noun); APPOSITIVE NP:MOD OF N; NOMINATIVE ABSOLUTE:MOD OF CLAUSE (e.g. *The wind knocked down our tent, **an event that ruined our camping plans***).

11.3 Adverbials

An adverbial is a constituent (phrase or clause) that provides adverb-like information and that is functioning in a role or slot that could be filled by an ADVP. We defined adverb-like information or adverb meaning back in the discussion of adverbs and ADVPs: an ADVP generally tells *when, where, why, how, how much, how often, how long*, and other versions of those sorts of information. Adverbials may take several forms, including ADVP, PP, ADVCL, NP (especially NPs that name times or places), and PROADV in dependent clauses and questions, as well as PARTP and INFP (see Chapter 12). Adverbials have a number of functions: they can modify verbs, adjectives, adverbs, and clauses, and they can complement a verb as an SC, LC, MC, TC, or OC.

We have so far avoided two problems with adverbials: first, there are times when it is not clear whether an adverbial following a verb functions as a modifier or a complement of that verb. Second, we have used the term "sentence modifier" or "clause modifier" loosely to identify any adverbial that falls outside the subject-predicate structure of the clause and that can be moved to the beginning or end of the clause or to the slot between subject and verb; but there are, as we shall see, a variety of clause-modifying adverbials with distinctly different characteristics. To more adequately organize and identify the adverbials we have so far studied, we need to develop some new concepts and some new terminology. These new ideas should complement and enrich our understanding of adverbials and augment our ability to identify them.

11.3.1 Scope[1]

Until now, we have described adverbials as either complements of verbs or as <u>modifying</u> verbs, adjectives, other adverbs and clauses. We have defined a "modifier" as a constituent in a clause that can be removed without altering the grammatical well-formedness of the clause. In those terms, all the constituents that we have so far labeled as sentence modifiers or clause modifiers are, by definition, modifiers: if we delete them, the sentences or clauses are still well formed.

But we have also talked about a modifier as being effectively subordinate to the term it modifies. Thus, in an NP, a noun functions as the <u>head</u>, while ADJPs, DPs, and adjectival post-modifiers are <u>dependents</u> of the head and so secondary or subordinate to it. From the start though, we have seen that what we call "sentence modifiers" are not really subordinate or secondary to the clause; rather, they stand on a pretty equal footing with the clause: they fall outside the clause structure, not functioning as part of the subject or predicate. And rather than "modifying" the clause, in terms of being secondary, it would be more apt to say that the sentence modifiers we have looked at <u>contextualize</u> the clause, providing information about the context within which the actor named in the subject performed the action named in the predicate. In the sentence *On Tuesday, we went to the mall*, the PP *on Tuesday* is "oriented toward" or "related to" or "provides information about" the whole clause. Linguists often use the term "scope" to describe the relationship between what we commonly call a modifier and the constituent it modifies. Haussamen elaborates:

> To say that an adverb has a certain word or words in its scope is to say that it colors our understanding of those words. The idea of adverbial scope is effective because, unlike modification, it suggests that the adverb can be directed at words and word groups of various kinds and sizes, and that though the adverb is in a relationship to them, the relationship is not necessarily one of subordination.[2]

The scope of the adverbial PP *on Tuesday* is the entire clause since the PP frames the time in which the whole event named in the clause took place, telling not only when the *going to the mall* occurred but when <u>we went</u>.

The concept of scope allows us to distinguish several categories of adverbials, among them SENTMODS. We can use these categories as an addition to the language we already have for talking about adverbials and their function and placement within sentences. These categories include subjunct adverbials, adjunct adverbials, disjunct adverbials, conjunctive adverbials, and sentence modifiers, all of which have different kinds of scope and different constraints on movability.

11.3.2 Subjunct Adverbials

"Subjunct" literally means "joined below." Citing Quirk, et al. in the *Comprehensive Grammar of the English Language,* Haussamen describes subjuncts as words or phrases that are "less important than the subject, verb, or [verb] complement. They amplify or intensify or diminish another sentence element, and they carry less weight than it does."[3] In short, subjuncts conform to our usual idea of an AdvP as a constituent that modifies another; subjuncts commonly indicate degree:

1.   *Terry, you are so cute.*[4]
2.   *I just started practicing.*[5]
3.   *If not for gravity, we'd scarcely know up from down.*[6]
4.   *This is not going to go the way you think.*[7]

The scope of a subjunct is very narrow: the subjuncts in these examples only relate to an immediately neighboring constituent: *so* only relates to *cute*; *just* relates to the verb *started practicing*; *scarcely* relates to *know*; *not* relates to the verb *is going to go.*

The subjuncts give adverbial information: *so* tells *how cute*; *just* tells *how recently the practicing started*; *scarcely* tells *how much* or *the degree of knowing*, as does *not*, which indicates *a zero-degree of going to go.* We can thus identify subjuncts by asking adverbial questions, but, typically, a subjunct will not stand as an acceptable or complete answer to such a question:

1.a. *Terry, how cute are you? *So.*
2.a. *When did you start practicing? *Just.*
3.a. *How would we know up from down? *Scarcely.*
4.a. *How is this going to go the way you think? *Not.*

And subjuncts cannot be moved from their location in the sentence without altering the meaning of the sentence or creating a grammatically ill-formed sentence:

*You are so cute. *So you are cute. *You so are cute. *You are cute so.*

Adverbials commonly stay close to the constituents that are in their scope. Otherwise, their reference becomes vague, ambiguous, or shifts to a different constituent. The scope of a subjunct is so small that, typically, it cannot be moved at all.

11.3.3 Adjunct Adverbials

"Adjunct" literally means "joined to." An adjunct is not subordinate or second-ary to other major clause elements but roughly equal in the weight of its mean-ing. As we shall see, adjuncts may be what we have previously called either complements *or* modifiers. As a simple guide, all adverbial complements of verbs (SC, LC, TC, MC, OC) are adjuncts, but we would classify some adjuncts as modifiers. Consider the following sentences:

5. *She put the fish in the refrigerator.*[8]
6. *I slept well.*
7. *I slept in the bathtub.*[9]

Until now, we have said that the PP *in the refrigerator* is functioning as an adverbial complement of the verb *put*—specifically, as an adverbial OC. We can see that the PP has a weight nearly equal to the subject and the verb, since the sentence is incomplete without it, and the meaning of the PP is essential to the meaning of the whole. At the same time, using our new concept of "scope," we can see that the scope of reference of the PP *in the refrigerator* is not the entire clause but just the NP:DO *the fish* and the verb *put*, in that *in the refrig-erator* tells where the fish is and where the action of *putting* took place. The PP *in the refrigerator* does not tell where *she* was. We also don't ordinarily move the PP to create a sentence like:

5.a. *In the refrigerator she put the fish.*

Moving *in the refrigerator* to the front of the sentence is an inversion: we have taken one of the verb complements out of its typical position at the end of the sentence and moved it to the beginning. Although the inversion may sound off, we may use it for stylistic reasons, to set up a contrast with another clause, as when we say something like, *In the refrigerator she put the fish. In the pantry she put the rice.* In the context of these two sentences, the adjunct PP becomes a conjunctive adverbial (see 11.3.5), extending its scope beyond the single sentence, using the PP to connect one sentence to another. We know that, in sentence 5, the PP *in the refrigerator* is not a SENTMOD because:

- Its scope is much but not all of the sentence: it tells *where the fish was put* (but not *where she was*).
- Moving it to the front of the sentence feels odd: it is an inversion (when we move a SENTMOD there should be no sense of creating an inversion).
- When we move it, we will likely change the scope of its reference.

By contrast, in the sentences *I slept well* and *I slept in the bathtub*, the verb, *slept*, is intransitive: it requires no complement. In our earlier discussions, we would have said that, in these sentences, the ADvP *well* and PP:ADVERBIAL *in the bathtub* were both functioning as modifiers of *slept*: we can drop them and still have a well-formed sentence (*I slept*), and we cannot move them.

6.a.   ?*Well I slept.*

is a poetic inversion, or simply non-Standard; and

7.a.   ?*In the bathtub I slept.*

is an inversion and could be used to set up the same sort of contrast as in 5.a. In neither 6.a. nor 7.a. is the adverbial a SENTMOD. Furthermore, we find that the scope of each adverbial is the whole clause: *well* describes my state and the quality of the sleeping; *in the bathtub* tells both where I was and where the sleeping occurred.

Sentence 8 offers a subtler example:

8.   *She lived in Chicago.*[10]

We could say that *in Chicago* is a PP:ADVERBIAL:LC. We might also argue that we can hear an intransitive reading of the verb *lived*: that *She lived* is, by itself, a well-formed sentence and that *in Chicago* is a PP:ADVERBIAL:MOD of "lived." We could also argue that *in Chicago* is nearly as essential to the clause as the subject and verb: after all, her living *in Chicago* is distinctly different from the mere fact of her living.

The scope of *in Chicago* includes both the subject and the verb: *in Chicago* doesn't just tell where *she* was or where some act of *living* went on. Rather, it tells where *she lived*—it answers the test question, *Where did she live?* By this reading, *in Chicago* is more like a sentence modifier than a verb complement in that it provides context for the subject and verb. If we move it to the beginning of the clause, we have the same sort of inversion that we saw in 5.a., 6.a., and 7.a:

8.a.   ?*In Chicago she lived.*

The inversion also seems to suggest a change in how we construe the meaning of "lived": in the original sentence 8, "lived" is likely to mean "resided"; while in the inverted sentence 8.a., "lived" means something like "throve" (c.f. *In Chicago she really lived*). But the inversion is less common than the uninverted sentence.

We now have a new class of adverbial constituent, one that stands nearly equal with subject and verb but which is not movable and so is not a SENTMOD. It may have the whole clause in its scope, as in sentence 8. It may also have only some of the major constituents of the clause in its scope, as in sentence 5. It may be, to use our earlier terminology, an adverbial complement of the verb, as in sentence 5; or it may be in the hazy zone between complement and modifier, as in sentence 8, or it may be an adverbial modifier:

9.   *She kissed her mother on the cheek.*

In sentence 9, the PP *on the cheek* is a modifier: we can drop it and still have a well-formed sentence. Haussamen observes that the PP *on the cheek* provides information about the kissing and the mother:[11] it does not tell us where the subject, *she*, was (*she* was not, after all on her mother's cheek) and so only includes the predicate in its scope. By contrast, consider:

10.   *She kissed her mother on the platform.*

In sentence 10, *on the platform* tells where the whole event took place; the PP includes the whole clause in its scope—it tells where *she* was while kissing her mother. And while the PP can be moved in 10, it cannot be moved in 9:

9.a.   **On the cheek she kissed her mother.*
10.a.   *On the platform she kissed her mother.*

In sentence 9, *on the cheek* is an adjunct adverbial. As we shall see below, in sentence 10, *on the platform* is a true SENTMOD.
    Haussamen also cites the following sentence as containing an adjunct:

11.   *He was killed by a terrorist.*

Sentence 11 is in passive voice, and *by a terrorist* is a PP:AGENTIVE that, like a modifier, can be dropped from the sentence. However, the PP has the same weight as both the subject and the verb because the PP contains the NP:PREPCOMP that names the agent of the sentence. The scope of the PP is just the verb: *how was the killing done? By a terrorist.* In sentence 11, moving *by a terrorist* clearly creates an inversion—and an odd one at that: the sentence:

11.a.   ?*By a terrorist he was killed.*

sounds distinctly like Yoda.
    And so we have three characteristics of adjunct adverbials: first, they are generally not movable and are usually limited in scope to only part of a clause. They are, therefore, different from SENTMODS. Second, while all adverbial complements are adjuncts, sometimes adjuncts can be deleted, like modifiers, leaving behind a well-formed clause:

9.b.   *She kissed her mother.*
11.b.   *He was killed.*

Third, an adjunct typically has only part of a clause in its scope—although a larger part than a subjunct usually does—or it may have the whole clause in its scope—as do SENTMODS.

11.3.4 Disjunct Adverbials

As the name implies, disjuncts are adverbial constituents that are less closely joined to the sentence or clause. Their scope is the entire clause: they stand outside the clause structure and refer to the whole clause, providing a context for it. Typically, that context is the speaker's opinion or observation about the content of the clause.

Disjuncts can be thought of as a type of SENTMOD: like SENTMODS, they can typically (though not always) be moved; but unlike full-fledged SENTMODS, one cannot make a disjunct the focus of a question.[12] Let's look at some examples:

. 12. *In fack, confidentially, nothin' like this never happened to me before.*[13]
13. *For knowledge is limited, whereas imagination embraces the entire world, stimulating progress, giving birth to evolution. It is, strictly speaking, a real factor in scientific research.*[14]
14. *Obviously, we butchered it.*[15]
15. *Whatever she says, don't argue.*[16]

In all of these examples, the disjunct adverbial can be moved to the beginning or end of the sentence. But just try making the disjunct the focus of a question:

14.a. How did we butcher it? **Obviously.*

By contrast, a SENTMOD can always be the focus of a question formed from the clause it modifies:

15. SENTMOD:

> *The nation's political leaders vacated their homes in the city because of the epidemic.*[17]
> *Why did the nation's political leaders vacate their homes in the city? Because of the epidemic.*

Haussamen observes that, while one cannot frame a question around a disjunct, when the disjunct is not itself a clause one can frame a clause around the disjunct, a clause in which the actual sentence is included as a dependent clause:

12.a. *In fack, I tell you in confidence that nothin' like this never happened to me before.*
13.a. *I am speaking in a strict manner when I tell you that it is a real factor in scientific research.*
14.b. *It is obvious to us that we butchered it.*

The disjunct typically offers the speaker's opinion about what the clause says. We see this in 12.a, 13.a, 14.b in that it is the speaker who is "speaking confidentially," "speaking strictly," and to whom "it is obvious." We find the same characteristics in 15, where it is the speaker who is saying, "I tell you in spite of whatever she says, ..."

That famous bugaboo, the word *hopefully*, is an example of "a typical disjunct":[18] it can easily be paraphrased by framing it in a clause that includes the actual sentence as a dependent clause:

16. *Hopefully, that doesn't ever happen again.*[19]
16.a. *I am hopeful that it will not ever happen again.*

A disjunct typically has a whole clause in its scope; it can usually be moved around the clause; and it cannot be the grammatically well-formed answer to a question.

11.3.5 Conjunctive Adverbials

Conjunctive adverbs are a well-established category in traditional grammar. Unlike the three categories of adverbials that we already examined, conjunctive adverbials do not have part or all of a clause in their scope. "Instead, they establish a relationship between that clause and the previous clause"[20] and sometimes a following clause as well. Here are some of the most common conjunctive adverbial words and phrases:

accordingly	first ... then ...	moreover	therefore
also	furthermore	nevertheless	thus
anyhow	hence	next	in fact
besides	however	nonetheless	in other words
consequently	indeed	so	on the one hand
finally	instead	still	on the other hand
first, second, etc.	likewise	then	to conclude

Conjunctive adverbials are so named because they relate clauses to each other much as CCONJS can; the conjunctive adverb *however* is even often mistaken by students for a CCONJ because its meaning is very similar to that of the CCONJ *but*. However, unlike *but*, when a conjunctive adverbial is placed at the beginning of a clause, it must always be separated from the clause by a comma; a clause-initial *but* is typically not followed by a comma. And while *but*, preceded by a comma, may be used to conjoin two clauses, *however* can never be used to conjoin two clauses with only a comma preceding: *however* must always be preceded by a semicolon or a period:

He's doing great, but he needs to talk a little less.[21]
He's doing great; however, he needs to talk a little less.

> *He's doing great. However, he needs to talk a little less.*
> **He's doing great, however he needs to talk a little less.*

Conjunctive adverbials also provide additional, adverbial information about the clauses they relate; in this way, they are akin to SConjs. But unlike other adverbials, conjunctive adverbials do not hold a relationship with one clause but direct or express a relationship between two or, sometimes, more clauses (or even paragraphs) as in the case of a set like *first . . . second . . . third . . .* or *first . . . next . . . finally.* Typically, conjunctive adverbials are movable within a clause, and, usually, we can't frame a question around the container clause in such a way that the conjunctive adverbial will be its answer.

As Haussamen observes, we might see conjunctive adverbials as one end of an adverbial continuum, with their scope extending beyond the clause; the other end of the continuum could be seen as subjunct adverbials, with their extremely narrow scope.

Although conjunctive adverbials are movable, it is best to keep them at or very near the beginning of a clause: since they mark how the reader is supposed to relate the clause that follows to the clause that precedes, if the conjunctive adverbial appears later in the second clause, the reader may have to backtrack to reconstruct the relationship between the clauses. Anything that forces the reader to backtrack disrupts the flow of reading and therefore should typically be avoided in formal essay writing and even in personal, informal writing.

In general, we can't frame a question around a conjunctive adverbial:

17. *However, the debt level can not go much higher.*[22]
    ?When/how/why can't the debt level go much higher? *However.

A partial exception can be found in those conjunctive adverbials that include ordinal numbers:

18. *First, I added more brown stripes at the cheeks. Second, I added a line on either side of my nose and extended it above my eyebrows. Last, I followed that line and curved it into my eyelid.*[23]

    When did you add more brown stripes at the cheeks? First.
    When did you add a line on either side of your nose and extended it above your eyebrows? Second.
    When did you follow that line and curve it into your eyelid? Last.

11.3.6 Sentence Modifiers and Clause Modifiers

I now venture away from Haussamen in establishing a category of adverbial expressions called "sentence modifiers" (SentMod) or "clause modifiers" (e.g. NClMod). A defining feature of SentMods is that they can always be moved to the beginning or end of the clause to which they are related and may often be moved to the slot between the subject and verb. One can always make a SENTMOD the focus of a question, and, because the scope of a SENTMOD is the entire clause, the question will need to include the entire clause.

19. *Because of the epidemic, the nation's leaders vacated their homes.*
19.a. *The nation's leaders vacated their homes because of the epidemic.*
19.b. *The nation's leaders, because of the epidemic, vacated their homes.*
19.c. Why did the nation's leaders vacate their homes? *Because of the epidemic.*

SENTMODS are movable because they fall outside the subject-predicate structure of the clause and, unlike adjuncts, they always have the whole clause within their scope; however, like adjuncts, they have a weight roughly equivalent to the rest of the clause. In general, a SENTMOD provides contextualizing information relevant to the entire clause, such as concurrent action, preceding or causative events, or following or resultative action:

Concurrent Action:

20. *While we were waiting, they would carry me up and down the platform.*[24]

Preceding or Causative Events:

21. *After reading Dave Eggers's* A Heartbreaking Work of Staggering Genius, *he was inspired to write nonfiction.*[25]

Following or Resulting Action:

22. *The day before the party, Serena and Teri brewed some vanilla chai tea.*[26]

Because the sentence-modifying adverbials provide a context that seems to surround the main clause, my spring 2005 students proposed that they should be called "circumjuncts" since they are "joined around" their container clause. The same sort of clause-modifying adverbials can also modify dependent clauses. Like a SENTMOD, the clause modifier can appear at the beginning or end of the clause and often between the SUBJ and PRED; but a clause modifier of a dependent clause must appear after the subordinator or complementizer, within the boundaries of the dependent clause that contains it:

Adjective Clause Modifier (ADJCLMOD):

15.a. *I remember the time when*[RELPROADV]*, because of the epidemic*[ADVCL:ADJCLMOD]*, the nation's political leaders vacated their homes in the city.*

Noun Clause Modifier (NCLMOD):

15.b. *We knew that*[SUBORDINATOR]*, because of the epidemic*[ADVCL:NCLMOD]*, the nation's political leaders vacated their homes in the city.*

Adverb Clause Modifier (ADVCLMOD):

15.c. *When*_[SCONJ], *because of the epidemic*_[ADVCL:ADVCLMOD], *the nation's political leaders vacated their homes in the city, we too left.*

But the relationship of a clause modifier to a dependent clause—its scope, its movability, the question that can be framed around its container clause with the clause modifier as an answer—is the same as the relationship of a SENTMOD to a sentence.

SENTMODS and clause modifiers come in a great range of forms. In fact, any form of adverbial—ADVP, PP, ADVCL, NP:ADVERBIAL, PROADV, PARTP:ADVERBIAL, INFP:ADVERBIAL—can function as a sentence- or clause-modifying adverbial.

The following table sums up the identifying qualities of all five different kinds of adverbials:

Adverbial Type	Movable?	Frame a question around it?	Scope
Subjunct adverbial	No	Rarely	One or two words; the complete verb
Adjunct adverbial	Not easily	Usually	Part of or whole clause
Disjunct adverbial	Yes, typically	No	Whole clause
Conjunctive adverbial	Yes	No	Multiple clauses
Sentence/clause modifier (Circumjunct adverbial)	Yes	Yes	Whole clause

Haussamen sums up his discussion of adverbials by noting that teaching students that the adverb is subservient to the verb is misleading. Subjuncts are the least common type of adverbial. For a better model of an approach to adverbials, Haussamen quotes Shuan-Fan Huang's 1975 *A Study of Adverbs*: "[A]dverbs may be described as the principal ways in which the language user characterizes the conditions and circumstances[,] the hows and wherefores of actions and events."[27] Haussamen concludes that:

> Such a definition replaces the traditional statement about syntax [that adverbs only modify other parts of speech] with a pragmatic and rhetorical characterization. It describes the role that adverbs play in communication by describing the kind of information they convey. . . . It avoids exaggeration of the adverb's relation to the verb; instead, by referring to "actions and events," it connects the adverb to the whole clause without eliminating the verb as a focal point.[28]

In Chapter 12, this characterization of adverbs, and adverbials more generally, will help in discussing the roles they play in relation to non-finite verb phrases.

Key Points

- **Nominals** are phrases and clauses that (1) perform nominal functions (SUBJ, AGENT, PCOMP, DO, SC, IO, OC) and (2) provide noun-like information (telling *who* or *what*). When it is performing a nominal function, a complete nominal can be identified by the pronoun replacement test.
- **Adjectivals** are phrases and clauses that (1) perform adjectival functions (MOD OF N, SC, OC, ADJCL:MOD OF CLAUSE, NOMINATIVE ABSOLUTE:MOD OF CLAUSE) and (2) provide adjective-like information (telling *which* or *what kind of*). Not all "adjectival forms" can perform all adjectival functions.
- **Adverbials** are phrases and clauses that (1) perform adverbial functions (thus far identified as modifier OF V, ADJ, ADV, and SENT/CLAUSE and verb complement, including SC, LC, MC, TC, OC) and (2) provide adverb-like information (telling *when, where, why, how, how much, how often, how long,* and other versions of those sorts of information).
- Adverbials can also be categorized in terms of their scope, movability, and whether they can serve as the focus of or answer to a question. Based on those criteria, adverbials can be categorized as subjuncts, adjuncts, disjuncts, conjunctive adverbials, and sentence modifiers (circumjuncts).

11.4 Exercises: Nominals, Adjectivals, and Adverbials

A. Nominals: real-world sentences: use the passage from Exercise 1.3B on pages 27–28, "Dog Belonging to Princess Anne Attacks Royal Maid." For each sentence, identify each complete nominal and, for each nominal, identify its form (NP, PRON, RELPRON, NCL and, if you can, PARTP:NOMINAL, INFP:NOMINAL) and its function (e.g. SUBJ, PCOMP, DO, etc.).

Example: (1) A dog belonging to Princess Anne—NP:SUBJ of "attacked"

B. Nominals: more real-world sentences: use the following passage[29] and use the same instructions as in Exercise A.

(1) If you're late for work, a driver using a cell phone may be to blame. (2) U.S. researchers said on Wednesday that people who use cell phones while behind the wheel impede the flow of traffic, clog highways and extend commute times. (3) "It's a bit like breaking wind in the elevator. Everyone suffers," Peter Martin of the University of Utah's Traffic Lab said in a telephone interview. (4) Prior studies have equated the risk of driving while talking on a cell phone with driving while drunk. (5) Some 50 countries have banned use of hand-held phones while driving. (6) The latest study shows the impact of cell phone use on traffic patterns. (7) "It has to do with the reaction to changes in speed," said Martin, who teaches civil and environmental engineering. (8) "When a driver who is not distracted is in a traffic stream and the vehicle in front slows down, the driver

will brake in response. (9) When a vehicle speeds up in front, the driver will respond and speed up," he said.

C. Adjectivals: real-world sentences: Use the passage from Exercise 1.3B on pages 27–28, "Dog Belonging to Princess Anne Attacks Royal Maid." For each sentence identify each complete adjectival and, for each adjectival, identify its form (ADJP, PP:ADJECTIVAL, ADJCL, and, if you can, PARTP:ADJECTIVAL, INFP:ADJECTIVAL) and its function (e.g. MOD OF ___, SC, etc.).

Example: (1) belonging to Princess Anne—PARTP:ADJP:MOD OF "dog"

D. Adjectivals: more real-world sentences: use the passage on cell phone users from Exercise 11.B, and use the same instructions as in Exercise C.

E. Adverbials: made-up sentences: use the passage beginning, "Today my brother Jim and I shopped for dictionaries," from 8.4, Exercise A on page 181. For each sentence identify each complete adverbial and, for each adverbial, identify its form (ADVP, PP:ADVERBIAL, ADVCL, NP:ADVERBIAL, PROADV, and, if you can, PARTP:ADVERBIAL, INFP:ADVERBIAL) and its function (subjunct, adjunct, disjunct, conjunctive adverb, sentence modifier, or clause modifier).

Example: (1) Yesterday—NP:ADVERBIAL:SENTMOD

F. Adverbials: real-world sentences: use the passage from Exercise 1.3B on pages 27–28, "Dog Belonging to Princess Anne Attacks Royal Maid," and use the same instructions as in Exercise E.

G. More real-world sentences: use the passage on cell phone users from Exercise 11.B, and use the same instructions as in Exercise E.

Notes

1. For the substance of the following discussion, I am heavily indebted to the chapter on adverbs in Brock Haussamen. *Revising the Rules: Traditional Grammar and Modern Linguistics.* 1st ed. Dubuque, IA: Kendall/Hunt, 1993.
2. Ibid. 122–123.
3. Ibid. 113. See also Randolph Quirk, Sidney Greenbaum, Geoffrey Leech, and Jan Svartvik. *A Comprehensive Grammar of the English Language.* New York: Longman, 1985.
4. Jordan Peele. "*Get Out* Sprung from an Effort to Master Fear, Says Director Jordan Peele." *Fresh Air.* NPR. 15 Mar 2017.
5. John Grisham. *The Rainmaker.* New York: Doubleday, 1995. 406.
6. Will Hunt. "Getting Lost Makes the Brain Go Haywire." *theatlantic.com.* 21 Feb 2019.
7. Luke Skywalker. *Star Wars: The Last Jedi.* Lucasfilm/Disney. 2017.
8. Eliza Factor. *Love Maps.* New York: Akashic Books, 2015. 6.
9. "Journalist Elizabeth Neuffer Discusses Her Career." *Fresh Air.* NPR. 3 Dec 2002.
10. Leslie Baldacci. "Author Tallies Toll of Breakups on Society." *Chicago Sun-Times.* 12 Jan 1997.
11. Haussamen, op. cit. 114.

12. Ibid. 114–115.
13. Oda Mae (Whoopi Goldberg). *Ghost*. Paramount. 1990.
14. Albert Einstein. "On Science." "Opinions and Aphorisms." *Einstein on Cosmic Religion and Other Opinions and Aphorisms*. Mineola, NY: Dover, 2009. *COCA*. 25 May 2019.
15. Alejandro Villanueva. Qtd. in Justin Terranova. "Steelers Desperately Try to Get Out of Anthem-protest Spotlight." *New York Post*. 26 Sep 2017.
16. Jack Hettinger. "Keeping the Faith." *Arkansas Review: A Journal of Delta Studies* 26:1–4 (1994): 302.
17. Sandy Hingston. "11 Things You Might Not Know About Philly's 1793 Yellow Fever Epidemic." *phillymag.com*. 2 May 2016.
18. Haussamen, op. cit. 115.
19. Sam Belden. "The Yankees' New Third Baseman Hit into a Triple Play in His First At Bat at Yankee Stadium." *Insider.com*. 26 July 2017.
20. Haussamen, op. cit. 115.
21. Lynn Kirkle. "Nearly Two Decades of Parent-teacher Conferences and I'm Still Learning." *Omaha World-Herald*. 9 Feb 2017.
22. Anna Fountain Clark. "Emergency Financial Management in Small Michigan Cities: Short-Term Fix or Long-Term Sustainability?" *Public Administration Quarterly* 41.3 (Fall 2017): 556.
23. Rochelle Barlow. "Turn into a Cat (with Makeup)." Website posting. *aslrochelle.com*. N.d.
24. Amy Leinbach Marquis. "The Voice of the Glacier: Ranger Doug Follett Reflects on 50 Years at Glacier National Park." *National Parks* 84.2 (Spring 2010): 10+.
25. Sharyn Jackson. "A Minnesota Teacher of the Year Shares Wisdom in Teaching Tell-all." *Minneapolis Star Tribune* 3 May 2017.
26. David Masello. "Prairie Party." *Country Living* 30.3 (Mar 2007): 119. *COCA*. 25 May 2019.
27. Shuan-Fan Huang. *A Study of Adverbs. Janua Linguarum*. Series minor: 213. The Hague: Mouton, 1975. 30.
28. Haussamen, op. cit. 117–118.
29. Julie Steenhuysen, "Cell Phone Users Tie Up Traffic: Study." 2 Jan 2008. *Reuters*. <www.reuters.com/article/us-usa-phones-traffic/cell-phone-users-tie-up-traffic-study-idUSN0210822520080102>.

Chapter 12

Non-Finite Verb Phrases

It is time now to turn our attention to what is in many ways the most slippery but most useful part of English grammar: non-finite verb phrases. The finite forms of verbs are the two tensed forms: the present and past, which may each stand alone as the MV of a clause. The three other forms are called "non-finite" because they are not tensed and so cannot stand alone as the main verb of a clause:

Finite		Non-finite		
Present	Past	Present (-ing) Participle	Past (-ed) Participle	Infinitive
drive(s) walk(s)	drove walked	driving walking	driven walked	to drive to walk

Until now, we have only dealt with the non-finite forms of verbs in the context of their use in multi-word finite verbs (see Chapter 6). But non-finite verbs can function in other roles within clauses: like dependent clauses, both participle and infinitive phrases can function as nominals, adjectivals, and adverbials. And just as an NP can consist of a noun by itself, so a participle phrase (PARTP) or an infinitive phrase (INFP) can consist of a participle or infinitive alone.

> *Embarrassed, I felt like the neo-pro I was.*[1]
> *Cue the laughing trombones.*[2]
> *To err is human.*[3]

In the first sentence, *embarrassed* is a participle functioning adverbially as a disjunct (PARTP:ADVERBIAL:DISJUNCT). In the second sentence, *laughing* is a participle functioning adjectically as a modifier of *trombones* (PARTP:ADJECTIVAL:MOD OF "trombones"). And in the third sentence, *to err* is an infinitive functioning nominally as the subject (INFP:NOMINAL:SUBJ).

Like dependent clauses, non-finite verb phrases have their own internal constituent structures. Non-finite verbs often act as the heads of phrases that comprise a participle or infinitive plus modifiers and/or complements:

*The jockey **checking her saddle** is my sister.*
***To prepare her horse**, the jockey first checked her saddle.*

In the first sentence, the PartP, *checking her saddle*, functions adjectivally as a modifier of the noun *jockey* (PartP:Adjectival:Mod of "jockey"): it is a constituent of the NP, *The jockey checking her saddle*. At the same time, the PartP has an interior constituent structure of its own: the verb *checking* is followed by the NP *her saddle*, which functions as a DO.

In the second sentence, the InfP *to prepare for the race* functions as an adverbial modifying the sentence *the jockey checked her saddle* (InfP:Adverbial:SentMod). Within the InfP, the verb *to prepare* is followed by the NP *her horse*, which is functioning as a DO.

Non-finite verb phrases have agents. Even though a verb is non-finite, in use, it will still have an agent, which may be stated or implied. In the last two examples, the explicit agent of both *checking* and *to prepare* is *the jockey* since it is the jockey who is doing the checking and preparing. In *To err is human*, the implicit agent of the infinitive *to err* is a generic person, sometimes stated as *one*. It is important to be able to identify the agent of a non-finite verb: writers who fail to do so can make the reference of the non-finite verb phrase unclear. The result of that lack of clarity is what is sometimes called a dangling modifier.

Furthermore, like finite verbs in dependent clauses, non-finite verbs can take modal and imperfect semi-auxiliary verbs and perfect, progressive, and passive auxiliaries. We will look at examples below. Because of their similarity to clauses, non-finite verb phrases are sometimes called "participle clauses" and "infinitive clauses." But because they do not have finite verbs and cannot have subjects that agree with them in number and person, we will refer to them as phrases.

Non-finite verb phrases are an important stylistic device in writing. Although they are the parts of English grammar that are typically given the least coverage in textbooks, non-finite verb phrases are important and relevant to teaching and thinking about writing. Along with dependent clauses and such sentence-rearranging devices as passive voice and *it* extraposition, non-finite verb phrases allow us to rearrange the delivery and flow of information by further reducing independent and dependent clauses and incorporating them as dependent elements within or attached to clauses. Non-finite verb phrases are thus part of a spectrum of devices running from independent clauses all the way down to prepositional phrases:

Sentence: *The woman was wearing the red dress. The woman went to the party.*
Adjective Clause: *The woman who was wearing the red dress went to the party.*

Participle Phrase: *The woman <u>wearing the red dress</u> went to the party.*
PP: *The woman <u>in the red dress</u> went to the party.*
PP: *The woman <u>in red</u> went to the party.*

Despite the changes in form, the meaning of each underlined constituent is much the same, and the function of each remains the same: each is an adjectival post-modifier of the noun *woman*. And yet, each form creates a different rhetorical effect: using fewer words reduces the weight and significance of the idea being expressed, making it more secondary to the main point of the sentence. The change in structure also changes the rhythm of the sentence, allowing us to manipulate the pace of the sentence and paragraph: shorter sentences read faster and so may have sharper impact when contrasted with longer sentences. We can see this in the following pair of sentences, the first of which uses a dependent clause that, in the second, is reduced to an infinitive phrase:

When one makes an error, one is being human.
To err is human.

PARTPs and INFPs can sometimes function in the same slot in a sentence, but they commonly carry different meanings. Consider these two sentences:

Though they'd met before at the cafe, a formal visit would secure an important relationship, necessary for a woman in Kabul <u>running</u> a business.[4]
Though they'd met before at the cafe, a formal visit would secure an important relationship, necessary for a woman in Kabul <u>to run</u> a business.

The participle *running* implies that the woman is already operating a business (or at least she has very real prospects of doing so), while the infinitive *to run* implies that she is not yet running the business but hopes to. That is, the participle implies a realized—or at least more potentially real—state of affairs, while the infinitive marks the event is irreal or hypothetical.

Analyzing non-finite verb phrases: PARTPs and INFPs can often be analyzed in terms of how their form and function are similar to those of dependent clauses, and we will have recourse to those similarities. However, as we've already seen, non-finite verb phrases also bear a strong resemblance to verb phrases that function as predicates. These similarities will prove useful in helping us analyze the function of various constituents—especially adverbials—within non-finite verb phrases.

12.1 Participles (PART) and Participle Phrases (PARTP)

A PARTP consists of a present or past participle, either alone or with complements and/or modifiers:

1. _Driving_ is one of the great pleasures of my life.[5]
2. _Driving my '65 Mustang_ is one of the great pleasures of my life.
3. _Driving my '65 Mustang on the highway_ is one of the great pleasures of my life.

In sentence 1, _driving_ is a PARTP:NOMINAL:SUBJ of the container clause _Driving is one of the great pleasures of my life_. The implied agent of the participle _driving_ is "I" since, if we ask, "Who is the speaker talking about doing the _driving_?" the answer will be "him- or herself." In relation to the speaker, the agent of _driving_ is "I."

In sentence 2, _driving my '65 Mustang_ is a PARTP:NOMINAL:SUBJ of the container clause _Driving my '65 Mustang is one of the great pleasures of my life_. Within the PARTP, there are other constituents: along with the participle _driving_, there is an NP, _my '65 Mustang_, which is functioning as the DO of "driving": the NP answers the question, "Someone is driving what?" Again, the implied agent of the PARTP _driving my '65 Mustang_ is "I."

In sentence 3, _driving my '65 Mustang on the highway_ is still a PARTP: NOMINAL:SUBJ of the container clause _Driving my '65 Mustang on the highway is one of the great pleasures of my life_, and within the PARTP, _my '65 Mustang_ is again an NP:DO of "driving." But we have one more constituent within the PARTP: the PP _on the highway_, which answers the adverbial question, "Where is your '65 Mustang being driven?" which seems to indicate that the PP is some kind of adverbial locating the action named in the PARTP. To determine what type of adverbial it may be, we need to determine what its scope is and whether it is movable. The scope seems to be the whole PARTP since the entire activity of _driving my '65 Mustang_ occurs _on the highway_. Thus, the PP might be a participle phrase modifier (PARTPMOD), or it might be an adjunct. The major distinction between the two is movability. We will find that adverbial constituents of a PARTP cannot usually be moved from the end of the PARTP to the slot before the participle without changing the scope of the adverbial or simply making an ungrammatical sentence:

> _Driving my '65 Mustang <u>on the highway</u> is one of the great pleasures of my life._
> _<u>On the highway</u> driving my '65 Mustang is one of the great pleasures of my life._

By my reading, moving the PP changes its scope, so it may no longer just be telling about _driving my '65_ Mustang but could also be about "being one of the great pleasures of my life." That is, perhaps on the highway, driving my '65 Mustang is one of the great pleasures of my life. But, by contrast, on the city streets, riding my Vespa scooter is one of the great pleasures of my life. Since we cannot move the adverbial PP _on the highway_ without changing its scope, in the original sentence, it is functioning as an adjunct.

PARTPMOD: Occasionally, an adverbial constituent of a PARTP will be movable within the PARTP:

> *Quickly beating the eggs, he consulted the recipe.*
> *Beating the eggs quickly, he consulted the recipe.*

The adverb *quickly* also has the whole PARTP, *beating the eggs*, in its scope since it is the not just the beating but the beating of the eggs that is happening quickly. Therefore, *quickly* is functioning as a PARTPMOD. The whole PARTP *quickly beating the eggs* is, in turn, functioning as a SENTMOD.

As we just saw, a **PARTP may start not with the particple** but with an adverbial functioning as a PARTPMOD or as a subjunct that modifies the participle:

> **Subjunct:** *Hardly knowing what he was doing, he took it from her.*[6]
> **PARTPMOD:** *Quickly beating the eggs, he consulted the recipe.*

PARTPs can function as nominals, adjectivals, or adverbials:

> Nominal: *Driving my '65 Mustang*[PARTP:NOMINAL:SUBJ] *is one of the great pleasures of my life.*
> Adjectival: *The woman driving my '65 Mustang*[PARTP:ADJECTIVAL:MOD OF "woman"] *is Imelda.*
> Adverbial: *Driving my '65 Mustang*[PARTP:ADVERBIAL:SENTMOD], *Imelda headed for Rockford.*

PARTPs functioning as nominals are, in traditional grammar, called "gerunds" or "gerund phrases." The term "participle" is, in traditional grammar, reserved for PARTPs functioning as adjectivals. Traditional grammar does not recognize participles as having an adverbial function. The words "participle" and "gerund" both come from Latin. "Participle" comes straight from the Latin *participium*, meaning "a word having the characteristics of both a verb and an adjective," hence the term's use in traditional grammar to refer to the *-ing*, *-ed* or *-en* forms of verbs when they are used as adjectives. "Gerund" is derived from the Late Latin *gerundus* which is the verbal adjective (participle) form of *gerere*, meaning "to bear" or "carry on." A gerund bears or carries on by presenting an action as a thing: in Latin, and later in English, "gerund" comes to refer to a verbal noun: the *-ing* form of the verb used as a noun. The term "participle" is still often used to refer to a PARTP functioning as an adjectival and the term "gerund" used to refer to a PARTP functioning as a nominal. At the same time, you will see the *-ing* form of a verb referred to as the present participle form and the *-ed* or *-en* form of a verb (the form that follows the AUX *have* to form the perfect aspect) referred to as the "past participle" form. We will stick with calling both the *-ing* and the *-ed* forms "participles" and talking about how they function as nominals, adjectivals, and adverbials.

12.1.1 Nominal Participle Phrases

Rarely in English grammar can we say that something is always true, but here is one of those moments: when a PARTP functions as a nominal, the participle is always a present participle (the *-ing* form):

> *Baking is my favorite activity.*
> **Baked is my favorite activity.*
> *Driving my '65 Mustang is one of the great pleasures of my life.*
> **Driven my '65 Mustang is one of the great pleasures of my life.*

Since past participles cannot function as nominals, we always know that a PARTP with a past participle must be functioning as an adjectival or an adverbial.

A PARTP:NOMINAL can perform the whole range of functions filled by other nominals, with the notable exception of OC:

> SUBJ: *Driving my '65 Mustang is my favorite activity.*
> AGENT: *A composite score was created by summing the five items.*[7]
> DO: *I love driving my '65 Mustang.*[8]
> SC: *One of the great pleasures of my life is driving my '65 Mustang.*
> PCOMP: *Imelda has a plan for driving my '65 Mustang on the highway.*
> IO: *KDKA-TV's Jon Delano gave driving a truck a try with the able help of Paul Bulick, who is the director of All-State Career School.*[9]

As with all nominals, we can use the pronoun replacement test to identify each complete PARTP:NOMINAL.

In Chapter 7, we saw that V + NP:DO + PARTP is a verb complementation pattern all its own, different in its nature from V + DO + OC. We will look at that pattern more closely below. First, we need to look at PARTPs functioning as nominals that are functioning as SCs and IOs.

Nominal PARTP functioning as an SC: A copular *be* followed by a nominal present PARTP functioning as a subject complement, as in, *One of the great pleasures of my life is driving my '65 Mustang*, looks like a *be* AUX followed by the present participle marking the progressive aspect, as in, *Imelda is driving my '65 Mustang*. The difference is simple: when we have BE + V-*ing* marking the progressive aspect of a verb, we can drop the *be* AUX, change the V-*ing* to a present or past form, and still have a grammatically well-formed sentence:

> *Imelda is driving my '65 Mustang.→Imelda drives my '65 Mustang.*

But when the MV is copular *be* followed by a nominal PARTP:SC, we cannot make the same change and still have a well-formed sentence:

> *One of the great pleasures of my life is driving my '65 Mustang.*
> **One of the great pleasures of my life drives my '65 Mustang.*

Nominal PARTP functioning as an IO: Only a limited set of verbs take as their complement NOMINAL:IO + NOMINAL:DO (or its alternate, NOMINAL:DO + TO/FOR + NOMINAL:IO). Of these verbs, an even more limited set can take a nominal PARTP as the IO.

> *Jon Delano gave driving a truck a try.*
> *?Jon Delano gave a try to driving a truck.*
>
> *Debbie gives helping others her whole heart.*
> *Debbie gives her whole heart to helping others.*[10]

Other verbs that can take IO + DO do not easily take a nominal PARTP as the IO. Rather, putting the nominal PARTP in the first complement constituent slot tends to make the second complement an OC; you can try making up examples with verbs like *make* and *find*. Remember that in the NOMINAL:IO + NOMINAL:DO complement pattern, the two nominals always name different objects, while in the NOMINAL:DO + NOMINAL:OC complement pattern, the two nominals always name or refer to the same object. When we place a nominal PARTP in the first complement slot after the MV, in most cases, the NP in the second complement slot will name or refer to the same object as the nominal PARTP in the first complement slot.

A nominal or adjectival PARTP cannot function as an OC: Consider:

> *I found Imelda driving my '65 Mustang.*
> *We saw children playing a game of some sort.*[11]
> *I left Archie watching the fight.*[12]

It may at first appear that we have an NP:DO (*Imelda; children; Archie*) followed by a nominal or adjectival PARTP:OC. But as we saw in Chapter 7, in none of these sentences can the PARTP be construed as a nominal. The pronoun replacement test does not work at all with the PARTP (**I found Imelda it*).

Also, the PARTP after the NP:DO does not seem to be an adjectival functioning as an OC since the PARTP does not in any way tell us *which* or *what kind* of person or thing the NP:DO is, and NP:DO + PARTP does not seem to be parallel in sense with clear examples of NP:DO + ADJP:OC verbs such as:

> *I found Imelda friendly.* vs. *I found Imelda driving my '65 Mustang.*
> *I left Archie content.* vs. *I left Archie watching the fight.*

We might also parse the PARTP in this context as parallel to an ADVERBIAL:OC. Consider:

> *I found Imelda in my '65 Mustang.* vs. *I found Imelda driving my '65 Mustang.*
> *I left Archie at the fight.* vs. *I left Archie watching the fight.*

Just like the PP:ADVERBIAL:OC, we might construe the PARTP as telling *how* or *in what state* I found Imelda and *how* or *in what state* I left Archie (we might also construe the ADJS *friendly* and *content* in the same manner: as telling *how*, *in what state*, or *in what manner*).

Perhaps a better analysis lies in the fact that the NP:DO is the agent of the following participle. This can easily be seen by paraphrasing the NP:DO + PARTP with an NP:DO + dependent clause:

PARTP: *I found Imelda driving my '65 Mustang.*
NCL: *I found that Imelda was driving my '65 Mustang.*
NON-ESSENTIAL ADJCL: *I found Imelda, who was driving my '65 Mustang.*
ADVCL: *I found Imelda while she was driving my '65 Mustang.*

PARTP: *We saw children playing a game of some sort.*
NCL: *We saw that children were playing a game of some sort.*
NON-ESSENTIAL ADJCL: *We saw children, who were playing a game of some sort.*
ADVCL: *We saw children as they were playing a game of some sort.*

PARTP: *I left Archie watching the fight.*
NCL: None—try it!
NON-ESSENTIAL ADJCL: *I left Archie, who was watching the fight.*
ADVCL: *I left Archie when he was watching the fight.*

Each paraphrase of the PARTP (NCL, ADJCL, ADVCL) highlights a different implied meaning for the original PARTP:

- The NCL paraphrase emphasizes the PARTP as implying a discovered fact or thing.
- The non-essential ADJCL paraphrase, like the ADVCL paraphrase, implies that the action named by the PARTP is concurrent with the action of the container clause, but the information contained in the PARTP is not essential for identifying the person named in the NP:DO.
- The ADVCL paraphrase highlights that the PARTP implies concurrent action.

Only the larger context will tell us which meaning of the PARTP is the most appropriate parse, and it may be difficult to discern a difference—which points to another strong connection among nominal, adjectival, and adverbial meaning: metaphorically, we understand "the time when someone is performing an action" (the adverbial parse) as "an object that can be *found* or *seen* or *left*" (the nominal parse); at the same time, we understand "an action being performed by someone" as "a characteristic of the person performing the action" (the adjectival parse).

Summing Up the Predicate Participle Problem: Given the pattern V + NP:DO + PARTP:VC, is it best:

- To parse the PARTP as a nominal, adjectival, or adverbial functioning as an OC?

• Since the NP is the agent of the participle, to parse the NP + PARTP as a "non-finite clause" (a "participle clause")?
• And, if we understand the NP + PARTP combination as somehow being clause-ish, to parse the NP + PARTP combo as an adverbial of concurrent action, a nominal, or a non-<u>essential</u> adjectival?

What do we gain with each analysis? What do we lose? Which one seems to you to work best? Why? Write some notes on your thoughts about this problem: you'll want to refer to them when we meet it again in parsing the pattern V + NP:DO + infinitive phrase.

One last note: There are many verbs in English that take the complement pattern **NP:DO** + PARTP:VC, particularly verbs of sensation (*smell, hear, feel,* etc.) and discovery or observation (*discover, observe, admire, catch* [in the sense of *perceive*]), as well as the verb *send*; here are a few more examples:

He heard **Belafonte** <u>singing the same line over and over again</u>.[13]
Even a simple glide across the bay becomes more exciting when you can feel **the engine** <u>rumbling underneath you</u>.[14]
I watched **the bees** <u>buzzing from flower to flower</u>.[15]
I caught **the kids** <u>raiding my candy bucket</u>.[16]
Her strong throw sent **the rock** <u>sailing over the wall</u>.[17]

12.1.2 Adjectival Participle Phrases

When a PARTP functions as an adjectival, like other adjectival constituents, it can be a modifier of a noun. A participle alone may function as a pre-modifier of a noun, taking the adjective slot between the DP and the noun. Effectively, a participle in the pre-modifier position is indistinguishable from any other adjective; some words that end in -*ing* (e.g. *interesting*) function primarily or solely as adjectives. We can check how well established a participle is as an adjective by whether it can take a degree subjunct like *very*:

an interesting book→a very interesting book
a sleeping dog→*a very sleeping dog

An adjectival PARTP may also function as a post-modifier of a noun, in which case the PARTP can include the participle as well as complements and/or adverbials more complex than a subjunct.

An adjectival PARTP can function as an SC. However, like an adjectival PARTP functioning as a pre-modifier of a noun, the PARTP:ADJECTIVAL:SC is indistinguishable from any other ADJ and can only consist of the participle by itself, or with a degree subjunct like *very*. We can use this distinction to indicate the difference between a PARTP:ADJECTIVAL:SC and a verb in the progressive aspect:

MV in present progressive:

Detective Gibson is lying.[18]
*Detective Gibson is very lying.

V + PᴀʀᴛP:Aᴅᴊᴇᴄᴛɪᴠᴀʟ:SC:

This is exciting.[19]
This is very exciting.

When a PᴀʀᴛP:Aᴅᴊᴇᴄᴛɪᴠᴀʟ modifies a noun, <u>typically</u>, if the participle is by itself (without complements, or adverbials more complex than a subjunct), it appears as a pre-modifier of the noun, in the AᴅᴊP slot between the DP and the noun (though we will see exceptions below). Present participles can always appear as an Aᴅᴊᴇᴄᴛɪᴠᴀʟ:ᴘʀᴇ-Mᴏᴅ ᴏꜰ N, and some are used more frequently as adjectives than as MVs in the present progressive (e.g. *interesting* and *exciting*):

> PᴀʀᴛP:Aᴅᴊᴇᴄᴛɪᴠᴀʟ:ᴘʀᴇ-Mᴏᴅ ᴏꜰ N: *This is a <u>very interesting</u> story.*
> PᴀʀᴛP:Aᴅᴊᴇᴄᴛɪᴠᴀʟ:SC: *The story is <u>very interesting</u>.*[20]
> MV: *It is important for the nurse to understand that there is a difference between what <u>is interesting</u> the public and what is in the public interest.*[21]
>
> PᴀʀᴛP:Aᴅᴊᴇᴄᴛɪᴠᴀʟ:ᴘʀᴇ-Mᴏᴅ ᴏꜰ N: *We anticipate a <u>very exciting future.</u>*
> PᴀʀᴛP:Aᴅᴊᴇᴄᴛɪᴠᴀʟ:SC: *The future outlook is <u>very exciting</u>.*[22]
> MV: *Today, a unique cross-genre blend of history and fantastic fiction <u>is exciting</u> authors and enticing readers.*[23]

Those participles that are used more frequently as adjectival pre-modifiers of nouns than as MVs are precisely those that are most readily used as SCs.

If the PᴀʀᴛP:Aᴅᴊᴇᴄᴛɪᴠᴀʟ includes not only the participle but complements and/or adverbials more complex than a subjunct, then the PᴀʀᴛP:Aᴅᴊᴇᴄᴛɪᴠᴀʟ is typically a post-modifier of the noun. A PᴀʀᴛP:Aᴅᴊᴇᴄᴛɪᴠᴀʟ functioning as a post-modifier of a noun may be either an essential or a non-essential modifier.

1. <u>Pre-modifier:</u> *All that stands between a <u>speeding</u> car and a cliff is a concrete barrier.*[24]
2. <u>Essential post-modifier:</u> *Like a car <u>speeding down the interstate</u>, a boat creates its own breeze.*[25]
3. <u>Non-essential post-modifier:</u> *Mere hours later, Coombs had us jammed into a convoy of rental cars, <u>speeding toward Switzerland</u>.*[26]

In sentence 2, the PᴀʀᴛP *speeding down the interstate* is an essential modifier because it provides information the reader or hearer needs in order to distinguish which particular car is being referred to by this use of the word *car*. If, in sentence 2, we drop the participle phrase functioning as an essential modifier (*speeding down the interstate*), the sentence will still be well formed (*Like a car, a boat creates its own breeze*), but the scope of reference of *a car* will be less specific and potentially less clear.

In sentence 3 above, the PARTP *speeding toward Switzerland* is a non-essential modifier because it describes the cars, or possibly the caravan, or "us," and it describes action that is coincident with the action described in the container clause (*We were jammed into a convoy of rental cars* and were, coincidentally, *speeding toward Switzerland*); but if we drop the PARTP:ADJECTIVAL that is functioning as a non-essential modifier, the scope of reference of the NP that the PARTP modifies remains clear: with or without the PARTP, we know which particular people are being referred to by the PRON "us" and which particular *convoy of rental cars* is being referred to by that NP.

In an adjectival PARTP, the participle may be either a present participle or a past participle:

4.a. PRESPART: *The hiding demons walked into the firelight.*[27]
4.b. PASTPART: *The hidden demons are less predictable.*[28]

Not all past participles can be used as pre-modifiers of nouns:

5.a. *The lying snake looked her right in the eye.*[29]
5.b. **The lied snake looked her right in the eye.*

In more complex PARTPs (such as 2 and 3), there is a close parallel between the adjectival PARTP and an ADJCL, and there is a parallel between the non-essential modifiers and an ADVCL—specifically an adverbial of concurrent action:

PRESPART (essential):

2. PARTP: *Like a car speeding down the interstate, a boat creates its own breeze.*
2.a. ADJCL: *Like a car that is speeding down the interstate, a boat creates its own breeze.*

PRESPART (non-essential):

3. PARTP: *Mere hours later, Coombs had us jammed into a convoy of rental cars, speeding toward Switzerland.*
3.a. ADJCL: *Mere hours later, Coombs had us jammed into a convoy of rental cars, which was speeding toward Switzerland.*
3.b. ADVCL: *Mere hours later, Coombs had us jammed into a convoy of rental cars, as it was speeding toward Switzerland.*

PASTPART (essential):

6. PARTP: *A black car driven by the masked Racer X forces the truck to pull over.*[30]

6.a. ADJCL: *A black car **that was** driven by the masked Racer X forces the truck to pull over.*

PASTPART (non-essential):

7. PARTP: *Earnhardt Ganassi Racing parked its iconic No. 8 car, driven by Aric Almirola, after the season's seventh race, in April.*[31]

7.a. ADJCL: *Earnhardt Ganassi Racing parked its iconic No. 8 car, **which was** driven by Aric Almirola, after the season's seventh race, in April.*

7.b. ADVCL: *Earnhardt Ganassi Racing parked its iconic No. 8 car, **when it was** driven by Aric Almirola, after the season's seventh race, in April.*

The PARTP:ADJECTIVAL with the present participle looks very much like an active voice ADJCL with the RELPRON:SUBJ and the progressive *be* AUX deleted, while the PARTP:ADJECTIVAL with the past participle followed by a BY-PP:AGENTIVE looks like a passive voice ADJCL with the RELPRON:SUBJ and the passive *be* AUX deleted. This parallel between the PARTP and the dependent clause provides us with a test for identifying the form of the PARTP:ADJECTIVAL:

> **The adjective clause test for an adjectival participle phrase**: To test whether a PARTP following a noun is a PARTP:ADJECTIVAL:MOD OF N, turn the PARTP into an ADJCL by adding an appropriate RELPRON:SUBJ and an appropriate *be* AUX. If the ADJCL is a fair paraphrase of the PARTP, then the PARTP is adjectival.

Also, as with nominal participle phrases, paraphrasing the PARTP:ADJECTIVAL as an ADJCL can help us identify the functions of constituents within the PARTP, especially adverbials.

Occasionally, a PARTP:ADJECTIVAL that includes not only a participle but its complements and/or adverbials more complex than a subjunct can appear in the slot between DP and noun, but note the use of quotation marks by the author to flag the self-conscious oddness of the usage:

8. *This "sticking your head in the sand" mindset eventually catches up to individuals down the road.*[32]

This kind of construction is rare and very limited as to where it is appropriate. Similarly, in certain contexts, a single word PARTP:ADJECTIVAL may appear after the noun it modifies:

9. *Heav'n has no rage like love to hatred turn'd/Nor hell a fury like a woman scorn'd.*[33]

10. *A penny saved is a penny earned.*[34]

This usage is a poetic inversion: we would more commonly speak of *a scorned woman*. But it works just like any construction with an adjectival past-participle-phrase functioning as a post-modifier of a noun: the noun being modified by the PARTP is the patient—the DO—of the participle. We can always see this by using an ADJCL to paraphrase the NP that contains the PARTP:

9.a. *Heaven has no rage like love to hatred turned/Nor hell a fury like a woman who has been scorned (by someone).*

→*Someone has scorned a woman.*

10.a. *A penny that was saved (by someone) is a penny that is earned (by someone).*

→*Someone saved (a penny). Someone earned a penny.*

A noun modified by a present PARTP names the agent of the participle—the actor performing the action named by the participle. A noun modified by a past PARTP names the patient of the participle: the person, place, or thing immediately affected by the action. Either way, as with other adjectival modifiers, a PARTP:ADJECTIVAL typically needs to be close to the noun it modifies. This last point becomes even more significant in discussing adverbial PARTPs and the relationship between an adverbial PARTP and an adjectival PARTP that functions as a non-essential adjectival modifier.

12.1.3 Adverbial Participle Phrases

Depending on whether they can be moved to both the beginning and end of their container clause, adverbial PARTPs may function as sentence or clause modifiers, or adjuncts:

PARTP:ADVERBIAL:SENTMOD:

11. *More than a dozen other musical acts, hoping to be popular, recorded "I'll Smile Again."*[35]

PARTP:ADVERBIAL:CLAUSE MODIFIER:

12. *The weather took a distinct turn for the worst as Scott began his final dash, hoping to be the first to reach the South Pole.*

PARTP:ADVERBIAL:ADJUNCT:

13. *Shunned by the other parents, Stephanie takes up with the glamorous, elusive and mysterious Emily Nelson.*[36]

PartPs often appear in the three positions in clauses that we have come to associate with sentence and clause modifiers:

11.a *Hoping to be popular, more than a dozen other musical acts recorded "I'll Smile Again."*
  More than a dozen other musical acts, hoping to be popular, recorded "I'll Smile Again."
  More than a dozen other musical acts recorded "I'll Smile Again," hoping to be popular.

12.a. *The weather took a distinct turn for the worst as, hoping to be the first to reach the South Pole, Scott began his final dash.*
  The weather took a distinct turn for the worst as Scott, hoping to be the first to reach the South Pole, began his final dash.
  The weather took a distinct turn for the worst as Scott began his final dash, hoping to be the first to reach the South Pole.

Sometimes, however, they cannot:

13.a. *Shunned by the other parents, Stephanie takes up with the glamorous, elusive and mysterious Emily Nelson.*
  Stephanie, shunned by the other parents, takes up with the glamorous, elusive and mysterious Emily Nelson.
  *Stephanie takes up with the glamorous, elusive and mysterious Emily Nelson, shunned by the other parents.

The movement of the PARTP is blocked, in part, by the presence of the second NP, *the glamorous, elusive and mysterious Emily Nelson*, which names another animate actor who could, conceivably, *be shunned*. Our default is to read the agent of the PARTP as the closest reasonable NP.

Sometimes movement of a PARTP:ADVERBIAL just seems to be blocked by distance:

14. *Buffeted by the storm, the ship struggled to safety.*
  The ship, buffeted by the storm, struggled to safety.[37]
  ?The ship struggled to safety, buffeted by the storm.

15. *Approaching the curve near San Diego City College, the trolley slows almost to a stop.*[38]
  The trolley, approaching the curve near San Diego City College, slows almost to a stop.
  ?The trolley slows almost to a stop, approaching the curve near San Diego City College.

The third version of these sentences may be grammatically well formed, but they are stylistically weak because of the separation between the present PARTP and its agent or the past PARTP and its patient.

Nonetheless, whether they can be moved to all three slots, and thus are clearly SentMods, or cannot be moved away from their agents or patients, and thus must be considered adjuncts, these PARTPs all have the entire container clause in their scope and provide adverbial contextualizing information for the characters and action in the container clause, commonly telling *why* or *when* the action occurred.

Adverbial PARTP in the middle of a clause: When a PARTP is placed between the NP:Subj and VP:Pred of the container clause, and is separated from the agent by commas, it may be paraphrased by either a non-<u>essential</u> AdjCl or an AdvCl:

AdjCl paraphrase:

11.b. *More than a dozen other musical acts, <u>who were</u>* **hoping to be popular**, *recorded "I'll Smile Again."*

AdvCl paraphrase:

11.c. *More than a dozen other musical acts, <u>because they were</u>* **hoping to be popular**, *recorded "I'll Smile Again."*

As we have already seen, there is a connection between non-essential adjectival information and adverbial information: both can provide context or framing for the action of the container clause. Because both of these paraphrases work, we must conclude that when the apparently adverbial PARTP is placed between the Subj and Pred, both sorts of meaning may be available to the reader.

12.1.4 The Agent—or Patient—of the Participle

So far, we have talked very loosely about present participles having agents and past participles having patients. It is important to understand the relationship between the participle and its agent or patient for two reasons: first, in revising a PARTP into a dependent or independent clause, we need to be able to identify the logical agent of a present participle, or patient of a past participle, to make it the subject of the clause. Second, to use PARTPs to clearly convey meaning, we have to be careful about locating the PARTP near its agent or patient: when a PARTP is located too far from its agent or patient, the reference or meaning of the PARTP can become unclear or ambiguous, and, with adjectival and adverbial PARTPs, if the agent or patient of the PARTP is absent, the result can be a dangling participle.

The agent or patient of the participle is typically explicit in the container clause, especially with adjectival and adverbial PARTPs; the agent is often implicit with nominal PARTPs (remember: nominal PARTPs always use present participles). In adjectival and adverbial PARTPs, the agent or patient of the participle is an important constituent of the container clause that anchors the PARTP, linking it to the container clause and helping to make clear what the function of the PARTP is within the container clause. A true "dangling participle" is always an adjectival or adverbial PARTP whose agent or patient has been deleted from the container clause.

The agent of a nominal PARTP can be explicit:

16. *Running the team has been O'Malley's full-time job.*[39]

To find the agent of the PARTP, we ask the same kind of question we would ask with a finite verb: "Who or what is PARTP?" "Who or what is running the team?" The answer, *O'Malley*, is the agent of the PARTP.

The agent of a nominal PARTP is often implicit:

17. *Running a team takes time and effort.*[40]

There is no stated agent of the PARTP *running a team*, no NP that answers the question *who is running a team?* The two available nouns, *time* and *effort*, aren't the actors performing the action named in the PARTP. Rather, the agent of the PARTP is an implied, abstract person, and the subject/topic of the container clause is that abstract person's abstract act of *running a team*. However, we have a related construction in which the PARTP is preceded by a possessive determiner:

17.a. *One's running a team takes time and effort.*

In this sentence, the PARTP *running a team* behaves like a single noun, and its nominal status is further marked by the possessive determiner
    The agent or patient of a PARTP:ADJECTIVAL or PARTP:ADVERBIAL generally must be explicit. If a PARTP:ADJECTIVAL is an <u>essential</u> modifier, then the <u>agent</u> or <u>patient</u> of the PARTP is the noun being modified by the **PARTP** and that agent or patient must be explicit. Consider the sentence:

18. *The people **walking in darkness** have seen a great light.*[41]

If we try to remove the agent of the participle in these sentences, we get nonsense: * *Walking in darkness have/has seen a great light*. Because the <u>essential</u> PARTP is a modifier functioning as a constituent within an NP, to remove the agent of the PARTP is to remove the head noun of the NP—and so to make a grammatically ill-formed sentence.
    When the PARTP functions as a <u>non-essential</u> adjectival modifier, or as an adverbial, the agent or patient should be explicit in order to make the

reference of the PARTP clear. Unfortunately, we can delete the agent or patient of the PARTP if two conditions both hold: (1) if the agent or patient of the PARTP is the same as the subject of the container clause and, (2) if the MV in the container clause is transitive; we then can put the MV into passive voice and delete the agent of the container clause, thus also deleting the agent or patient of the PARTP. The result is almost invariably either a PARTP with vague or ambiguous reference or a dangling participle.

Consider the following sentences in which the agent (11.a) or patient (13.a) of the PARTP is explicitly stated, and the agent or patient of the **PARTP** is the NP:SUBJ of the container clause:

11.a. ***Hoping to be popular***, *more than a dozen other musical acts*[AGENT OF "HOP-ING"; SUBJ OF "RECORDED"] *recorded "I'll Smile Again."*

13.a. ***Shunned by the other parents***, *Stephanie*[PATIENT OF "Shunned"; SUBJ OF "takes up with"] *takes up with the glamorous, elusive and mysterious Emily Nelson.*

Each of these PARTPs may be functioning as a non-essential adjectival modifier or an adverbial SENTMOD. Let's put the container clause in passive voice (11.d and 13.b) and then delete the agent of the container clause, thus removing the agent (11.e) and patient (13.c) of the PARTP:

Passive voice:

11.d. ?*Hoping to be popular*, *"I'll Smile Again" was recorded by more than a dozen other musical acts.*

13.b. ?*Shunned by the other parents*, *the glamorous, elusive and mysterious Emily Nelson is taken up with by Stephanie.*

Passive voice, agent deleted:

11.e. **Hoping to be popular*, *"I'll Smile Again" was recorded.*

13.c. **Shunned by the other parents*, *the glamorous, elusive and mysterious Emily Nelson is taken up with.*

The passive voice versions of these sentences are distinctly awkward and unclear, forcing the reader to backtrack and decipher that, no, in fact, "I'll Smile Again" is not the agent of *hoping* and that it is not "Emily Nelson" who was *shunned*. When we delete the agent form the passive voice container clause, we get true dangling participles, in that the first option for an agent or patient for the participle is ridiculous, and there is no second option with which to make sense of the participle's meaning. One of the reasons that some teachers warn so strongly against using passive voice is that passive voice is involved in dangling both participles and other modifiers. However, the passive voice verb is not, in itself, the problem: passive voice merely aids and abets the "crime" of dangling participles.

The agent of a PARTP can appear in several different places in the container clause. We have already seen that the agent of a PARTP can appear as the subject of the container clause and as a possessive determiner. It can also appear in the complement of the MV in the container clause:

19. *Playing in the band* *has also helped* <u>Olsen</u> *stay out of trouble.*[42]

Olsen is the one who is *playing in the band.* The agent of a PARTP can even be the whole container clause:

20. *Someone dashes into the frame at the last minute, **ruining the shot.***[43]

Here, it wasn't just *someone* that ruined the shot; rather, the whole clause is the agent of the PARTP, a relationship that can be paraphrased by:

20.a. *Someone dashing into the frame at the last minute ruins the shot.*
20.b. *Someone who dashes into the frame at the last minute ruins the shot.*

Having the whole clause be the agent of the PARTP is much like having an entire clause be the antecedent of a RELPRO-WORD, as in:

20.c. *Someone dashes into the frame at the last minute, **<u>which</u> ruins the shot.***

The RELPROCLAUSE <u>which</u> refers back to the whole preceding clause, *Someone dashes into the frame at the last minute.*

12.1.5 PartPs With Auxiliary and Semi-Auxiliary Verbs

It is very common for <u>present</u> participles to take AUX and semi-AUX verbs that mark perfect and imperfect aspect and passive voice. However, <u>past</u> participles cannot take auxiliaries. Remember that, in finite verbs, the first word in the complete verb marks the tense of the verb. Likewise, in a PARTP where the participle includes AUX and/or semi-AUX verbs, the first word of the complete participle takes the present participle form. For the verb *drive, driving* is the present participle, and *having driven* is the perfect present participle. Native English speakers have many of these forms in our repertoire of ordinary usage. Here are some examples of the perfect, imperfect, and passive <u>present</u> participle. The present participle does not take the progressive aspect: we cannot have two *-ing* forms next to each other in the same verb:

Present Participle: *<u>Driving</u> home to Evanston, he felt his years had not been wasted.*[44]

Perfect Present Participle: *You imagine all the folks upstate who, <u>having driven</u> home from their parties on state-funded highways, are snug in their beds.*[45]

Imperfect Present Participle: *Drivers stop at the Wayside Service Station across the street to fill up before <u>starting to drive</u> home.*[46]

Passive Present Participle: *While <u>being driven home</u>, Mikaela ponders why a super advanced robot would transform into a "piece-of-crap Camaro."*[47]

Perfect Imperfect Present Participle: *The impression from the simulator studies discussed above is that sleepiness soon after <u>having started to drive</u> reaches levels high enough to result in a crash.*[48]

Perfect Passive Present Participle: *When Churchill got there, <u>having been driven</u> through a city undergoing an aerial assault, he found about 100 people drinking champagne in the shelter below ground.*[49]

Modal auxiliaries have no participle form, so they cannot appear at the beginning of a multi-word participle. However, semi-modal verbs do have *-ing* forms, so we can have forms of the modal present participle and combinations of the modal present participle with aspect and passive voice auxiliaries and imperfect aspectual verbs:

Modal Present Participle: *Earnhardt said last month he hopes Washington fans don't "disown" him for <u>having to drive</u> the Eagles car.*[50]

Modal Perfect Present Participle: *Salita is such a careful, reined-in fellow that one comes away <u>wanting to have seen</u> much more of the men around him.*[51]

Modal Imperfect Present Participle: *Sedentary folks could improve their health without <u>having to start running</u> marathons.*[52]

Modal Passive Present Participle: *Eventually <u>having to be driven</u> everywhere and realizing how circumscribed my life would be if I didn't learn forced me to try again.*[53]

Of course, the more complicated these modal present participle phrases get, the less common they are in actual English usage. But we can and do use the simpler ones fairly often.

12.1.6 PartPs Preceded by a Subordinator

A PartP may sometimes be preceded by a subordinating conjunction:

21. <u>*When*</u> **shown the best techniques**, *students improve.*[54]
22. <u>*Although*</u> **shown as Under Construction on the map**, *the Dining Center opened in Fall, 2007.*[55]

We only find this construction with a select list of SConjs: *although, as if, as though, even though, if, though, unless, when, whenever, while*. With those subordinating conjunctions that commonly also function as prepositions, it makes more sense to parse them as PPs with a nominal PARTP functioning as a PCOMP. We can test for whether we have an SCONJ with a PARTP or a preposition with a PARTP:NOMINAL:PCOMP by using the pronoun replacement test:

21. *When* [shown the best techniques], students improve.
21.a. **When* [it/that], students improve.
22. *Although* [shown as Under Construction on the map], the Dining Center opened in Fall, 2007.
22.a. **Although* [it/that], the Dining Center opened in Fall, 2007.
23. *After* [being shown the prototype and how to use it], Somers loved it.[56]
23.a. *After* [that], Somers loved it.

Words like *after* are considered prepositions when followed by a clear nominal but are SCONJs when followed by a clause or PARTP that does not allow for the pronoun replacement test. Words like *when* and *although* are almost always SCONJs since only rarely can they be followed by a nominal alone.

A PARTP preceded by an SCONJ is always adverbial, functions like an ADVCL:SENTMOD, and can always be paraphrased by an ADVCL:

> *When* (they are) **shown the best techniques**, children improve.
> *While* (she is) **being driven home**, Mikaela ponders why a super advanced robot would transform into a "piece-of-crap Camaro."

12.2 Infinitives (INF) and Infinitive Phrases (INFP)

Infinitive phrase forms: Most commonly, the infinitive appears as the particle *to* plus the base form of the verb:

> **To err** is human.
> It's easy **to get** kids **to run** a marathon.[57]

However, the word *to* is commonly deleted from the **infinitive** following the DO after certain <u>verbs</u>:

> I just <u>saw</u> you **kick** her.[58]
> She <u>felt</u> the baby **move**.[59]
> <u>Watch/help/make/let</u> me **climb** the tree!

We label the infinitive without *to* as the "bare infinitive" rather than describing it as a tensed form because the NP preceding the infinitive does not have to agree with the verb in person and number, as it would if the verb were finite. We also have constructions with the **to-infinitive** that closely parallel those with the bare infinitive:

> Reaching down, he <u>helped</u> me **(to) climb** up and onto the seat between them.[60]

The quotidian problems of everyday life <u>could</u> actually <u>help</u> your sister (to) heal.[61]

The infinitive appears in four different formal contexts:

1. The **to-infinitive**—*to* + the base form of the verb.
2. The **bare infinitive**—the base form of the verb.
3. The **in order to infinitive**—*in order to* + the base form of the verb.
4. The **for-to infinitive**—*for* + Nominal + *to* + the base form of the verb.

We will find that the *in order to* infinitive construction helps us in identifying adverbial INFPs, while the *for-to* infinitive construction will help us identify the agent of an infinitive.

Like PARTPs, INFPs may appear as the infinitive by itself or as an infinitive plus complements and/or adverbials:

> **To govern** *is to choose.*[62]
> **To govern a country** *requires one to choose and accept actions that are necessary evils.*[63]
> *The art of parliamentary government is* **to govern the country by means of continuous conversation.**[64]

In each of these sentences, the highlighted INFP functions as a nominal, which functions, respectively, as the SUBJ in the first two container clauses and an SC in the third. In the second sentence, the NP *a country* is the DO of the infinitive *to govern*. In the third sentence, the PP *by means of continuous conversation* is an adverbial functioning as an adjunct: it is adverbial in meaning (telling *how* the country will be governed); we cannot move it; and it has a weight roughly equal to the other constituents of the INFP.[65]

Infinitive phrase functions: INFPs can function as nominals, adjectivals, or adverbials:

> Nominal: <u>To govern</u>[INFP:NOMINAL:SUBJ] *is to choose.*
> Adjectival: *The candidate* <u>to watch in the California governor's race</u>[INFP:ADJECTIVAL:MOD OF "candidate"] *is None of the Above.*[66]
> Adverbial: *Are electric vehicles ready* <u>to go mainstream</u>[INFP:SUBJUNCT/MOD OF "ready"].[67]

12.2.1 Nominal Infinitive Phrases

INFPs <u>cannot</u> perform the whole range of nominal functions. They consistently and clearly function as subjects, agents, and SCs:

> SUBJ: <u>To govern</u> *is to choose.*

AGENT: *It's so easy to fall in love.*[68]

SC: *The art of parliamentary government is to govern the country by means of continuous conversation.*

When an infinitive phrase functions as an SC, it is always nominal:

The art of parliamentary government is [*to govern the country by means of continuous conversation*].
The art of parliamentary government is [*this*].

Nominal infinitive phrase functioning as a DO? As we saw in Chapters 6 and 7, it is an interesting question as to whether a nominal INFP can function as a DO. Let's puzzle over this a bit more:

1. *I want to work on the project.*
2. *I began to work on the project.*
3. *I began working on the project.*

So far, I have argued that in sentence 1, *want to* is a semi-modal verb and the complete verb is *want to work*. Likewise, in sentences 2 and 3, I have argued that *began to* and *began* are imperfect aspectual Vs and the complete verbs in these sentences are *began to work* and *began working*.

At the same time, we might also follow traditional grammar in parsing these sentences so that everything after the first verb (*want*; *began*) is a NOMINAL:DO. This seems to be verified by the pronoun replacement test since we can reasonably paraphrase sentences 1–3 as follows:

1.a. *I want it.*
2.a. *I began it.*
3.a. *I began it.*

Which is the "right" parse? I don't know. But if we look at the way different verbs are actually used, some verbs seem to be more like semi-AUX Vs in this position and some less so. *Want to* can be paraphrased by *may*, and thus parsing it as a semi-modal verb seems fruitful. And *begin/begin to* seem to name an action that is integral with the action named by the following verb (c.f. the progressive AUX *be*, as in *I am running*), and thus parsing them as aspectual semi-AUX Vs seems fruitful. Now consider:

4. *I love to work on the project.*
5. *I love working on the project.*

Here is an instance where meaning and usage may clearly impact parsing. Using the verb "love" in such contexts seems to presuppose some object of the verb: a thing or person that is loved, a "beloved." While the action expressed by *love*/*love to* may seem aspectual (inseparable from the action named by the following verb), because feeling "love" presupposes an object of that love, it may be more fruitful here to parse *to work*/*working on the project* as a NOMINAL:DO—that is, as the literal and grammatical object of that love. At the same time, when we put these sentences into passive voice, we get:

4.a. ?*To work on the project is loved by me.*
5.a. ?*Working on the project is loved by me.*

Perhaps parsing *love*/*love to* as imperfect aspectual Vs is the better answer. Try to think of more verbs in English that can be followed by *TO* + V or by V + -*ing*. Which analysis seems to work better? Why?

INFPs as verb complements: INFPs don't function as IOs and PCOMPS because the word *to* gets in the way. The particle *to* that marks the infinitive can also be a preposition and is also often implied with the IO (remember the *to-for* test for the IO). Instead, in the PCOMP and IO positions where we might like to use a nominal INFP, we use a PARTP. Note the similarity between the two sentences *I like to drive on the highway* and *I like driving on the highway*. In many contexts, we can use either a PARTP or an INFP to convey essentially the same meaning. In contexts where we cannot use an INFP, we can often use a PARTP instead:

*INFP:NOMINAL:PCOMP: **The young colonel had devised a plan _for_ to drive the Spanish out of the Bahamas' capital.*
PARTP:NOMINAL:PCOMP: *The young colonel had devised a plan _for_ driving the Spanish out of the Bahamas' capital.*

Nominal and Adjectival INFPs don't functions as OCs. As we saw in 7.1.3.5, there is a verb complementation pattern in which the *to*-infinitive does not immediately follow the MV of the container clause. Instead, we have the MV followed by an NP:DO and an **INFP:VC**:

The law requires _you_ to signal a turn or lane change with your turn lights or hand signals at least 100 feet (30 m) ahead.[69]
His doctor persuaded _him_ to take time off.[70]
The medical staff convinced _him_ to take time off.[71]
I forced _him_ to tell the truth.[72]

As with PARTPs in the same position, at first blush, we might think that these sentences have the INFP functioning as an OC. The OC renames the NP:DO or ascribes an attribute to the NP:DO, and the test for identifying an OC is whether you can put an appropriate form of copular *be* between the NP:DO and the OC. As we saw back in 7.1.3.2, *We elected him president* implies *he is president; president* is an NP:OC. *Nancy found rock climbing exciting* implies that *rock climbing is exciting. Exciting* is an ADJ:OC.

This test does not work persuasively with an INFP in the OC slot. Yes, in the sentence *The law requires you to signal a turn*, we can insert a form of *be* between the NP:DO and the INFP to get, *You are to signal a turn*. But in such a sentence, the INFP does not rename or ascribe an attribute to the NP:DO. The verb *be* is not, here, copular; rather, *are to* is a semi-modal verb. Like the modal AUX *must, are to* implies a command. If *You are to signal a turn*, then *You must signal a turn*.

And, as with the DO + PARTP:VC complement pattern, when a verb takes a DO + INFP as its complement, the DO names the agent of the INF. The relationship between the INF and its agent is very close, and the location of the INFP in the sentence is still controlled by the location of its agent. As with PARTPs, the close relationship becomes even more evident when we look at adjectival INFPs.

12.2.2 Adjectival Infinitive Phrases

An adjectival INFP can only consistently function as a post-modifier of a noun:

The urge to sneeze was becoming unbearable.[73]
The coach saw my desire to succeed.[74]

We can use the pronoun replacement test to identify whether an INFP is functioning as an adjectival post-modifier of a noun and is therefore part of an NP:

[*The urge to sneeze*] *was becoming unbearable.*
[*It*] *was becoming unbearable.*

The coach saw [*my desire to succeed*].
The coach saw [*it*].

Unlike a PARTP:ADJECTIVAL, an INFP:ADJECTIVAL can only be a post-modifier of a noun—regardless of whether the INF stands alone or has complements and/ or adverbial dependents.

While an adjectival present PARTP typically modifies the noun that is the agent of the participle, and an adjectival past PARTP typically modifies the noun that is the patient of the participle, as Christer Geisler points out in his monograph, *Relative Infinitives in English*, the noun being modified by an INFP:ADJECTIVAL may be the agent of the infinitive, but it is not necessarily, or even typically, so. The noun that the INFP modifies may have other roles:

- **Agent of the infinitive:** *She had a number of friends to help her out. Friends* is the agent of *help*. You could paraphrase the NP including the INFP as . . . *friends who would help her out*.

- **DO or patient of the infinitive:** *This is **the method** to adopt. The method is the DO or patient of *adopt*. You could paraphrase the NP including the INFP as *One should adopt **this method**.*
- **PCOMP within the INFP:** *This is **the place** in which to discuss it. In which* would be rewritten as *in this place* and would be an adverbial in the paraphrase, *One should discuss it **in this place***; or *They had many items to choose from*, which could also read, *They had many items from which to choose*—*One could choose from **many items***.[75]

The noun being modified by the adjectival INFP always has a function within the INFP.

The agent of the INFP:ADJECTIVAL is often not explicitly stated. In the four examples just given, only the first one has an explicit agent for its infinitive (*friends*); the other three have implied agents (some words are added for clarity):

> *This is the method for one to adopt.*
> *This is the place in which one is to/should discuss it.*
> *They had many items for one to choose from.*

The implicit agents are best paraphrased as indefinite (*one*), as they refer to no definite person or actor. Geisler notes that not only are the agents of INFPs typically indefinite but also a majority of the nouns modified by adjectival INFPs are indefinite, indicating that adjectival INFPs are generally used to introduce new or unfamiliar information—to talk about general cases or abstractions, rather than definite, specific instances.[76] This is consistent with our previous observation that V-*TO*-V constructions, and other constructions with *TO* + V in them, are very often modal or imperfect in meaning, naming hypothetical, not fully realized, or abstract actions.

Identifying an INFP:ADJECTIVAL functioning as a post-modifier of a noun: In trying to identify an INFP:ADJECTIVAL, it is often useful to paraphrase the INFP with an ADJCL, as we did with a PARTP:ADJECTIVAL functioning as a post-modifier of a noun. If the INFP:ADJECTIVAL is a non-essential modifier, its agent will always be explicit, and to paraphrase it with an ADJCL will only require adding an appropriate RELPRON and AUX:

Non-essential INFP:ADJECTIVAL:

> *He reset jury selection, to have started this week, for Nov. 21.*
> *He reset jury selection, **which was** to have started this week, for Nov. 21.*[77]

Likewise, when the INFP:ADJECTIVAL is an essential modifier and the agent is explicit:

Essential INFP with explicit agent:

> *She had a number of friends to help her out.*
> *She had a number of friends **who were** to help her out.*

The agent of the <u>essential</u> INFP:ADJECTIVAL is often implicit, as we have seen above. When the <u>agent of the INFP</u> is implicit, we also need to supply a subject for an ADJCL paraphrase:

Essential INFP with <u>implicit agent</u>:

This is the method to adopt.
*This is the method **that** <u>one</u> **is** to adopt.*

We can always use an ADJCL to paraphrase an INFP:ADJECTIVAL that is functioning as a post-modifier of a noun.

12.2.3 Adverbial Infinitive Phrases

INFPs functioning as adverbials are more flexible and have a broader range of functions than do adverbial PARTPs. Adverbial INFPs may function as:

* Sentence and Clause Modifiers.
* Adjuncts.
* Disjuncts.
* Subjuncts in ADJP:SC and ADJP:OC.

We can distinguish an INFP:ADVERBIAL from nominal and adjectival INFPs, as well as from V-*TO*-V constructions by using:

The ***in order*** **test for adverbial infinitive phrases**: Given a sentence with *TO* + V, if we insert the words *in order* before the word *to* and the sense of the sentence does not change, then the combination *TO* + V marks the beginning of an INFP:ADVERBIAL.

Consider the following examples:

INFP:ADVERBIAL

Pseudonyms were used <u>to insure</u> the confidentiality of all participants.
*Pseudonyms were used **in order** <u>to insure</u> the confidentiality of all participants.*[78]

INFP:ADJECTIVAL

The urge <u>to sneeze</u> was becoming unbearable.
The urge **in order <u>to sneeze</u> was becoming unbearable.*

INFP:NOMINAL

<u>To govern</u> is to choose.
**In order <u>to govern</u> is to choose.*

INFP:ADVERBIAL:SENTMOD: Adverbial INFPs are commonly used as sentence modifiers:

> *In order to form a more perfect Union, we the people of the United States do ordain and establish this Constitution for the United States of America.*
>
> *We the people of the United States, in order to form a more perfect Union, do ordain and establish this Constitution for the United States of America.*
>
> *We the people of the United States do ordain and establish this Constitution for the United States of America in order to form a more perfect Union.*

We can obviously move the INFP *in order to form a more perfect Union* without changing the meaning of the sentence, and we can easily frame a question around the INFP: "Why did we ordain and establish this Constitution?" *In order to form a more perfect Union.* The scope of the INFP is the entire container clause since *we the people* do the *forming*, and *to form a more perfect union* is *why we the people ordain and establish this Constitution.*

INFPs can also function as dependent clause modifiers:

INFP: ADVERBIAL:NCLMOD:

[That, to score a goal, Franz ran the length of the field] was hardly unusual.

INFP:ADVERBIAL:ADJCLMOD:

The player [who ran the length of the field to score a goal] is Franz.

INFP:ADVERBIAL:ADVCLMOD:

[Since Franz, to score a goal, had run the length of the field], he was out of breath.

INFP:ADVERBIAL:ADJUNCT: Infinitive phrases are often used as adjuncts:

> *I am a single mom of 2 boys, and I work to support us.*[79]
> *I just slipped and fell when I was running to see Einstein.*[80]

Despite having the combination V-*TO*-V, in these sentences we do not have a semi-modal followed by a verb, as shown by the *in order* test:

> *I work in order to support us.*
> *I was running in order to see Einstein.*

Both of these INFPs have the whole container clause in their scope: in each example, the NP:SUBJ of the container clause is the agent of the INFP; in each case, the INFP gives a reason (why) for the predicate. In neither of these sentences is the INFP easily moved without sounding like Yoda:

?To support us I work. *I, to support us, work.
*To see Einstein I was running. *I, to see Einstein, was running.

In the following two sentences, the INFPs are adjuncts within, respectively, a PARTP and an INFP:

*There was Franz, running the length of the field **to score a goal**.*
*To run the length of the field **to score a goal** requires stamina and skill.*

In these two sentences, if the containers for the adjuncts were clauses instead of non-finite verb phrases, then the adjuncts would be clause modifiers. Because the containers are non-finite verb phrases, in both cases, we cannot move the INFP *to score a goal*. Therefore, in both sentences, the INFP is an adjunct with, respectively, the PARTP *running the length of the field* and the INFP *to run the length of the field* in its scope.

 INFP:ADVERBIAL:DISJUNCT: Like a SENTMOD, a disjunct can be moved within the container clause to the beginning, end, or the slot between subject and predicate, and disjuncts have the whole container clause in their scope. However, we cannot frame a question around a disjunct. The disjunct also gives the speaker's opinion of or observation about the content of the container clause; this is clear in the case of an INFP:DISJUNCT because the agent of the INFP will be *I*. INFPs form disjuncts using a simple but highly productive pattern:

To be totally honest, *my first emotion was annoyance.*[81]
Not to say craft cider can't surprise you, *but, usually, if you can smell it, you will taste it.*[82]

In the first example, the INFP:ADVERBAL:DISJUNCT can be easily moved to the other slots in the sentence, while in the second example, the disjunct is not easily moved (try it). And we cannot frame a question around either the non-negated nor the negated INFPs functioning as disjuncts (try this, too).

 An **INFP:ADVERBIAL** can commonly function as a **SUBJUNCT** in an **ADJP:SC** or **ADJP:OC**:

INFP:ADVERBIAL:SUBJUNCT IN AN ADJP:SC

Congress was <u>ready</u>[ADJP:SC].
*Congress was <u>ready **to fund it**</u>*[ADJP:SC].[83]

This kind of book is <u>hard</u>[ADJP:SC].
*This kind of book is <u>hard **to read rapidly**</u>*[ADJP:SC].

INFP: ADVERBIAL: SUBJUNCT IN AN ADJP: OC

The low price made Franz happy[ADJP:OC].
The low price made Franz happy to buy a new soccer ball[ADJP:OC].

These INFPs tell *how* or *in what manner* about the ADJs in their scope; the INFPs are not movable; and their scope is tightly limited. It seems reasonable to label them as subjuncts.

12.2.4 The Agent of the Infinitive

As we noted above, the agent of an infinitive is often implicit and best paraphrased by an indefinite pronoun. For example, in the sentence *This kind of book is hard to read rapidly*, the agent of the infinitive *to read* is implicit, and the sentence is not talking about some specific person reading. The agent of the infinitive is best named by an indefinite pronoun such as *one*: *One is/wants to read (this kind of book) rapidly*.

Less often, the agent of the infinitive is explicitly stated in the container clause, as in the sentence *The low price made Franz happy to buy a new soccer ball*. The agent of the infinitive is *Franz* since he is the one who will *buy a new soccer ball*. We can thus paraphrase the INFP with the sentence *Franz is/wants to buy a new soccer ball*.

There is a common, conventional structure of the form *FOR*-NP-*TO*, in which the agent of the infinitive is stated explicitly:

He reset jury selection, to have started this week, for Nov. 21. (for jury selection[AGENT] *to have started)*
It's hard to read this kind of book rapidly. (for me[AGENT] *to read)*
It takes a lot of courage for scientists[AGENT] *to speak out.*[84]

The NP between *for* and *to* is the agent of the infinitive. Notice that if the agent of the infinitive following *for* is a personal pronoun, it takes the objective form: in this context, *for* behaves like a preposition and so demands the objective form. In some contexts, it is tempting to read the *FOR* + NP as a PP. But part of the point of the sentence involves the close relationship between *for me* and *to read rapidly*. If we analyze the two as separate constituents, then we change their scope and lose the agent-verb connection between *me* and *read*. It is more useful to analyze the *FOR* + NP + *TO* + V construction as a particular sort of complete INFP with an explicit agent.

Even in sentences without the *FOR* + NP explicit agent of the INFP, and in which you cannot insert *FOR* + NP, this construction can help serve as a test for identifying the agent of the infinitive:

I work to support us.
I work for whom to support us?

For me to support us.

*The low price made Franz happy **to buy a new soccer ball**.*
*Happy **for whom** to buy a new soccer ball?*
***For Franz** to buy a new soccer ball.*

To err is human.
***For whom** to err is human?*
***For one** to err is human.*
***For us** to err is human.*

The FOR-NP-TO structure for identifying the agent of an infinitive also works with the phrase *in order to* that we have used to check if an INFP is adverbial. Combining the two gives us *in order FOR-NP-TO*:

> *Pseudonyms were used **to insure the confidentiality of all participants**.*
> *Pseudonyms were used **in order to** insure the confidentiality of all participants*
> *Pseudonyms were used **in order for the researchers to** insure the confidentiality of all participants*

Being able to identify the agent of an INFP is important both for revising sentences for clarity and for changing the order of information within sentences to maintain the topic of a paragraph from sentence to sentence.

12.2.5 InfPs With Auxiliary and Semi-Auxiliary Verbs

As with present participles, it is very common for infinitives to take AUX Vs that mark perfect and progressive aspect; passive voice; and imperfect aspectual Vs. In such multi-word infinitives, the first word in the string takes the infinitive form. Thus, *to drive* is the infinitive, and *to have driven* is the perfect infinitive. Here are some examples of the perfect, progressive, imperfect, and passive infinitive:

> Infinitive: *Salles walks to her car to drive home at the end of her workday.*[85]
> Perfect Infinitive: *Males were more likely to have driven while drunk.*[86]
> Progressive Infinitive: *It doesn't make any sense for people like that to be driving for Uber or Lyft.*[87]
> Imperfect Infinitive: *Pick the right time to start driving on the highway.*[88]
>   *She took advantage of that to get into the car and to start to drive away.*[89]
> Passive Infinitive: *McBride and a handful of other workers were ushered into a temp agency van to be driven to a factory job in west suburban McCook.*[90]

Perfect Progressive Infinitive: *The researchers found that teens were less likely to have been driving a large pickup.*[91]

Perfect Imperfect Infinitive: *The agents thought it unusual for a traveler, such as Mr. Rivero, to have begun driving in Las Cruces.*[92]

The changes that we have induced are therefore likely to have started to drive the epithelial 293T cells toward full pluripotency.[93]

Perfect Passive Infinitive: *How disheveled I was, and miffed at my date, not even to have been driven home and given a kiss good-bye.*[94]

Progressive Imperfect Infinitive: *It would be too dangerous for any vehicle at all to be attempting to drive.*[95]

Modal auxiliaries have no infinitive form, so they cannot appear at the beginning of a multi-word infinitive. However, semi-modal verbs do have infinitive forms, so we can have forms of the modal infinitive and combinations of the modal infinitive with aspect and passive voice auxiliaries and semi-Aux Vs:

Modal Infinitive: *It is in our nature as Americans to want to drive everywhere.*[96]

Modal Perfect Infinitive: *It's the stupidest thing I've ever felt, to want to start fighting off death at thirty-four like my father does, with drugs and daily runs and a strict diet (he has utterly turned his life around), to want to have inherited the same system that grabbed his heart from the inside and squeezed it like a vise.*[97]

Modal Imperfect Infinitive: *It's the stupidest thing I've ever felt, to want to start fighting off death at thirty-four like my father does.*

Modal Passive Infinitive: *It would have been extremely impolite to expect to be paid for helping an uncle.*[98]

As with the more complicated PartP constructions, the more complicated the verb of the InfP, the less common they are in actual English usage. However, we can and do use the simpler ones fairly often.

12.2.6 InfP Preceded by a Subordinator

Nominal, adjectival and adverbial InfPs may sometimes be preceded by a subordinator:

Nominal Infinitive Phrase with a Subordinator: With nominal InfPs, we cannot use the subordinators *that* or *if*, but we can use *whether* and nearly the whole list of *wh*-words. As with *wh*-NCLs, in *wh*-nominal InfPs, the *wh*-word has a function within the InfP.

*I didn't know **whether to laugh or cry**.*[99]

*For years I never had to think about **what to do** or **when to do it**.*[100]

*I want to learn **how to play** "Here Comes the Sun" by The Beatles.*[101]

In the preceding examples, *what* is a ProN:DO of "to do." *When* and *how* are ProAdvs and require a little more analysis.

One of the easiest ways to analyze the InfP is to paraphrase it with a clause. *When to do it* becomes *When one ought to do it.* To analyze the function of the ProAdv, it is simplest to turn it into a substantive adverbial, such as *today*. This gives us *Today one ought to do it.* The adverbial is movable, at least to the end of the clause: *One ought to do it today.* *?One, today, ought to do it.* We can frame a question around the adverbial: *When is one to do it? Today.* And the scope of the adverbial is the whole InfP: both the subject (*one*) and the predicate are contained in the timeframe of the adverbial (*today*). All of this information helps us label the function of *when* within the InfP. The one significant difference between *today* and *when* is that *when* cannot be moved in the same way that we can move *today*. Since *when* has the whole InfP in its scope, but we cannot move *when*, we can conclude that *when* is a ProAdv:Adjunct.

If we do the same sort of analysis of *how to play "Here Comes the Sun,"* we find that the substantive adverbs we may substitute for the word *how* are, like *how* itself, hard to move. Remember that *wh*-pro-words are commonly taken from their place in SVC clause order and moved to the front of a dependent clause. So in paraphrasing the InfP with a clause, we may need to restore the ProAdv to the slot it fills in the default SVC clause: *I am to play "Here Comes the Sun" how.* Replacing *how* with a substantive adverbial, we get something like *I am to play "Here Comes the Sun" well,* or, *I am to play "Here Comes the Sun" on the guitar.* We already know that the adverbial is not movable; and the scope of the adverbial is the whole InfP since the AdvP (*well; on the guitar*) characterizes the "playing of 'Here Comes the Sun'"—effectively a whole predicate—and has a broader scope than we find with subjuncts. Therefore, we determine that *how* is a ProAdv:Adjunct.

Here is a list of **wh-subordinators that can precede an InfP**: *how, what, when, where, which, who, whom, why.* InfPs beginning with these *wh*-words are always nominal and can function in all of the roles fulfilled by nominals except OC:

Subj: *Whom to invite is a big minefield.*[102]
    What to avoid is what someone once called the definition of hell: truth realized too late.[103]
Agent: *There is what to investigate.*[104]
DO: *I want to learn how to play "Here Comes the Sun."*
    Terry asked her in 2000 how she decided what to print and whom to trust.[105]
IO: *We do give some thought to what to wear.*[106]

PC<small>OMP</small>: *This cultural framework consists of ideas about <u>when to fight</u> and <u>when to compromise</u>.*[107]
SC: *The real question is <u>what to tolerate</u>.*[108]

W<small>H</small>-P<small>RO</small>-<small>WORD</small> functions: Within the I<small>NF</small>P:N<small>OMINAL</small>, the *wh*-words function in all of the ways we have already seen with interrogative and relative pro-words, and with *wh*-subordinators in NC<small>LS</small> and A<small>DV</small>C<small>LS</small> (10.2.1.1; 10.2.2), but for one exception: the *wh*-P<small>RO</small>N<small>S</small> cannot be the agent of the I<small>NF</small>P (try it!). In an I<small>NF</small>P, a *wh*-P<small>RO</small>N can only be the complement of the infinitive or a PC<small>OMP</small>.

Adjectival I<small>NF</small>P with a subordinator: An I<small>NF</small>P with a subordinator can function as an adjectival only with the subordinator *whether* and therefore, reasonably, in idioms with nouns that express the idea of having a choice:

*It will leave to the politicians the question **<u>whether to keep, trim or discard the mortgage-interest and charitable write-offs</u>**.*[109]
*They will have to make a decision **<u>whether to participate or not to participate</u>**.*[110]
*Parents need a genuine choice **<u>whether to stay at home and take care of their children</u>**.*[111]

It is curious that these I<small>NF</small>P:A<small>DJECTIVAL</small> constructions take *whether* as a subordinator because this word is never used to mark an A<small>DJ</small>C<small>L</small>. Despite their adjectival meaning and function, there is no way to paraphrase these I<small>NF</small>Ps as A<small>DJ</small>C<small>LS</small>. The answer may be that they are derived from sentences like the following, in which *whether* + I<small>NF</small>P functions as a N<small>OMINAL</small>:PC<small>OMP</small>:

*The question **of** <u>whether to keep</u>. . . .*
*They will have to make a decision **about** <u>whether to participate</u>. . . .*
*Parents need a genuine choice **for** <u>whether to stay home</u>. . . .*

Adverbial I<small>NF</small>P with a subordinator: We also have a very limited set of idioms in which we can place an SC<small>ONJ</small> in front of an I<small>NF</small>P, creating an adverbial. The SC<small>ONJ</small>s that can appear with infinitive phrases are *as if* and *as though*:

*He shrugged, **<u>as if to say, Miles and I are friends, too</u>**.*[112]
*Several times Thornton started, **<u>as though to speak</u>**, but changed his mind.*[113]

These adverbial SC<small>ONJ</small> + I<small>NF</small>P constructions can be paraphrased by A<small>DV</small>C<small>LS</small>: *He shrugged, **as if** <u>he were going to say</u>. . . . Several times Thornton started, **as though** <u>he were going to speak</u>.* The adverbial SC<small>ONJ</small> + I<small>NF</small>P construction always functions as a S<small>ENT</small>M<small>OD</small> or a clause modifier.

Key Points

- Non-finite verb phrases—participle and infinitive phrases (PARTPs; INFPs)—may comprise a non-finite verb alone or may include modifiers and complements. Thus, like dependent clauses, they have both a complex internal structure and function as a single constituent within a container phrase or clause.
- PARTPs and INFPs may be nominal, adjectival, or adverbial and can perform most of the functions of other nominals, adjectivals, and adverbials.
- In structure, PARTPs and INFPs are like partial or incomplete predicates.
- A PARTP or INFP always has an agent, which may be explicit or implied. To ensure that the reference of a PARTP or INFP is clear and to avoid dangling modifiers, a reader must be able to easily identify the agent.
- The complete participle or infinitive may include perfect, progressive, and passive AUX verbs and semi-modal and imperfect aspectual verbs.
- PARTPs and INFPs may be preceded by a limited variety of subordinators.

12.3 Exercises: Participle and Infinitive Phrases

A. PARTPs: a mix of real-world and made-up sentences:[114]

- Identify each **complete PARTP**.
- For each PARTP, identify whether it is functioning as a nominal, adjectival, or adverbial, and identify its function in or in relation to the container clause.

    - For adjectival PARTPs, where relevant, note whether the PARTP is an **essential** or **non-essential** modifier.

- For each complete PARTP:

    - Identify the complete participle.
    - Identify the agent and, as relevant, the patient of the participle.
    - Identify the modifiers and complements of the participle.
    - For each modifier or complement, identify its form and function within or in relation to the PARTP.

- **Remember**: a PARTP may consist of a participle without any modifiers or complements.
- **Also**: note any participles (or apparent participles) that are part of finite verbs, and note the tense, modality, aspect, or voice that causes the verb to include a present or past participle form.

(1) "Going out there in South Carolina and taking the gloves off would not be my preference," Huckabee said of the prospects of a tough encounter with McCain.

(2) But neither of them is reluctant to throw punches if he is confronted: McCain did it directly, by airing ads in New Hampshire that called Romney a phony.

(3) In South Carolina, Huckabee is leading all other candidates in the polls and it is there that the contest with McCain is likely to be head-on. (4) Huckabee is already exploiting an issue that could be damaging to McCain—immigration—by running ads in the state that promote his tougher proposal for treating illegal immigrants.

(5) Romney's greatest concern is not splitting conservative voters with Huckabee and thereby opening a path to victory for McCain.

(6) Last week's Iowa caucuses delivered handsome victories to Democrat Barack Obama, bidding to be the first Black president, and Republican Mike Huckabee, a Baptist preacher and former governor banking on doing well in South Carolina. (7) But Tuesday's New Hampshire primaries muddied the waters by handing the Democratic spoils to former first lady Hillary Clinton and to Senator John McCain for the Republicans.

(8) Nonetheless, something different appears to be afoot, as campaigns trafficking in optimism brace for the venerable machinations that typify this state's bare-knuckle politics.

(9) "White, college-age kids in South Carolina are flocking to work for Obama, and this was happening before he became popular," said local historian Walter Edgar, acknowledging the lingering racial divide in this former slave state where Blacks account for about half of Democratic primary voters.

(10) South Carolina is one of the more impoverished states in the union, with just over four million people, nearly 30 percent of whom are African-American.

(11) Looking further back in history: On January 4, 1912, the British explorer Robert Scott, taking four men with him, began his final dash to the pole, hoping to be the first to reach the South Pole. (12) Leading Scott by sixty miles, a Norwegian expedition commanded by Roald Amundsen was moving swiftly. (13) The sleds used by both teams grew lighter as their provisions dwindled.

(14) Reaching the pole on January 17, the British found the Norwegians had already been there. (15) Weakened by scurvy, frostbite, and exhaustion, the five explorers, knowing they had very little hope of survival, set out on the 800-mile journey back to their base ship.

B. PartPs: real-world sentences:[115] use the following text and the same instructions as in A. **By my count, there are 34 PartPs in this article.**

(1) Regan, Jim. "Sometimes less is more." csmonitor.com. Posted Aug. 29, 2002. www.csmonitor.com/2002/0829/p25s01-stin.html. Accessed Sep. 15, 2018.

(2) It's an unfortunate fact that the very features that make many exceptional websites worth viewing contribute to the viewer's impatience,
as he or she waits for large files to trickle their way down the Internet
pipeline. (3) This week's review will introduce a pair of sites that are
a bit friendlier to dial-up modems—one providing amusement and the
other enlightenment—and will close with a special case that proves that
some material is worth almost any wait.

(4) First is a site that sets the standard in low-bandwidth interactivity. (5)
5k is an annual contest where designers are invited to create websites
or web applications using HTML, JavaScript, Flash, or whatever they
want—as long as the complete project weighs in at less than five kilo-
bytes. (6) (Which means that you could fit more than 250 of these exper-
iments on a single floppy disk.) (7) Leading by example, even the host
site is minimalist in appearance, using only two colors (black and white)
in its design, leaving it looking a bit like a late-'80s Macintosh interface.

(8) Now in its third year, 5k attracted 366 entries for the 2002 competition,
and some of the results are genuinely impressive. (9) The collection of
winners includes an experiment in single-cell reproduction (as well as
a multi-cell flagellate simulation), a kaleidoscope, and a rather unique
version of Pong.

(10) The grand-prize winner was a simple but attractive browser "toy,"
activated by dragging one's pointer across the screen. (11) My favorite
was Night Waltz, an app that allows the surfer to "dance" with trees.
(12) Each entry is given its own page, with scoring statistics, an introduction from the author, and an area for public discussion of the merits
or shortcomings of the design. (13) Links to the 2000 and 2001 competitions are available at the top of each page.

(14) Unless you're a designer, you're not likely to spend a great deal of
time here, and there's a good chance that not all the entries will work
on your computer (even the website's own links to the previous years'
competitions had a way of randomly changing from buttons to nearly
invisible lines as I toured the site), but it is interesting to see that so much
can be done with so little. (15) And it's always satisfying to be able to
spend more time viewing a page than waiting for that page to appear.

(16) Next, is the The Memory Hole, a site dedicated to "rescuing knowledge and freeing information." (17) The Memory Hole makes an interesting complement to the better-known The Smoking Gun, but while
The Smoking Gun favors uncovering sources of amusement (certain
stars' unusual contract riders) and personal transgressions (an America
West pilot's bar tab), The Memory Hole deals with documents that gov-
ernments and corporations would rather that you didn't see.

(18) Launched in July, The Memory Hole is another basic black-and-white
site (with just a touch of red), so it's as easy to view as 5k. (19) Examples include:

—A less than encouraging report of a GAO test of security measures at federal office buildings in Atlanta, Georgia. (20) ". . . They were able to move freely and extensively throughout these facilities during both day and evening hours and were not challenged by anyone . . ."

—An article which was posted, and then removed, from the NewsMax website, in which a CIA official calls for "Sending SWAT Teams into Journalists' Homes," to combat leaks of classified documents

—A map of the Arctic National Wildlife Refuge (deleted from the USGS site) that depicted caribou calving grounds in areas that the administration wanted to open to oil exploration

(21) In each case, the material is described in brief, with links to relevant websites and related information. (22) In addition to the Memory Hole's own collection, the site also provides offsite links to similar coverage in the commercial media, such as an *Atlantic Monthly* piece about the long history of attempts to destroy embarrassing information—linked to Enron's recent paper shredding spree.

(23) The Memory Hole demonstrates how powerful a tool the Web can be when it comes to the retrieval and dissemination of information (especially information that certain parties would prefer to suppress), and this final offering demonstrates the same principle, albeit in an entirely different context.

(24) While I'm not aware that Leonard Nimoy is actively trying to inhibit the online display of his '60s music video The Ballad of Bilbo Baggins (which I stumbled across at MetaFilter), there's a good chance that he would rather it had vanished along with go-go boots and Nehru jackets. (25) And yet, while the Web exists, so shall this unfortunate attempt to step out of Mr. Spock's shoes. (26) The QuickTime movie won't load as quickly as 5k or Memory Hole, but if you need a laugh, this will definitely be a case of time invested rather than time spent.

C. INFPs: made-up sentences:

- Identify each complete INFP.
- For each INFP, identify whether it is functioning as a nominal, adjectival, or adverbial, and identify its function in or in relation to the container clause.

    - For adjectival INFPs, where relevant, note whether the INFP is an **essential** or **non-essential** modifier.

- For each complete INFP:

    - Identify the complete infinitive.
    - Identify the agent of the infinitive.
    - Identify the modifiers and complements of the infinitive.

- For each modifier or complement, identify its form and function within or in relation to the INFP.
- **Remember**: an INFP may consist of an infinitive without any modifiers or complements.
- **Also**: note any semi-modal or imperfect aspectual verbs that consist of V + TO that are part of finite verbs, and note the tense, modality, aspect, or voice of the complete finite verb.

1. It's so easy to fall in love.
2. To see the world in a grain of sand takes a discerning eye.
3. To tell you the truth, I actually love Malomars.
4. For me to have the money to buy Malomars would be heaven.
5. My assignment was to carefully read all of the text on a box of Malomars.
6. In relating my obsession with Malomars, I try to present a true picture of my childhood.
7. To tell the truth of my experiences is my aim.
8. Researchers have found many ways to eat a Malomar.
9. To write better advertising, I had to take on a new career.
10. I desired to communicate my true feelings about Malomars to my readers.
11. In my commercial work I have been able to express great emotion.
12. You cannot appreciate the depth of my desire for you to succeed.
13. I have counted on you to be a good source of information.
14. Unquestionably, what I need is to buy a stack of new CDs.
15. My quest is to dream the impossible dream.
16. I like to eat apples and bananas.
17. I know how to play tennis.

D. INFPs: real-world sentences:[116] use the same instructions as in C. **By my count, there are 14 INFPs in this passage**.

¶1 (1) Discipline, it has been suggested, is the means of human spiritual evolution. (2) This section will examine what lies in back of discipline—what provides the motive, the energy for discipline. (3) This force I believe to be love. (4) I am very conscious of the fact that in attempting to examine love we will be beginning to toy with mystery. (5) In a very real sense we will be attempting to examine the unexaminable and to know the unknowable. (6) Love is too large, too deep ever to be truly understood or measured or limited within the framework of words. (7) I would not write this if I did not believe the attempt to have value, but no matter how valuable, I begin with the certain knowledge that the attempt will be in some ways inadequate.

¶2 (1) One result of the mysterious nature of love is that no one has ever, to my knowledge, arrived at a truly satisfactory definition of love. (2) In an effort to explain it, therefore, love has been divided into various categories: eros, philia, agape; perfect love and imperfect love, and so on. (3) I am presuming, however, to give a single definition of love, again with the awareness that it is likely to be in some way or ways inadequate. (4) I define love thus: the will to extend one's self for the purpose of nurturing one's own or another's spiritual growth.

¶3 (1) At the outset I would like to comment briefly on this definition before proceeding to a more thorough elaboration. (2) First, it may be noticed that it is a teleological definition; the behavior is defined in terms of the goal or purpose it seems to serve—in this case, spiritual growth. (3) Scientists tend to hold teleological definitions suspect, and perhaps they will this one. (4) I did not arrive at it, however, through a clearly teleological process of thinking. (5) Instead I arrived at it through observation in my clinical practice of psychiatry (which includes self-observation), in which the definition of love is a matter of considerable import. (6) This is because patients are generally very confused as to the nature of love. (7) For instance, a timid young man reported to me: "My mother loved me so much she wouldn't let me take the school bus to school until my senior year in high school. (8) Even then I had to beg her to let me go. (9) I guess she was afraid that I would get hurt, so she drove me to and from school every day, which was very hard on her. (10) She really loved me." (11) In the treatment of this individual's timidity is was necessary, as it is in many other cases, to teach him that his mother might have been motivated by something other than love, and that what seems to be love is often not love at all. (12) It has been out of such experience that I accumulated a body of examples of what seemed to be acts of love and what seemed not to be love. (13) One of the major distinguishing features between the two seemed to be the conscious or unconscious purpose in the mind of the lover or non lover.

¶4 (1) Second, it may be noticed that, as defined, love is a strangely circular process. (2) For the process of extending one's self is an evolutionary process. (3) When one has successfully extended one's limits, one has then grown into a larger state of being. (4) Thus the act of loving is an act of self-evolution even when the purpose of the act is someone else's growth. (5) It is through reaching toward evolution that we evolve.

¶5 (1) Third, this unitary definition of love includes self-love with love for the other. (2) Since I am human and you are human, to love humans means to love myself as well as you. (3) To be dedicated to human spiritual development is to be dedicated to the race of which we are a part, and this therefore means dedication to our own development as well as "theirs." (4) Indeed, as has been pointed out, we are incapable of loving another unless we love ourselves, just as we are incapable of teaching our children self-discipline unless we ourselves are self-disciplined. (5) It is actually impossible to forsake our own spiritual development in favor of someone else's. (6) We cannot forsake self-discipline and at the same time be disciplined in our care for another. (7) We cannot be a source of strength unless we nurture our own strength. (8) As we proceed in our exploration of the nature of love, I believe it will become clear that not only do self-love and love of others go hand in hand but that ultimately they are indistinguishable.

Figure 12.1

Notes

1. Michael Barry. "The Razor's Edge." *Bicycling* 52.6 (Jul 2011): 82.
2. "On Sesame Street, 'C' Is for Controversy, Too." *Talk of the Nation*. NPR. 12 Nov 2009. 25 May 2019.
3. Alexander Pope. *An Essay on Criticism*. Ed. John Sargeaunt. Oxford, UK: Clarendon Press, 1909 (1711). Part II.525. 21.
4. Deborah Rodriguez. *The Little Coffee Shop of Kabul*. New York: Ballantine Books, 2012. 8.
5. Clea Simon. *When Bunnies Go Bad*. Scottsdale, AZ: Poisoned Pen Press, 2016. 9.
6. Olga Grushin. "The Daughter of Kadmos." *Partisan Review* 69.3 (Summer 2002): 385.
7. Kathleen L. Lane, et al. "The Efficacy of Phonological Awareness Training with First-Grade Students Who Have Behavior Problems and Reading Disorders." *Journal of Emotional and Behavioral Disorders* 9.4 (Winter 2001): 224.
8. Traditional grammar would choose this interpretation. But, as we saw earlier, depending on context, we might also interpret the verb *love driving* as having the imperfect aspect.
9. Jon Delano. "New Truck Drivers Being Highly Sought After." *KDKA-TV* (Pittsburgh, PA). 12 Mar 2012. <https://pittsburgh.cbslocal.com>.
10. Lee Ann Branham. *Greenup Learning Center*. Online posting. 22 Nov 2016. <www.greenuplearningcenter.com>.
11. Douglas Coupland. "Clone, Clone on the Range." *Time* 149.10 (10 Mar 1997): 74+.
12. Chris Lynch. *Shadow Boxer*. New York: Harper Collins, 1993. 213.
13. Norm Clarke. "King Brings His Wit to Wynn Las Vegas." *Review-Journal* (Las Vegas, NV). 17 Jun 2009.
14. "Boat & Jet Ski Rentals in Ocean City, MD." *The Official Site of Ocean City, Maryland*. 2019. <https://ococean.com/>.
15. ohlovelykay. "#beespollinating." Aug 2018. <www.picomico.com/tag/beespollinating>.
16. prairiefisherman. "Kids Looting a Candy Bucket." *Reddit*. 1 Nov 2015.

17. Cynthia Reeg. "The Three Sisters." *Faces* 21.9 (May 2005): 42+.
18. David Robinson. "Mystery on the Mississippi." *Dateline*. NBC. 6 Oct 2017.
19. Russell Newman. "Wonder Boy: A Story of Transformation." *20/20*. ABC. 17 Nov 2017.
20. Harry Smith. *The Early Show*. CBS. 28 Apr 2010.
21. Helen Caulfield. *Vital Notes for Nurses: Accountability*. Malden, MA: Blackwell, 2005. 151. Examples of such uses of *interesting* as part of a finite transitive verb are extremely rare.
22. Niall Gaffney. Qtd. in Wes Gardner. "UT Hires Former Hubble Scientist." *The Austin* (TX) *Statesman* (4 May 2013): B2.
23. Mort Castle. "Blend History & Imagination." *Writer* 121.8 (Aug 2008): 39.
24. Kelsey Atherton. "THE Testers." *Popular Mechanics* 192.6 (July 2015): 88.
25. Daniel Drollette. "Australia's Solar Sailor." *Technology Review* 101.4 (Jul/Aug 1998): 54.
26. David Gonzales. "'Get Me Doug Coombs!'" *Skiing* 56.2 (Oct 2003): 92.
27. Robert Reed. "Raven Dream." *Fantasy & Science Fiction* 101.6 (Dec 2001): 5+.
28. "The Hidden Costs of Claims: Big Bites from Your Bottom Line." *Louisiana Workers' Compensation Corporation*. 26 Sep 2014. <www.lwcc.com>.
29. Janet Chapman. *Tempt Me If You Can*. New York: Pocket Star Books, 2010. 12.
30. "Speed Racer." *Scholastic Action* 31.14 (12 May 2008): 10.
31. Seth Livingstone. "Economic Woes Cast Cloud over Racing's Big Weekend." *USA Today*. 21 May 2009.
32. Fisher Investments. "Employee 401(k) Empowerment Tools." 2017. <www.fisher 401k.com>.
33. William Congreve. *The Mourning Bride: A Tragedy. Bell's British Theatre. Consisting of the Most Esteemed English Plays*. Vol. XIX. London: George Cawthorn, 1797 (1697). III:ii. 63.
34. Attributed to Benjamin Franklin.
35. David Hajdu. "Tearing Up the Pop Charts." *The New Republic* 246.2/3 (Mar/Apr 2015): 64.
36. Katie Walsh. "Stylish *Simple Favor* Doesn't Ask Too Much of the Audience." *The San Diego Union Tribune*. 14 Sep 2018.
37. John Warriner. *English Grammar and Composition*. Fourth Course. Orlando: Harcourt Brace Jovanovich, 1982 [1948]. 69.
38. Linda Rovin Cooper. "This Trolley Driver Has a Line on San Diego." *The San Diego Union-Tribune*. 4 Apr 1988.
39. Roy S. Johnson. "Take Me Out to the Boardroom." *Fortune* 136.2 (21 Jul 1997): 42.
40. Vzzdak. "NCSoft: City of Heroes Can't Be Saved." Online posting. *The Escapist*. 3 Oct 2012. <https://v1.escapistmagazine.com>.
41. Isaiah 9:2. *New International Version* (NIV). New York: Biblica, 2011.
42. Corey Binns. "They're in the Band: Mom and Son Bond over Rock Music." *today.com*. 13 Jun 2013.
43. Tim Moynihan. "The Coolest New In-Camera Features." *PC World* 28.6 (Jun 2010): 46.
44. Joseph Epstein. "Dubinsky on the Loose: A story." *Commentary* 106.6 (Dec 1998): 46.
45. Macy Halford. "What to Read on the Subway When Service Is Cut." *newyorker. com*. 29 Mar 2009.
46. Tokheim Oil Tank and Pump Co. Advertisement. *Motor Age* 38.13 (23 Sep 1920): 74.
47. Josef Steif. "In the Eye of the Beholder." *Transformers and Philosophy: More than Meets the Mind*. Eds. John R. Shook and Liz Stillwagon Swann. Chicago: Open Court, 2009. 59.
48. David Sandberg, et al. "The Characteristics of Sleepiness During Real Driving at Night—A Study of Driving Performance, Physiology and Subjective Experience." *Sleep* 34.10 (1 Oct 2011): 1318.

49. Danna Harman. "In Churchill's Footsteps." *The Christian Science Monitor*. 28 Jan 2004.
50. Marissa Payne. "NFL Saves Dale Earnhardt Jr. from Having to Drive an Eagles Car at Pocono." *washingtonpost.com*. 2 Jun 2017.
51. Ella Taylor. "Review of *Orthodox Stance* (2008)." *L.A. Weekly. rottentomatoes. com*. 10 Apr 2008.
52. Clint Talbot. "If 'Sitting Is the New Smoking,' Can Desk Workers Snuff Out Risk?" *Colorado Arts and Sciences Magazine* (University of Colorado, Boulder). 28 Feb 2017.
53. Emily Yoffe. "Fear the Road." *Slate.com*. 14 Jan 2013.
54. Patricia Beckham, et al. "Working Together for Music Education." *Music Educators Journal* 79.5 (Jan 1993): 40.
55. "VUMC Information Technology." Vanderbilt University Medical Center. Website. 15 Apr 2016. <https://it.vanderbilt.edu>.
56. Landon Hall. "Squeezeplay." *The Orange County Register*. 5 Dec 2013.
57. Janine DeFao. "At-risk Students Running for Their Lives." *The San Francisco Chronicle* (19 Mar 2006): B1.
58. David Young. "Public Display of Rage: Would You Stop an Abuser?" *PrimeTime Live*. ABC. 17 Aug 2010. *COCA*. 28 May 2019.
59. Juniperberry. "Anyone Find Out They Were Pg When They Felt the Baby Move?" Online posting. *mothering.com*. 25 May 2011.
60. Wendell Berry. "Return to Port William." *The Christian Century* 124.1 (9 Jan 2007): 20.
61. Amy Dickinson. "Ask Amy: Grieving Mother Diminishes Others' Problems." *LaCrosse* (WI) *Tribune*. 19 Apr 2019.
62. Jonathan Schell. "The Folly of Arms Control." *Foreign Affairs* 79.5 (Sep/Oct 2000): 23.
63. JonF. Online comment to Rod Dreher. "Flake Flakes." *theamericanconservative. com*. 30 Oct 2017.
64. Alan Ryan. "In a Conversational Idiom." *Social Research* 65.3 (Fall 1998): 483.
65. Occasionally, an adverbial constituent of an INFP will be movable within the INFP:
*To **quickly** catch the suspect, law enforcement agencies pooled their resources.*
*To catch the suspect **quickly**, law enforcement agencies pooled their resources.*
The ADV *quickly* also has the whole INFP, *to catch the suspect*, in its scope since it is the not just the catching, but the catching of the suspect that is happening quickly. Therefore, *quickly* is functioning as an INFPMOD. The whole INFP *quickly catch the suspect* is, in turn, functioning as a SENTMOD. Generally, an Adverbial:INFPMOD cannot appear before the to of the infinitive.
66. B. Drummond Ayres, Jr. "The 1994 Campaign: In Race for California Chief No Candidate Is Favorite." *The New York Times* (19 Sep 1994): A1.
67. William Brangham. *The NewsHour*. PBS 19 Jul 2017.
68. Buddy Holly and Norman Petty. "It's So Easy." 1958.
69. "Chapter 5: Intersections and Turns." *Drivers' Manual*. Department of Motor Vehicles, New York State. N.d. <https://dmv.ny.gov/>.
70. Paul Rogers. "Sam I Am." *Golf Magazine* 56.6 (Jun 2014): 99.
71. Dan Toman. "Cardinals' Carpenter on Fatigue Issues: 'My Body Wasn't Working on all Cylinders.'" *thescore.com*. 13 May 2015.
72. Patrick J. Duffley. *The English Infinitive*. New York: Longman, 1992. 19–20.
73. Michael Sears. *Long Way Down*. New York: Putnam, 2014. 203.
74. Henry Unger. "5 Questions for the Boss." *The Atlanta Journal Constitution* (5 Oct 2015): 1D.
75. Christer Geisler. *Relative Infinitives in English*. Acta Universitatis Upsaliensis. *Studia Anglistica Upsaliensia* 91. Uppsala, Sweden: Uppsala University, 1995. 4.

76. Ibid. 4.
77. Kevin Sack. "Charleston Judge Orders Competency Evaluation of Dylann Roof." *The New York Times*. 8 Nov 2016.
78. Leslie Podlog. "Perceptions of Success and Failure Among University Athletes in Canada." *Journal of Sport Behavior* 25.4 (Dec 2002): 368+.
79. "Readers Write." *Ms.* 16.3 (1998 Fall): 6+.
80. Peter Lopatin. "Nathan at the Speed of Light." *Commentary* 128.3 (Oct 2009): 51.
81. Amy Krouse Rosenthal. "The Wreck." *Parenting* 19.2 (Mar 2005): 157.
82. Francine Maroukian. "The Rebirth of Hard Cider." *Popular Mechanics* 192.4 (May 2015): 23.
83. Neil deGrasse Tyson. "Naming Rights." *Natural History* 112.1 (Feb 2003): 24.
84. Brad Knickerbocker. "Conversations with Outstanding Americans: Jane Lubchenco." *The Christian Science Monitor*. 15 Aug 1997.
85. Mandy Oaklander. "Life/Support." *Time* 186.9/10 (7–14 Sep 2015): 50.
86. Sheila Sarkar and Marie Andreas. "Acceptance of and Engagement in Risky Driving Behaviors by Teenagers." *Adolescence* 39.156 (Winter 2004): 697.
87. Jeffrey Meitrodt. "Cities Give Pass to Sketchy Uber, Lyft Drivers." *Minneapolis Star Tribune*. 18 Dec 2016.
88. "7 Tips for Driving on the Highway for the First Time." *Now from Nationwide*. 9 Feb 2018. <https://blog.nationwide.com>.
89. Bob Ratterman. "Oxford Man Charged After Pulling Knife During Dispute with Wife." *Journal-News* (Oxford, OH). 15 Jun 2017.
90. Annie Sweeney. "Nonviolence Is a Choice." *Chicago Tribune*. 25 May 2017.
91. "Study: What Kind of Car NOT to Buy a Teen Driver." *Time.com*. 18 Dec 2014.
92. U.S. v. Rivero. No. 2:17-cr-1915-KG. United States District Court, D. New Mexico. *Leagle.com*. 2 Oct 2017.
93. Thierry Bru, et al. "Rapid Induction of Pluripotency Genes After Exposure of Human Somatic Cells to Mouse ES Cell Extracts." *Experimental Cell Research* 314.14 (15 Aug 2008): 2634+.
94. Abby Frucht. *Polly's Ghost: A Novel*. New York: Scribner, 2000.
95. Eve Guevara and Stuart Taylor. "Tift Prepares for Hurricane Irma." *The Tifton* (GA) *Gazette*. 9 Sep 2017.
96. Paul Theroux. "The Long Way Home." *Smithsonian* 40.6 (Sep 2009): 70+.
97. Ross McCammon. "Heart." *Esquire* 153.6/7 (Jun/Jul 2010): 120+.
98. Daniel A. Offiong. "Traditional Healers in the Nigerian Health Care Delivery System and the Debate over Integrating Traditional and Scientific Medicine." *Anthropological Quarterly* 72.3 (Jul 1999): 120.
99. David Ehrlich. "How Should Lin-Manuel Miranda Structure the Film Adaptation of *Hamilton*." *Slate.com*. 8 Jan 2016.
100. Oprah Winfrey. "What I Know for Sure." *O, The Oprah Magazine* 16 (1 Apr 2015): 130.
101. "Music Lessons Build Skills and Confidence for Students of All Ages." *The Chicago Tribune*. 10 Jun 2016.
102. Jennifer Ludden. "A Guide to an Insanity-Free, 'Practical Wedding.'" *Talk of the Nation*. NPR. 26 Jan 2012.
103. Tom Junod. "E.O. Wilson." *Esquire* 151.1 (Jan 2009): 113.
104. Ruth Schuster. "Analysis 'New Organ' Discovered in Human Body Sends World Wild, Too Bad It's Not True." *Haaretz*. 4 Jan 2017.
105. David Bianculli. "Remembering Syndicated Gossip Columnist Liz Smith." *Fresh Air*. NPR. 17 Nov 2017.
106. Esther Schindler. "What (Not) to Wear on an IT Job Interview: 6 Real-life Examples." *IT World*. 30 Jun 2014.

107. Sally E. Merry. Qtd. in Polly O. Walker. "Decolonizing Conflict Resolution: Addressing the Ontological Violence of Westernization." *American Indian Quarterly* 28.3/4 (Summer/Fall 2004): 546.
108. J. Eric Hazell. "The Trouble with Tolerance." *Humanist* 59.6 (Nov/Dec 1999): 35.
109. Jeffrey H. Birnbaum. "Secrets of the Kemp Commission." *Time* 147.2 (8 Jan 1996): 34.
110. Arthur Kropp. "Ralph Reed, Executive Director, Christian Coalition, and Arthur Kropp, President, People for the American Way, Discuss School Prayer." *Face the Nation.* CBS. 20 Nov 1994.
111. "Marian Wright Edelman: An Interview with the Mother Marian." *Psychology Today* 26.4 (Jul/Aug 1993): 77.
112. Vani Mohindra. "Playing Sevens." *New Moon Girls* 24.5 (May/Jun 2017): 27.
113. Jack London. *The Call of the Wild.* New York: Grosset and Dunlap, 1912. 151.
114. Sentences 1–5 taken or adapted from "Analysis: McCain and Huckabee now rivals." The Associated Press. Jan 10, 2008 by Jim Kuhnhenn. Copyrighted 2004–2008. Associated Press. 298811:0519PF. Used by permission.

    Sentences 6–10 taken or adapted from Porter Barron. "South Carolina the Next Contest." *The Age* (Australia). 9 Jan 2008. Sentences 11–15 based on Warriner, op. cit. 69.
115. Jim Regan. "Sometimes Less is More." *The Christian Science Monitor.* 29 Aug 2002. Used by permission.
116. From M. Scott Peck. "Love Defined." *The Road Less Travelled.* New York: Simon and Schuster, 1978. 81–83. Used by permission.

Chapter 13

A Grand Review Exercise

The remainder of this book is taken up by a review exercise in which you will take the text of a single essay from a popular magazine and identify all of the phrase and clause structures we have discussed. This will serve not only to review and reinforce what you have studied but to show you how much you have learned. It will also show you just a smattering of the ways in which grammatical structures—patterns, repetitions, contrasts, embedding of structures within structures—help to create the rhythms, textures, and rhetorical effects that are commonplace in effective prose.

Real-world sentences: Using the entire text of the article below, do the following series of review exercises.

A. **Noun Phrases**: Identify each complete NP; for each NP, identify its function; for each NP, identify the head noun.

B. **Prepositional Phrases**: Identify each complete PP; for each PP, identify whether it is adjectival or adverbial; identify its function.

C. **Adjective Phrases**: Identify each complete ADJP; identify its function.

D. **Determiner Phrases**: Identify each complete DP; for each determiner, identify its type (e.g. possessive determiner, quantifier, etc.); for each DP, identify the noun it specifies.

E. **Pronouns**: Identify each PRON and PRONP; identify its form (e.g. personal, possessive, relative, indefinite, etc.); identify its function; and, **where relevant**, identify the attributes of the PRON (case, number, person, gender, animateness).

F. **Adverb Phrases**: Identify each complete ADVP and, for each, identify its function using **both** sets of terminology we have discussed: modifier and complement **and** subjunct, adjunct, etc.

G. **Conjunctions**: Identify each Coordinating Conjunction (CONJ) and Correlative Conjunction (CCONJ), and, for each, identify the complete constituents it conjoins. Identify each item of conjunctive punctuation (commas, semicolons, colons, dashes, hyphens, parentheses, virgules) and, for each, identify its function using the list in 9.2.7.

H. **Verbs**: Identify each **complete finite V**; for each, identify its tense, mood, aspect, and voice.

I. **Verb Complements**: For each **complete finite VP**, identify its complete complement(s), and identify its complement pattern using the list in 7.2. **Also**, identify each **complete phrasal verb** and its pattern using the list in 7.2.

J. **Independent and Dependent Clauses**: For each independent and dependent clause, identify its complete SUBJ and PRED and each simple SUBJ and PRED. If the sentence is not in SVC order, identify how it has been rearranged (e.g. interrogative, passive, expletive *there*, etc.).

K. **Dependent Clauses**: For each dependent clause, identify the complete clause and whether it is an ADJCL, NCL, or ADVCL. Identify its function within its container clause, and:

- For each ADJCL, identify the relative pro-word; identify the form of the relative pro-word; and identify its function within the ADJCL. If there is no relative pro-word, state what pro-word is implied and what its function would be within the ADJCL. **Also**, for each ADJCL, where relevant, note whether the PARTP is an **essential** or **non-essential** modifier.

- For each *wh*-NCL, identify the *wh*-subordinator, its form, and its function within the NCL.

- For each ADVCL, if the SCONJ is a *wh*-word, identify its form and its function within the ADVCL.

L. **Participle Phrases**:

- Identify each complete PARTP.
- For each PARTP, identify whether it is functioning as a nominal, adjectival, or adverbial, and identify its function in or in relation to the constituent that contains it.

    - For adjectival PARTPs, where relevant, note whether the PARTP is an **essential** or **non-essential** modifier.

- For each complete PARTP:

    - Identify the complete participle.
    - Identify the complete agent of the participle. If the agent is implied, name it, and state that it is implied.

- For a PartP with a past participle, indicate both the agent and patient. If the patient is implied, name it, and state that it is implied.

    - Identify each immediate constituent of the PARTP (modifiers and complements of the participle).
    - For each constituent, identify its form and function within or in relation to the PARTP.

- **Remember**: a PARTP may consist of a participle without any modifiers or complements.

- **Also**, note any participles (or apparent participles) that are part of finite verbs, and note the tense, modality, aspect, or voice that causes the verb to include a present or past participle form.

M. **Infinitive Phrases**:
- Identify each complete INFP.
- For each INFP, identify whether it is functioning as a nominal, adjectival, or adverbial, and identify its function in or in relation to the container clause.
  - For adjectival INFPs, where relevant, note whether the INFP is an **essential** or **non-essential** modifier.
- For each complete INFP:
  - Identify the complete infinitive.
  - Identify the complete agent of the infinitive. If the agent is implied, name it, and state that it is implied.
  - Identify each immediate constituent of the INFP.
  - For each constituent, identify its form and function within or in relation to the INFP.
- **Remember**: an INFP may consist of an infinitive without any modifiers or complements.
- **Also**, note any semi-modal or imperfect aspectual verbs that consist of *TO* + V that are part of finite verbs, and note the tense, modality, aspect, or voice of the complete finite verb.

N. **Nominals**: Identify each nominal constituent, its form, and its function.
O. **Adjectivals**: Identify each adjectival constituent, its form, and its function. Where relevant, note whether the adjectival is an **essential** or **non-essential** modifier
P. **Adverbials**: Identify each adverbial constituent and, for each, identify its form and whether it is functioning as a subjunct, adjunct, disjunct, conjunctive adverbial, SENTMOD, clause modifier, PARTPMOD, or INFPMOD.

(1) Is It Time to Dump Him?

Posted by David Zinczenko, editor-in-chief of *Men's Health* on Tue, Mar 20, 2007, 11:39 am PDT

(2) "Mysteries of the Sexes Explained," provided by *Men's Health*. http://health.yahoo.com/experts/menlovesex/25031/is-it-time-to-dump-him;_ylt=AptEXD01JR2bOQNWmEZ4E1OrJNIF. Accessed March 21, 2007.
(3) This won't come as news to women: Men aren't all that good about breaking up. (4) Sometimes a man will half-heartedly try ("things just

aren't clicking"). (5) Sometimes a man will force you to make the first move ("well, if you think things aren't working out then"). (6) Sometimes a man will stew in a bad relationship for years before actually having the guts to break it off. (7) Why? (8) For lots of reasons—one of them being that many men, even if they don't like the relationship anymore, don't want to be immortalized (to you and all your friends) as The Bad Guy. (9) Not an excuse, but it's what men tend to do. (10) When you consider a recent national survey showing 21 percent of men say they're on the lookout for a better relationship while they're in a relationship—then it's all the more important that women know the signs of a guy who's looking for the exit before he's even in the room.

(11) Dump-worthy: He ignores. Not dump-worthy: He doesn't listen.
(12) There is a difference. (13) The way I see it, the guy who doesn't listen is the guy who spaces out on TV when a woman is asking if he liked that night's chili. (14) A guy who doesn't listen is a guy who forgets to cap the toothpaste despite the fact he's been told 12 times in the last six days. (15) Annoying? (16) Sure. (17) Deal-breakers? (18) No. (19) On the other hand, a guy who ignores is the kind of guy who always puts himself first by ignoring the things that are important to you—like chronically forgetting an anniversary or birthday, or not asking how a doctor's appointment went, or choosing his golf game over her family get-together. (20) Once in a while may be fine, but when it happens all the time, it means that his priorities don't include you.

(21) Dump-worthy: He has two cell phones (one of which you didn't know about). Not dump-worthy: He won't tell you his password.
(22) Oh, if I had the surefire formula for catching a cheater, I'd be using 100-dollar bills as napkins. (23) While cheating is, in many cases, the obvious relationship-ender, the trickier issue is gathering up the signs that a guy is indeed borrowing sugar from the neighbor. (24) I will tell you this: A guy who's protecting his e-mail password isn't necessarily cheating; he just thinks that there still should be some semblance of his privacy (plus, he's not too keen on you seeing the internet photos his co-worker buddy may have sent over). (25) But when a guy hasn't told you about an extra cell phone, it's a pretty likely sign that there's somebody calling it who darn well shouldn't be.

(26) Dump-worthy: He won't apologize. Not dump-worthy: He goes silent.
(27) A man who clams up during a fight or a discussion isn't necessarily just trying to make you mad (though some are). (28) He's thinking, he's debating, and he's being cautious about what he says—because he knows you're listening (and perhaps ready to pounce on his arguments). (29) A guy will eventually open up, if you can give the issue some time to settle down, or even approach him in a setting where he's

more comfortable talking (like the car). (30) The real power play comes not from the silent treatment, but from a man who can't utter a "sorry"; that's not only a sign of stubbornness, but a sign he's not ready to give any ground. (31) If he's not willing to show a little weakness early in the relationship, chances are it'll only grow worse as the relationship grows—if it even gets that far.

(32) Have your own relationship deal-breakers and stories? Fess up here.

Index